RONA

From 1939 to Today

**Bibliothèque et Archives nationales du Québec
and Library and Archives Canada cataloguing in publication**

Main entry under title:

RONA: from 1939 to today

Issued also in French under title: RONA : de 1939 à aujourd'hui.

ISBN 978-2-922068-17-7

1. RONA (Firm) - History. 2. Hardware stores - Québec (Province) -
History. 3. Business people - Québec (Province) - Biography. I. RONA
(Firm). II. Title.

HD9745.C34R66 2010b   381'.45683065714   C2010-941540-X

RONA: From 1939 to Today

Legal deposits
Bibliothèque nationale du Québec
National Library of Canada

Project supervision: Daniel Richard, Rona
Editorial coordination: IQ Press
Writing-consultation: Daniel Larouche and Patrice Servant
Archival managment: Sylvie Lebel
Historical research: Georges Langlois
Data entry: Élaine Gusella
Profile interviews and writing: Évelyne Deshaies and Aralie-Maude Thibault
Translation: Soludoc
Linguistic revision: Keren Penney
Profile photographs: Quentin photographe
Graphic design and page layout: Derome Design
Printing: Friesens, Canada

1 2 3   12 11 10

RONA

From 1939 to Today

Under the direction of
Robert Dutton

Table of contents

My earliest memory of RONA is my father's feeling of pride. The year was 1971. He had just finished hanging the banner outside the little hardware store he owned in Sainte-Dorothée that provided our family's livelihood. At that time, joining RONA was really something. In a way it represented success. Because you had to be financially sound. The large wholesalers made their profit by extending credit to the dealers. But there was no credit at RONA. The terms were net 10 days. The result was that RONA dealers stood out from the crowd. Their businesses were well run. They were able to offer the best prices. And they were proud of their banner. The years passed, but the pride in being a RONA dealer never faded.

I wanted to tell the RONA story because this is a business like no other. It is unique. Its origins go back more than 70 years, to a Quebec experiencing a dawning self-awareness. It was founded by people who thought differently and who continue to do so; businesspeople who felt that a company should first provide an honourable living for its workers, and who believed that profit was not an end in itself, but a just reward for a job well done.

Those men are no longer with us, and there are not many among us now who knew them in their day. And yet, their imprint remains. They instilled in the organization a way of seeing and growing that continues to guide the development of RONA, a company that today has close to 700 stores, nearly 30 000 employees, and annual retail sales of more than $6 billion.

With a third generation of dealers now taking over the reins in many of our stores, and new dealers all across Canada joining the company, I felt the moment was right to pay tribute to our founders and to the people who crafted the business for the benefit of those who today, perhaps without realizing it, carry the torch handed on by Rolland and Napoléon.

Let me tell you the story.

Robert Dutton

Once upon a time •

THE TRADE OF HARDWARE STORE OPERATOR HAS BEEN AROUND FOR A LONG TIME, AS WITNESSED BY THESE PHOTOS FROM ANOTHER ERA.

❶ Joseph-Arthur Dorval was the son of Philippe Dorval, chief of the Quebec City fire brigade from 1877 to 1906. In 1901, Joseph-Arthur founded the hardware store that bore his name. Around 1904, he moved it to the corner of D'Aiguillon and Sutherland streets in Quebec City, where it still exists today.

❷ Joseph-Arthur Dorval in front of his hardware store in 1925. Back then, it was an ironworks store that also sold tools, fishing tackle, a few kitchen utensils, and paint.

❸ In 1912, with the help of his wife, Germaine, Octave Bélanger converted a store on La Fontaine Street in Montreal into an ironworks business. Soon after, in 1916, his son Eugène soon took over the reins and ran Ferronnerie Eugène Bélanger Ltée.

❹ In the 1930s, Eugène Bélanger bought several hardware stores that were in trouble, including this one on Masson Street in Montreal, photographed around 1935.

Before RONA

❺ In 1935, Zoé Bougie and Joseph Anctil bought a Victorian house in Saint-Denis-de-Brompton. They turned a portion of it into a general store that would eventually become Matériaux J. Anctil.

❻ The general store that had been in operation on Des Écossais Road since 1935 first sold firewood, sugar, sacks of flour, and hardware articles. In 1995, at the age of 95, Zoé was still able to recall that their very first sale was a box of mothballs!

❼ Alarm clocks, thermometres, scissors, and kettles are neatly displayed on the shelves behind the merchant at this Revelstoke store in Hairy Hill, Alberta, during the first decades of the 20th century.

❽ The Revelstoke Lumber Company was created in 1901 with the purchase of a mill on the Columbia River, near Revelstoke in British Columbia. The company was bought in 1905 by Samuel H. Bowman, and renamed the Revelstoke Sawmill Company Ltd. The photograph of this store in Burstall was taken in 1921.

❾ Starting in 1906, the Revelstoke Sawmill Company began opening lumberyards in towns that had sprung up along the railroads that ran through Alberta and Saskatchewan. Employees at the Wymark Yard in Saskatchewan transport lumber in 1916.

AFTER THE SECOND WORLD WAR, the 1940s saw the hardware stores stocked full of all sorts of new products: utensils, pots and pans, irons, Flo-Glaze paint, rope and wire, and toilet seats. Philippe Dorval is on the left with Mr. Lortie, an employee.

A company is born
1939 - 1954

1

In 1939, a half-dozen hardware store dealers formed a company called Les Marchands en Quincaillerie Ltée, for the purpose of pooling their purchases in order to improve access to supplies, secure better prices, and break their dependence on the wholesalers who were monopolizing the hardware industry and engaging in practices that were questionable at best. After making it through the lean war years, they joined forces to overturn a boycott by manufacturers orchestrated by the large wholesalers, who took a dim view of these neighbourhood dealers trying to shake up the established order. Fifteen years after it was founded, the company had a hundred member dealers throughout Quebec. Internal tensions led to the resignation of the president and co-founder Émery Sauvé, and the company was taken over by its other co-founder, Rolland Dansereau, who invested his personal fortune in the business.

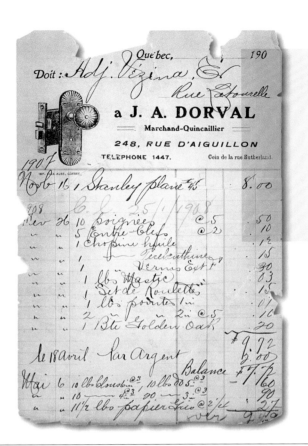

IN THE 1900s, the J.A. Dorval hardware store provided loyal service to the residents of the Saint-Jean-Baptiste neighbourhood in Quebec City. In 1907 and 1908, we know that a Mr. Vézina bought, among other items, door handles, oil, and casters, all for under $10!

THE ÉDOUARD MORENCY HARDWARE STORE on Durocher Street in Quebec City's Saint-Sauveur district opened its doors in 1907. A record of clients' accounts was kept in a large, bound ledger. In 1927, Mr. Bédard bought some LePage glue.

The name RONA made its appearance much later. Originally known as Les Marchands en Quincaillerie Ltée, the company came into being on a very dark day in world history, on September 1, 1939, the day Hitler's armies invaded Poland, sparking the outbreak of the Second World War.

The hardware trade was a difficult one in those days. Materials were extremely hard to come by, and labour was almost as scarce. It was to resolve this supply problem that a handful of hardware store dealers in Montreal, headed by merchant Émery Sauvé, joined forces with businessman Rolland Dansereau.

They were two extraordinary men, and their meeting proved decisive.

Rolland Dansereau was the son of a grocer. His father, Camille, was one of the originators of a small buying group called Les Épiceries Modernes. You could say that this is where the young Rolland drew some of his inspiration. A graduate of the École technique de Montréal, Rolland Dansereau learned the electrical trade before becoming a representative for some American manufacturers and criss-crossing Canada from Halifax to Vancouver. Worn out from his travels, he decided to go into business for himself and set up shop on De la Commune Street. Dansereau had a head for figures; he was an entrepreneur who was good at breaking down barriers. Nothing stopped him, and he

would often remind his "English" acquaintances that he had "never had cause to feel ashamed of his language."

Émery Sauvé, a man who was never at a loss for words himself, was a hardware dealer in Ville-Émard, now a neighbourhood of Montreal. He was a merchant through and through and knew every one of his clients by name. He was a leader, and also a bit of an eccentric, always ready to defend ideas that ran counter to general opinion. He would say, "My competitors can't be my competitors all the time and in all things. There has to be some common ground for agreement on which we can all grow." At a time when competition pitted neighbourhood against neighbourhood, it took a lot of nerve to speak out in favour of a strategic alliance.

When reading accounts of the very earliest days of RONA, it is amusing to see that in some people's eyes, Rolland Dansereau was the heart and soul of the new company, while others saw Émery Sauvé as its vital force.

Nowhere is this more apparent than in two anecdotes about how the partnership between the two men came about.

According to the first, Dansereau, having borrowed $3 000 from his mother, suggested to Sauvé that he go to Toronto to pick up a load of brooms, in exchange for a 2% commission.

According to the second, it was Sauvé who took the initiative, suggesting that they form a buying group for

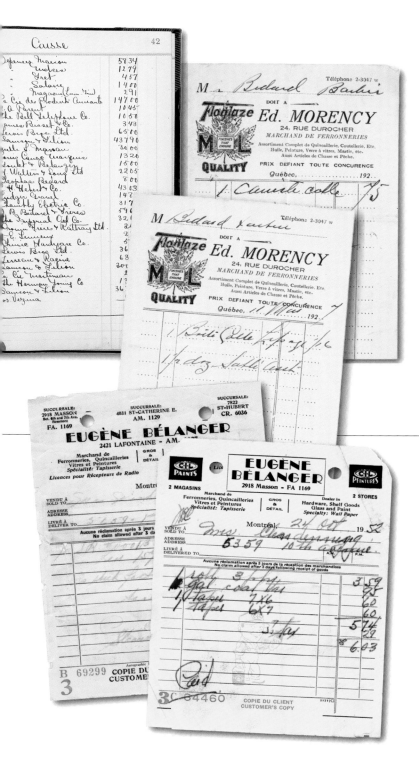

NEAR THE END OF THE 1930s, Ferronnerie Eugène Bélanger Ltée had stores on several Montreal streets: La Fontaine, Saint-Hubert, Sainte-Catherine, and Masson. Only the Masson Street store would remain.

1939

Across the planet, the year 1939 was forever marked by the outbreak of the Second World War. In the wake of military aggression by Germany against Czechoslovakia, Italy against Albania, and Japan against China, the descent into war gathered momentum sharply in late August. At that time, Hitler achieved a masterstroke, signing a non-aggression pact with Stalin, leader of the Soviet Union, which enabled him to move forward with his plans for conquest, both in Poland and in Western Europe, free of any interference from the USSR. One week later, on September 1, the die was cast: the German invasion of Poland sparked the greatest conflict in human history.

With the Canadian government's declaration of war on Germany on September 10, Quebec Premier Maurice Duplessis decided to take advantage of the situation to call an early provincial election, the focus of which was conscription, or mandatory military service. In an attempt to restore an image that had become more than a little tarnished since his election in 1936, Duplessis sought to present himself as the bulwark of French Canadians against conscription.

He was soundly defeated, winning only 15 seats to the 70 won by Adélard Godbout's Liberals. At a time when there was no Quebec Liberal Party—it would not be founded until the 1950s—federal Liberal ministers had involved themselves extensively in the provincial campaign, solemnly pledging their opposition to conscription for military service overseas. It was, as we know, a promise that would be broken.

1940

Bolstered by the devastating successes of Hitler's armies, the war cast a shadow over the whole of 1940. Norway and Denmark fell in April, and, on May 10, a general offensive against the Netherlands, Belgium, and France was launched. While the first two countries surrendered after a few days, France resisted during a month of chaotic and desperate fighting before seeking an armistice.

The conditions imposed by the victor were harsh: occupation of two thirds of the territory, payments of 400 million francs per day, 10 000 head of cattle per week, and 700 000 tonnes of coal per month for the maintenance of the occupation troops. Unwilling to accept such humiliation, General Charles de Gaulle took refuge in England and, from there, delivered his appeal of June 18 calling for resistance; he then established a government in exile, which would be referred to as "Free France."

Then came the Battle of Britain. For three long months, the German air force pounded the ports, airfields, and cities of England with thousands of tonnes of bombs, in the hope of forcing London to seek an armistice. Galvanized by their prime minister, Winston Churchill, and defended by an air force of superior quality, the English held firm; towards the end of the year, Hitler redeployed his forces to other theatres of operation. He had just experienced his first defeat.

1941

1941 saw the geographical extension of the war. After invading Yugoslavia and Greece, and sending Rommel's *Afrikakorps* into Libya to advance towards the Suez Canal, Germany attacked the Soviet Union on June 22, without warning and in blatant violation of the non-aggression pact of 1939. Caught unawares, the Soviets retreated on all fronts, and, by the beginning of December, the Germans were 30 kilometres from Moscow. Victorious but exhausted, they would face there what the Russians always referred to as their top general, "General Winter."

It was the United States' entry into the war that would turn this conflict into a "world" war. Although he was sympathetic to the Franco-British cause, President Roosevelt was compelled to remain neutral by an isolationist Congress. Nevertheless, that did not prevent him from meeting with Prime Minister Winston Churchill in early August aboard a warship anchored off Newfoundland, and there, they signed the Atlantic Charter recognizing the right of all peoples to self-determination.

It was Japan that drew America out of its isolationist shell with a surprise attack on the U.S. Pacific fleet at Pearl Harbor, Hawaii, on December 7 📷. The following day, the United States entered the war, against Japan, Germany, and Italy simultaneously. The war had now truly become a "world" war.

LES MARCHANDS EN QUINCAILLERIE LTÉE

was issued letters patent and officially created in 1939.
The first shareholders of Les Marchands en Quincaillerie Ltée
met in Montreal. The first officers were elected on
October 13, 1939.

CANADA
PROVINCE DE QUÉBEC
GEORGE VI, PAR LA GRACE DE DIEU, ROI DE
GRANDE-BRETAGNE, D'IRLANDE ET DES TERRI-
TOIRES BRITANNIQUES AU DELA DES MERS,
DEFENSEUR DE LA LOI, EMPEREUR DES INDES.

Lettres Patentes
constituant en
corporation

" Les Marchands en
Quincaillerie
Limitée "

ENREGISTREES LE
10 octobre 1939.
Libro 175.
Folio 174.

Le sous-registraire
de la Province:

A tous ceux que les présentes lettres
concerneront ou qui les verront,

SALUT :

ATTENDU que la première partie de la
Loi des Compagnies de Québec, statue que
le lieutenant-gouverneur peut, au moyen
de lettres patentes expédiées sous le
grand sceau, accorder à trois personnes ou
plus qui en font la demande par requête, une
charte les constituant en corporation pour
certains objets relevant de l'autorité législative de cette Province, excepté pour
la construction et l'exploitation de chemins
de fer, pour les affaires d'assurance, et
pour les affaires de fidéicommis ;

ATTENDU que les personnes ci-après désignées ont demandé par requête une charte
qui les constitue en corporation pour les
objets ci-après décrits :

ATTENDU que les dites personnes ont
rempli les formalités prescrites pour l'obtention de la charte demandée, et que les
objets de l'entreprise de la compagnie projetée sont de ceux pour lesquels le lieutenant-gouverneur peut accorder une charte ;

A CES CAUSES, Nous avons, en vertu des
pouvoirs qui Nous sont conférés par la dite

E.S. -1-

—7—

Minutes d'une assemblee generale des actionnaires de "Les Marchands
en Quincaillerie Limitee" tenue dans un salon de l'Hotel Queens,
Rue Windsor, a Montreal, a 8.30 du soir, le 13 Octobre, 1939.

La renonciation suivante a l'avis de convocation d'assemblee,
est lue et signee par tous les actionnaires.

Nous, soussignes, etant tous et les seuls actionnaires de Les
Marchands en Quincaillerie Limitee, renoncons par la presente a
tout avis de l'heure du jour, de l'endroit et des motifs de la
deuxieme assemblee generale des actionnaires de la Compagnie, a
etre tenue au salon de l'Hotel Queens, rue Windsor, a Montreal,
ce 13eme jour d'octobre, 1939 a 8.30 du soir.

Signe a Montreal, ce 13eme jour d'octobre, 1939.

E. Sauve .... S.E.Bonneville

Les minutes de la derniere assemblee sont lues, acceptees et signees.
Sont presents Messieurs Emery Sauve, Sylva Bonneville et Rolland
Dansereau.

Mr. Emery Sauve fut elu president de l'assemblee et Mr Rolland
Dansereau fut elu secretaire de l'assemblee.

Il fut alors resolu a l'unanimite que 50 des actions communes
de la Compagnie soient offertes en vente immediatement; la ba-
... que sur appro-

E.S. —8—

La compagnie sera administree par un bureau de Direction compose
de cinq membres; chacun de ces membres devra etre detenteur d'au
moins une action commune de la compagnie.

Le quorum pour toutes les assemblees du Bureau de Direction sera
de trois membres.

Il fut resolu a l'unanimite qu'aucun actionnaire ne pourra etre
detenteur de plus de deux actions privilegiees chacun.

L'on proceda alors a l'election des officiers de la Compagnie
qui seront elus pour la periode d'un an. Le resultat suivant fut
rapporte par le Secretaire.

Mr Emery Sauve, fut elu President.
Mr. Sylva Bonneville, fut elu 1er Vice-President.
Mr. Damase Desjardins, fut elu 2eme Vice-President.
Mr. Rolland Dansereau fut elu Secretaire-Tresorier.

Comme la compagnie ne se compose que de quatre actionnaires, le
Bureau de Direction fut alors autorise de se completer lors de sa
prochaine assemblee; un directeur devant y etre elu.

Le Secretaire soumet alors divers projets de Reglements lesquels
il faudrait accepter ou modifier le plus tot possible. Il fut alors
resolu unanimement que ceci soit differe a la prochaine assemblee,
afin de donner le temps necessaire aux actionnaires de les bien etudier.

L'assemblee est alors ajournee sine die.

E. Sauve
President

Secretaire.

... par Mr Emery
... par Mr Sylva
... par Mr
... par Mr
... Desjardins
... tte assemblee.
... rees necessaires
... ttre des certi-
... derniers auront

QUINCAILLERIE A. CHAMPAGNE was built in 1907, in Saint-Honoré-de-Shenley in the Beauce region. It started out as a general store, but developed quickly and, from the 1940s, purchased its supplies through Les Marchands en Quincaillerie.

SERVICE ABOVE AND BEYOND is old hat to a hardware merchant! At the dawning of the 1930s, Philippe Dorval, who had been helping his father in the hardware store for several years already, dressed up as Santa Claus.

which Dansereau would act as representative, earning a 2% commission on sales.

What is not in doubt, however, is that Dansereau and Sauvé were bound by a mutual admiration, and both knew that their meeting would change the course of their lives.

To my mind, these differing accounts show that, right from the very beginning, RONA already had the main ingredients for success: a natural inclination for trade, the ability to work together, business skills, and a gift for thinking differently.

Les Marchands en Quincaillerie Ltée received its letters patent on October 6, 1939. The applicants were Alphonse Lemay, accountant, Rolland Dansereau, manager, and Laurent Fauteux, lawyer, all from Montreal. Each purchased one common share in the company, and they were appointed as its provisional directors.

The mission of the company was to "engage in wholesale and retail trade as hardware and ironworks merchants." The share capital was set at $10 000, divided into 100 common shares worth $1 each, and 99 preferred shares worth $100 each. Preferred shares were entitled to a dividend of 5% per year with priority over dividends on common shares, but they carried no voting rights.

The head office of the new company was located in suite 411 of the Confederation Building, at the intersection of St. Catherine Street and McGill College Avenue.

The first meeting was held on October 13, with the election of a board of directors. Émery Sauvé was appointed president. Two other dealers, Sylva Bonneville and Damase Desjardins, were appointed vice-presidents. Rolland Dansereau was secretary-treasurer.

And thus was born a truly original company, an incorporated business like many others, but with this unique difference: its shareholders were also its clients, and the business existed solely for their benefit.

That was the fundamental characteristic of Les Marchands en Quincaillerie Ltée and, seven decades later, it remains an essential component of RONA's culture: by the dealers, for the dealers. And if the dealers are well-organized, properly financed, and suitably equipped, they will be in a better position than anyone else to provide good service to their clients. This is the principle that has shaped RONA's entire history.

Everybody in the hardware business was talking about the company, and new members were joining each week. The company soon outgrew its office in the Confederation Building. In January 1940, a sample room was rented at 7 Notre-Dame Street East, in an area that was still too young to be called "Old Montreal." A year later, a first warehouse was rented a short distance away, at 104 St. Paul Street East, followed by a second nine months later at 296 Place d'Youville, a building formerly used as a stable.

1942

Around the world, 1942 marked both the point of maximum advance for the German and Japanese empires, and the beginning of a shift in the balance of power in favour of the "Grand Alliance" between the United States, Great Britain, and the Soviet Union. The Japanese were on India's doorstep, while the Germans were at the gates of Egypt, in North Africa, and Stalingrad, in Europe. In August, the poorly coordinated raid on Dieppe by Canadian and British commandos ended in bloody defeat, although it did provide lessons that would prove valuable for the future invasion of the continent.

But the tide was clearly turning. In the Pacific, the Japanese fleet was defeated at Midway in June. In November, Rommel was halted at El Alamein, in North Africa, and the Allies landed in Algeria and Morocco. By December, the Germans were surrounded on all sides in Stalingrad. The reconquest had begun.

In Canada, 1942 witnessed the most serious crisis since Confederation between the "two founding nations." Mackenzie King's Liberal government held a national plebiscite asking the Canadian population to allow it to rescind its promise not to impose conscription for mandatory military service overseas, a promise that had been made by the federal Liberals during the 1939 Quebec provincial election. The result was unsurprising: French Canadians voted NO overwhelmingly; the response from English Canada was an equally vigorous YES. The government was thus released from its promise. But this development cast a stark light on the division between the French and the English, the effects of which can still be felt today.

1943

1943 was another year dominated by developments in the ongoing global hostilities. The German and Japanese empires retreated further. In Stalingrad, nearly 300 000 German soldiers surrendered after being completely surrounded; Hitler's most significant defeat to date, it took on a symbolic value. In North Africa, the Italian-German forces surrendered in the spring; the Allies subsequently landed in Sicily, in July, and in Italy, in September. In the Pacific, the Americans were gaining ground one island at a time.

The Italian defeats in North Africa and Sicily led to the fall of Mussolini, who was overthrown by his own cabinet and imprisoned under orders from the king, and eventually to Italy's surrender in September. But the Germans had already replaced the Italians on the country's defense lines, blocking the Allies' way to Rome.

During this time, chiefs of state were meeting with increasing frequency, to try to keep alive an alliance that was rife with internal tensions, particularly between the USSR and the West. Churchill and Roosevelt held consultations with one another, on one occasion meeting in Quebec City, in August, before finally meeting with Stalin in Tehran, in November, at which time they resolved to stage a landing in France the following year.

1944

The Second World War entered its fifth year in 1944. It was the decisive year: in the Pacific, the Americans advanced systematically from one island to the next and, by year's end, were able to launch their first aerial assaults on Japan itself. In Europe, following Italy's defection, Germany found itself alone and surrounded on all sides, and it would gradually have to abandon nearly all the territories it had conquered since 1939.

The famous Normandy landing on June 6 is recognized as the military event of the year. In the largest naval and air operation in history, close to 7 000 vessels, 15 000 planes, 95 000 vehicles, 210 000 tonnes of material, and 619 000 soldiers were mobilized, arriving on the beaches of Normandy from England over a 10-day period. The operation, as risky as it was massive, proved successful and opened the way to Germany for the Western Allies, who gained a foothold there in October. Meanwhile, the Soviets had liberated their entire territory and had made headway into Poland and Romania.

In July, 44 allied nations signed the Bretton Woods Agreements in the small New Hampshire village of the same name. These agreements created the World Bank and the International Monetary Fund. While it sent an observer, the Soviet Union did not sign on.

In Canada, Saskatchewan elected North America's first socialist government, the CCF (Co-operative Commonwealth Federation), led by T.C. "Tommy" Douglas. Many of this government's progressive policies were subsequently adopted by the federal government and the other provinces.

In Quebec, 1944 is remembered for the electoral defeat of the Liberals. In spite of such significant achievements as women's suffrage and the creation of Hydro-Québec, Godbout's government alienated the nationalists when it broke its 1939 anti-conscription promise and surrendered some of the province's powers of taxation to the federal government to help finance the war effort. Maurice Duplessis stepped forward as the champion of provincial autonomy and took back the reins of power, which he held until his death in 1959.

OTHER COMPANIES THAT SOLD BUILDING MATERIALS were established in Quebec during the time of Les Marchands en Quincaillerie Ltée. P.H. Desrosiers founded LaSalle Ltée in 1933 and Val Royal, in Montreal, in 1951.

At the same time, the business adopted a structure that would remain in place until the mid-1950s. In 1941, three members were added to the board of directors: J.J. Girouard, Henri Lemoine, and Lucien Lamarre. The board now consisted of seven people: a president, two vice-presidents, three directors, and a secretary-treasurer, a role still filled by Rolland Dansereau. A prospectus sent to the "Secretary of the Province of Quebec" in the summer of 1940 reported that there were 50 common shares and 14 preferred shares. The authorized share capital at the time was $49 900, rising to $99 900 in 1946.

That year Les Marchands en Quincaillerie Ltée started a tradition that would continue for many years, contributing significantly to the group's renown, and representing a show of strength by these associated dealers in the face of their rivals. In 1946, on the first floor of the Atwater Market, in a room redolent of fish, Les Marchands en Quincaillerie Ltée held its first-ever annual exhibition. It was a trade fair at which new products were presented to dealers. Over the years it has become a must-attend event. Many people were there, and it provided an opportunity to recruit new members.

Les Marchands en Quincaillerie Ltée was emerging from the shadows. In the photo taken at the opening of the seventh annual members' convention (p. 22), there are no fewer than 93 hardware dealers and, in the front row, the

THE REVELSTOKE SAWMILL COMPANY
continued its expansion into Western Canada. In
1940, it was well established in the new communities,
including Ponteix, in Saskatchewan, where the
Canadian Pacific railroad had run since 1913.

president, Émery Sauvé, is seated next to Camilien Houde, the all-powerful mayor of Montreal.

The arrival of Napoléon Piotte

During that period, politics and religion were never far from the forefront. It is therefore not surprising that an event organized by the Frères du Sacré-Cœur provided the setting for an encounter that would prove to be another significant moment in the young history of Les Marchands en Quincaillerie Ltée.

The year was 1947. One of the guest speakers was a gentleman by the name of Napoléon Piotte. A high school teacher at Le Plateau school, he was also a devout Catholic and a fierce French Canadian militant. Rolland Dansereau, attending the event, was awed by Piotte's powerful skills as an orator. It did not matter that he knew nothing about business or hardware, he had a manner of speaking and an energy that impressed Dansereau, who saw in him a natural "propagandist." This word has, over the years, taken on a negative connotation, but at that time, it was the name given to someone who was in charge of recruiting, the first task assigned to Piotte.

After one of his talks, Dansereau went straight up to him and said: "You can start on Monday morning." To Piotte, this came as a bolt out of the blue. He found the venture tempting, but he already had 30 years of teaching

under his belt, his retirement was not far off, and business was not always highly regarded as a profession in Catholic circles. Piotte himself told this story on stage many years later, at the 20th convention of Les Marchands en Quincaillerie Ltée:

> "As long as I live I will never forget the day when I found Rolland Dansereau, whom I barely knew, waiting for me at the door of the school at lunchtime. He was there to ask me to go to work for him and take over from a childhood friend of mine.
>
> This put me in a very awkward spot. On one hand, I knew nothing whatsoever about your group, let alone about hardware; on the other, I would have to take over from a friend. I therefore asked Mr. Dansereau for permission, before I made any sort of commitment, to go and see my predecessor and ask him why he had resigned from a position which, at first glance, seemed to me to be quite well paid.
>
> I got my interview. Another former employee was there also. There were many insinuations but no specific accusations. No obstacles were put in the way of my acceptance, but, based on what they knew about me, some people predicted I would last no more than six months. As I had been given a list of some former as well as some active clients, I took the liberty of paying each one of them a visit.

The parent company's premises •

THE FIRST YEARS WERE MARKED BY NECESSITY AND GROWTH. FROM VERY HUMBLE BEGINNINGS, SPACES WERE ADDED ON ONE AFTER THE OTHER; SOME WERE USED AS DISPLAY ROOMS, OTHERS AS OFFICES, WHILE OTHERS STILL SERVED AS WAREHOUSES.

❶ 296 D'Youville Place. Photo taken before 1962.

❷ 104 Saint-Paul Street East. Photo of Saint-Paul Street looking east, from the corner of Saint-Gabriel Street. Today, that is the address of Le Deux Pierrots. The building is located on the right, just beyond the fire hydrant.

❸ 7 Notre-Dame Street East. The photo was taken from the southwest corner of the intersection of Saint-Laurent and Notre-Dame streets. Landry et Berthiaume, a store that sold cash registers, is located at number 1.

Between the years 1939 and 1948, the company moved from 7 Notre-Dame Street East to 104 Saint-Paul Street East, and finally to buildings located at 296 Place d'Youville, which formerly housed the stables belonging to the Sœurs de la Charité, a community founded by Marguerite d'Youville at the beginning of the colonization period. This final location looked out onto a large courtyard, and today's discriminating diners will recognize it as the site of the renowned Gibbys Restaurant, where you can still see the arches through which the horses entered.

These stables, which dated back to 1740, were only renovated in 1967. Marielle Luchesi, who began working with the company as secretary and bookkeeper in 1959, says that, prior to then, "the offices were made of bare lumber; they were quite primitive." They rode a freight elevator with a metal grille to travel between floors! Marielle worked as an assistant, along with three other co-workers, under the supervision of Robert Tétreault, the accountant. She had been hired by Napoléon Piotte, whom she had met as a result of their mutual involvement with various worthy causes. Back then, he was the "voyageur," the travelling sales representative, for the group. "A very nice man," Marielle would note fondly. Only Rolland Dansereau's office was completely closed off. And, picture this... even the door was upholstered with padded leather! But he watched the employees carefully. Rolland wanted to succeed and was anxious to make sure

18

From one expansion to another

the employees were doing their jobs properly. The moment devices like interphones and cameras appeared, he had them installed.

It was no wonder that, in 1960, the company's small group of employees considered their De la Savane Street premises to be the height of contemporary office design. For starters, they had everything they could possibly want: a large display room, the warehouse in the basement, and a beautiful staircase leading up to the offices, which could be admired from the outside through a large glass window. And everything was state-of-the-art, including all the office equipment. Marielle even had a 'bookkeeping machine'—there was no longer any need for wooden pencils! Nonetheless, a degree of interpersonal austerity was still maintained. The offices were bordered on either side by the large display room. Rolland had his office at the back, in the middle, and, adjoining it was the accountant's office, which Napoléon also used. The atmosphere was of an ultra-organized beehive.

Opposite this area was the printing room, where the catalogue that was indispensable to the merchants was produced, ad nauseam. Michel Gendron worked there, and he explains how they used a Gestetner duplicating machine to assemble and print the illustrations, cut-outs, and photos. In spite of the relative modernity of the premises and equipment, they still put together all their advertising material by hand; week after week, a human assembly line would gather around the table preparing the price catalogues.

Marc St-Pierre, Michel's boss, joined the company in 1962, in the early years on De la Savane Street. The workers were still in the process of gutting the inside of the building, pulling out nails and taking down shelving. A total of 42 people worked there at the time. One peculiar detail that required some getting used to was that everyone worked to

❹ In April 1961, the publication *Le Quincaillier* reported that Les Marchands en Quincaillerie Ltée had just moved "to the ultra-modern building on De la Savane Street that houses a sample room, a warehouse, and offices over some 72 000 square feet of space."

❺ In 1967, Lise Pichette was working in the De la Savane Street offices as a secretary-receptionist.

❻ Members of Marchands Ro-Na Inc. meet in the De la Savane Street offices, now grown too cramped, for the annual shareholders' meeting in 1972.

20

❼ Beginning in 1974, visitors to the Nobel Street head office in Boucherville were received in a large room facing the computer centre.

❽ From the end of the 1970s, the store decoration and display department at the head office of Marchands Ro-Na Inc. on Nobel Street in Boucherville designed and produced the displays for the Rona banner stores.

the sound of bells, which indicated each worker's movements. Everyone had a lot of space to move around in, but, due to the company's growth, this would not last long.

The De la Savane Street location was close to imploding. Pierre Forget arrived at the warehouse in 1971. At 67 people, the group was still quite small. But so significant had been the increase in the number of members, suppliers (300), and products the company carried (8 000), that the situation was reaching a boiling point. Orders were still being taken over the phone and filled by hand, box after box. Finally, they annexed the building next door

and linked it to the main offices via a tunnel, which provided them with approximately 100 000 sq. ft. (9 300 m²) more floor space. But it wasn't enough. "We had to walk on top of pallets piled high with merchandise to get a piece of equipment," Pierre relates.

The decision, in 1973, to build the Nobel Street facilities was not reached without careful consideration. The company relocated there the following year and the number of employees rapidly swelled to 200. The computer centre was described as 'the most advanced in the entire country.' Within the company, everyone took great pride in this huge accomplishment, which was realized through a cooperative effort. They rejoiced and celebrated, the festivities lasting from March 3 to 6, 1974. Employees, merchants, and suppliers all assembled for the official opening, with the spring/summer collection of toys and decorations on display to greet everyone. It was just the start of the boom, of the larger scale of things to come. Eventually, however, and in spite of having already built one addition, even these new premises proved too small. In the last years there, the pressure to expand was becoming increasingly intense. It became necessary to rent warehouse space elsewhere, which significantly slowed the process of receiving merchandise.

"The trials and tribulations of growth," Pierre would recall serenely. The first months in the new

Du Tremblay location were indescribable; no words could express the feeling of exhilaration tinged with panic as people strove to get technology and expansion working in sync. But they all pulled together... and they succeeded. The company grew, it streamlined its operations, and they all prayed that they wouldn't have to move again! In 2010, the distribution centre in Boucherville accommodated 1 200 employees, a daycare, the Rona Academy—a permanent training school—and a warehouse, which is close to a kilometre long. But that's another story.

❾ 220 Du Tremblay Road in Boucherville is an immense building that houses both Rona's head office and a huge distribution centre.

Ouverture du 7ième Congrès Annuel   Les Marchands en Quincaillerie Limitée
Montréal, les 26-27-28 février 1946

After a couple of weeks of talking to people here and there, I was no closer to an answer. There was only one solution: step into my predecessor's shoes and get acquainted with the situation myself. Twelve years have passed since that memorable day, and, so far, I feel neither regret nor remorse."

And so began the long and successful partnership between Rolland Dansereau and Napoléon Piotte, whose first names are forever joined together under the RONA banner.

Napoléon Piotte started his career with the associated dealers not long after the end of the war. As mentioned before, the company had grown during those dark years, but in business terms, they were still lean times. Severe rationing was strangling trade, and its full force was intensely felt by the hardware dealers. Metal of any kind, in particular, was being channelled towards the defence industry. Finding any bit of lead piping at that time was a real feat.

Piotte's arrival coincided with a gradual easing of rationing restrictions. The economic situation was improving, and the whole world, including Quebec and Canada, was entering into a period of strong growth stimulated by the rebuilding of war-ravaged Europe.

The time was right to recruit new members, and the indefatigable Napoléon spared no effort, putting in countless hours at work and on the road. In just a few months, he transformed the group by turning it into a Quebec-wide entity. Up until then, Les Marchands en Quincaillerie Ltée

had essentially been a Montreal-based concern, and that metropolitan affiliation made the group less than popular in places like Quebec City and the rural areas. But while Napoléon Piotte also had the "shortcoming" of being a Montrealer, it could be said in his favour that he was a devout Catholic, and this opened not only heaven's doors to him but many others too. He travelled the length and breadth of Quebec. Many dealers in Quebec City joined, and the group quickly spread to other parts of the province.

Napoléon Piotte's arrival was a real shot in the arm for the group. But this development at Les Marchands en Quincaillerie Ltée, coming just as the economy was finally starting to pick up, proved troubling in certain quarters. The large wholesalers who had a stranglehold on the hardware sector did not look very favourably on these neighbourhood dealers who took clients away from them and thought they could overturn the established order. In fact, these wholesalers, like Lewis Brothers and Prud'homme et Fils, were in a fairly strong position. They set themselves up as ineluctable middlemen between the manufacturers and the retailers, and many abuses occurred. It was not unusual, for example, for a dealer ordering a barrel of 2 ½-inch nails—the best-selling size—to be obliged to also purchase an equal quantity of 4-inch nails, for which he had no use. That was the law of the wholesalers who, in many cases, were also retailers themselves, competing with their own clients.

THE 1946 CONVENTION brought together merchants from several regions, including Jean-Paul Pion from Saint-Damase, Eugène Bélanger from Montreal, and Charles McKenzie from Drummondville. Sitting in the middle is Camilien Houde, the mayor of Montreal, and third from the left of the mayor is Rolland Dansereau.

DEALER ROBITAILLE'S TICKET for the 1946 convention. The Marchands' directors had decided that on February 26, access to the convention would be reserved for members of the organization, while the next two days would be open to retailers from across the province of Quebec.

The initiator

Émery Sauvé
Former Merchant and First Chairman of the Board

It is thanks to the vision of Émery Sauvé and his fellow pioneering hardware merchants—Sylva E. Bonneville, Damase Desjardins, J.J. Girouard, Henri Lemoine, Lucien Lamarre, J.O. Roberge, Léopold Lamarre, and Olaüs Latendresse—that the story began. His vision was one of cooperation between members, of a united effort. To this day, it is still an integral part of the fabric of Rona.

Émery Sauvé was chairman of the board of directors of Les Marchands en Quincaillerie Ltée from the signing of the letters patent in October 1939 until 1953. He not only provided the driving force behind this vast collective, but he dedicated 14 years of his life to sustaining it.

Born in 1877 in Coteau-du-Lac, he moved to Montreal in 1903 with his young bride, Emma. In 1908, he opened an ironworks shop, Maison Émery Sauvé, in Ville-Émard, now part of the Sud-Ouest borough of Montreal, and, long before today's dollar stores had come into fashion, he added a five-and-dime store to it. En 1926, he opened a second store in the same neighbourhood, following the same hybrid formula.

His businesses quickly turned into a family affair. In 1956, É. Sauvé became É. Sauvé Inc. His son Jean-Marie headed the company, and his grandsons, Roger and Rolland, came aboard as managers. They acquired Queen Mary Hardware in 1967. The first hardware store, on Monk Street, was transformed into a shopping centre in 1970.

Émery Sauvé's story goes far beyond that of the businessman he was; it is rather a story of community. The list of organizations he either founded or belonged to is dizzying. In 1913, he was a school commissioner in Ville-Émard. That same year, he presided over the local chapter of the Saint-Jean-Baptiste society. In 1921, he established the Property Owners League of Montreal and headed it until 1935. He would go on to found the Ligue des propriétaires de la province de Québec, and served as its president for seven years. In 1922, he was named president of the Retail Merchants Association of Canada, where he would retain a permanent position as senator. From 1933 to 1950, he served as a director at Université de Montréal. He was elected municipal councillor six times between 1940 and 1957, representing the citizens of Saint-Henri, Sainte-Cunégonde, and Saint-Paul. In 1952, he was sent to Rome as a delegate of the City of Montreal for the elevation to the rank of cardinal of His Eminence Paul-Émile Léger. Upon his death, in 1961, the flag at City Hall was lowered and flown at half mast. La voix populaire, his neighbourhood's local publication, would say of him: "The benefactor of a host of humanitarian causes, Mr. Sauvé always demonstrated his concern for the cause of the common good."

A Knight of the Equestrian Order of the Holy Sepulchre of Jerusalem, a Knight of Columbus, a Justice of the Peace, and a warden for the parish, he was the staunch supporter of a great number of charitable organizations. Just a few paces from his businesses and his home is a commemorative park that bears his name, a reminder to everyone of the importance of his social involvement.

1945

In some respects, 1945 stands as a watershed year in the 20th century and one of the most significant of the entire modern era. It marked the end of the Second World War and, with it, the end of Europe's dominance in the world, which had endured for more than 200 years. The future now belonged to two superpowers, the United States and the Soviet Union 📷.

But the end of the war brought with it a deep spiritual and moral malaise that gripped humankind. Indeed, the close of this chapter in history was itself accompanied by unimaginable acts of barbarism, and not only on the part of the vanquished, who continued to cause bloodshed throughout their interminable retreat. The victors, too, spread death and destruction, often cruelly and without justification, as evidenced in a spate of horrific bombings that claimed hundreds of thousands of civilian lives (200 000 in Tokyo alone, for example) and the atomic bombings of Hiroshima and Nagasaki, which offered a staggering glimpse into the scientific and technological capacity for self-destruction now in man's possession. Furthermore, the revelation to the world of the largest genocide in history, the Jewish Holocaust in Europe, seemed to challenge the very notion of humanity.

There were, nonetheless, a few glimmers of hope. New legal concepts of "war crimes" and "crimes against humanity" emerged to contribute to humankind's moral progress, while the establishment of the United Nations would encourage the peaceful resolution of conflicts between states.

1946

January 10 marked the opening of the first session of the General Assembly of the United Nations (UN). Other international organizations came into being during the year, with more or less direct ties to the UN: the International Court of Justice (ICJ) 📷, the World Health Organization (WHO), and the United Nations Children's Fund (UNICEF).

But cracks were beginning to appear in the wartime alliance between the United States and the Soviet Union. In a famous speech delivered on March 5, Winston Churchill coined the term "iron curtain." The Cold War was already looming on the horizon, and Canada was plunged into it with the Gouzenko affair, when an attaché from the Soviet Embassy in Ottawa claimed political asylum and exposed the names of several Soviet spies who were active in Canada. The government of Mackenzie King shrouded the entire affair in mystery, and Gouzenko's face was never seen; to prevent reprisals, he always appeared with a hood over his head, leading people to wonder at times if he actually existed.

Towards the end of the year, the bombing of Haiphong by the French Navy heralded the beginning of the French Indochina War against Vietnamese nationalists, a conflict that would continue for close to 10 years. Decolonization was under way.

1947

In 1947, the Cold War began in earnest. While the USSR set up Soviet-influenced governments in the satellite states of Eastern Europe (Poland, Hungary, Bulgaria, and Romania), U.S. President Harry Truman proclaimed the doctrine that bore his name, with its focus on containment. The aim was to block the advance of communism everywhere in the world by providing financial, material, and military aid to countries under threat.

In conjunction with the Truman Doctrine, the U.S. developed the Marshall Plan, an extensive program of economic assistance for Europe totalling more than $13 billion in dollars of the day, most of it in the form of gifts. This assistance was immediately declined by the Soviets.

In Asia, Great Britain finally resigned itself to giving up the "pearl" of its empire: India. But the intractable conflict between Muslims and Hindus led to the colony's division into two states along religious lines: the Indian Union, which was primarily Hindu, and Pakistan, which was primarily Muslim. Massive population displacements, combined with bloody massacres on both sides, cast a shadow over the attainment of independence.

1947 also saw the signing of the General Agreement on Tariffs and Trade (GATT), the goal of which was to reduce tariffs and liberalize trade among signatory countries. This agreement would play a vital role in the evolution of the global economy in the 50 years that followed.

In Canada, Saskatchewan's CCF government introduced the first universal public hospital insurance program. Thus was laid the first building block of what would become the health care program Canadians today consider an integral part of their identity. One would have to wait until 1961 for the remaining provinces to adopt equivalent hospital insurance programs.

1948

The Cold War intensified with the Berlin Blockade. At the end of the war, Germany had been divided into four occupation zones (United States, Great Britain, France, and the USSR). Due to its strategic importance, the city of Berlin, while located wholly within the Soviet zone, was itself subdivided into four sectors. To reach their respective sectors in that city, Western powers had to pass through the Soviet-occupied zone in Germany. On June 14, the Soviets suddenly blocked all access to the city, stranding West Berlin, which soon ran short of essential supplies. The three Western Allies responded with a massive airlift that sent planes to the city carrying as much as 6 000 tonnes per day of goods of all kinds, from coal to potatoes. The blockade would last for close to a year.

A new nation appeared on the map on May 14: Israel. It was a country whose birth was accompanied by ethnic cleansing operations conducted against native Palestinians by Zionist terror organizations. The intervention of neighbouring Arab states sparked the first Arab-Israeli war, during which Israel seized new territories, while nearly a million Palestinians ended up in refugee camps in adjacent countries.

The year closed with the adoption, on December 10, by the United Nations General Assembly of the Universal Declaration of Human Rights, ushering in a new phase in the emergence of a moral conscience for humankind.

On November 15, the Liberal Party accepted the resignation of W. Lyon Mackenzie King, the longest serving prime minister since 1935. At the party's leadership convention, his successor, Louis S. Saint-Laurent, was sworn in as party leader and prime minister of Canada.

1949

There was further consolidation of the two blocs in the Cold War. The Soviet Union and its satellites formed the Council for Mutual Economic Assistance (COMECON) to counter the Marshall Plan, while the Western nations created the North Atlantic Treaty Organization (NATO), a defensive military alliance that was vigorously condemned by the Soviets. In the meantime, the Berlin Blockade was lifted; Stalin had realized his error in failing to anticipate that a large city could now be supplied entirely by air, and could not risk precipitating a war by attempting to intercept the unarmed planes taking part in the airlift.

With the crisis over, each superpower set about building its own Germany: the Western nations merged their occupation zones, creating the Federal Republic of Germany, while the Soviets established the German Democratic Republic in their zone.

At the same time, tensions between the blocs kicked up several notches with the construction of a Soviet atomic bomb in September, a development that broke America's atomic monopoly, and the communist victory in China in October, which brought to a close a protracted civil war that had raged for 20 years. The Cold War now engulfed the entire world, and the adversaries faced the realization each had the ability to destroy the other side—and themselves in the process.

Canada added its 10th province on April 1 when Newfoundland joined Confederation following a second referendum in which 52% of voters were in favour of becoming part of Canada.

NAPOLÉON PIOTTE enjoyed meeting people. He shakes the hands of the crew aboard the *SS Homeric*.

AS THE 1940s DREW TO A CLOSE,
LES MARCHANDS EN QUNICAILLERIE LTÉE

were already like a little family. They participated in social activities together, like this cruise aboard the *SS Homeric*.

The battle of Toronto

At the start of the 1950s, the wholesalers decided to crush this group of troublemakers by organizing a boycott. Manufacturers were forbidden to sell anything at all to Les Marchands en Quincaillerie Ltée under threat of losing their wholesaler clients. Stanley, Black & Decker, Pyrex, and many others would cut all ties with the associated dealers. The group's very existence was in danger.

But Les Marchands en Quincaillerie Ltée would not back down. For the first time in their history, they would have to take on an adversary bigger than themselves. In years to come, this would become routine.

The conflict with the wholesalers came to an end with a confrontation that has remained famous in the annals of RONA. It is still referred to as "the battle of Toronto." In a way, it was a baptism of fire for our founders, a defining moment when they gained a conviction that would inform the entire culture of the organization, the idea that nothing could stop them if they stood united in their efforts.

The story played out in Toronto, over a period of two or three consecutive years, at the Canadian Hardware Show, the major annual exhibition organized by the Canadian Retail Hardware Association. The Quebec hardware dealers' trips to Toronto have become legendary at RONA. A hundred or so dealers would leave by train on Saturday evening, party the night away, and then rather rowdily take over an entire floor in a downtown hotel.

Rolland and Napoléon had come up with a plan that would force the manufacturers to do business with them. All of the dealers took part in the offensive. Rolland had given his instructions: "Go and buy whatever you need. But buy double the amount. We'll keep the surplus for the warehouse."

So the dealers went up and down the aisles and placed huge orders. At the end, the manufacturers asked which wholesalers they did business with.

— With Les Marchands en Quincaillerie Ltée.

— Then I can't take your order.

— That's okay, just tear it up.

Ten, twenty, thirty, eighty orders were torn up by salesmen who were furious that their time had been wasted and their large commissions lost.

Napoléon was on the floor coordinating the operation, which continued throughout the five days of the show. Rolland was in the hotel room and answered the phone call that was not long in coming:

— Mr. Dansereau, we have to talk.

It was in this way, with the participation of all the dealers, that the boycott was broken. It had taken two years, three for the more recalcitrant among them, but all the manufacturers eventually gave in, regardless of what the large wholesalers had to say about it.

Rolland Dansereau and Napoléon Piotte •

THEIR NAMES FOREVER UNITED UNDER THE RONA BANNER.

Rolland Dansereau first learned about the principles and benefits of cooperation from his father, Camille, the mastermind behind the Épiceries Modernes chain of grocery stores. During that period, Rolland would attend meetings held by a small group of merchants who pooled their orders to obtain better prices. He would not forget this lesson in economy.

Rolland graduated from the École technique de Montréal and learned the trade of electrician before signing on as a sales representative for various American manufacturers from Halifax to Vancouver. He subsequently went on to found his own business on De la Commune Street, in Old Montreal.

In 1939, when the hardware merchants were looking for an agent to negotiate prices and make purchases for them, they naturally turned to Rolland. He accepted, even if the commission offered him was, relatively speaking, quite modest. He was one of three applicants to whom the company's letters patent were issued on October 6, 1939. Jean-Paul Morency, Charles' younger brother, stated that Rolland was a businessman "with great foresight, who had understood that the company was destined for greatness." Indeed, taking advantage of the upheaval that world war had created, his wealth, and his intuition, this astute businessman purchased the participating merchants' shares, little by little, until he had become the majority shareholder.

In 1947, Rolland Dansereau, a numbers man, invited Napoléon Piotte, an articulate man and a renowned speaker, to become the 'propagandist'—a term used in days gone by—for Les Marchands en Quincaillerie Ltée. It was a decision that would one day lead to the cooperative system.

A talented student, Napoléon had studied to become a teacher in Quebec and Vermont. He began his teaching career in an elementary school in Montreal, after which he became a school inspector in Saint-Jean-sur-Richelieu, before returning to teach at a high school in Montreal. But he was also a fervent Catholic and community activist. As a young man, he belonged to the Association catholique de la jeunesse canadienne-française (ACJCF). As an adult, he was the right arm for Monsignor Forget, a French priest, collaborated on the launch of *Le Richelieu* newspaper, founded the charitable organization Œuvre des terrains de jeux, contributed to the Saint-Jean-de-Lalande retirement home, established the Fédération des amicales des Frères du Sacré-Cœur, organized the second fund-raising campaign for the Immaculée-Conception parish centre, and on the list went.

As a speaker, he was much in demand. A member of the Ordre des commandeurs de Jacques-Cartier (the Order of Jacques-Cartier), a secret society unknown to the public, which was founded at the beginning of the 1920s, Napoléon defended the Order's causes until its dissolution in the mid-1950s. This group sought to promote the involvement of Francophones in the federal civil service and to maintain the vitality of the French language in various areas, including product labelling—on cigarette packages, for instance—and the designation of public places—such as Château Champlain or the Jacques-Cartier Bridge.

Rolland would say, "I am never embarrassed by my faith nor by my native tongue, and my business keeps on growing." It was easy to see that the two men, though not alike, shared common values.

From 1949 to 1952, Rolland built the Palais du commerce, on Berri Street, where, each year, thousands of visitors would browse the manufacturers' kiosks. And, of course, he continued to grow his business. He was a man who managed his staff with an iron hand, as was common practice in those days. His employees worked at various stations in a large square room, and the products were on display in the centre of the room. Cameras and interphones allowed him to keep track of each

The founders

Rolland Dansereau

Napoléon Piotte

Rolland Dansereau was a founding member of Les Marchands en Quincaillerie Ltée in 1939. He first acted as intermediary and secretary-treasurer, until 1954, when he became president.

In 1947, Napoléon Piotte was responsible for recruiting new members for Les Marchands en Quincaillerie Ltée. In 1962, he led a group of hardware store dealers in acquiring the organization, and then became its president.

employee's involvement. When Napoléon became president, he would follow suit… except without the cameras.

During this period, Napoléon travelled throughout the province, holding meetings with the hardware store dealers in each region, talking to them, listening to them, and convincing them. Through his efforts, the work force increased as well.

In 1960, the two men created Ro-Na, a new entity whose name was created using the first two letters of each of their given names. In 1962, Napoléon and nine merchants bought out Rolland's shares and re-established the cooperative system, at least from the financial aspect. André Dion remembers:

"When I started there in 1966, it was a cooperative. At the end of the month, and especially at the beginning of the year, Mr. Piotte would go around distributing the annual rebates in the form of bank notes. He would say, "Here's the breakdown: this is what it cost the administration, these are the prices we paid, these are the prices you were charged, and this is what's left over; this is your rebate."

Napoléon was a businessman who dreamed of building, because for him, that gave life meaning. He constantly thought of building for others, his French-Canadian brethren, his friends. On September 30, 1968, he left the office and was admitted to hospital, where he died eight days later. To this day he is remembered as a man who was good, firm, and kind, someone who was committed and had the ability to persuade others. Rolland died only months later.

A storehouse of knowledge

Pierre Piotte
Former Merchant and Former Member of the Board of Directors

As a teen, he would do the dusting at the offices of Les Marchands en Quincaillerie Ltée, at Place d'Youville in Montreal... It was the end of the 1940s, and Pierre Piotte, Napoléon's son, was already immersed in the world his father had created a few years earlier. His father played a hugely influential role in his son's life, and Pierre held him in the highest esteem. But this modest and easy-going man also has a story to tell.

Fresh out of college in 1951, and acting on the sound advice of Rolland Dansereau, he got a job at the Mont-Royal hardware store to learn the ropes of the retail trade. He then returned to the head office for a while to work as an order clerk, but he had been bitten by the retail bug—and he missed the contact with customers—so he joined Modelectric, where he worked as manager for the next 10 years. In 1966, he purchased the company with partner Marcel Robillard, eventually selling it in 1992 with the intention of retiring... which he never did. Instead, he returned to work for André Gagnon, who had bought the store from him, and, since 2001, has had a variety of responsibilities at the Quincaillerie Beaubien. A never-ending adventure of service, enthusiasm, and personal relations: the story of his life.

During all those years, Pierre kept ahead of the times. He was the first merchant to set up an Ambiance Boutique, a new concept for presenting decorating ideas, which attracted a female clientele from far and wide... of course, he didn't let that interfere with his family life! His commercial initiatives were widely acclaimed at the time.

He also became closely involved in the inner workings of Rona. In 1975, when he was presiding over the first trade convention, the company introduced a new rule making it mandatory for the group's name to cover at least 50% of the surface of a merchant's outdoor sign. Around the same time, they also launched an innovative and motivational advertising strategy. From 1977 to 1982, Pierre served as a member, then as vice-chairman, of the board of directors.

Between 1983 and 2003, he sat on the advisory committee of the Canadian Retail Hardware Association, the Quebec Employers' Council, and the Conseil québécois du commerce au détail (Quebec retailing council). If you ever need information on the hardware or retail trade, just talk to Pierre. His mind is a vast storehouse of knowledge, which he is always happy to share!

A decade later, in the early 1960s, Les Marchands en Quincaillerie Ltée would put a similar strategy into action... this time to obtain services in French.

The painful departure of Émery Sauvé

Through all its ups and downs, the company continued to progress. There were now a hundred member dealers, and sales reached $1.758 million in 1951, although that number dropped slightly in the two years that followed, falling to $1.528 million in 1952 and $1.410 million in 1953. Overall, business was fairly good, but a number of dealers were in precarious positions, and dissatisfaction was on the rise, with dealers complaining about the high prices they had to pay for their purchases.

Throughout 1953, the minutes of the various meetings reported the interminable discussions that took place on this topic. In the fall of that year, tensions started to mount. The search was on to "find some way or ways to make the members' transactions with the company more profitable for the members" (October 26). The president, Émery Sauvé, suggested hiring an additional employee, but the directors felt that the company could not afford this (November 16). There were calls for "a new mode of selling," and some wanted to "liquidate the stock we currently have on hand" (November 24). On November 30, the minutes report that "the meeting was long," but no decision was made and the president was harshly criticized.

The breaking point came in January 1954. An account of the situation can be found in a document dated January 19.

The facts

"For the last year [we have been hearing] complaints from members who are highly dissatisfied with the present situation and the profits they are earning. It has been observed that sales at the large stores are dropping off because the prices offered are not satisfactory. However, there is also a decline in business at the small stores, because there is not enough merchandise in stock to fill orders when needed and thus ensure their clients' satisfaction. In both cases, the solution lies in increasing our capital […]:

a) the members refuse, as they already have around $500 invested;

b) the directors who have incurred personal liability, and have done so without remuneration, do not wish to pay more, and rightly so, as they cannot obtain administrative liability in relation or in proportion to their investment;

c) the managing director [Rolland Dansereau] offered to put up the necessary money, to a maximum of an additional $200 000, on the

1950

On the international stage, 1950 was a year dominated in every way by the Korean War, which broke out in June and threatened to plunge the world into another global conflict a mere five years after the end of the Second World War.

On June 25, Soviet-aligned North Korea invaded South Korea without warning and seized almost the entire country in the space of a few months. The United States responded by sending in an expeditionary force, sanctioned by the UN Security Council and commanded by General MacArthur, which repelled the aggressors and then in turn invaded North Korea, advancing as far as the border with China by October. China then decided to intervene. 200 000 Chinese volunteers were deployed along the front from end to end; they took back all of North Korea and advanced again into the South. The American forces, although bolstered by contingents from other nations (including Canada), were in complete disarray.

The Cold War was at its height. A veritable anticommunist psychosis gripped the U.S., where Senator Joseph McCarthy was making charges of communist infiltration in every sphere, from the State Department to the film industry, which saw many of its writers, actors, and directors blacklisted. Even Charlie Chaplin was not exempt from suspicion. Disgusted, he left the U.S. to go into exile in Europe.

1951

The Korean War continued to dominate world headlines in the early months of 1951. Facing a stalemate in the field, General MacArthur urged President Truman to take the war into Chinese territory, using nuclear weapons if necessary—a suggestion the president wisely rejected. In the face of increasingly public criticism from his general, Truman relieved him of all his duties. MacArthur was given a hero's welcome upon his return to the U.S. As the front had more or less stabilized around the 38th parallel, lengthy armistice negotiations commenced and would continue for two years.

A first step was taken on the road to European unity with the creation of the European Coal and Steel Community (ECSC), of which there were six member countries (France, West Germany, Italy, Belgium, the Netherlands, and Luxembourg).

In Great Britain, Winston Churchill was re-elected prime minister. Although he had been a great inspiration to the British people during the war and one of the architects of the victory over Nazi

Germany, he had lost the 1945 election and, in fine Churchillian tradition, had assured his fellow citizens that he would return. Six years later, against all expectations, he succeeded. He was 77 years old. He retired four years later, and, in 1965, died at the age of 90.

1952

The entire decade of the 1950s was characterized by anti-colonial struggles. In Asia, the Indochina war raged on, with France becoming increasingly mired in the conflict. In North Africa, bloody incidents were on the rise in the French possessions of Tunisia and Morocco. Nationalist leaders were arrested and sometimes expelled from the country; violent confrontations pitted European colonists and native Arabs against one another. In Kenya, Great Britain faced an uprising by a particularly militant political-religious movement known as the Mau Mau.

Although no longer a British colony, Egypt was still grappling with European imperialism over the Suez Canal. The Canal Zone was under Anglo-French control and was occupied by the British army. There had previously been riots, even pitched battles, directed against the occupiers, and, on July 23, a revolutionary council made up of nationalist officers from the Egyptian army deposed King Farouk, who was seen as being both corrupt and pro-British.

In the United States, the presidential election put an end to 20 years of Democratic dominance when the presidency was won by the Republican candidate, General Dwight D. Eisenhower, who had commanded with such success on the Western Front during the Second World War.

In Canada, the *Old Age Security Act* came into force on January 1, providing each Canadian with a pension of $40 a month beginning at age 70. To finance and administer this new program, the federal government had to obtain a constitutional amendment from London.

In Quebec, Maurice Duplessis led his Union Nationale party to a third consecutive electoral victory.

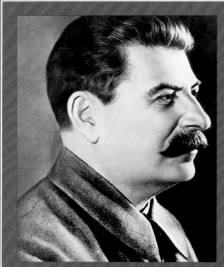

1953

The major event of 1953 was undoubtedly the death of Joseph Vissarionovich Dzhugashvili, better known as Stalin . He had come to power in the Soviet Union in 1929 and went on to establish one of the most terrible dictatorships in modern history. His death truly marked the end of an era, both domestically and internationally. Within the Soviet Union, there followed a relative softening of the regime and a certain refocusing of the economy on improving the living conditions of the country's population. On an international level, a definite easing of Cold War tensions could be felt. The Korean War finally ended in an armistice, with each side back where it started. Another pointless war...

In Iran, the crisis that had erupted with Great Britain two years previously over nationalization of the country's oil industry came to a head with the overthrow of the Mossadegh government, in the wake of spurious "mass" riots that had in fact been covertly orchestrated by the CIA. With Mossadegh in prison, the Shah instituted a pro-West dictatorship that would remain in place for close to 30 years.

In Quebec, this was the year of the Coffin affair, named for the prospector from the Gaspé who was accused of killing three American hunters. He would be hanged three years later.

With the publication in 1958 of the book *Coffin était innocent,* by Jacques Hébert, the notion that Coffin had been the victim of a judicial error and even a miscarriage of justice gained acceptance. The Coffin affair would contribute to the abolition of the death penalty in Canada.

Canada's first indoor shopping mall, the Lawrence Plaza, opened its doors in Toronto.

1954

The first half of the year was dominated by the Indochina War. On May 8, the French army suffered a massive defeat by the Viet Minh at Dien Bien Phu (4 000 killed or injured and 8 000 taken prisoner). The event resounded like a thunderclap around the world. For the first time since the dawn of European imperialism nearly 500 years earlier, a colonized people had achieved a decisive victory in a pitched battle against a Western colonial power .

Two months later, the Geneva Accords brought the war to an end. Vietnam was to be divided provisionally into two states along the 17th parallel, and elections were scheduled in two years for the reunification of the country. The other two parts of French Indochina, Laos and Cambodia, became neutral sovereign states.

But France's problems were not over yet. No sooner had the Indochina War ended than the Algerian War erupted, with a series of attacks launched in various parts on the country on All Saints' Day, on November 1.

In Guatemala, the democratic and progressive government of Jacobo Arbenz Guzmán, which had expropriated land from the United Fruit Company, was overthrown by a military putsch funded by the CIA. The country would remain, in the strictest sense of the term, a banana republic.

AFTER THE SECOND WORLD WAR, the hardware merchants resumed their regular activities, and the members of the Marchands met to talk strategy. The meeting took place in 1949, at the Royal York Hotel in Toronto.

condition that he be allowed to manage the company and its money. [...]

The members approved this solution unanimously, insisted on getting the opinion of the president, and called upon him at the end to give his decision, but his only answer was and remains total silence.

Between these meetings in late November and early January, some of the members, having learned of the situation through previous meetings, requested interviews with the president. He refuses to see anyone at all. [...]"

The board of directors met again on January 30. The president, Émery Sauvé, was not in attendance. He had sent a letter of resignation which the directors accepted "unanimously but regretfully."

And so RONA's co-founder and first president, Émery Sauvé, left the stage in circumstances clouded by discord. Henri Lemoine and J.J. Girouard, who had also been with the company since its earliest days, departed as well. Rolland Dansereau became the president. Assisting him were J.O. Roberge, first vice-president, Lucien Lamarre, second vice-president, and Olaüs Latendresse, first director, who was already a member of the board of directors. Two people were added: Médard Leduc, who became third director, and, rather surprisingly, Ronald Dansereau, the son of the new

DURING THE 1950s, members of the Marchands en Quincaillerie Ltée would visit the exhibitions in Toronto each year. Rolland Dansereau is with Napoléon Piotte and Léonce Côté at the Lord Simcoe Hotel.

president, who became second director and secretary of the company. This new team remained unchanged until 1962. Almost at once, a series of by-laws controlling sales to the member dealers was abolished and new rules were instituted in accordance with the wishes that had been expressed to no avail in the preceding months.

These various changes were ratified at a special general meeting of shareholders on February 5, 1954. However, only five people were present, as Rolland Dansereau had obtained a proxy from all the other shareholders, including Émery Sauvé. Immediately afterwards, at a special general meeting of the directors, Rolland Dansereau, who at that time owned 10 shares, informed his colleagues that he had purchased from various other shareholders a total of 83 common shares and that he wanted to sell one common share to his son Ronald and another to Médard Leduc, retaining 91% of the common shares for himself and becoming thus the sole controlling power of Les Marchands en Quincaillerie Ltée.

This crisis left many with a bitter taste in their mouths, and contradictory views of the situation abounded. But one thing was certain, the great friendship between Rolland Dansereau and Émery Sauvé, the two co-founders of RONA, was forever broken.

According to Émery Sauvé's grandson Marcel, Rolland Dansereau did some backroom manoeuvring to seize control of the company by buying out the dealers' shares for an amount equal to 10 times the price they had paid. "He would go to the dealers and say: 'Don't tell anyone, I'll buy them from you for $1 000. This won't change anything for you, you can still be a member.' Then one day, Dansereau announced to my grandfather that he now had the majority and he did not need him anymore. It was nearly the death of my grandfather."

But to many member dealers, and to Napoléon Piotte as well, who had spoken out against Sauvé's indecisiveness as president, Dansereau's power play ensured the survival of the business, put its finances back on solid footing, and resolved a major operational issue that was in the process of destroying it.

Dansereau's fortune

There is another aspect of this episode that must not be overlooked. When he took control of the business, in addition to buying nearly all of the common shares, Rolland Dansereau put up $200 000 of his own money to fund the company's working capital. Not bad for a man who, 15 years before, had borrowed $3 000 from his mother for a shipment of brooms. So how did he come to have such a tidy sum?

For the answer, we have to go back a few years. During a trip to Germany, Dansereau had visited a large exhibition hall and thought that such a place would be very useful in Montreal because it would ensure Les Marchands en

An early bloomer

Éloïse Paquin

Horticultural Expert, Comptoir Richelieu, Botanix,
Sorel-Tracy, Quebec

As a young girl visiting the family's Botanix store with her mother, Éloïse would tell herself, "When I grow up, I want to have greenhouses too." Today, it's a dream come true, as she is now a co-owner of the garden centre with her father and her sister.

From the tender age of 12, she spent her summers working at the store. From there, she went on to study ornamental horticulture at the Institut de technologie agroalimentaire (agri-food technology institute) in Saint-Hyacinthe. Since she was not allowed to do her internships at the family business, she trained in Quebec City and at Reford Gardens—a plant-lover's paradise. Never once did she doubt her career choice: this was what she was destined to do. But while deeply attached to her work, wherever it took her, she says that whenever she returned to the store, "I felt like I was home."

Though it can be physically demanding, Éloïse finds the work extremely gratifying. Her favourite time of the year is the start of the propagation season. You're still in the depths of winter, surrounded by all that snow and ice, but in the greenhouse, life is beginning; tiny seeds and cuttings are all starting to grow. Every year, during the nine off-season months, they get ready for the three months of summer. Éloïse visits trade shows looking for new varieties, and tests the annuals she's found to select the prettiest, hardiest, and easiest to reproduce. Something new and exciting crops up every year, and, as she's not a person who likes to do things the same way twice, that suits Éloïse down to the ground!

THE EXTENDED DORVAL FAMILY enjoying a ride in 1925, in the J.A. Dorval hardware store's delivery cart. This cart had to negotiate the steep hills of the Saint-Jean-Baptiste neighbourhood in Quebec City.

IN THE 1920s, CARS BEGAN TO REPLACE HORSES. J.A. Dorval bought a 1927 Chevrolet truck, which his son Philippe had to operate because he himself did not know how to drive.

IN 1944, the Ford Panel truck was an integral part of daily activities at the Anctil family store in Saint-Denis-de-Brompton.

BY THE END OF THE 1930s, Eugène Bélanger already owned several delivery vehicles, including three 1936 Stewart Panel trucks.

Quincaillerie Ltée would never again be short of space for their annual show. It was a project that consumed him and one that he would undertake personally, while pursuing his activities with the associated dealers.

Through his connections with the mayor of Montreal, Camilien Houde, Rolland Dansereau acquired a large lot on Berri Street for $1. He then persuaded a man by the name of Firmin Bédard and a lawyer, who was the brother-in-law of Minister Paul Sauvé (the same Paul Sauvé who would serve a brief term as premier of Quebec in 1959-1960), to invest $5 000 each. Dansereau himself invested $40 000. He then obtained a commitment from the provincial government that it would lease the second floor of a future building on a long-term basis. It was more than enough to complete the financing. The year was 1951. In a few months, the Palais du commerce was built, a structure that would be a Montreal highlight for decades to follow.

For two years, the place was a hive of activity nearly 24 hours a day. It even served as a venue for concerts by American rock groups in the evenings. Dansereau's and Piotte's sons acted as doormen there on the weekends. The Palais du commerce proved highly profitable. Rolland Dansereau had an enormous office with huge windows there. One day, some employees went to see him and told him they were planning to unionize. "You've probably been thinking about this for a long time," he said to them. "Give me the weekend to mull it over." On Monday morning, he fired all the employees and put the building up for sale. The Palais du commerce was promptly bought by financier Jean-Louis Lévesque. And that was how Rolland Dansereau came by the money that later enabled him to take control of Les Marchands en Quincaillerie Ltée.

It was therefore an experienced businessman, capable of playing hardball, who single-handedly took over the reins of Les Marchands en Quincaillerie Ltée. At a time when the company was going through an unprecedented crisis, he did not think twice about investing what must have been a very substantial portion, if not the entirety, of his recently acquired fortune. Rolland Dansereau had an unshakable faith in the group he had helped to found, and it was he who would give it the momentum it needed to truly soar.

A family portrait · The extended clan

1954

Sales: $1 586 580

Affiliate stores (members): approximately 400

The Spring Show •

AT THE HEART OF THE NETWORK, AND IN EVERY HEART, THE DEALER SHOWS HAVE ALWAYS HELD A PLACE OF CAPITAL IMPORTANCE. CEMENTING RELATIONSHIPS, FOSTERING CONNECTEDNESS, ENCOURAGING INNOVATION, SHOWCASING PRODUCTS, PROVIDING A FORUM FOR DIRECT INTERACTION BETWEEN SUPPLIERS AND DEALERS, A PLACE TO MEET AND TO REFLECT... EACH SHOW IS A MILESTONE ALONG A CONTINUING JOURNEY.

❶ "The role of an exhibition is to put manufacturers and dealers in contact with one another and to make sure they are surrounded with the very best and latest in merchandise and services," said Rona's president, Charles Morency, reporting on the 1969 Spring Show that was held in the De la Savane Street sample room.

❷ Dealers and consumers discovering the new products at the 2009 Spring Show, held in Toronto in the fall of 2008.

While, from the outset in 1940, the merchandise has been the focal point in the exhibit halls and the offices, it is the relationships between people, and their desire to serve their clients, that give meaning to the event. Over the years, a variety of different formats have been used in facilities in Old Montreal, the Atwater Market, the Palais du commerce, and, finally, the Palais des congrès de Montréal; sometimes the shows alternate with Quebec City. There have been Christmas shows, spring and fall hardware shows, gift, sporting goods, dishware, and toy shows, and the list goes on.

The show marked its 65th anniversary in 2010. For the last twenty or so years, it had always been referred to as the Spring Show. Held in the fall, it served to introduce the new products that would be sold the following spring. At first the shows were more traditional, bringing dealers and suppliers together, without any real negotiations taking place. Later, only the best products, preselected by the merchandising team and with prices discussed in advance, were presented.

In recent years, the Spring Show assumed a different look and feel. Now, it is essentially a showcase for new products. And then there are also the displays, the equipment, and of course, the marketing plan. "Back then, it was as though we were building a warehouse," recalls Danielle Savard, who is responsible for coordinating the show and who has been with Rona for over 30 years. Sometimes we erect entire facades of a house! There is an eco-responsible section, a Rona by Design section... Normand Dumont calls it "creating a store within the show." With fewer suppliers and better prices, the result is closer to what consumers are looking for.

In 2008, the show was held in Toronto for the first time. And now that the group has a Canada-wide presence, the shows will be mounted in

34

A major happening

turn in various major cities around the country: Montreal, Toronto, Calgary, Vancouver... Requiring the services of 200 people, the logistics will be more demanding, but the results well worth it. The show is attended by more than 2 500 dealers, suppliers, and store employees, sometimes along with hundreds of store customers, who come together on that Sunday for a blow-out "consumer day."

The dealers each receive a booking catalogue, customized to reflect their purchasing history. It serves as a sort of personal guide to the exhibition, and it is accessible via eRONA, which allows them to prepare in advance. It includes everything from the layout of the 130 000-sq. ft. (12 000 m²) show, to delivery policies, product release dates, etc.

Several vice-presidents are on hand to present the company's future directions, marketing plans, and advertising initiatives, greet potential member dealers, affiliated dealers, and dealers from the big-box stores and banners, in an ongoing round of meetings and presentations. Discussion groups on topics such as paint, service, and displays are also organized.

In addition to the show and the presentations, there are three key events. First is the opening breakfast, attended by 1 000 guests, at which the president gives a talk and welcomes the participants. This is followed by the introduction of the new dealers (those who joined the group during the year), who are given a joyful welcome against a rousing musical backdrop.

On the first evening of the show, the Excellence Gala is held, to recognize and celebrate employees from across the network who have been named Service Champions.

The show's closing event is the President's Banquet, attended by more than 2 500 guests. Guests are entertained by well-known artists such as Gregory Charles, with variety shows, the *Rona Star* show—the format varies from year to year. It is a marvellous opportunity for dealers and their spouses, suppliers, and employees to meet and mingle.

The highlight of this full evening is the president's speech. You can almost hear a pin drop. Everyone present waits with bated breath for this moment. There will be talk of passion, ethics, dreams... words and ideas to motivate and mobilize the group for the entire year!

❸ The president's speech was a rousing moment of the Spring Show's closing banquet. Robert Dutton refreshed and revitalized Rona's values during the economic and socially turbulent times of 2008.

The Man Who Planted Trees is one of the speeches that had the greatest impact on the audience. The year was 2006. Robert Dutton had drawn his inspiration from a charming short story of the same name, written by Jean Giono, which had been beautifully adapted into an animated film by Frédéric Back. The main character, Elzéard Bouffier, plants so many trees, day after day, that a magnificent forest rises up and whole villages are repopulated. "There is an urgency to act, but the vision calls for patience," he said, paying tribute to the men and women at Rona who, each day, "work with the same quiet urgency, their eyes set firmly on the future."

Warehousing and distribution •

PRODUCTS, SIZE, AND SUCCESS BEYOND IMAGINATION!

❶ André Bernard and Napoléon Piotte in the parking lot of the warehouse on De la Commune Street in Montreal in the 1950s.

❷ In 1969, the director of advertising, Marc St-Pierre, talks about the various divisions in the De la Savane Street warehouse to French wholesalers visiting Quebec.

Pierre Forget has been around long enough to have witnessed much of Rona's impressive expansion. In his 38 years with the warehouse, he has watched the company grow from 7 000 products, 300 suppliers, and 72 000 sq. ft. (6 700 m²) of combined warehouse and office space, to 36 000 products—90 000 in total across the network—2 500 suppliers, and 926 000 sq. ft. (86 000 m²) of warehouse space at the location on Du Tremblay Road in Boucherville alone. He has learned a myriad of different technologies over the years. Fortunately, he is still here to tell us about it, because otherwise, it would be hard to believe.

In 1971, when he started at the warehouse on De la Savane Street, in Montreal, everything was done manually, from telephone orders, to managing and transferring materials, to billing. Between the offices and the warehouse, there were 67 employees. Stock was kept on pallets that were stacked

three high, while backup reserves (used when the front-line storage units were empty) were set out on sheets of cardboard or paper. Approximately 7 000 items were managed completely by hand. When items were taken from the reserve, the lot was crossed out on the paper that was kept in the storage unit.

To meet dealers' needs, Rona did business with close to 300 suppliers. Their trucks delivered merchandise, which was unloaded into one of the warehouse's three sections: A, for giftware; B, for tools; and C, for plumbing and hardware. Orders were filled in each section, new boxes were packed and marked with the number of the dealer to whom they were to be sent, the contents were checked by a colleague assigned to that task, then it was on to the packaging area, and, finally, shipping, where the boxes were placed on the ground in the specific area set aside for each client. There were no

In the nerve centre of the organization

❸ The two levels of small merchandise storage at the Nobel Street warehouse had a total of 1.25 kilometres of shelving stocked with over 12 000 different products.

❹ The head office and distribution centre on Nobel Street in Boucherville.

❺ The mini-rail system at the Nobel Street warehouse operated at a rate of 400 carts an hour, allowing more than 1 600 orders to be filled every day.

electric carts, only dollies pushed by hand. Other trucks, often belonging to the dealers themselves, would leave the warehouse in the afternoon, filled with boxes of merchandise.

In the last year on De la Savane Street, a 100 000 sq. ft. (9 300 m²) building was annexed. It was connected by a tunnel that was perpetually congested with pallets. That was where shipping took place. The company had a few trucks. But Rona was expanding so quickly that it soon outgrew the facilities it had. It was time to leave.

In 1974, the company moved to Nobel Street, in Boucherville. The building was brand new, modern, computerized, and, most importantly, there was lots of space... at first, anyway. There were, in fact, 225 000 sq. ft. (20 900 m²), and pallets could be stacked four high! A short time later, a lumberyard was even added at the back. The carts now ran on a mini-rail system, and as they were computerized,

they moved along the tracks by themselves to allow orders to be filled section by section. The warehouse still had three sections, but as a sign of the changing times, they were now organized differently, with one general section covering giftware to electrical, one section for tools, and the "full case" section for major clients. As computer technology developed, processes improved, leaving less room for human error and reducing the need for cross-checking. But the carts in the reserve area still had to be pushed, which meant that some physical exertion was still required!

The fleet of trucks grew, more and more clients were being served, and the territory that had to be covered expanded. In the late 1980s, for reasons of efficiency, the decision was made to eliminate the fleet and work instead with transportation companies. This was a shock to the company's truck drivers; the tendency had always been for people

	Indoor area	Outdoor lumberyard
Boucherville, Quebec	926 000 sq. ft. (86 000 m²)	
Terrebonne, Quebec	380 000 sq. ft. (35 300 m²)	
Saint-Hyacinthe, Quebec	100 000 sq. ft. (9 300 m²)	125 000 sq. ft. (1 200 m²)
Halton Hills, Ontario	45 000 sq. ft. (4 200 m²)	477 000 sq. ft. (44 300 m²)
Calgary, Alberta	491 000 sq. ft. (45 600 m²)	
Calgary, Alberta (TOTEM)	104 000 sq. ft. (9 700 m²)	375 000 sq. ft. (34 800 m²)
Edmonton, Alberta	185 000 sq. ft. (17 200 m²)	
Surrey, British Columbia	85 000 sq. ft. (79 000 m²)	378 000 sq. ft. (35 100 m²)
Total	**2 131 000 sq. ft. (198 000 m²)**	**1 540 000 sq. ft. (143 000 m²)**

⑥ There is a continuous stream of employees and goods at the Du Tremblay Road warehouse: managing 36 000 products requires order and efficiency.

there had to be shipped twice, which was how things operated during the last two or three years in that location.

In 1999, the company moved one more time, although not very far. It stayed in Boucherville, still close to the major highways, but now a comfortable 650 000 sq. ft. (60 400 m²) were available. It was both a huge relief and the beginning of a nightmare that would continue for eight long months. All at once, there was a changeover to a completely new computer system, thousands of tonnes of merchandise had to be relocated, the number of stores to be served was skyrocketing, and new methods had to be learned and implemented.

The new computer system alone created considerable turmoil and necessitated numerous meetings and adjustments. Each item first had to be accurately measured, as the innovative box manufacturing system provided for optimal stacking of merchandise in terms of weight and volume. A screwdriver, a hammer... and a lot of stress for workers who were already overwhelmed by the move itself. With his supervisor, Claude Vallée, Pierre remembers working 12 to 14 hours per day, seven days a week, for eight months straight. For a time, the dealers were asked to place only their most urgent orders.

Fortunately, at the time of the expansion that increased the space to 926 000 sq. ft. (86 000 m²), these issues were long resolved and everything

to stay with Rona a long time. But the impact of this decision was mitigated to the greatest extent possible, as arrangements were made to ensure the drivers would be hired by the transportation companies under the same conditions as they had with Rona.

In 24 years, the company grew three times. First it expanded to 352 000 sq. ft. (32 700 m²), then to 450 000 sq. ft. (41 800 m²), but, eventually, it ran out of space again. There was nothing the 200 employees could do to squeeze in any more merchandise. They were often 200 to 300 entries behind, as there was simply not enough room. An additional warehouse had to be rented, and everything stored

38

was running smoothly. Today, approximately 36 000 products are managed at the Boucherville distribution centre, and it truly is a marvel to behold the carts that run "intelligently" from one location to another, the men and women moving through the nearly kilometre-long corridors in electric carts or on bicycles, the incoming containers that are constantly arriving—some 2 000 of them from Asia alone in just a few days in the spring, delivering gardening supplies—and the merchandise stacked five pallets high to a towering 25 ft. (7.5 m). There is continuous activity, but the atmosphere is one of calm and order, like a carefully choreographed dance.

The administrative centre is responsible for supplying the distribution centres and the big-box stores in Quebec, Ontario, and the Atlantic Region. All stores are supplied centrally via the supply systems. The same is true for the other distribution centres across the country.

As expansion continued, a large and very modern 320 000-sq. ft. (29 700 m²) warehouse was opened in Calgary in 2004. In 2006, a new 380 000 sq. ft. (35 300 m²) warehouse in Terrebonne was put into service exclusively for the big-box stores, which mostly order merchandise to be shipped directly on pallets. This helped to ease congestion in the Boucherville warehouse which, once again, was threatening to run out of space!

At the time of the major acquisitions, the company also retained existing warehouses in Ontario

(Halton Hills), in Alberta (Calgary and Edmonton), and in British Columbia (Surrey), bringing the total indoor and outdoor surface area to more than 3 670 000 sq. ft. (340 900 m²).

Today, the nine distribution centres use the latest technologies in inventory management and make it possible for Rona to be present across the entire country, providing fast, efficient service while minimizing the environmental impact of transportation.

GEORGES LANOUETTE JR., on the right, by the counter, took over the reins of the Notre-Dame hardware store in Montreal.

From Rolland to Napoléon to Ro-Na
1954 - 1962

2

In 1954, Rolland Dansereau stood alone at the helm. He had invested his fortune to keep Les Marchands en Quincaillerie Ltée afloat. Some, however, were less than happy with his control over the company. Napoléon Piotte tried to reassure the dealers and persuaded Dansereau not to convert the company into a wholesaler like all the rest. Feeling caught in the middle between Dansereau and the dealers, Piotte left the organization. He would return a few months later, at Dansereau's insistence. Despite friction and conflict, business continued to grow. In 1960, Rolland and Napoléon agreed to form a chain of retailers, Ro-Na, open to the members of Les Marchands en Quincaillerie Ltée. With this banner, the dealers found themselves with a powerful advertising and promotion tool that contributed to the growth of their business. Due to failing health, Dansereau had to resign himself to selling Les Marchands en Quincaillerie Ltée. After lengthy negotiations, Napoléon and a group of dealers bought Rolland out; they then restructured the business to include a management company (Gestion La Savane Inc.) and established operating rules that would prevent takeovers in future. Ownership of the business was once again in the hands of the dealers.

The time was early 1954. With a comfortable majority of the company's voting shares behind him, Rolland Dansereau acquired sweeping powers in such areas as sales methods, employee hiring and salaries, and the admission and suspension of members. In short, he carried a lot of weight.

But he had taken a big risk. He had invested what must have been a good part of his personal fortune in order to save the company from going under. We need only look at the facts: this project was his life's work, and he wanted above all else to make it a success. At his stage in life, this man, who was long past the first flush of youth, should have been going home to the big house in Outremont he had recently acquired, and living comfortably off his capital. But when no one else was willing to chip in another cent, he refused to throw in the towel.

This was quite a reversal. Overnight, the dealers who had pushed Sauvé from the presidency for his indecisiveness found themselves under the leadership of a man who wielded full power and authority, with a personality that was every bit as forceful.

Those who had called for stronger leadership were soon complaining that they no longer had any say in matters. There were rumblings of discontent. Many members wondered what had become of the principles of mutualism on which Les Marchands en Quincaillerie Ltée had been founded.

Moreover, barely 18 months had passed before Dansereau came up with a plan for converting the company into a wholesaler just like all the rest. He shared his thoughts with Napoléon Piotte, his faithful ally, who was still acting as a recruiter on a salary of $110 per week. To Piotte, the whole idea was unacceptable. Indeed, how could they consider turning the associated dealers into "just another wholesaler" when the very impetus for forming the group was a desire to break the stranglehold the large wholesalers had on the dealers?

Napoléon stands up to Rolland

On July 5, 1955, Napoléon Piotte wrote a long letter to Rolland Dansereau. He looked at the matter from all angles, taking infinite precautions, and told his friend and president of the gossip that was making the rounds about him and the danger that lay in such a drastic restructuring.

Dear Sir,

These last few weeks, I have spent a lot of time thinking about your suggestion of converting "Les Marchands en Quincaillerie Ltée" into a wholesale firm along the lines of "Lewis" and the others...

[...] The first problem that comes to mind, and it is the most important one, is the matter of the preferred shares. This is the critical issue. Some will readily agree to give up their claim on the value of their shares, but many others will cling fiercely to it.

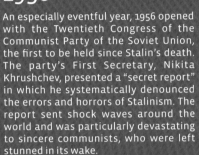

1955

One of the year's key events was the Bandung Conference. Held in April and named for the Indonesian city in which it took place, it signaled the arrival of the Third World on the international scene. The participating countries—nearly all of them former European colonies that had recently gained their independence—strongly asserted the equality of all nations and the right of all peoples to self-determination, in addition to calling for disarmament and a ban on nuclear weapons, and proclaiming themselves "non-aligned" with or against any of the Cold War power blocs.

Nevertheless, that war persisted, with the signing of various pacts that further consolidated each bloc: the Warsaw Pact for the Soviets, and the Baghdad Pact and Southeast Asia Treaty for the West. Despite this, however, a summit meeting was held in Geneva in July, the first since 1945, during which initial discussions on disarmament were broached.

On December 1, an African-American seamstress in Montgomery, Alabama, refused to give up her seat on a bus to a white passenger. This sparked the sweeping civil rights movement and the drive towards black emancipation in the United States that would culminate in the election of Barack Obama as president in 2008.

Closer to home, in Montreal, March 17 was the date of the famous "Richard Riot" at the Forum, triggered by the suspension of star hockey player Maurice Richard from the playoffs, a move that French Canadians felt was an insult to them.

1956

An especially eventful year, 1956 opened with the Twentieth Congress of the Communist Party of the Soviet Union, the first to be held since Stalin's death. The party's First Secretary, Nikita Khrushchev, presented a "secret report" in which he systematically denounced the errors and horrors of Stalinism. The report sent shock waves around the world and was particularly devastating to sincere communists, who were left stunned in its wake.

This was the beginning of de-Stalinization, and it would have tragic consequences in Hungary. In October, a massive, armed popular uprising overthrew the government and attacked Soviet troops. Close to a thousand Soviet tanks then rolled into Budapest 📷, but it would take 15 days of fighting and 25 000 deaths to finally crush the revolution, while 500 000 Hungarians fled, many of them eventually finding refuge in Canada.

At the same time, the West was grappling with the Suez Crisis. Following Egyptian leader Gamal Abdel Nasser's nationalization of the Suez Canal, an Anglo-French expedition attempted to regain control over the canal, while Israel attacked across the Sinai Desert. In the face of widespread condemnation, the aggressors agreed to the cease-fire called for by the UN. At the suggestion of Canada's delegate, Lester B. Pearson, then Minister of External Affairs 📷, the Security Council sent in the first contingent of "blue berets" to act as a buffer between the opposing forces. This initiative would earn Pearson the Nobel Peace Prize the following year.

[...] Now, you know as well as I do that your actions have sparked jealousy and envy, and that past difficulties within the company have turned members who once enjoyed the fruits of your work into slanderers who have felt no compunction about tarnishing a reputation. [...] All these whisperings and rumours are going to grow even stronger and more widespread if the change currently being considered is made [...].

Will the change under consideration help us to achieve more? [Piotte refers here to increasing sales and profits] At the moment it is more difficult to sell than ever before, because there is less money in circulation [...]; then, there is overproduction, and manufacturers and wholesalers alike are selling on whatever terms they can get, as long as they sell. But the buyers, the retail stores, which have problems of their own, are carrying credit and suffering under competition from the chain stores and hawkers, and they are looking for opportunities and are taking advantage of the pressure to obtain concessions from the suppliers... and therefore they buy from whichever one will give them the best deal, with no concern for past favours.

Piotte's allusion to a difficult economic context is surprising, as the letter was written at a time when Canada's economy was booming, following the downturn in 1954.

43

Women in the hardware business

"THERE ARE ALWAYS STORIES ABOUT WOMEN IN THE HARDWARE BUSINESS," SAYS GEORGES LANOUETTE, A DEALER IN MONTREAL. HE IS THINKING, OF COURSE, OF HIS GRANDMOTHER ALBERTINE, WHOSE STRENGTH OF CHARACTER COMMANDED THE RESPECT OF THE ENTIRE FAMILY. "BUT YOU KNOW WHAT? SHE WAS RIGHT MOST OF THE TIME. AND THAT'S STILL WHERE WE ARE TODAY."

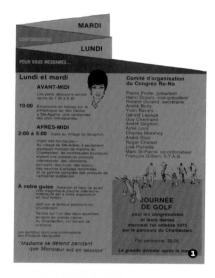

❶ In 1975, the convention program included activities especially "For the ladies..."

For the benefit of the younger people among us who would not remember, here is just one example, going back to 1975, of many that illustrate how the importance of women was recognized. In his opening speech at Rona's first convention, held at the Chantecler in Sainte-Adèle, then President Charles Morency paid tribute to them in this way:

"Gentlemen, with your permission—which I trust you won't refuse me—I would like to say a special 'thank you' to the ladies who so graciously agreed to accompany you this evening. The tables tonight may be abundantly laden with all sorts of mouthwatering dishes, but they are further embellished by the charm and elegance of the ladies who have joined their husbands and whose very presence lends a sparkling brilliance to this opening dinner."

And in the convention brochure:

Especially for the ladies, an evening of entertainment in the Cocorico Room—Provided by the Le Patriote nightclub, Tex Lecor, Guy Trépanier, and their band. With the ladies' permission, gentlemen may also attend.

That was 35 years ago. But make no mistake, the role of women in the hardware business largely reflects the role of women in our society. It would not be until the 1980s that their role was recognized, as it was in all spheres of society. And yet, as we know, hardware stores were often built by couples and developed by whole families, sometimes over several generations.

In a more recent account, Henri Drouin recalls a convention that took place in 1984:

"Part of my speech had focused on the role of women in our stores. Male employees were paid on an hourly basis, but women were paid weekly, even though they might work 70 hours for the same pay. They owned no shares. But they always played a part in the major decisions of the business... There was dead silence. There were about 500 or 600 people in the room, so 250, 300 couples. The men weren't too sure where I was going with this. But the women were listening..."

A group of women held a meeting at that same convention, and out of that came the realization that they connect more with seniors and young people, they have a greater awareness of beauty. They were here, and here to stay. Prejudices around their hardware knowledge and skills, however, would take a bit longer to go away. After all, construction, and all that goes with it, had long been considered a man's job.

Carmen Grégoire is 46. She remembers a time when she would give a client some advice, and the client would immediately go and double-check what she had said with one of her male colleagues. Today, she manages and is expanding the hardware store that her grandfather and father started in Matane, in 1947. After obtaining a bachelor's degree in business administration and working for three years, she felt the lure of the hardware business calling her back, and so, in 1990, she rejoined her aging father. He was still set on his idea of expanding but could see no way to make it happen. Carmen, however, was thinking big, but the D'Amour Street location proved too small. She completely redesigned and redecorated the store, but realized more space was needed than the 3 600 sq. ft. (330 m²) she had to work with. She wanted to be the first to offer the region all the things she felt were missing: lighting fixtures, garden furniture, Christmas decorations, bathroom fittings... She turned to Rona for advice and, in 1995, at the age of 31, built her first store. She designed it and knew everything about the 12 000 sq. ft. (1 115 m²) establishment, down to the last bolt. In 2003, she was ready to start selling building supplies. So she

A retail affair

added a 13 000-sq. ft. (1 200 m²) warehouse, again, with help from Rona, as well as the expertise of some colleagues in New Brunswick to whom she had paid a visit. Her elegant store, brimming with specially selected items in a range of bold colours, attracted a female clientele who really appreciated having a place like this to shop. As for the men, it has been a long time since any of them double-checked her advice. "These days, men are more accustomed to working with women. That wasn't necessarily the case when I was hiring in the 1990s," she says. On display in her office are numerous trophies and awards, both local and national. She takes great pride in these.

Today, the Rona network and the country as a whole benefit from the talent of dealers like Dianne Clarke, Monique Bélanger, Peggy Godfrey, Jacqueline Marsolais Prud'homme, Lise Joanes, Éloïse Paquin, Caroline Fradet, and the hundreds of women of all ages in this profession, whose goal is to fill their clients' lives with beauty... and run successful businesses.

At the administrative centre, Renelle Anctil, a hardware dealer, was the first woman member dealer to sit on Rona's board of directors, which she did from 1994 to 2000. Other well-known business women have also joined the board of the publicly-traded group: Louise Caya from 2002 until the present, Monique F. Leroux in 2003, and Doris Joan Daughney since 2007.

Members of Rona's executive committee include Linda Michaud, vice-president, Information Technologies, from 1992 to 2008; Suzanne Duchesneau, director, Orders Department, from 1962 to 1981; Michèle Roy, vice-president, Communications and Public Affairs, since 2007; and Marie-Claude Soucy, vice-president, Internal Auditing and Continuous Process Improvements, since 2008.

There are a lot of women at Rona. They can be found in every role, particularly in marketing and merchandising, where they make most of the decisions. As in the rest of society, practicing a profession or trade at this company is no longer a matter of gender, but one of talent and aspiration.

❷ In the mid 1980s, Rona collaborated with the YWCA to offer women training workshops on using tools.

❸ Renelle Anctil manages the Matériaux Carrefour hardware store. Along with a Rona L'entrepôt in Sherbrooke, it was ranked among the 50 best-managed businesses in Canada by the *Financial Post*.

❹ Sylvie Turcotte, director of Customer relationship management, Rona, Boucherville.

❺ Suzanne Maggi, director of Merchandising, Rona, Boucherville.

IN 1952, EMPLOYEES OF QUINCAILLERIE MODELECTRIC pose for the camera. Specializing in household appliances, the store was located on Canora Road in Montreal. Pierre Piotte, who had been working there as a clerk since 1951, recalls that it had a full post office, and that they would provide demonstrations of the lawnmowers right in the store's yard!

It is possible, however, that the dampening effect of the recession on people's spirits lingered on.

Napoléon continued:

[...] In my humble opinion, I believe that our sales will hold steady and even grow if, instead of increasing expenses, we continue to guarantee for our members: a) monthly rebates; b) flawless delivery on regular stock; c) improved payment terms.

Which just goes to show how deep-rooted the basic principles of distribution are!

Piotte then discussed each of these three points, stressing the importance of the rebates for the dealers, describing the missed deliveries that were a source of frustration to them, and pleading that members be allowed at least the time it took for their goods to arrive before being required to pay for them. He concluded:

Whatever your final decision, you will find me ever at the ready to serve as faithfully as possible.

I trust that you will see in this only the disinterested concern I have in what is best for you and yours, and I remain, dear Sir, most respectfully yours,

N. Piotte

This letter from Napoléon Piotte suggests that Dansereau's prosperity was engendering jealousy at a time when, from what he writes, many dealers were struggling to stay afloat. Dansereau had the power of money behind him, and Piotte urged him to use that power with restraint, for the good of the company and its dealers.

A dealer of that time recalls:

"At the end of the 1950s, some manufacturers (one of them an American company that made pots and pans) went to see Dansereau and made the following proposition: 'If we can sell in your stores, we will give you a volume discount' (possibly 1, 2 or 3%). That discount should have been passed on to the dealers, but it was pocketed by Dansereau. And Dansereau put those products in the flyer so that the dealers would be forced to buy them. So the guys started grumbling and it was Piotte they went crying to, complaining that they'd been reduced to selling pots and pans!"

In Dansereau's defence, it should be said that over the preceding several years, he had helped the company to balance its profits and losses by waiving part of the remuneration provided for in the contract signed in 1939. Although his annual salary was $1, he was remunerated by commission on the sales of Les Marchands en Quincaillerie Ltée. Of course, what was a modest payment for the fledgling company of 1939, 20 years later amounted to some $60 000—a tidy sum for 1959 and the equivalent of approximately $500 000 today! But Dansereau nonetheless

DURING THE 1950s, member dealers had to place their orders with Les Marchands en Quincaillerie Ltée using a catalogue like this one that came out once a month.

Magasin No

Nom

Adresse

(rue)

(ville)

No de téléphone :

Edition Novembre

Les Marchands en Quincaillerie Limitée

295 de la Commune
MONTRÉAL

No 4—1953

Moyen de transport désiré :

Adresse du transport à Montréal

Téléphone du transport à Montréal

N.B. — Les prix ci-dedans indiqués sont sujets à changement sans avis.

½ H.P. — 1800 R.P.M. — Ball Bearing .... ch. 27.20
¼ cheval-vapeur — 1800 R.P.M. coussinet sur billes
½ H.P. — 1800 R.P.M. — Ball Bearing .... ch. '56.85
60 cycles

9-B
LESSIVEUSES — INGLIS — WASHING MACHINES

Imperial avec Pompe automatique — cuve en porce-
laine — modèle effleurant le sol
Imperial with automatic Pump — Porcelain Tub — ch. 146.36
covered bottom

Royal avec Pompe automatique — cuve en porce-
laine — Royal with automatic Pump — porcelain ch. 127.09
Tub — regular model

N.B.—Tous ces articles seront expédiés
directement de nos fournisseurs

10-B
RÉVEILLE-MATIN & HORLOGES — INGRAHAM —
ALARM CLOCKS & ELECTRIC CLOCKS

Réveille-matin 40 heures — 40 hour Alarm Clocks

Ace — plain   Ace — plain .... ch. 2.19
Ace — lumineux   Ace — radium .... ch. 2.63
Canadian Call — plain   Canadian Call — plain ch. 2.50
Canadian Call — lumineux Canadian Call — lumin. ch. 3.00
Pal — plain   Pal — plain .... ch. 3.66
Pal — lumineux   Pal — luminous .... ch. 4.33
Challenge — plain   Challenge — plain .... ch. 2.63
Challenge — lumineux   Challenge — luminous . ch. 3.30
Little Star — plain   Little Star — plain .. ch. 3.96
Little Star — lumineux Little Star — luminous ch. 4.63
Westerner — animé   Westerner — animated . ch. 2.63

Réveille-matin 8 jours — 8 Day Alarm

Dawn — plain   Dawn — plain .... ch. 4.32
Dawn — lumineux   Dawn — luminous ...... ch. 5.00

.... ch. 3.67
.... ch. 4.33
...ben Corner .... ch. 4.63
...Mantel, Clock,
.... ch. 6.63
...cel Case .... ch. 7.30
...el Walnut
.... ch. 7.97

Alarm Clocks
...dsor Alarm .... ch. 4.63
...dsor Alarm — lu-
.... ch. 5.30
...SA 20 Memo — plain ch. 5.30
SA 20 Memo — lumineux SA 20 Memo — plain .. ch. 5.30
Winston Boitier en bois Winston Wood case .. ch. 8.63

Horloges électriques de cuisine —
Electric Kitchen Clocks

SK 21 Globe   SK 21 Globe .... ch. 5.00
SK 16 Dinette   SK 16 Dinette .... ch. 5.30
SK 18 Kitchen Korner SK 18 Kitchen Korner ch. 5.67
SK 174 Wafer — chromé SK 174 Wafer chromed ch. 5.96

Carillons électriques — Electric Striking Clocks

Croydon — Carillon Croydon — Cathedral Strike
noyer ou érable   — Walnut or Maple .. ch. 23.33

Horloge commerciale — Commercial Clock

Bristol — Horloge de bu- Bristol Square Office
reau, carrée   Clock .... ch. 11.96

Montres-Bracelets — Wrist Watches

Roy Rogers — uni   Roy Rogers — plain .. ch. 4.33
Westerner   Westerner .... ch. 4.33
Diamond chrome — ca- Diamond Chrome Plain
dran uni   Dial .... ch. 5.00
Diamond chrome — ca- Diamond Chrome Luminous
dran lumineux   Dial .... ch. 5.67
Diamond Gold — uni   Diamond Gold — plain ch. 5.67
Diamond Gold — lumineux Diamond Gold — lumin. ch. 6.33
Dart Chrome — uni   Dart Chrome — plain . ch. 5.30
Dart Chrome — lumineux Dart Chrome — luminous ch. 5.96
Dart Gold — uni   Dart Gold — plain ... ch. 5.96
Dart Gold — lumineux Dart Gold — luminous ch. 6.63

Montres de poche — Pocket Watches

Ingraham — Boitier   Ingraham — Plated
plaqué   Case .... ch. 2.63
Westerner   Western .... ch. 3.00
Roy Rogers   Roy Rogers .... ch. 3.00
Black Watch — lumineux Black Watch — lumin. ch. 3.30
Sentinel Sweep   Sentinel Sweep ..... ch. 3.30

Assortiment de Montres de Poche avec étalage —
Assortment Pocket Watch with Display Stand

No. 3 Assortiment de Montres de poche —
Pocket Watch Deal .... ch. 17.86

Assortiment de Montres-Bracelet avec étalage —
Assortment Wrist Watch with Display Stand

No. 6 Assortiment de Montres-bracelet
Wrist Watch Deal .... ch. 34.52

5

A man of many colours

Alfred Flageole Jr., aka "Junior"

Paint Expert, Rona L'entrepôt, Charlemagne, Quebec

The best way to make a new house feel like home is to paint it in your favourite colours. First stop: the paint department. But what do you choose? Latex, oil, gloss, flat, mildew-resistant? Eggshell, orange, yellow? How much paint do you need? What accessories should you buy? Brushes, rollers... the choice is bewildering! Never fear—help is at hand in the form of Alfred Flageole Jr., or simply "Junior" to his friends.

You could say he was born into it. His parents ran a paint store in Grand-Mère, in the Mauricie region. In those days, of course, they had nowhere near the 4 000 shades offered today. You bought basic white paint and mixed tubes of pigment into it, which meant no two gallons were ever the same. The tubes were later replaced by pouches—like little packets of soy sauce—which still produced fairly inaccurate results. At long last, the colour-dispensing machine made its appearance, making it possible to guarantee colour uniformity.

But you're still left with the problem of having to choose a colour. Today, fortunately, technology comes to the aid of the humble home decorator. Forget fiddling for hours with tiny colour swatches; bring in your favourite cushion, and Junior will scan it to match the exact colour!

Over the years, Junior has seen it all. He could talk to you for hours about the strange requests that people make and some of their unusual ideas. One day, a man came in holding a clipping from a cedar hedge. "I need a spray paint in this colour!" he declared. Since the range of aerosol colours was rather limited, Junior asked him what he wanted it for. "We've got friends coming this weekend and my wife doesn't like the yellow patches on the hedge, so I have to paint them over!"

47

Bring on the projects!

André Harvey

Quincaillerie Arthur Harvey, Rona L'Express,
La Tuque, Quebec

After holding the fort for the past 48 years, André sums up his experience simply by saying, "This is a terrific profession to be in!" He adds, "When you finally become an owner, you have room to move, you have options; you can always reorganize your store to reflect your values and personality." Since 1950, the Rona store in La Tuque has certainly seen its fair share of changes. That was the year when André's father, Arthur Harvey, purchased a grocery store in the town centre for $2 500! The grocery store evolved into a hardware store, but also housed a motorbike and snowmobile dealer, and even a Radio Shack within its 4 000 sq. ft. of space!

André started to work with his father in 1962, at the same time that the Harveys joined Rona. He went to study for a certificate in administration in Quebec City, but spent more time on the ski slopes than in the classroom. Come exam time, he decided to jump on a bus and return to work at the store! And he proved that he had a flair for business. Back then, a set of ski equipment sold for $49, but he ordered 10 pairs of Head skis at $100 each—a small fortune! That might well have been André's last day on the job, were it not for the fact that, since he was still a devoted ski enthusiast and always at hand when others took a tumble and broke their equipment, he provided the repair shop with a steady influx of customers! That made him appreciate the clients of the hardware store even more. "They're not people with problems, they're people with projects!"

In La Tuque, everyone knows everyone else, and André says his store is like home to him. His clients are his friends, and they often confide in him. One thing is certain: his warm and friendly nature was the reason that today he can say with pride, "We survived!" With a two-hour drive to the nearest city of Trois-Rivières, sources of inspiration are few and far between for this self-taught businessman. But every time he comes home from a visit to the Canadian Tires and Home Depots of this world, he says, "Life's good at Rona!"

48

IN 1952, OLIVETTE AND HENRI ANCTIL took over the family hardware store in Saint-Denis-de-Brompton. It was while they were at the helm that the business joined Les Marchands en Quincaillerie Ltée.

waived part of it, although the exact amount of the portion he declined to accept is rarely mentioned. The minutes of the February 1958 annual general meeting show, however, that Rolland Dansereau gave up $15 800 of the commissions to which he was entitled under his contract for 1957—a not inconsiderable amount, to say the very least. And it was out of his personal compensation, not the company's funds, that he paid the employees their annual bonuses. Also, it is possible that the discounts of 1, 2 or 3% mentioned by the dealer were in fact not volume discounts, but rather cash discounts for prompt payment. And Dansereau might have argued that the company could not receive any cash discounts because he was funding its working capital. By 1959, his investment, in the form of a loan, had reached $380 000, an amount on which the company paid him interest of 5% "if any profit remained at the end of the year," according to the minutes of the meetings of the board of directors.

And yet there were, so to speak, no profits, as that was not the company's reason for being. The company existed to secure products for the dealers at competitive prices. The dealers therefore received "trade discounts"—that is, discounts on the suggested retail prices in the catalogue—which were calculated according to a complex structure and varied depending on the category to which the dealer belonged and the number of preferred shares he owned. For example, under the structure in place in 1959, the price

THE LANOUETTE FAMILY ran a hardware store in the Saint-Henri district in Montreal since 1889. Georges Lanouette and his son stand behind the counter.

certain dealers paid for their merchandise was the exact price that Les Marchands en Quincaillerie Ltée paid to the manufacturer, as long as they had paid the company a fixed annual amount of $1 200 to cover their share of the administrative expenses. For the dealers, it was not a bad arrangement, to say the least.

Be that as it may, Piotte's opinion seemed to have carried some weight, because Les Marchands en Quincaillerie Ltée did not become just another wholesaler.

But discontent continued to grow, and the situation became difficult for Napoléon Piotte. He found himself in a real dilemma, caught between his loyalty to Dansereau and his fondness for the dealers who had turned to him when they needed someone to listen to their frustrations.

In 1957, after 10 years with the associated dealers, Piotte accepted an offer he had received to become the president of the Ligues du Sacré-Cœur de Montréal. There he would be assigned two major projects, the first of which was coordinating the celebrations for the 75th anniversary of the Ligues du Sacré-Cœur, to be hosted by the Ligues de Montréal. These celebrations would culminate in a massive convention held in June 1958, attended by some 50 000 participants from every corner of the country. In addition, during his presidency, the Ligues, with the very public support of the Archbishop of Montreal, Cardinal Léger, conducted a vigorous campaign to stamp out obscenity in literature and the press.

1957

1957 saw the creation of the European Economic Community (EEC), an initiative intended to establish a common market among the member countries, of which there were six at the time: France, Germany, Italy, Belgium, the Netherlands, and Luxembourg. This represented a decisive step on the road to European unity.

In the ongoing confrontation between the world's two superpowers, the Soviet Union took the lead in the field of space technology. In August it launched the first intercontinental missiles, with a range of 5 000 kilometres. The Soviets could now deliver a direct strike on American soil. However, it was the launch in October of Sputnik, the world's first artificial satellite, that captured imaginations everywhere. And the Soviets made history again the very next month when they sent the first animal, Laika the dog, into space. The U.S. was stunned to find itself trailing behind.

The political scene in Canada, too, was rocked by the electoral victory of John Diefenbaker's Conservatives, marking the end of a Liberal hegemony that had lasted since 1921 (with only a brief interruption between 1930 and 1935). But it was a minority government, with Louis Saint-Laurent's Liberals winning more votes than the Conservatives.

In Quebec, the very long and difficult Murdochville strike fuelled growing anti-Duplessis sentiment.

1958

For much of the year, the international spotlight was focused on France. In May, French settlers in Algeria—the "pieds-noirs"—taking the view that French policy in Algeria was too soft on the Algerian rebels, rose up and called for the return to power of Charles de Gaulle, who had retired from politics several years earlier. Carried along on an irresistible wave of popularity, and in a climate of dread at the prospect of a civil war, de Gaulle became President of the Council (prime minister) and was given broad powers to resolve the crisis. He quickly proposed a new constitution, which was adopted by referendum in September, with 80% of votes in favour. Thus was born the Fifth Republic, which is still in place today, and de Gaulle became its first president in December.

In Canada, Prime Minister John Diefenbaker, at the head of a minority government, called a snap election and won by the biggest landslide in Canadian history, securing 208 out of 265 seats.

With the support of Maurice Duplessis, he even swept Quebec, which had not voted Conservative since 1917.

This was also a year of events at the extreme ends of the earth: the first crossing of Antarctica via the South Pole, the first commercial flight over the North Pole (Paris–Tokyo), and the first transit across the North Pole, completed by the Nautilus, an American nuclear-powered submarine.

1959

The year opened with a major event in the history of the Americas: the victory of Fidel Castro's guerrilleros in Cuba, causing the dictator Fulgencio Batista to flee the country on January 1. The island was immediately engulfed in a true revolution, the likes of which the Americas had never seen before. In May, Castro announced the nationalization of the land and its redistribution to farmers, an act that struck a serious blow to the immense sugar cane plantations of U.S. companies like United Fruit. From that point on, relations with the United States quickly deteriorated.

The Soviets held their lead in the development of space technology, scoring three consecutive firsts: the first man-made object to be propelled beyond the Earth's gravitational field, the first rocket to reach the Moon, and the first photographs of the dark side of the Moon. Secure in these achievements, the Soviet government embarked on a charm offensive in the form of an extended visit by Nikita Khrushchev to the U.S., where he won the public over with his vitality, his enthusiasm, and his affability.

On April 25, following five years of construction, the St. Lawrence Seaway opened to navigation. Inaugurated on June 26, in the presence of Canadian Prime Minister John Diefenbaker, U.S. President Dwight D. Eisenhower, and Queen Elizabeth II, the waterway now provided a link for commercial shipping from the Atlantic Ocean all the way to the western head of Lake Superior, some 3 700 kilometres inland.

In Quebec, the death of Duplessis profoundly changed the political landscape. His successor, Paul Sauvé, announced plans for free education and the development of public secondary education. With the Radio-Canada producers' strike taking place at the same time, the Quiet Revolution was just on the horizon.

Regional development •

THE HEART OF A HARDWARE DEALER HAS ALWAYS BEAT TO THE PULSE OF HIS REGION.

❶ During the 1998 ice storm, Rona donated chainsaws to people in the Montérégie region, including citizens of the town of Saint-Luc.

The ice storm that battered Quebec in 1998 provides many examples of the retailers' commitment to their community and the support the administrative centre provides. It is worth remembering that the administrative centre itself is located in the famous triangle that bore the brunt of the storm. And although the power outage at the centre did not last very long, many of the employees there were affected. They had to look after their families. For some, the blackout continued for several weeks. Rona had to cope with that, while at times running on generators. "It was back to basics," says Jean Émond, the retired vice-president of People and Culture. "All our activities were focused on one thing: survival."

On a broader scale, the dealers in the region also needed support, and the administrative centre responded by sending them the merchandise that was needed most urgently: generators, firewood, lamp oil, candles, snowblowers, gas stoves... The buyers concentrated on the products that were absolutely essential. They received 65 generators,

but the dealers were asking for 500. How were they going to distribute them? How could the company help where it was needed the most? Rona also contributed directly to the operation by donating firewood and de-icing salt, and by supplying power saws for lumberjacks from the Gaspé Peninsula who had come to help the people of Saint-Luc, some 20 minutes from Montreal. At the same time, the company made sure there was food available for all employees at the cafeteria, and it provided support to their families. This was a time to reinforce the importance of ethical behaviour on everyone's part, to ensure that people were not exploited in their time of weakness and that business practices remained sound.

To Claude Bernier, the executive vice-president of Marketing and Customer Innovations, Rona's role is to help the dealer become the most important player in his or her local market and, thus, a strong economic and social stakeholder:

> "When they join us, we give them tools they won't get anywhere else. We are used to competing with North American players. We give them the same tools that a North American or international company would provide: products—including the ECO line—training, marketing... the same as a large corporate store."

Acquisitions strengthen this position further by providing the opportunity to create synergies, an important factor in sustainable development, to build a relationship with the community, and to deliver the right product at the right time and at the right price to the members of that community.

But there's nothing new about a hardware dealer playing a central role in the life of the region. Charles Morency had this to say about the hardware store where he worked with his father Édouard, long before he was president of Rona:

50

Worthy causes and vital jobs

"Customers back then were in much less of a hurry; they didn't pressure the storekeeper. I remember that in the winter, customers would come in and gather around the huge stove in the centre of the store and chat. Then eventually, one of them would say to me, 'When you have a minute, Charles, would you mind getting such and such for me...' The hardware store became a sort of meeting place, a spot where people would come to discuss politics, hear the latest gossip... and sometimes even inquire about what was new in hardware."

Tucked away in the memories of the Anctil family of Saint-Denis-de-Brompton, Quebec, is a portrait of the way things would have been in 1937, when they were just starting their business:

"A lilac hedge blooms along the side of a large Victorian-style house, while a group of children play in the countryside on Des Écossais Road. A grey Monarch pulls up to the White Rose gas pump, and Joseph Anctil chats with the driver, whose wife and children go into the general store. They all marvel at the diversity and sheer quantity of the products available: fabric by the yard, shoes, wool, work clothes, tools, wrought iron objects, groceries, penny candy... There is truly something for everyone! Outside, the men swap advice about the spring planting, while inside, Zoé measures out some cloth and expresses amazement at the birth of her

client's fifteenth child. "Can we put this on a tab, Mrs. Anctil?" "Well, of course, with spring planting in full swing and you with another mouth to feed on top of that..."

The Rona stores, the distribution centres, and the administrative centres employ just under 30 000 people in Canada and support several thousands of causes.

❷ The J. Anctil store was a gathering place in the town of Saint-Denis-de-Brompton in the 1930s.

❸ Settlements in Western Canada benefitted from Revelstoke's presence, because they supplied building materials, as shown in this 1924 photograph taken in Calgary. Rona bought Revelstoke at the same time as it acquired Revy, in 2001.

❹ During the 1950s, the Édouard Morency hardware store was located in the heart of the community in Quebec City's Lower Town, near Saint-Vallier Street.

51

Go with the flow

Éric Dupuis

Plumbing Merchandising Expert,
Administrative Office, Boucherville, Quebec

In 1986, Éric was studying business in college. He began working at a Brico store. As he was moved from one department to another, he gained experience and was finally offered a management position in the store. What began as a part-time student job blossomed into a career and, more importantly, a passion. Or, as Éric says with a smile, "I was hooked." Brico subsequently became Réno-Dépôt, and Éric continued to learn about the various aspects of sales, customer relations, and renovation. By 2005, he was responsible for 60 employees and the marketing for four huge departments in the Réno-Dépôt in Brossard. Days flew by at a frenetic pace to the soundtrack of "If you're not satisfied, call Éric!" Between the clients, the employees, and the thousand-and-one problems to be solved, he developed valuable on-site expertise. When the position of assistant merchandiser in plumbing for the Réno-Dépôt division became available at Rona, Éric took the next natural step along his career path.

The first day, sitting in his small office, he asked himself, "What am I doing here? All my life, I ran throughout the stores, and now I'm sitting alone in front of a computer." The answer came soon enough: as a merchandiser, Éric was on the front lines. He had to juggle clients' demands, marketing, finances, and keep everybody happy in the process! And all that had to be achieved while providing clear leadership and making informed decisions. It didn't matter what kind of a game plan you worked out in the morning, "there would always be an email waiting for you to let you know that the earth has stopped turning!"

Éric is able to maintain a delicate balance between analysis and intuition, speed and thoroughness, and he keeps things running smoothly, which is a good thing if you're in plumbing!

NOTES for a speech by Charles Morency.

Piotte's departure left a void. Rolland Dansereau realized that he could not sail the ship alone. He was not by nature the sort of person who could act as a unifying force for the independent dealers, to whom Piotte had been an advisor, confidant, and collaborator. While Dansereau was a formidable businessman, it soon became clear that Piotte had been the soul of the organization.

Rolland Dansereau persuaded Napoléon Piotte to return to the fold. It was now February 1959. Little is known about the terms under which Piotte rejoined the company. But one thing is certain, he secured improved conditions for himself, and in all likelihood it was during those negotiations that the idea of creating a true chain of retailers was first put forward by Napoléon Piotte.

While these events were taking place, the company's sales nonetheless continued to grow, rising from under $2 million in 1958 to close to $3 million in 1959. It was not always smooth sailing, but there was a definite upward trend all the same.

Napoléon as Rolland's equal

It was in this context of sunshine and cloud that Les Marchands en Quincaillerie Ltée celebrated its 20th year in business. To mark the anniversary, Rolland Dansereau arranged a huge celebration for the dealers and their wives. Napoléon Piotte took to the stage to pay a glowing tribute to Dansereau. He could not resist the temptation to give the dealers present a bit of a lecture.

AFTER HIS FATHER, LOUIS, ALPHONSE CHAMPAGNE ran the family hardware store, located in Saint-Honoré-de-Shenley in the Beauce region, until 1955, when his son Guy officially took over the business.

NEAR THE END OF THE 1940s, GUY CHAMPAGNE MET NAPOLÉON PIOTTE, who had come to present the new products to the store owners in the Beauce. The A. Champagne hardware store had been one of the early ones to join Ro-Na, as witnessed by the logo in his store window (at the top, on the left).

In particular, Piotte said:

"Since the company's founding, Mr. J.R. Dansereau has been its managing director, and for nearly five years now, its president. What have these last 20 years been like for him? Certainly not a bed of roses. [...] I have found many among us who were more concerned about what Mr. Dansereau might earn from his job than about the savings he could help them to achieve.

Mr. J.R. Dansereau has been a good-hearted and generous man, one who is quick to forgive. How many of you have had occasion, for one reason or another, to knock on his door asking for a favour [...] and did not receive what they asked?

Mr. J.R. Dansereau has been and continues to be an incomparable leader, and many companies I know would give a fortune to have him go and accomplish for them the great things he accomplishes for you."

Then, at the close of his speech, Piotte addressed Dansereau directly:

"Mr. Dansereau, some two months ago, finding that you were depressed, your doctors strongly advised you to resign your post. You gave notice to your board of directors accordingly. Since then, I have, on my own initiative, visited each of our good members, some of whom are here this evening, and, in the hope of keeping you at the helm of this company, I requested of them an unprecedented act of trust. I can tell you that 98% of the members I visited agreed to my request and have given me the means to allow you to do a thorough cleanup— something that is an absolute necessity—and to ensure that your task in future is less difficult, less exhausting, less demoralizing. It is therefore my pleasure to give you the shares thus collected for the same amount that I paid to acquire them. And here is a list of the donors and the size of their gifts..."

That was a lot of information in very few words!

Dansereau, ill. A transfer of shares for his benefit. And what about this "cleanup" that was an "absolute necessity"?

Let's see if we can shed some light on what was happening.

As will be recalled, Piotte returned to the fold at the insistence of Dansereau, who had realized that his "propagandist" had a way with words that was vital to the company's success. This quite probably put the relationship between the two men on an entirely different footing. Piotte was no longer relegated to a secondary role. He now addressed Dansereau as his equal. This is seen clearly in the closing words of his speech on that 20th anniversary evening.

Economic development •

THE PROCESS OF ECONOMIC DEVELOPMENT IS LIKE A CHAIN REACTION. THE CHAIN ALLOWS SMALLER MEMBERS TO GROW BECAUSE THEY ARE SUSTAINED AND SUPPORTED BY LARGER ONES THAT RECOGNIZE THE QUALITY OF THEIR PRODUCTS AND DISTRIBUTE THEM.

❶ Roland Boulanger & Cie had manufactured its mouldings and doors in Warwick since 1942. It entered into business with Rona in 1975.

At Rona, there are countless examples. Moulding manufacturer Roland Boulanger & Cie, of Warwick, Quebec, is one of them. It is the largest employer in town, with a staff of several hundred. Had it not been for Rona, which made the little company a preferred supplier and distributed its products outside the province of Quebec, it would not have grown to the size it is today. Robert Dutton remembers the excitement of the president, Guy Boulanger, when he brought his 82-year-old mother to see a display of their mouldings in Ontario. The company, which has been in business for 60 years, is now one of the largest manufacturers of mouldings in the country.

The same happened with Duchesne, in Yamachiche, Quebec. Founded in 1927, the company, today, is headed by Françoise Duchesne, a third generation Duchesne. It has become a Canadian symbol of excellence in the field of building materials. Rona helped foster its development and expansion by buying its nails, wire mesh, and siding products.

An especially eloquent example is that of Sico paint, long a featured product in the Rona network, which is itself a major paint retailer. Normand Dumont, the executive vice-president of Merchandising, explains the impact of this chain:

"Over time, we contributed significantly to Sico's development. It is thanks to Rona that Sico is the player it is today. Without Rona, it would never have had the presence it currently enjoys in Western Canada. It's a question of reflex. Today we can put a name to it; we call it sustainable development. In the past, we didn't express it that way. But that kind of environmental awareness has always been there.

For example, over ten years ago, we launched a paint recovery program in Quebec. Back then, that sort of thing wasn't very trendy. But we felt it was important. Because when you sell products that have an impact on the environment, you also have to do your part to deal with the resulting waste properly... which, in the end, means recycling it. So it was a great initiative. It meant we were the first to start recovering paint in Ontario, in 2008. Communities there really appreciated this program, and it worked well, because it doesn't matter where people are, everyone is stuck with their bits of leftover paint they don't know what to do with or how to get rid of. We're really proud of this.

When it comes to forest products, we buy everything locally in Canada. We'll never buy products in one province and then ship them to another, unless, of course, it's a specialty product. Otherwise, everything is bought

The driving force behind a long chain of partners

locally. This is, in fact, part of our wood products policy, which we unveiled at the Spring Show in November 2008."

A series of specific targets is included in Rona's Wood Products Procurement Policy, which states that, by the end of 2010, 100% of the commodity lumber (spruce, pine, fir) it sells will come from certified forests. Rona and its suppliers will be subject to a rigorous assessment program, and the policy will be reviewed on an annual basis.

In the time since Rona established a Canada-wide presence, many quality brands have achieved broader distribution: H. Paulin & Co. fasteners and parts (Toronto, Ontario); Exchange-A-Blade recycled power tool accessories (Delta, British Columbia); Garant tools (Saint-François, Quebec); Ove bathroom products (Laval, Quebec); René Corriveau patio furniture (Montmagny, Quebec); Quickstyle flooring products (Montreal, Quebec); Globe Canada light bulbs (Montreal, Quebec); Bélanger-UPT faucets and plumbing accessories (Saint-Laurent, Quebec); Reliable fasteners (Toronto, Ontario), and Moulding & Millwork decorative mouldings and Columbia Skylights skylights (Western Canada), to name but a few.

❷ The Garant business was born with the construction of a forge in 1895, in Saint-François de Montmagny. In the 1960s, Rona's merchants and employees visit the site where tool handles and other products were manufactured.

❸ Sico products were attractively displayed at Rona, as seen by this 1980s demonstration display.

❹ A long-time collaborator, Normand Dumont joined Rona in 1989. In 2000, he was appointed vice-president and, in 2004, executive vice-president of Merchandising.

Four generations later...

Claude Bélanger

Quincaillerie C. Bélanger, Rona Le Quincaillier, Montreal, Quebec

THE J.A. DORVAL HARDWARE STORE underwent renovations in 1953. The interior was remodelled and the office was moved towards the back of the shop. The store remained crammed full of products and articles of all kinds!

Let's take a trip back in time with Claude Bélanger, to the turn of the 20th century, to be more precise. In 1912, there was no such thing as Les Marchands en Quincaillerie Ltée; that was when Claude's grandparents, Octave and Germaine, took over the store on La Fontaine Street in Montreal, where it all began.

Four years later, they handed over the reins to their son Eugène. He was quite the entrepreneur, buying up failing businesses and selling off the stocks for a profit. In 1933, a property came up for sale in the up-and-coming neighbourhood of Rosemont. Realizing the location's potential, he decided to take the plunge; he bought it and opened the hardware store that still operates there today.

Claude started working full time with his father in 1952. It was a passion for him. In 1960, when he was just 25, Eugène named him manager. Claude's priorities were advertising, customer service, and his employees' well-being. He also liked to design his own flyers, which already had a circulation of 200 000! Sales soared...

Then, on December 6, 1979, disaster struck when a fire destroyed the building. Claude had been on his way to work, oblivious to what was happening. He remembered letting the firetruck pass him that morning, thinking, "They're in more of a hurry than I am!"

At the time, a battle was raging between the local merchants and the owners of a nearby lot. Claude became actively involved in the struggle. He didn't want to rebuild his store without the assurance that no commercial premises would go up on that site. The Masson Street merchants finally triumphed, and the way was clear for Claude. On November 11, 1981, he celebrated the reopening of his hardware store. Rona had supported him enormously throughout the whole transition process.

In 1989, his son Dominique heeded the call of the family business and also joined the team. He, in turn, became manager seven years later.

With some reluctance, Claude gradually withdrew from the day-to-day operations and finally retired in 2003, though he would still put in an occasional appearance. After all, turning your back on something that's been a part of you for 58 years isn't so easy!

Piotte began by paying tribute to Dansereau and his genius for business. I have no doubt that he sincerely meant every compliment. But he also made a point of disclosing Rolland Dansereau's fragility by revealing that he had been weakened by illness. Then, with a single stroke, he demonstrated both his loyalty to Dansereau and his influence within the organization.

Working behind the scenes, completely unbeknownst to Dansereau, Piotte had arranged for many of the dealers to assign their preferred shares to Dansereau.

But what is the connection between this financial transaction and the "thorough cleanup" that was "an absolute necessity," in Piotte's words?

It could not have been a question of control. These shares had no voting rights. Furthermore, in 1956, the board of directors had given Rolland Dansereau absolute control over the operations of Les Marchands en Quincaillerie Ltée, including the power to "set the prices at which our merchandise is sold to our various clients, and also set the terms of sale for clients." And that is to say nothing of the power he had to hire or fire any employee or travelling salesman "with or without cause" and to decide their pay.

Indeed, the preferred shares seemed to be a source of dissatisfaction and criticism among the dealers. The minutes of the meetings held in that era contain no indication that any dividends whatsoever were paid on these shares. It is true that the dealers who owned at least five of these

PRIOR TO THE ADOPTION OF THE FAMOUS BIRD IN 1964, this logo—seen here in the window of Édouard Morency's hardware store in Quebec City, 1962—was used in correspondence and for identification purposes by the members of Quincaillerie Ro-Na.

THE EXTERIOR OF J.A. DORVAL'S STORE has not changed: the round windows that existed on the building in 1959 are still there today.

shares got a better price for certain categories of products. But these were fairly narrow categories, which limited the economic benefit associated with the shares.

In addition, when the company stopped acting as an intermediary between sellers and buyers in 1954, there was no longer a market for these shares. No return on the shares, no market for them, and yet buying them was mandatory—no wonder the dealers felt they had been had. It had reached the point where many of these shares were still not fully paid for, even though in some cases they had been purchased more than five years previously.

As the company at that time existed for the benefit of its members, and its balance sheet was less than robust, it could not afford to redeem the shares. In fact, only Dansereau, who was already advancing considerable funds to the company, had the means to buy them, regardless of the price.

Be that as it may, on February 4, 1960, the board of directors held a meeting. The minutes confirm the transfer to Rolland Dansereau of 580 preferred shares that had been owned up until that time by some hundred individuals. Approximately a hundred additional shares would be transferred to him over the weeks that followed. The par value of the shares was set at $100, but no transfer price was mentioned.

Ro-Na makes its appearance!

A few months later, on July 20, 1960, a new company was formed under the name Quincaillerie Ro-Na inc. / Ro-Na Hardware Inc.

Its share capital was set at $25 000. Following the first meeting of the board of directors of the new company, on October 6, 25 shares were issued and put into circulation, for a total value of $2 500. Of these shares, Les Marchands en Quincaillerie Ltée owned 20, or 80% of the share capital, and Rolland Dansereau, Napoléon Piotte, J.O. Roberge, Gaston Tétreault, and Médard Leduc owned one share each. Rolland Dansereau, as the agent of Les Marchands en Quincaillerie Ltée, thus controlled the majority of the Ro-Na Hardware Inc. shares.

Even today, controversy still surrounds the origin of the name "Ro-Na." It would appear to be a combination of Rolland's and Napoléon's first names. According to one version of the story, it was Piotte who came up with the name "Ro-Na." Piotte supposedly convinced Dansereau by saying that "Ro-Na" could just as easily suggest "Robert and Ronald," Rolland Dansereau's two sons, as "Rolland and Napoléon."

On the other hand, it was in fact Dansereau and not Piotte who registered the "Ro-Na" trademark personally before selling it to the new company—a fact that would seem

THE EUGÈNE BÉLANGER HARDWARE STORE
on Masson Street suffered significant
damage in a fire in 1956.

to corroborate the other version of the story, according to which Dansereau was the man who came up with the name.

But really, none of that matters. What counts is that the spirit shown by Rolland and Napoléon lives on in the company today, 50 years later.

The new company's first board of directors consisted of J.O. Roberge, chairman; Gaston Tétreault, vice-chairman; Napoléon Piotte, secretary; and Médard Leduc, treasurer. Napoléon was also appointed manager of the company, which set up its offices at 295 De la Commune Street, in Old Montreal.

The mission of the new company was to promote business through cooperative advertising and the organization of promotions. The independent retailers who became the "Ro-Na dealers" would be recruited exclusively from among the members of Les Marchands en Quincaillerie Ltée.

They would have to commit to taking part in the advertising program and the discounts promoted by the company. They would be required to sell the products offered by Les Marchands en Quincaillerie Ltée in preference to any other products. And they would also have to concentrate their purchases there, as Les Marchands en Quincaillerie Ltée was the only supplier officially recognized by the new chain of hardware stores. In addition, the Ro-Na dealers would have to help with the funding for advertising campaigns, contributing 1% of their purchases up to $100 000 per year and 0.5% above that

amount. The contribution amount could not be less than $120 per year. They would also have to pay $5 rent per month for the use of the Ro-Na banner.

At this first meeting, the directors of Ro-Na decided to form an advisory committee of dealers, "to submit suggestions to the executive concerning the effective functioning of the company's operations." This advisory committee mirrored a similar committee already in existence, whose members were dealer clients of Les Marchands en Quincaillerie Ltée. It would remain a vital part of life at Ro-Na for many years to follow.

After 20 years in business, the associated dealers had the leverage they needed for real growth: a buying group for securing better prices from suppliers, and a banner to serve as a focus for promotion and a visible symbol of their membership in a group like no other.

The huge blue sign that is today displayed on hundreds of stores all across Canada was still far in the future, but the train had left the station and there was no stopping it now.

The creation of this chain of retailers meant the restructuring of certain activities. In order for the new banner to inspire confidence, it had to be supported by a dependable supplier and a flawless supply system. More space was needed. Rolland Dansereau therefore acquired, under his own name, a large building located at 5200 De la Savane Street, in the northern part of the city. The two companies were headquartered there, and 40 employees worked at

THE 1956 FIRE PROVIDED EUGÈNE BÉLANGER WITH AN OPPORTUNITY TO GROW, because he was able to increase his retail space by buying up adjacent properties that had been damaged in the blaze.

this location. Many of them had never seen such a large warehouse space. And yet that was just the beginning...

The initial financial statements for Ro-Na Hardware were positive. As at December 31, 1961, after a full year in operation, the business reported earnings of $40 755. This consisted primarily of the contributions paid by the members, representing 1% of their purchases from Les Marchands en Quincaillerie Ltée. Expenses totalled $38 531 and consisted essentially of advertising costs. Although still in its infancy, the new entity generated revenues that were substantial for that time, and it reinvested more than 90% of those earnings in advertising and promotion initiatives. These initiatives helped to build business for Les Marchands en Quincaillerie Ltée, whose sales that year totalled more than $3.8 million.

The wheels had been set in motion, and they were turning ever faster.

The immense challenge of taking over from Rolland

At this time, Rolland Dansereau's health continued to be fragile. In 1961, he suffered a heart attack. He recovered, but he knew he would have to slow down, and he resigned himself to the idea of selling Les Marchands en Quincaillerie Ltée. Reinvestment was required in order to expand inventories and give the dealers the more varied product ranges they wanted. In addition, the first computers were starting

A smile that lights up the room

Ana Da Silva
Electrical Expert, Rona Brampton, Ontario

The first thing you notice when you meet Ana is her smile. It's not just the fact that she's smiling, it's that her smile is at the very heart of her philosophy of life and her work ethic. She believes work is a little like cooking. You prepare a dish you like, but by using some favourite ingredients and herbs to spice it up, you turn the whole thing into something thoroughly pleasurable! Sometimes, the spice is a kind word, a special attention, a moment with your team, but often, it's simply... a smile! Because, for Ana, the only way to work is to be passionate about every aspect of her job, whether sweeping the floors or finding a solution for a client with a 'special' character.

Ana's journey is evidence of how she devotes herself completely to all she does. After having raised two girls, she felt she needed to do something for herself. And what could be more natural for someone who loves human contact than to return to her first line of work, customer service? She couldn't imagine working alone; even though today she has the title of manager, she considers herself first and foremost to be part of a team.

Ten years ago, she saw an ad for the position that she still holds today at the Rona Home & Garden in Brampton, which, at the time, was a The Building Box store under construction. When she was hired, her first assignment was to help set up the store. She smiles whenever she stands in front of the construction materials aisle, recalling the support beams and the shelves she installed herself!

But her fondest memory is of Robert Dutton. In 2004, at the time of the merger, Ana proudly gave him a tour of their facilities. While they were chatting, she happened to mention that her daughter was about to undergo an operation. Six months later, at the Spring Show, he made a beeline for Ana and asked for news of her daughter, saying he had thought about her a lot. Do you know many company presidents like that?

Tools • State-of-the-art products

SINCE THE DAYS OF THE FIRST HARDWARE STORES, ALMOST NOTHING HAS REMAINED UNCHANGED. EVEN THE HUMBLE SCREWDRIVER IS NOW MORE ERGONOMICALLY DESIGNED AND MORE DURABLE, TO SAY NOTHING OF THE INVENTION OF THE NAIL GUN, WHICH HAS REVOLUTIONIZED THE WORK OF BUILDERS!

But what most strikes the eye and the mind of a visitor is the evolution in the way articles have been displayed, organized, and made accessible. From those venerable old general stores with their disorganized jumbles of bolts and agricultural objects, we have progressed to what can be considered veritable shopping centres that are brightly lit, where shoppers can circulate freely among the impressive displays of products arranged by areas of activity.

❶ In the 1940s and 1950s, hardware dealers published their own ads illustrating their various products and tools. Back then, it was common to assign traditional gender roles in a bid to attract the customer: revolutionary new kitchen utensils were aimed at the female homemaker; saws and hammers, at the male handyman...

❷ In the 1960s, ads for drills and saws were still targeted to men, while pots and coffeemakers were aimed at women... Also during the 1960s, Quincaillerie Ro-Na began to publish a common flyer for all its members.

❸ Dealers continued to be responsible for their own in-store merchandising displays until the 1970s. A few, including R. Deslongchamps & Fils, already offered neatly organized displays of tools...

❹ ...while other opted for more improvised presentations!

❺ From the end of the 1970s, Rona began to develop various types of displays and invited its member dealers to use them. Sanders, saws, and other tools of the handyman were now arranged in neat rows along the walls.

❻ In the 1980s, gender distinctions began to blur, and tools were becoming more universal. Motorized tools were no longer the exclusive preserve of men!

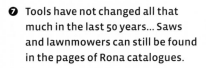

❼ Tools have not changed all that much in the last 50 years... Saws and lawnmowers can still be found in the pages of Rona catalogues.

❽ Still, a few new items made their way into the pages in the 1980s, such as these portable cassette players.

❾ In the 1990s and 2000s, the Rona flyers were standardized across Canada. The trusty hammer was always a stock item!

10 With the emergence of big-box stores, tools became a mainstay in every Rona.

LA VENTE DE "LES MARCHANDS EN QUINC. LIMITEE"

C'est le 4 janvier 1962, que M. J.-R. Dansereau offrit en vente, au soussigné, la Compagnie "Les Marchands en Quincaillerie Ltée. Le projet sérieusement examiné semble très réalisable. Toutefois il faudra procéder avec beaucoup de discrétion de façon à ne pas donner l'éveil aux manufacturiers.

Après examen de la liste il est convenu que M. Nap. Piotte intéressera quelques marchands, le plus petit nombre possible, pour réaliser un montant comptant de $120,000.00. Comme conséquence d'une demande assez générale des membres de bâtir "quelque chose" pour eux, on aurait été plutôt sous l'impression que ramasser $120,000.00 eut été un jeu d'enfants. Mais l'expérience confirme une fois de plus qu'il y a "loin de la coupe aux lèvres".

Sur un simple coup de fil, M. Charles Jalbert de Chicoutimi et M. Jean-Yves Gagnon de Roberval, y vont chacun de $1,250.00. Bon départ. - Québec consulté également par téléphone, nous recevons de M. Philippe Dorval $15,000.00 et de M. Hector Durant $10,000.00. De Montréal, M. Olaüs Latendresse promet $25,000.00, qu'effectivement nous recevons. M. J.O. Roberge souscrira volontiers $5,000.00, mais ne se portera garant de rien. Et les coups de fil se continuent pour nous garantir $5,000.00 de chacune des personnes suivantes: Messieurs Jacques Adam, André Dufour, Paul-Emile Chevrier, Joseph Dion et Nap. Piotte. Nous sommes déjà onze d'intéressés et nous n'avons souscrit que $10,500.00.

Plus de membres intéressés compromettrait la bonne marche future de "Les Marchands en Quincaillerie Ltée."; par ailleurs le capital souscrit n'est pas suffisant; toutefois il y a lieu de convoquer les intéressés et de tenir une réunion préliminaire. - Elle sera convoquée pour 2 hres p.m., mercredi, 31 janvier au domicile du soussigné soit à 2890, Est Boul. St-Joseph.

NAPOLÉON PIOTTE takes over the helm of Les Marchands en Quincaillerie Ltée from Rolland Dansereau in March 1962.

LETTER
explaining the sale of Les Marchands en Quincaillerie Ltée.

to appear at the company, and, gradually, Dansereau, the pioneer, came to feel that his time had passed.

Dansereau first approached his son Ronald, who was 34, to take over for him. But he declined, saying that he did not have the strength it would take to make the business develop and grow. His other son, Robert, was only 18 and was therefore too young.

While Dansereau was weighing various possible scenarios, he had a meeting with Gaston Tétreault, a leading dealer from Granby who was considering joining some Quebec City dealers with plans to form a rival group, given their dissatisfaction with their profits and with the situation in general. Dansereau suggested that he buy Les Marchands en Quincaillerie Ltée, but the discussions did not go far; neither Tétreault nor the dissatisfied dealers in Quebec City were able to come up with the necessary capital.

On January 4, 1962, Rolland turned to Napoléon. He proposed selling everything to him: both companies (Les Marchands en Quincaillerie Ltée and Ro-Na Hardware Inc.), the existing inventory, and the building on De la Savane Street. He added that there were other buyers in the wings, including some Americans.

Napoléon immediately got on the phone and set out on the road in an effort to convince some of the dealers to take part in this new venture. He needed to come up with at least $120 000 as quickly as possible. He threw all his energy into it and used his powers of persuasion to the fullest, but succeeded in collecting only $105 000 from 11 participants, including Olaüs Latendresse, who alone was willing to invest $25 000.

A meeting was nonetheless arranged with Rolland, who set out his conditions:

a) *Les Marchands en Quincaillerie Ltée and Ro-Na Hardware Inc. for $120 400 in cash, representing 93 common shares (out of a total of 100) and 778 preferred shares (out of 1 482), as well as all furnishings and lighting fixtures;*

b) *Repayment of loans granted by Rolland Dansereau to Les Marchands en Quincaillerie Ltée for the purchase of goods in inventory, representing a total amount of $245 000;*

c) *Purchase of the building at 5200 De la Savane Street for $720 000, or a 10-year lease with an annual rent of $72 000, plus $14 000 for municipal taxes.*

The first condition posed no problem. The second was more difficult to fulfill, as it would require any prospective buyers—that is, the dealers—to personally endorse a bank loan. As for the price of the building, it was deemed to be too high. A counter-offer for $650 000 was made and was promptly rejected by Rolland, who again hinted at the presence of other interested buyers, although he would not say who.

PHILIPPE DORVAL was one of six businessmen who bought back Les Marchands en Quincaillerie Ltée in 1962. He and his father had been partners since 1929, and in 1951 he became the owner of the J.A. Dorval hardware store in Quebec City.

WHEN HE DECIDED TO JOIN NAPOLÉON PIOTTE IN THE RONA ADVENTURE IN 1962, Charles Morency already had thirty years of experience in the hardware business under his belt, having been in charge of the family-run business of Édouard Morency Ltée.

Napoléon returned to the task. He was able to negotiate a loan for $300 000 with the Provincial Bank of Canada—which, in 1979, would merge with the Banque Canadienne Nationale to form the National Bank of Canada—in return for a letter of guarantee to be signed by all those who would eventually be appointed directors of Les Marchands en Quincaillerie Ltée. But while he battled on, others were giving up the fight: four of the dealers who had said they were interested went back on their decision. Napoléon travelled from Montreal to Quebec City, to Chicoutimi, to Sherbrooke, and to Granby, looking for others to take their place. He made a renewed appeal to Olaüs Latendresse, but when he went to see him, Latendresse was in bed, ill and waiting to be taken to hospital. He asked Napoléon to release him from his promise, he who had been his biggest investor. But Napoléon Piotte did not give up. It was as though he was on a mission, and he was willing to do anything to keep the company from falling into American hands.

Finally, on March 1, 1962, the goal was reached. He had collected 10 signatures and secured the required capital. These 10 dealers—all of whom no doubt a little crazy—pooled their efforts and their marbles to buy the company, and they must be remembered. I salute the following dealers who, in a way, were responsible for the "refounding" of RONA: Napoléon Piotte, J.O. Roberge, Jean-Yves Gagnon, Réal Gendron, Philippe Dorval, Hector Durand, Charles Morency, Charles Jalbert, Joseph Dion, and Gaston Tétreault.

In taking this step, they were in a sense going back to their roots and reaffirming the principle of solidarity and mutual aid on which the business had originally been founded 23 years earlier.

A special meeting of the board of directors was held on March 7, 1962. Its members were appointed as follows: Napoléon Piotte, president; J.O. Roberge, first vice-president; Philippe Dorval, second vice-president; Charles Morency, first director; Gaston Tétreault, second director; and Jean-Yves Gagnon, third director.

The celebrations did not last long, as reality soon caught up to them. Each of the new owners had expended considerable effort in the endeavour to buy out Rolland Dansereau. But it was not enough. Even more money was needed to support the company's growth and develop the business. Shareholders' equity was needed to prevent the debt load from becoming untenable. But how could they ensure a sound capital position for a business that for years had been financed out of Rolland Dansereau's own pockets?

The solution was right in front of them: the building on De la Savane Street. It was a tangible asset that could provide good financial leverage. But Dansereau was not willing to let it go for a song.

So the company's new owners, with Napoléon Piotte as their leader, would have to employ some clever tactics if they were to acquire it for a good price.

1960

International tensions rose sharply in May, when an American U-2 spy plane was shot down over the Soviet Union, just before the scheduled opening of a summit meeting in Paris involving the "Big Four" (the United States, Great Britain, France, and the USSR). When the conference opened, Khrushchev demanded that the U.S. acknowledge the incident as an act of aggression against the USSR and suspend all reconnaissance flights over Soviet territory. The U.S. rejected these demands, and Khrushchev returned to Moscow, effectively abandoning the conference.

Decolonization turned into tragedy in the Belgian Congo, which gained national independence only to descend immediately into chaos, with the massacre of Europeans and intertribal conflicts. Prime Minister Lumumba, who was not well thought of by the West, was overthrown by the army and later assassinated.

In November, John Kennedy won a narrow victory to become president of the United States. He would be the first Catholic president and one of the youngest in his country's history.

Following unproductive discussions with the provinces, John Diefenbaker's federal government enacted the Canadian Bill of Rights. This statute is not, however, entrenched in the Canadian Constitution, and its effectiveness remains limited.

In Quebec, the June 22 election marked the beginning of the "Quiet Revolution," when Jean Lesage's Liberals came to power after 16 years of rule by the Union Nationale.

In other developments, 1960 saw the introduction on the market of the birth-control pill, which would play a key role in the liberation of women.

1961

April 1961 was an eventful month on the world scene. It opened with the Soviets further increasing their lead in the space race when they achieved the first human flight around the earth. Yuri Gagarin became the international star of the moment.

Four days later, the spotlight fell once again on Cuba. On April 17, Cuban anti-Castro forces, recruited, funded, trained, and transported by the CIA, landed at an area known as the "Bay of Pigs" to attempt to recapture the island. However, it turned into a lamentably botched operation after President Kennedy, who had taken office mere months before, refused to send in the U.S. Air Force. Wary of further invasions, Castro asked the USSR to assist with the country's defence, an initiative that would prove very dangerous indeed...

In the ongoing Cold War, events in the month of August defined 1961 as a key year. East Germany surrounded all of West Berlin with a 43-kilometre-long wall in an attempt to stem the flood of East Germans seeking refuge in the city by the hundreds of thousands each year. The "Wall of Shame" would stand for close to 30 years as a scandalous and hated symbol of the division of Europe.

The Legislative Assembly of Saskatchewan passed an act instituting a universal medical insurance program, the first in North America. The program came into force the following year. By 1972, all of Canada's territories and provinces had adopted similar programs.

1962

The space race gained momentum in 1962. The United States finally succeeded in sending a human into space in February, but still struggled to keep pace with the Soviets and their achievements. In August, the Soviets launched two manned spacecraft within a 24-hour period, one of which set a record for flight duration with a flight of 95 hours, covering a distance of 2.6 million kilometres. In contrast, John Glenn's mission had lasted less than five hours.

In October, the Cuban Missile Crisis brought the planet to the brink of a third World War. The USSR had started installing nuclear missiles in Cuba that were capable of striking every major city in the eastern part of North America, including Montreal and Toronto, and the United States responded with a naval blockade of the island. Over a period of seven days, the whole world held its breath, until a last-minute agreement was reached between Kennedy and Khrushchev. In exchange for a promise from the former not to invade Cuba, the latter agreed to dismantle the Soviet missile bases located there. So intense had been the feeling of alarm over the incident that, in its aftermath, tensions between the two superpowers finally started to ease.

In September, Prime Minister Diefenbaker officially opened the Trans-Canada Highway. It would only be completed in 1970 and would reach a total length of over 7 800 kilometres.

In Quebec, Jean Lesage's Liberals won the November general election, which had all the earmarks of a referendum on the nationalization of the province's electricity industry.

- A -

CANADA

PROVINCE DE QUEBEC

ELIZABETH DEUX, par la Grâce de Dieu, Reine du Royaume-Uni du Canada et de ses autres royaumes et territoires. Chef du Commonwealth, Défenseur de la Foi.

A tous ceux que les présentes lettres concerneront ou qui les verront,
SALUT:

Lettres patentes constituant en corporation

" GESTION LA SAVANE INC. "

ATTENDU que la première partie de la loi des compagnies de Québec, statue que le lieutenant-gouverneur peut, au moyen de lettres patentes expédiées sous le grand sceau, accorder à trois personnes ou plus qui en font la demande par requête, une charte les constituant en corporation pour certains objets relevant de l'autorité législative de cette province, excepté pour la construction et l'exploitation de chemins de fer, autres que les tramways existants et dont les voies ferrées ne servent qu'à un service exploité entièrement dans la province, pour les affaires d'assurance, et pour les affaires de fidéicommis;

Enregistrées le

2 novembre 1962

Libro 1146

Folio 88

ATTENDU que les personnes ci-après désignées ont demandé par requête une charte qui les constitue en corporation pour les objets ci-après décrits;

ATTENDU que les dites personnes ont rempli les formalités prescrites pour l'obtention de la charte demandée, et que les objets de l'entreprise de la compagnie projetée sont de ceux pour lesquels le lieutenant-gouverneur peut accorder une charte;

Le sous-régistraire de la province

Raymond Douville

A CES CAUSES, Nous avons, en vertu des pouvoirs qui sont conférés par ladite première partie de la loi des compagnies de Québec, constitué et, par les présentes lettres patentes, constituons en corporation les personnes suivantes, savoir:

GESTION LA SAVANE INC. is issued letters patent and formally created on November 2, 1962.

IN THE DE LA SAVANE STREET OFFICES, Napoléon Piotte, the new president of Les Marchands en Quincaillerie Ltée, meets a few members of the new administration: Hector Durand, Charles Morency, and Philippe Dorval, all Quebec City store dealers.

The first step was to restructure the business. The new owners created a management company, Gestion La Savane Inc. The name certainly made clear their intention of buying the building. Each of the dealer owners transferred his shares in Les Marchands en Quincaillerie Ltée to this new entity, the letters patent of which were registered on November 2, 1962. The business was defined as a management and holding company, investment firm, and hardware business. Its share capital was set at $500 000, divided into 5 000 common shares worth $10 each and 4 500 preferred shares worth $100 each.

A special rule was established: no one could own more than 500 common shares, or 10% of the new company's voting capital stock. The intent was clear. Such a rule was obviously designed to prevent any one person from seizing control of the business. The owners of preferred shares would be entitled to a preferential dividend of 7% per year. Any other dividend would be split between common shareholders and preferred shareholders in proportion to the number of shares they owned.

On November 26, the board of directors of Les Marchands en Quincaillerie Ltée passed a resolution intended to "guarantee the ownership of Ro-Na Hardware Inc. in perpetuity to Les Marchands en Quincaillerie Ltée provided that ownership of Les Marchands en Quincaillerie Ltée [passed] to Gestion La Savane Inc."

A by-law would subsequently be adopted stating that the directors of Gestion La Savane Inc., 10 in number, would all have to be hardware dealers, except for the president (as Napoléon Piotte was not a dealer; this exception would be abolished after his death). It would also be established that the company's charter could not be amended unless the owners of at least 65% of the common shares voted in favour. This rule, combined with the 10% limit on ownership and the fact that each director of the management company had to be a dealer, created a situation that was subsequently inviolable: the organization was under the collective authority of the hardware dealers. None of them, nor anyone else for that matter, would ever be able to take control without the consent of a substantial majority of the dealers.

The business now had an ownership structure that reflected its new reality: a holding company (Gestion La Savane Inc.) owned by dealers, which was itself the owner of a buying group (Les Marchands en Quincaillerie Ltée), whose members could become part of a chain of retailers (Ro-Na Hardware Inc.) in return for the rental of a banner and a contribution that was reinvested in shared advertising.

On paper, everything looked good, but the building on De la Savane Street still did not belong to Piotte and his partners. The business was ready; all that was needed now was to find it a home.

AT THE ÉDOUARD MORENCY HARDWARE STORE
in Quebec City, Charles Morency rewarded
his loyal customers with raffle prizes. In 1962,
under his watchful eye, his wife, Fernande, and
Father Dubé draw a winning ticket.

To accomplish this, the crafty Napoléon had to do two things: raise $270 000 from the dealers as a down payment on the building, and get the building at a better price than what Dansereau had to that point been asking.

While Napoléon put the finishing touches on his plan, Dansereau was in very low spirits. He regretted selling the company. Only a few weeks passed before he tried to have the sale revoked. But the contract contained no provision for doing so. For this tireless worker, boredom proved much more difficult to bear than his previous responsibilities.

A huge celebration was organized in Dansereau's honour. Many distinguished guests were in attendance: elected representatives, cabinet ministers, businesspeople. But Rolland himself was not there. He was in the hospital. The day before, he had suffered another heart attack. His son Ronald spoke on his behalf and read out a letter written by Rolland to the new owners:

Dear Sirs and Esteemed Partners,

[...] After 23 years of hard work, I am stepping down from the post I have held until now. My severely compromised state of health has forced this decision upon me. While I leave with a clear conscience, having always given the best of myself, I do not leave without regret... you have been not only partners and supporters, but real and genuine friends. My thanks go out to all of you!

If, in the course of our business dealings over the last 23 years, I have inadvertently hurt or offended you in any way, I apologize. Everything I have done has been with the common good in mind, and that is why I leave in peace, with no feelings of reproach or remorse. [...]

One final appeal, gentlemen, before I leave you: stick together, stand united, and your success is assured with LES MARCHANDS EN QUINCAILLERIE LTÉE! Be as true to this company as this company has been to you!

Sincerely,

J.R. Dansereau

Napoléon set out on the road once again to visit the dealers and persuade them to put more money into the company. He knew he would not receive a warm welcome. Many dealers felt they had been swindled in the past. Some of them even had the shares they owned hanging on their office wall, so convinced were they that the shares were worthless and that their investment had served only to make Dansereau rich. But Napoléon knew how to change their minds. He told them that this time, they would be investing in a new management company that would own a building. The building guaranteed their investment would have some value. One by one, the dealers got on board, and in the end Napoléon secured the necessary commitments.

"I felt like Superman"

Marc St-Pierre
Retired Administrative Employee, Former Advertising Director, and Former Marketing Director, Administrative Office, Boucherville, Quebec

When Marc St-Pierre arrived at Rona in 1962, with seven years' experience in the hardware business under his belt, it was two years before the advertising agency BCP would create the "oiseau rare" (rare bird) logo. He was one of just 42 employees at the De la Savane Street offices: "There weren't many of us," he recalls.

Three years later, after having moved from the warehouse to the ordering department, Marc was put in charge of advertising. He stayed there until he retired in 1989. At the beginning, he focused all his energy on strengthening the group brand. It's important to remember that in those days, the more well-known a hardware merchant was, the greater his decision-making power. Getting the other merchants to accept the idea of sharing a common image—and making joint decisions—proved quite a challenge. But he succeeded, and everyone was happy. Marc designed flyer upon flyer, as well as scores of calendars that the merchants bought to distribute to their clients. In those days, the Rona calendar adorned the walls of many a home!

Towards the end of the 1970s, the advent of easy-to-produce microfilm revolutionized the purchasing process. Television was one more tool in the direct advertising kit. Remember the ad where the young Napoléon and Rolland built a tree house? Effective, wasn't it? And then there were all sorts of other promotional "events": trade conventions that attracted hundreds of merchants; shows by star performers like Acadian singer-songwriter Édith Butler; conferences given by marketing specialist Gérard Virthe from the firm Cogem; carnivals in Quebec City; organized trips for merchants to Mexico, Brazil, and France; wine and cheese tastings; baseball games at Jarry Stadium; dances at École Meilleur, where Napoléon had studied; and, of course, a whole slate of golf tournaments... Marc was also in charge of preparing the trophies and the bronze plaques to award to everyone involved. A good time was guaranteed for all!

"All my life, I always felt a bit like a superman at Rona, because the guys at the top supported me in everything I did."

A family affair

The Anctil Family

Rona Anctil, Saint-Denis-de-Brompton; Rona L'entrepôt, Sherbrooke; and Rona Le Rénovateur, Magog, Quebec

You'll still find many Anctils working at J. Anctil hardware. All the main family members work there along with a good number of close and distant cousins.

In 1935, Joseph and Zoé were constantly coming to their neighbours' rescue with whatever supplies were needed, and they decided they might as well turn it into a business venture. That was how things started, and, from there, Henri and Olivette were the first to take over the reins, followed by Jocelyn and Francine, who have since passed the torch to their children, Caroline, Vincent, and David. The hardware gene seems to run in the family!

Rona Anctil is also a story about women. Jocelyn's sister, Renelle, runs a Rona L'entrepôt in Sherbrooke. Mothers, sisters, daughters, and wives have always played a key role in the business.

It's the perfect example of family solidarity. Everyone has their place, and each one has their job to do. In fact, that's their secret and the reason it all runs smoothly; advice is shared, but individual decisions are respected. And if there is an occasional difference of opinion, Francine has the last word. After all, she's still their mother—even at the store!

Of course, their staff is not made up exclusively of family members, and, few years ago, they sold 10% of their shares to the employees as an incentive. They own several stores: one in Saint-Denis-de-Brompton, a Rona L'entrepôt in Sherbrooke, and a Rona Le Rénovateur in Magog. As well, the family's business activities are becoming more diversified, with the opening of Usihome, a factory that manufactures prefabricated houses and walls for its clientele of general contractors. The Groupe Anctil also includes an environment division, which handles wastewater recycling, and the family is currently developing two residential projects. Phew!

Entrepreneurial flair is something that is acquired with time. Ever since the business opened, the hardware store has been the children's playground. "Here, the kids don't have play dough, they play with window putty!" So, though no one has ever been forced to join the team, though they've always been free to choose, the family has stuck together. But when you come from such a great family, it's hard to imagine wanting to work anywhere else!

IN WESTERN CANADA, Revelstoke was modernizing, and it opened stores like this one in Medicine Hat, Alberta. In 1961, Revelstoke Sawmill Company became Revelstoke Building Materials.

All that remained was to get the building for a lower price. Rolland Dansereau would not budge from his price of $720 000 for the building on De la Savane Street. For Napoléon and his partners, this was much too high. They sought the opinion of an agent from the company Morgan Trust, one Pierre Forest, who agreed with their view.

Pierre Forest and Napoléon Piotte decided together on the steps that would be taken next. Forest's interest in the matter was, of course, the sizable commission he would receive if the deal were to be completed to the satisfaction of Piotte and his associates.

It was now November 1962. Pierre Forest made an appointment to see Rolland Dansereau. He told him simply that the firm he represented was willing to purchase 5200 De la Savane Street. The interest expressed by such a prestigious financial institution as the Morgan Trust Company of Canada whet Dansereau's appetite, and he upped his price to $755 000, "and not a penny less."

Forest at once presented an offer for $600 000 along with a cheque for $25 000 as security. While they were talking in his office, the phone rang. Dansereau said a few words, then hung up. He told Forest that it was Piotte who had called and that he was planning to come in that very evening to close the sale. Forest, who was in league with Piotte, knew perfectly well that was not true.

Napoléon then set a trap for Dansereau. He had Dansereau's former secretary write a memo supposedly

5200 DE LA SAVANE STREET is located close to the Décarie Expressway in Montreal. From September 1960 until it was bought by the new administration in 1962, Les Marchands en Quincaillerie Ltée had rented the building owned by Rolland Dansereau.

intended for all the shareholders. He knew very well that she would tell Dansereau about this. The text went as follows:

> *Due to the impossibility of negotiating a sale between Les Marchands en Quincaillerie Ltée and Mr. Dansereau, you will find enclosed a cheque in the amount of _____ for the money you deposited in the name of Napoléon Piotte in Trust for the purchase of the property at 5200 De la Savane Street.*

The letter would, of course, never be sent. Its only purpose was to make Dansereau think that he no longer had a buyer.

A few days later, Pierre Forest of Morgan Trust knocked once again on Dansereau's door. He told him he was offering $625 000 this time, take it or leave it. Dansereau hesitated. He asked for 24 hours to think it over. When that time ran out, he asked for 24 hours more, on the pretext that his lawyer was out of town. Forest was not a man who was easily fooled. He checked and quickly determined that the lawyer in question was in fact in Montreal. He called Dansereau back and demanded that he accept immediately, otherwise the whole thing was off. Rolland gave in and signed.

Forest went straight to see Piotte and immediately sold the building to Gestion La Savane Inc. for a $25 000 commission.

The following day Napoléon Piotte, grinning from ear to ear, walked into Rolland Dansereau's office.

— What are you doing here?

— We are the ones who bought you out, Mr. Dansereau.

Gestion La Savane became incorporated on January 9, 1963.

After a year of negotiations, restructuring, and tactics, ownership of the business was now in the hands of the dealers. It was properly funded and ready to make a new start.

The lengthy partnership between Rolland and Napoléon was over. Napoléon, ever the second-in-command, had become president. It seemed that the idealist had learned from the old fox Rolland just how to do business.

The eventful, quarter-century-long association between the two men left as its legacy a fieriness of spirit, a drive to build, and a name, Ro-Na, which would come to symbolize daring and success. Most of all, it left, I think, a blend of idealism and pragmatism that is still a defining feature of our organization today.

A family portrait · The extended clan
1962

Sales: $5 094 730

Affiliate stores (members): approximately 300

DEALERS WISHING TO ADOPT THE "RO-NA" NAME also wanted their dress to reflect their new affiliation: in 1966, Marc St-Pierre and Conrad Thibault presented the dealers with brand new uniforms, including the famous red jacket.

Emergence
1963 - 1974

In 1963, Napoléon Piotte was president, after having bought the company from Rolland Dansereau along with a group of nine dealers. A wind of change was blowing across Quebec. It was the Quiet Revolution, and the winds of confidence also swelled the sails of the company. Under the guidance of Napoléon and his associates, the organization would begin to lay the groundwork for its success:

- an advertising campaign of unprecedented scope established the "rare bird" as the brand image of the Ro-Na dealers;
- an initial acquisition was made in the Quebec City area, and a first strategic alliance was formed with wholesalers in English Canada;
- a review of the rebate system provided the group with the funding needed for its development.

In fewer than six years, Napoléon transformed the organization. In September 1968, he collapsed at his desk and died a week later. Rolland Dansereau followed him a few months afterwards. The torch was passed to Charles Morency. Les Marchands en Quincaillerie Ltée became Marchands Ro-Na Inc., as Napoléon had wished a few weeks prior to his death. Ro-Na entered the computer age. The company moved into a huge administrative centre and ultramodern distribution centre that had been built in Boucherville. Ro-Na was now in the big leagues, with, in 1973, 388 member dealers and total sales of $26 million.

IN OCTOBER 1966, employees celebrated Napoléon Piotte's 64th birthday with an oyster party.

RO-NA HARDWARE DEALERS CONTINUE TO PROSPER. On June 17, 1967, in Saint-Denis-de-Brompton, the Anctil family inaugurated the reopening of their store following its expansion, with President Napoléon Piotte.

A wind of change

It was now 1963. A new wind was blowing through Quebec. The year before, Jean Lesage's Liberals had been re-elected. At the heart of this election, which for all intents and purposes amounted to a referendum, was the plan to complete the nationalization of private hydroelectric companies, a project championed by the popular Minister of Natural Resources, former journalist René Lévesque. In November 1962, the City of Montreal was awarded the 1967 World Exposition.

The province had embarked upon what would later be called the "Quiet Revolution." In the space of a few years, spurred on by the desire to take control of its economy, Quebec empowered itself with the means to advance its economic and social development, through the creation of such government agencies as the Régie des rentes du Québec, the Caisse de dépôt et placement du Québec, and the Société générale de financement du Québec. Education and health care, which until that time had been administered largely by religious orders, would henceforth be the responsibility of the government.

This was the context in which Napoléon Piotte took on the role of president of a group of nine dealers. The businesspeople of Quebec were also stirred by the excitement that bubbled through the province. It was a time for ambition. There grew in Quebec an appetite for success, a feeling of confidence. Napoléon Piotte would be the embodiment of that era. He who had for so long been Rolland Dansereau's second-in-command, he who had learned all he knew from the formidable Dansereau, now emerged as a visionary leader.

As I see it, it was at this time, under the guidance of Piotte and his associates, daring and determined dealers, that the company developed the foundations and capacities that have made RONA one of the biggest successes in Canadian business.

Let's take a look at how Napoléon Piotte set RONA on the path to success and steered our company through its own "quiet revolution."

A different style of leadership

Napoléon and his nine partners were now the joint owners of the holding company Gestion La Savane Inc., which owned all the common shares of the buying group Les Marchands en Quincaillerie Ltée, the members of which owned preferred shares. Les Marchands en Quincaillerie Ltée in turn owned all the capital stock of Ro-Na Hardware Inc., a subsidiary dedicated to marketing. The clients of Les Marchands en Quincaillerie Ltée could, if they so desired, display the Ro-Na banner.

Napoléon Piotte's style of leadership was different from Dansereau's. Ever since he first joined the organization, Piotte had always devoted the bulk of his time to relationships with the dealers. He was their collaborator, their

THOUGH A SERIOUS MAN WITH A COMMANDING PHYSICAL PRESENCE, Napoléon Piotte liked to have fun. In March 1968, he invited member dealers to the Hugues Desrochers sugar shack near Joliette.

confidant, their solace. He knew how to rally them and get this group of strong-minded individuals to pull together. Although he was now the president, he would continue to personally nurture those relationships, because, to him, the dealers were the heart of the company.

In addition, Napoléon continued to travel regularly to visit them... often with his suitcases full of banknotes! That was because he wanted to deliver the rebates to the dealers in person. The math was simple, recalls André Dion: "Here are the prices that were paid to buy the merchandise, and here are the prices at which it was sold to you. This is how much is left over, so this is how much we're giving back to you." It was not only money that changed hands; ideas were shared, too. These visits by Napoléon provided an opportunity to talk one-on-one about the business of the company, to sound out opinions and strengthen allegiances.

Napoléon was good-hearted and gave recognition where it was due. He handed out Christmas gifts and bonuses, thus making the connection between the employees and the company's good results. And he was a bon vivant who liked to have fun, laugh, and eat well. At the end of each meeting of his advertising committee, he would take everyone out to a restaurant. André Gagnon, who would serve as a member of the board of directors for 36 years, recalls:

"Our contribution was, of course, on a volunteer basis; our reward was going out for dinner with Mr. Piotte. Because he had been a teacher, he

From great-grandfather to great-grandson

Guy and André Champagne
Quincaillerie A. Champagne, Rona Le Quincaillier, Saint-Honoré-de-Shenley, Quebec

"My father is the Mick Jagger of Rona. I've lost count of the number of times I've heard him say 'This will be the last time!' He always comes back!" André Champagne's take on his father Guy's devotion to the business couldn't be more on the money.

Built in 1907 by Louis and taken over in 1942 by his son Alfonse, the store was bought in 1955 by Alfonse's sons, Guy and Jean-Paul. Back then, Guy was already a member of the Les Marchands en Quincaillerie Ltée organization, and he explains how they would meet Napoléon Piotte and other local merchants late in the evening in a school classroom to place their orders. "Napoléon would go back to Montreal the same evening to prepare everything. He was utterly driven!"

In the beginning, it was a general store that catered to all the needs of the residents of the small village of Saint-Honoré-de-Shenley, in the Beauce region. It even doubled as a farm supply outlet, as there was no other in the area. Groceries, hardware, work boots, seeds, livestock meal—you name it, they sold it!

In 1982, Jean-Paul left the business, and Guy had to decide quickly: either he bought him out or he closed the shop. Since there was no doubt in his mind that he wanted to carry on, he took out a bank loan to help him through and bought out his brother.

It was a very difficult period for Guy, but his son André was there to support him. In fact, that experience helped André decide that he wanted to stay on permanently—only not to sort potatoes like he did when he was little! Since his uncle had been the buyer, André would take over that role. What's more, with the advent of computerized systems, he was able to put his studies to good use! Ten years later, it had become obvious that, to stay viable, the company would have to specialize: it was time to choose between groceries and hardware. So, out went the fruit and vegetables and in came more construction materials.

In 1995, André took over the helm. But that didn't mean that Guy was out of the picture—gone for only two months, he returned to offer his services to his son. "I asked him for his CV and a few references," laughs André. For Guy, it was a matter of survival: "I came back because I couldn't bear being away. It's my passion!" he admits.

EACH YEAR, THE QUEBEC DEALERS ORGANIZED THE TOURNOI DES QUINCAILLIERS GOLF TOURNAMENT. In 1966, André Boily, Jean-Paul Morency, Jacques Deslauriers, and Gilles Laflamme shared a laugh as they looked at their scores!

always called us by our last names. He called me 'Gagnon,' never 'André.' I arrived at the restaurant— I remember it as if it were yesterday… 'Gagnon, what is the name of that flower over there?' There was a bed of flowers. So I said, 'Those there are lilies, Mr. Piotte.' And he would reply: 'I'll have you know, Gagnon, that those are petunias.' He had this booming voice…"

Napoléon shared many good times with the dealers. Apart from the annual trips to the Canadian Hardware Show in Toronto, which left indelible memories, there are numerous accounts of very lively social events. Dances, wine and cheese parties, sugaring-off parties, the president's annual dinner, golf tournaments… any occasion was a good excuse for a bit of a celebration. Once, while arrangements were being made for a big dance the following evening on the second floor of the building on De la Savane Street, the treasurer advised Napoléon to contact their insurance company, as he was not sure the floor would stand up under the assault of all the dancers and their partners!

It was in fact there, in the administrative offices on De la Savane Street, that Napoléon established his head-quarters. He occupied a large office with windows over-looking a huge area that was used as a sample room. He would often be found there early in the morning and late into the evening. Because, like Rolland, Napoléon was an untiring worker who expected those around him to be just as generous with their time. He was physically imposing, seemingly carved out of rock. His son Pierre describes him as a "big, strong man" who had "a serious demeanour" and "big hands… he could be intimidating."

Rough sailing in the first year

Although Napoléon enjoyed the esteem of the dealers and the trust of his associates at Gestion La Savane Inc., a few incidents came along to trouble his first year as president.

The minutes of the meeting of the board of directors held on January 28, 1963 describe some petty crimes that had taken place on De la Savane Street, as follows: "On November 23, theft of cash; on December 7, some sugar was thrown into the oil line of the boiler; and on December 18, it was discovered that the Gestetner [mimeograph machine] had been broken. The municipal detectives are still inves-tigating." The new president had to fire a few employees.

On December 12, 1963, a joint meeting was held of the boards of directors of Les Marchands en Quincaillerie Ltée and Gestion La Savane Inc. There it was resolved that a for-mal notice would be sent to a dealer accused of "spreading false and erroneous information to clients and suppliers."

Napoléon even faced an insurrection mounted by an organized group of dealers.

On May 7, 1964, a petition was received at the offices of Gestion La Savane Inc. It was signed by 28 dealers.

WAREHOUSE DIRECTOR ANDRÉ GALARNEAU, SALES DIRECTOR MAURICE MICHAUD, AND CONTROLLER ANDRÉ DION on a fishing trip at the Garant company club in 1969.

The document was a lengthy recitation of 16 points. The signatories called for a review of the company's ownership structure and share ownership framework.

According to their 8th point, full ownership of the company was theirs by right, and to support this position they offered an astonishing interpretation of the aim of those who bought the business from Rolland Dansereau:

> *"8—Whereas these dedicated Dealers [the nine co-founders and co-owners with Napoléon Piotte of Gestion La Savane Inc.] acquired the said Company with the goal of being of service to the members and clients of the company Les Marchands en Quincaillerie Ltée and with a firm resolve to deliver ownership of this Company to the latter in the near future;"*

The petitioners further submitted that the success of Les Marchands en Quincaillerie Ltée could not have been achieved without the contribution of its members, and this partnership would not be complete until the members had the right to elect the board of directors. The petition concluded with the following demand:

> *"That the charter of the company Gestion La Savane Inc. be amended to allow each Rona member who so desires to become an owner of common shares in equal numbers with his colleagues who are already shareholders."*

1963

The most memorable event of 1963 is without question the assassination of President John Fitzgerald Kennedy in Dallas on November 22 📷. More than 40 years later, the exact circumstances of the tragedy, and who was responsible for it, are still the subject of heated debate. The official theory of the lone gunman has not quelled the countless conspiracy theories that have surfaced involving a variety of suspects: anti-Castro groups, in disapproval of the president's supposed weak stance on Cuba; organized crime, in retaliation for the all-out war being waged on it by the attorney general, his brother Robert; white racists, in protest over his vigorous policies on racial equality; and even a combination of several of these elements.

Two days later, the alleged assassin, Lee Harvey Oswald, was shot dead at police headquarters in Dallas. The voice of the key individual in this event would now never be heard.

A few months earlier, during the "March on Washington for Jobs and Freedom," pastor Martin Luther King, Jr. had delivered his historic "I Have a Dream" speech in front of more than 200 000 people. The events in Dallas on November 22 dealt a terrible blow to the hope of an entire generation.

1964

The "Quiet Revolution" continued in Quebec. Following the nationalization of the province's electricity industry the previous year, 1964 saw the creation of a Ministry of Education that would bring under its authority a multitude of bodies and organizations active in the field of education, most of which were under the aegis of religious institutions. In October, a visit to Quebec City by Queen Elizabeth II resulted in what would become known as "Truncheon Saturday," when demonstrators were violently dispersed by police.

On August 4, an attack by North Vietnamese torpedo boats on two U.S. destroyers sparked a decisive escalation in the Vietnam War. One would learn later that this "incident" was a hoax and never happened...

In October 📷, Nikita Khrushchev was dismissed by the Central Committee of the Communist Party of the Soviet Union. As a sign of the changing times, however, he would not be executed and would live a quiet life in his Moscow-area *dacha* until his death in 1971.

In November, the Democratic U.S. president, Lyndon B. Johnson, was re-elected with the largest majority in the country's history, winning by a margin of 15.5 million votes and taking 486 electoral votes to the 52 won by Republican Barry M. Goldwater.

On December 15, nearly a century after it became a country, Canada finally adopted an official national flag, the maple leaf flag.

1965

The space race continued unabated in 1965, with the United States gradually closing the gap that separated them from the USSR. The Soviets successfully completed the first space walk in March, followed by the Americans in June. In December, two American Gemini capsules were launched and rendezvoused to within less than a metre of each other, without actually docking.

U.S. involvement in the Vietnam War intensified. The first aerial assaults on North Vietnam occurred in February, and the first Marines landed in March.

In Canada, the Laurendeau-Dunton Commission, established in response to growing nationalist sentiment in Quebec, produced a preliminary report stating that Canada was facing the most serious internal crisis in its history. The Commission would be the starting point for the entire policy around bilingualism in federal institutions.

On January 16, 1965, the Canada–United States Automotive Agreement, commonly referred to as the Auto Pact, was signed by Canada's prime minister and the president of the United States. This trade agreement transformed the North American car manufacturing landscape. It became the model for 'managed trade,' setting a precedent for broader free trade between Canada and the United States.

In November, Lester B. Pearson's minority Liberal government was returned to power, but it was still a minority. Canada had had a minority government since 1962, a situation that would not change until 1968.

In Quebec, the Quiet Revolution was still going strong, with the creation of the Régie des rentes du Québec and the Caisse de dépôt et placement, two key organizations of modern Quebec. Also in 1965, the province signed the first international agreement in its history, with France, relating to the field of education.

PRESIDENT NAPOLÉON PIOTTE,
meeting with manufacturers'
representatives at the 1966 exhibition.

A GARDEN HOSE LOGO!
The owners of Ferronnerie Paul A. Grégoire de
Disraeli take part in a window display contest
organized by Qunicaillerie Ro-Na in 1965.

This cut Napoléon Piotte to the quick. When he thought of the difficulty he had had finding nine dealers willing to reinvest in the company, when he thought of the risks they took, the bravery they showed... And now these people wanted to tear it all down in the name of some sort of divine right to ownership. Napoléon was enraged.

He decided to let a little time go by.

On September 30, the petitioners requested a meeting with the board of directors. It never took place. On October 11, the signers of the petition met at the Queen Elizabeth Hotel in Montreal. Some of them said they missed Dansereau's leadership and considered Piotte to be too controlling and more underhanded than his predecessor.

Napoléon's answer finally arrived. Eight closely-filled pages... and a clearly expressed feeling of anger.

He began by downplaying the importance of the petitioners, saying that 18 of the 28 were not, had never been, or would no longer be member dealers, as they had not signed their agreements for 1965.

He went on to dissect the points one by one, paying special attention to number 8:

> Here as well, those who drafted the petition have shown their <u>abysmal</u> ignorance [underscore Napoléon's]. Ten men bought Les Marchands en Quincaillerie Ltée in March 1962. They could have kept it all for themselves and no one would have had any right to say a word about it, because, of the 50 clients who had been approached, they were the only ones willing to take the risk. [...] Once [Gestion La Savane] was incorporated, in an unprecedented move, they transferred all the assets of Les Marchands en Quincaillerie Ltée and Ro-Na Hardware Inc., assets that they alone owned and had paid for with their own money, they transferred all these common shares to Gestion La Savane Inc. at cost. [...] Criticizing them is easy! Suspecting them is human perhaps, but cowardly certainly. Following their example of selflessness is something that you, in your self-centredness, will never be able to do.

Napoléon's response to the petitioners who wanted "complete security" was this:

> The preferred shareholders of Gestion La Savane Inc. [that is, all the member dealers] share in the profits of all three companies but are discharged from all financial and administrative liability.

And he did not hesitate to lecture them about their wish that they be allowed to elect the board of directors:

> Dearest democracy! What <u>crimes people commit</u> in your name! Especially when we know that <u>all it takes is one lunatic to create a schism</u> [underscore Napoléon's]. [...] The history of all our cooperatives in the last 40 years has proven that democratic elections were an obstacle to progress, they were the ruin of any sort of comprehensive plans, and they forced the cooperatives into

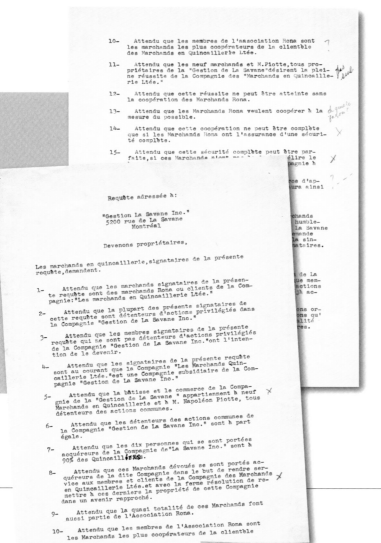

LIST of the dealers' "whereases."

A lasting attachment

Richard Provost

Quincaillerie Bernier, Rona L'Express, Montreal, Quebec

The very first Bernier hardware store opened its doors in 1912 on Saint-Laurent Boulevard in Montreal. It belonged to the Berniers for two generations before the Provost family took over when Mr. Provost senior, a store employee, went into partnership with Mr. Bernier junior. In 1948, they opened two new locations—one in the city's Verdun district, and one on Saint-Denis Street. In those days, the area to the north of Mont-Royal Avenue was a bustling, thriving community. From Thursday to Saturday, the streets were jam-packed. Cars lined up to pick up grocery orders from Steinberg's, moviegoers flocked to the Théâtre du Rideau Vert, a popular movie theatre back then, and diners provided the Plateau's La Binerie restaurant with a roaring trade. In the years that followed, the neighbourhood changed, retailers came and went, but Quincaillerie Bernier stayed firmly put. "Clients were attached to the store and the store was attached to them," and that's the true essence of a neighbourhood store.

Richard started working at the store when he was just 10 years old. His Saturday wages were 25 cents plus a tramway ticket. The money wasn't important; what mattered to him was discovering a world of people and products, and feeling useful. What's more, he says, "Working with my dad strengthened our relationship, and, in turn, working with my kids later on brought me closer to them." He wasn't just some stranger who would arrive home from work exhausted, whom you'd only see in the evenings and for a few hours on Sundays. Incidentally, Richard's father continued to work for the company until he was 89.

After working for Bétonel for a few years, Richard returned to the family business in 1973. His mind was made up: he believed that being your own boss offered you far more security. You're free to make your own decisions. As he puts it, "It's the story of my life: I wanted my own business, and now I have it!" And though he knows the store will stay in the family—his sons Yves and Stéphane are vice-presidents—Richard doesn't plan to throw in the towel any time soon. He'll stay there till the very end if he can. Like the Quebecois businessman Pierre Péladeau, he says, "Work is my second home; my office is my living room!"

The key to the company's success for the past five generations? They stock just about everything. People who can't find what they're looking for elsewhere come to Bernier, "… and if we don't have what they want, we'll get it for them within a couple of days." Clients like the fact that the person who serves them today will still be there next week; some employees have been there for over 30 years. The biggest challenge during all this time has been to remain open. When the big-box stores arrived, it was like we were being told "You guys are finished." But, as it turned out, there was room for everyone!

An expert hand and a good ear

Siavash Mahdieh
Kitchen Expert, Rona Toronto

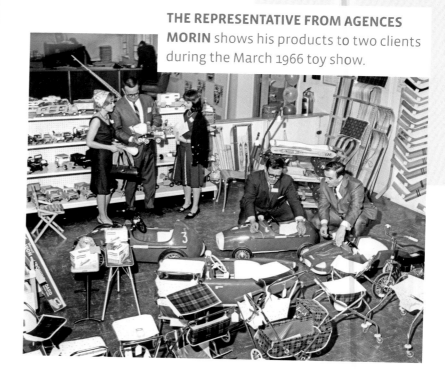

Four years ago, when Sia left Dubai and arrived in Canada, he felt ready for a career change. His work as an industrial engineer did not satisfy his artistic leanings or his hankering for creativity. So he embarked on a course of study in design and interior architecture. The International Academy appealed to him because if offered a hands-on rather than theoretical approach. During the three years he was in school, he worked at Rona as a kitchen designer.

Today, Sia is proud to say that he hasn't taken a vacation in eight years. When you are as passionate about your work as that, why deprive yourself of the chance to perfect your skills? In addition to the projects he heads at Rona, he has clients of his own... whom he steers toward the store for all their project needs! He appreciates the selection and quality of the products he works with.

The most important aspect of designing a kitchen isn't the client's budget. You can achieve miracles on a few thousand dollars. It's keeping in mind the myriad little challenges presented by each different project, whether it be an exposed column, an odd-shaped room, or a colour palette that's already been determined by another room. And you have to create a comfortable space. Creating a kitchen that's completely efficient means paying attention to a slew of details. That is primarily where a designer's expertise comes into play. For the rest, clients simply have to trust in their own taste. First of all, they usually have far more aesthetic sense than they believe, and second, it's their home!

Sia believes that the most important quality of a good designer is being able to listen. Then, they must always reinvent themselves and go beyond their limits. It's the same for any profession. Why be satisfied with basic knowledge when there are so many ways to learn and draw fresh inspiration?

a perpetual cycle of starting over and over again. [...] To operate a business like ours successfully, you have to have a comprehensive plan covering a period of at least five years, and you have to have peace and harmony among those in charge. [...] Les Marchands en Quincaillerie Ltée, originally founded in 1939, was restored three years ago to the purpose for which it was created, and it must continue to operate in a way that is true to the spirit of its founders. It is important not to let a democracy that can too easily turn into a demagogy divert this company from the specific ends for which it was created.

In the face of this point-blank refusal, some of the petitioners decided to pull up stakes and form a rival group, VISCO. Over the years that followed, members of the VISCO group found themselves returning to the Ro-Na fold. In 1974, the 22 remaining members of this group, nine of whom had in the interim become external clients of Ro-Na, asked to be allowed to rejoin the company. Most of them were reinstated in 1975, and VISCO was dissolved.

This was Napoléon Piotte's style, the forceful words and the torch of moral standards held high. In him we see the former teacher who could skilfully deliver a lesson. And we see the "propagandist" who pleaded his case and defended his position with vigour.

But there is something else to be seen in these words of Napoléon. It is worth taking a moment to reflect on it.

LES MARCHANDS EN QUINCAILLERIE LTÉE HELD THREE SHOWS:
a spring/summer show in January, a toy and Christmas show in March, and a fall/winter show in September only to begin with, followed by another in May, starting in 1971.

The impression is one of a man who had done his homework, who had given matters careful thought, and who had no doubt learned much from all those years spent at Rolland Dansereau's right hand. We also get some sense of the changes that were taking place in Quebec.

His criticism of the "pure" cooperative model is thus somewhat unusual. During the first half of the 20th century, cooperatives had been very popular in French Canada, where difficult access to capital and, no doubt, the persistence of traditional values had curbed the development of businesses based on the purely capitalist model. To many, cooperatives represented a financially accessible and morally acceptable way to do business. It is worth remembering here that Napoléon himself was a devout Catholic and that he had even "taken a break" from Ro-Na to work for an ecumenical undertaking. This dilemma between monetary affairs and the affairs of God was a familiar one to Napoléon.

As well, Napoléon remained a staunch defender of the founding values of Ro-Na, "restored three years ago to the purpose for which it was created," as he wrote, in a thinly veiled reference to the concentration of power and capital that had existed under Dansereau. At first glance his criticism of the cooperative movement seems rather surprising.

I think Napoléon Piotte believed in the values of the movement, but he was wary of the effects produced by the sort of diffuse accountability structure that was sometimes a feature of the cooperatives. Indeed, while the cooperative approach was an undeniable success in the sectors of finance (Les caisses populaires Desjardins, the mutual insurance companies) and agriculture (particularly the Coopérative agricole de Granby, which would later become Agropur), the results were less conclusive in other fields that had experimented with this business model. In fact, starting in 1948, the number of cooperatives and members in Quebec had systematically declined. Napoléon was no doubt familiar with this situation and wanted to prevent it from occurring at Ro-Na.

In his words we also glimpse the leader, the strategist. When Napoléon wrote about the necessity of "a comprehensive plan covering a period of at least five years," he expressed his desire to set the company on a firm footing, to steer it in the direction of growth and development, and to overcome the present trials and challenges once and for all.

And what becomes clear through all of this is that Ro-Na was not a company like all the rest. It was not a hierarchical organization in which the president's word was law and orders came down from the top, with no opportunity for anyone to express a differing opinion.

This company was first and foremost a community, a group of individuals who, each in their own way, were all exceptional people. It would have been necessary to spend some time with them, those dealers, to realize what a bunch of characters they were! They were all entrepreneurs. They all

Charles Morency • A focus on modernization

CHARLES MORENCY, A MERCHANT LIKE HIS FATHER BEFORE HIM, SUCCEEDED NAPOLÉON PIOTTE AND WAS THE PRESIDENT OF RONA FROM 1968 TO 1981.

❶ From his office on De la Savane Street—and on Nobel Street later—Charles Morency managed the affairs of Les Marchands en Quincaillerie Ltée and of Marchands Ro-Na Inc. from 1968 to 1981.

His father, Édouard, was a small hardware store operator in the region of Saint-Sauveur in Quebec, when Émery Sauvé, Aimé Lord, and a handful of other merchants banded together to circumvent the wholesalers and deal directly with the manufacturers, under the name Les Marchands en Quincaillerie Ltée.

When Édouard died in 1950, Charles, the eldest of thirteen children, continued the work his father had begun along with the help of his brothers. But it was difficult for several families to make a living off a single business, so, in time, they disbanded and went their separate ways. His brother, Jean-Paul, who was 15 years his junior, opened another hardware store on Sainte-Foy Road and, in 1971, became president of the Canadian Retail Hardware Association. His sons, Jacques and Guy, also became hardware store dealers.

Charles was one of the group of nine merchants Napoléon Piotte had joined that had bought out Rolland Dansereau's shares in 1962. A few days after Napoléon's death in 1968, Charles took over as president and chief executive officer.

André Dion remembers Charles as a man who was exceedingly open to people and ideas. He was very close to his employees; he respected them, showed his appreciation for their performance, and knew how to interact with them. The size of a person's wallet wasn't important to him, even though he was, first and foremost, a businessman. He respected the small and the large merchants equally, as long as they were faithful and loyal to the group. And he was very receptive to new methods.

Beyond those qualities, Charles was a man who liked to take risks. He would often visit the Blue Bonnets racetrack, where he would place a wager or two; he enjoyed the horse races and the betting. During the June 1960 provincial elections, he ran as the Liberal candidate in the riding of Saint-Sauveur, but was defeated by Francis Boudreau. Under his watch, operations were modernized, risks were taken; there was an overall change in outlook. People were invited to sit as members of the board of directors because they were forward-looking or because their ability to grow their businesses had not gone unnoticed. These included André Gagnon, Pierre Piotte, and Henri Drouin, among others. Purchasing was improved, but so was marketing, because that's what counted: the public image, the strength of product promotion. When Charles first arrived, it was a time when suppliers were beginning to warm to the idea of selling directly to Rona. This allowed the organization to move towards the next phase, one that was increasingly focused on the consumer, on people.

Their first policy conference was held in 1975. Charles' opening speech to the hardware store dealers was unequivocal. He urged them to "at

82

last show an economic pride that is our own, so that, in the future, Quebecers would not forever be client consumers [offered up to] out-of-province merchants." And he knew how to stir them to action: "The success of the national and international chains is not [the fruit of] what they are doing, but [of] what we are not doing." It wasn't surprising that at the close of these three days of discussions, the foundation had been laid for an entirely new way of thinking within the group.

Since then, awards have been presented annually to 20 members in recognition of their contribution to the group, as well as the quality of their public image. It has proved highly motivating and inspirational.

And the company just kept growing by leaps and bounds. "The greatest danger or potential pitfall for an organization like ours is to relax or to sit back on its laurels." In 1977, progress was such that the warehouse had to be expanded to 300 000 sq. ft. (27 900 m²). By 1978, it had grown to 450 000 sq. ft. (41 800 m²), and 360 employees were responsible for taking care of 455 members. Of the 12 000 products being offered, more than 1 000 were Ro-Na's own. When Charles stepped down as president in 1981, the company was boasting sales figures of $200 million.

Commerce magazine honoured Charles as 'man of the month' in August 1977. Gérard Virthe and Maurice Chartrand wrote: "His strength, it seems, is

in being able to convince others to decide for themselves what he believes is right for them, instead of simply dictating to them. In fact, he is a greater believer in discipline than in authority."

Charles was a man with great heart and vitality. He took part in many activities in his native region of Quebec, including serving as a municipal councillor from 1965 to 1969 and managing the Caisse populaire in Saint-Sauveur for 15 years. At the provincial level, he was president of the Association des groupements de distribution du Québec Agrodi; on the national level, he was president of the Quincailliers Grossistes Associés, a purchasing group that connected Rona to 1 800 other Canadian retailers; and internationally as director of Sapec, a buying cooperative of European hardware store dealers that provided Rona with the purchasing power it needed to reach the big leagues.

❷ Charles Morency enjoyed horse racing. While he was president, he organized evenings at the racetrack for Rona dealers and employees. André Gagnon, Philippe Dorval, and Jean-Yves Gagnon at the races in the 1970s.

❸ In 1979, on an outing to the Richelieu racetrack, Rona employees, including Charles Morency and his wife, Fernande, Robert Lavoie, and Laurent Héon study their betting cards attentively.

83

The logo over the years •

IT WAS NOT UNTIL 1965 THAT A COMMON LOGO WAS CREATED TO CONVEY A GROUP PHILOSOPHY AND IMAGE. THE FIRM OF BOUCHARD, CHAMPAGNE ET PELLETIER (BCP) HAD BEEN SELECTED TO CREATE A LOGO AND ORCHESTRATE AN ADVERTISING CAMPAIGN.

❶

❶ **The three companies that were an integral part of Rona's history each had their own logo through the years and successive changes in administration.**

1965. The January issue of *La Ronde Rona* described the rare bird as follows:

> A rare bird, in the 20th century, is a rare thing indeed. Really rare! And yet, we have recently catalogued a new species: the rare Ro-Na bird. Soon to be familiar throughout the province of Quebec, this rare bird is the emblem of hardware dealers of quality, the Ro-Na hardware dealers. A brief description will help you to spot him:
> • He is large and plump: he has everything you need.
> • He is colourful: there is nothing dreary or ordinary about him.
> • He stands sturdily on his feet: he is offering you proven products you can rely on.
> • He is looking towards the future: your well-being and success are important to him!

This was the start of the great wave that was to follow. Napoléon Piotte was excited about a project that had been in the works for several months already: a province-wide advertising campaign. He felt it was important to move with the times, to stay in step with his clients:

> "...to better understand them and sell to them, while continuing to adhere to the same principles of quality, courtesy, savings, and service for which we are known everywhere and which distinguish us as the rare birds we are."

The first phase of the advertising campaign focused on the common identity expressed in the new emblem, a symbol of so much hope. The large-circulation weekly publication *Perspectives* magazine alone ran 15 full-size ads in succession, totaling more than 8 million pages. This effort was soon followed by 145 billboard ads that were seen by 1.5 million passersby each day. The dealers then received advertising materials for their windows, displays, trucks, and products. Consistent signage was developed.

The ads for the stores and dealers stated the following:

> A Ro-Na hardware dealer is someone worth knowing. You'll notice he's a rare bird. He insists on sticking with business practices that seem a bit outmoded in this day and age... old-fashioned principles like quality, guarantees, reasonable prices, home delivery, first-rate service. [...]
> Offering quality products at affordable prices is precisely the reason why he has teamed up with other independent hardware dealers —other rare birds like himself—to form the Ro-Na chain. Together, they buy in volume to pay less... and, in turn, to sell for less.
> But what really sets the rare Ro-Na bird apart is the fact that he is a hardware expert, a serious guy who will never sell you a thingamabob when what you really need is a thingamajig.

1998. In an effort to update its brand image and bring it into line with market requirements, Ro-Na proceeded with a restructuring of its banners and gave its visual identity a fresh new look.

Each of the banners within the group was repositioned with greater precision in terms of square footage, market segment, and visual identity. Two banners, Le Quincailleur and Dismat, were eliminated, while two new ones, RONA L'Express and RONA L'Express Matériaux, were introduced.

The company's logo was redesigned, which had an impact on its visual identity in three ways:
• the Rona name was to carry a similar importance for all banners, with the exception of Botanix;
• there would be new outdoor signage for all stores;
• packaging for private brand products would be revamped.

The bird has taken flight

2010. Today, the Rona brand can be broken down into four major sectors:

1. Big-box stores

These stores offer an unequalled variety of products at the lowest prices. Everything is under the same roof: hardware, tools, building materials, articles for the garden, paint, decorating supplies, and seasonal items.

Generally, these stores vary in size between 60 000 sq. ft. (5 574 m²) and 165 000 sq. ft. (15 329 m²), and offer over 40 000 products.

2. Proximity stores

Proximity stores offer a wide range of seasonal products and a complete assortment of renovation and hardware items.

Generally, these stores vary in size between 5 000 sq. ft. (465 m²) and 60 000 sq. ft. (5 574 m²), and the bulk of their sales consists of lumber and construction materials.

TOTEM: These stores, which are exclusive to Alberta, serve mainly handymen and craftspersons looking for specialized products and services for home renovation projects. The size of these stores is about 30 000 sq. ft. (2 787 m²).

3. Specialized stores – Customers

These specialized stores were created to meet customers' hardware, seasonal products, and paint needs.

STUDIO by RONA: This innovative, almost 8 000-sq. ft. (743 m²), boutique concept is a first in Canada, and targets consumers as well as interior designers and professional painters, all in one location. Beyond paint and painting accessories, the Studio by Rona stores offer a vast selection of wallpaper, floor coverings, mouldings, window treatments, and bedding fabrics.

BOTANIX: These stores offer advice to customers on the choice of plants, maintenance, and landscaping. They stock a large variety of plants and articles for the garden.

4. Specialized stores – Commercial and professional market

Designed to meet the needs of commercial and professional customers, these stores offer a wide variety of specialized products in specific categories such as building materials and plumbing.

MATÉRIAUX COUPAL: Matériaux Coupal is a market leader in the sales of building materials for housing industry professionals in the Greater Montreal area, in Quebec.

NOBLE TRADE: This is one of the largest plumbing and heating supply wholesalers in Ontario, serving a commercial and professional customer base.

DICK'S LUMBER: Dick's Lumber is a top-ranking British Columbia lumber, building materials, and hardware specialist.

❷ Initially created as the visual identification for the member dealers of the company Quincaillerie Ro-Na Inc., the bird logo would subsequently be adopted for the Le Quincaillier banner and used until 1998.

❸ In the 1970s, the Marchands Ro-Na Inc. alternated between using the bird and the "Ro-Na" logotype as the company logo.

❹ In the 1980s, Rona began to update its image—as reflected in the company's logo—and make its first acquisitions.

❺ In 1998, the Ro-Na Dismat Group Inc. changed its name to RONA Inc. and introduced the logo that we know today. First used in conjunction with the logos of each individual banner, it increasingly stands alone on the signage of new stores.

An Asian accent

Bou Yeap

Commercial and Export Sales Expert,
Rona Home & Garden, Vancouver, British Columbia

Everyone knows that Canada is a bilingual country, but at the Grandview, Vancouver, store, the signs are also translated into… Mandarin! When we arrived, Bou Yeap, a commercial sales expert who hails from Malaysia, had just finished giving a tour to a group of translation students from Simon Fraser University. With his knowledge of several Asian dialects, Bou knows what he's talking about.

No matter what the field, selling is all about building a relationship of trust. To do that, you need to ask the right questions to properly understand what the client wants. In construction, you also need to assess the viability of a project, and if you think changes need to be made, you should discuss them with the client, who, obviously, has the final say. But Bou only gets involved in projects he thinks are feasible. "If you commit to something that can't work, it will always backfire on you! The client is free to go elsewhere, of course, but they'll often come back saying, 'You were right! I should've listened to you,'" he grins. A company that understands the value of good customer relations will guide clients throughout their projects and win their loyalty. Indeed, dispensing advise to his clients is what Bou likes best about his work. What one piece of advice would he give to everyone? "Be patient and rise to the challenges life throws your way!"

Because he worked in the construction industry in both Asia and Canada for many years—he even went to China to represent Revy on building sites—you can be sure that his words are based on a wealth of experience.

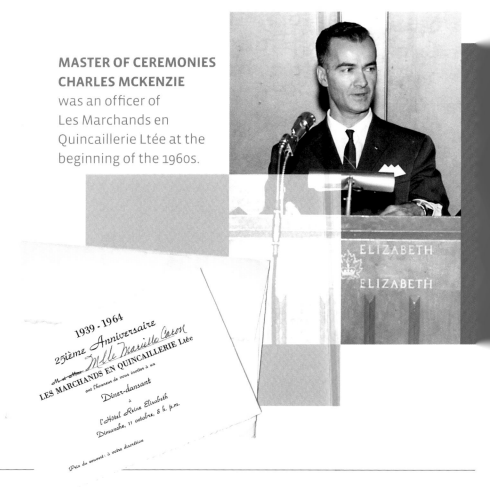

1939 - 1964
25ième Anniversaire
LES MARCHANDS EN QUINCAILLERIE Ltée
ont l'honneur de vous inviter à un
Dîner-dansant
à
l'Hôtel Reine Elisabeth
Dimanche, 11 octobre, 8 h. p.m.

Prix du couvert : à votre discrétion

understood their clients. They all understood their environment. They were all leaders, capable of thriving in a competitive climate. They knew how to run their hardware stores.

These were not the sort of men to be led by force or by ultimatums. To lead them required intelligence and respect. It required listening to them and taking their interests and ideas into account. It required helping them to see the advantage that lay in defining that zone where "every man for himself" exists alongside "all for one," where their independence would be strengthened through partnership.

Napoléon Piotte understood how to define that zone, to give substance to the company without compromising the independence of the dealers. He was able to deploy the political skills needed to ensure the operation of this uncommon and extraordinary group.

Napoléon's key projects

"Napoléon's key projects" is one way to describe the reforms he put in place, reforms that brought about a fundamental change in the company. Through these projects, Napoléon set in motion the transformation that would see the buying group evolve gradually into a retailer of hardware and renovation products. What happened was a sort of vertical integration. Up to this point, members had banded together in order to be able to buy better. Now, being together would also mean being able to sell better. But each member would sell in his own way, as each remained independent.

A SUMPTUOUS 25TH ANNIVERSARY FOR THE MARCHANDS.
Among the guests were Raymond Goyer, Aimé Lord, Hector Durand, Philippe Dorval, and their wives.

Napoléon undertook three key projects.

First, he turned advertising into a strategic lever for the development of the company. Second, he opened the door to the formation of alliances that would strengthen his group's purchasing power. And third, he provided the company with a system that would ensure sound funding for its development.

To my knowledge, there is no sort of "strategic plan" document in existence that sets out in black and white these projects and objectives. In most companies, it would take a few years for any formal planning to see the light. But each of these initiatives was too broad in scope, and the interplay between these reforms too powerful, for it all to have been mere chance or the result of a few isolated actions. It was obvious that Napoléon, who had written of the need for "a comprehensive plan covering a period of at least five years," had a clear vision of the puzzle he was about to assemble.

October 11, 1964 was a day of celebration. It was the day Les Marchands en Quincaillerie Ltée marked the 25th anniversary of the founding of the company. At that time, it had close to 300 member dealers, approximately 125 of whom displayed the Ro-Na banner. No fewer than 650 guests were in attendance at the Queen Elizabeth Hotel.

The keynote address for the evening was given by Charles McKenzie, a hardware dealer from Drummondville. He began with an overview of the company and summed up in just a few words what made it unique:

Always up for new challenges

Brad Dick

Rona Building Center, Portage-la-Prairie, Manitoba

In 2003, Brad Dick and his partners were looking for a new banner for their business that would help them expand while still allowing them to remain independent. Rona's marketing plan and growth attracted them. They would be the pioneers of Rona's independent merchants in the Prairies, with their first year bringing its fair share of challenges, including creating the right marketing programs and trying to fathom who did what in Boucherville. But their strong entrepreneurial spirit allowed them to rise to the task with brio; what's more, they derived great satisfaction from knowing they had contributed in some small way to the group's expansion out West.

Newton Enterprises began as a lumberyard in northern Manitoba in the 1940s and experienced considerable growth in the years that followed with the addition of a construction company and a store in Portage-la-Prairie.

Then, in 2007, a new store opened its doors in the premises of a former Wal-Mart. It had taken nine months of hard work to convert the dimly lit location with low ceilings into a bright, welcoming retail space of 45 000 sq. ft. Their efforts more than paid off. Brad said when they saw the reactions of clients arriving for the grand opening, they knew they'd "managed to create a 'wow' experience!" People looked around in wonder, saying, "At last! I don't need to drive to Winnipeg any more!" That day, the automatic doors never had time to close! Going to Rona was no longer just an errand the guys would run when they needed a box of nails or a two-by-four; now it was a family outing. Even the kids had their own shopping cart!

The next challenge? Like many others in the Rona family: to be the best in their market!

Like father, like daughter

Raynald Archambault

Ferronnerie Houle, Rona Le Quincaillier,
Saint-Jean-sur-Richelieu, Quebec

It all began for Raynald Archambault at 16, when his mother showed him an ad for a job at the local hardware store where his father had worked for 15 years. It was a quick and informal interview, conducted over the counter. Robert Houle, the son of the store's founder, Gabriel, asked the young Raynald if he often worked with his father. Raynald said yes, he was always with his dad. "You can start tonight, then!" the boss replied. A year later, the young man had earned the title of manager, with keys to the store... and the accompanying long hours. He worked tirelessly, unloading the products, pricing them by hand, and placing all the Rona orders... but Raynald was smitten! His boss gave him plenty of leeway, and that freedom made him even more enthusiastic and ambitious.

In 1991, just a little later than originally planned—he had wanted to own a hardware store by the time he was 25—he became a partner. The store expanded and Raynald was still as happy as could be. He himself admitted that his work was his hobby! And the secret to his success: putting in the hours, working hard, and being able to count on his family's support. His wife, Chantale, shared his dream.

All three of their children have worked at the store, but it's Audrey who has developed a true passion for the business. She joined the team as a young child. During the 1998 ice storm, they kept the hardware store running using generators, and the delivery man made daily return trips between Montreal and Saint-Jean to keep them supplied with propane gas. For six weeks, nine-year-old Audrey went round the neighbouring streets to help out clients, who, naturally, were charmed by the little girl. After a month without electricity, a visit from the Archambaults' adorable daughter was like a ray of warm sunshine! Twelve years later, when she finished school, Audrey became the assistant manager, attending trade shows with her father and already dreaming up her own plans for the store. She was just as ambitious as her father! "Audrey's the one coming with me!" her father would proudly declare. Instead of retiring at 55 as originally planned, he thinks he'll gradually cut back on his hours to continue providing support to his daughter. "Anyway," he adds, "doing 40 hours a week will feel like a vacation!"

"Manufacturers, agents of manufacturers, commercial travellers who come into contact every day with either the staff or clients [...] are amazed, astonished, impressed by the feeling of family that shines through in their business relationships. [...]

Your company is the only one that sells exclusively to its recognized clients, and no one can be a client without a hardware retailer's license. You do not compete with us for the business of the municipalities, manufacturers, contractors."

The speaker expressed the certainty that the company was destined for great success and that the name Ro-Na would soon be "as well known in Quebec as Maurice Richard"!

A professional approach to advertising

As it happened, Napoléon nearly took the joking remark of the dealer from Drummondville at face value, because it was on the occasion of this 25th anniversary that the upcoming launch of a major advertising campaign was announced, with an unprecedented budget—in terms of the company's finances—of $100 000. It would involve prestige advertising designed to highlight the service, quality, savings, and courtesy that consumers would find at Ro-Na hardware stores. It was intended both to persuade hardware dealers to join Ro-Na and to convince consumers to choose this banner for their purchases.

However, the project was not met with unbridled enthusiasm. It might even be said that a tough battle ensued. To many, all this advertising nonsense was a waste of money. Others expected to profit from the campaign directly, given that they were asked to contribute to its funding. Marc St-Pierre, who was in charge of advertising at the time, remembers the countless meetings that were held all across Quebec to convince the dealers of the importance of this promotional effort.

Ro-Na had already been advertising for a few years. That was even one of the purposes for which it was created. But for the first time ever, advertising creatives were brought in to formulate a strategy. The Montreal firm of BCP (Bouchard, Champagne, Pelletier) was selected. The concept was presented at a special meeting of the dealers held in Montreal. In front of the audience, the representative from BCP started drawing what looked like a cooking pot. From somewhere in the room, a dealer called out: "Not another pot! We're always getting stuck with pots!" Laughter erupted all around. But it was not a pot. It was the stomach of a bird, filled with tools: pliers, a wrench, a pair of shears... He had his eye open and his tricoloured tail was outspread. The advertising representative finished his drawing and said: "Why not promote Ro-Na as an exception among hardware stores? A rare bird!" The dealers expressed their immediate endorsement with warm applause.

The "rare bird" would soon be everywhere: in newspapers such as Montreal's *Dimanche-Matin,* Quebec City's *Le Soleil, Le Droit* in Ottawa-Hull, and *La Tribune* in Sherbrooke, in trade magazines like *Le Quincaillier* and *Hardware Merchandising,* and on more than 145 roadside signs in every corner of Quebec. Launched in January 1965, the campaign had such an impact that in March, it received a special mention for excellence from Publicité Club de Montréal.

Ro-Na now had a brand image, a slogan, and a personality all its own. For 25 years there had been a group of associated dealers, but now there was a retailer that took pride in being different and that drew strength from each of its member dealers.

The advertising campaign also had a significant effect on the members themselves, who acquired a new sense of pride in its wake, a feeling of belonging to the organization, as though each of them saw himself reflected in the ads and could declare himself to be "a rare bird."

From that moment on, advertising became a permanent part of Ro-Na's operations, with the formation of a dedicated committee that is still in place today. This foray into advertising was part of an approach to communications which, even at this early stage, was strategic and coordinated. Timed to coincide with the advertising campaign was the publication of the first issue of an internal newsletter, *La Ronde Ro-Na,* a tool that helped not only to keep the dealers up-to-date on company decisions but also to build a feeling of unity within the group and communicate

DEALERS MADE REGULAR VISITS TO TORONTO DURING THE 1960s.
Front row: Messrs. Coderre, Galipeault, and Thibault, Ms. Carrier, Messrs. Gagnon, Lord, and McKenzie. Back row: Messrs. Carrier, Beaulieu, Charest, Piotte, Hébert, Boutin, and Gagnon.

WHEN THE QUINCAILLIERS GROSSISTES ASSOCIÉS GROUP WAS FORMED IN 1965, they used the Ro-Na bird as their logo. In 1967, they adopted their own logo.

what was becoming a true "Ro-Na culture," centred around service and attention to the customer.

The debut issue carried this headline: "Ça y est, la vague Ro-Na déferle" ["Here we go, the Ro-Na wave is starting to roll"]. In his "Message from the President," Napoléon Piotte explained in detail the first advertising campaign and its importance for the dealers:

"Our advertising program is going to roll out all across the province. In one wave, the new face of Ro-Na will be unveiled for the general public to see, for **your** public to see [bold text original]. Our new advertising program is modern, comprehensive, appealing and, most importantly, it will be the source of increased profits for you. What we have done in the past has been excellent, as you know, but the times are changing, and we have to keep up with the times, we have to stay in step with our clients [...] The new year is the perfect moment for this kind of resolution. And remember, a resolution must always be kept, for two reasons: firstly, because it's good, and secondly, because we made it in the first place!"

In this way Napoléon and his partners imparted a distinctive image to the company, they implemented a structure specifically for advertising, and they steered the organization towards improved communication with the public and with its members.

This was the first of Napoléon's key projects.

An initial alliance, an initial acquisition

That same year, 1965, there was another important breakthrough. It seemed modest on the surface, but it carried with it the seeds of what would become one of the main avenues for Ro-Na's growth: strategic alliances and acquisitions.

First, Les Marchands en Quincaillerie Ltée entered into talks with Delino Inc., a hardware products distributor in the Quebec City area. Numerous meetings were held in Montreal and Quebec City, and formal negotiations commenced with a view to acquisition. Napoléon's objective was, of course, to take over that company's business volumes and recruit the dealers it had for clients.

Discussions were under way when Napoléon had a visitor to his office in Montreal, a certain André Dion, who was there to take on the position of controller. This young accountant, a native of Lac-Saint-Jean, had just completed his studies at Université Laval. He openly admitted that he found "the big city" intimidating. Piotte saw potential in this young fellow, who was both personable and bright, and whose father, like Napoléon himself, was a member of the Ordre de Jacques-Cartier. The apple doesn't fall far from the tree, the president undoubtedly thought to himself. Little did he know it then, but he had just hired the man who would become Ro-Na's fifth president!

The newcomer was thrust at once into the thick of the action, invited to take part in the discussions with Delino,

and would in the end be appointed interim director of that company. The transaction was finalized in the summer of 1966 by means of a share for share exchange, without a penny being spent.

From the initial approach through to analysis and negotiations, the transaction took approximately a year to complete. This first acquisition would firmly establish the "Ro-Na way," from which the company would never deviate: proceed with rigour, taking all the time required and exercising the greatest financial prudence.

While negotiations were taking place with Delino, there was a breakthrough on another front. In October 1965, Les Marchands en Quincaillerie Ltée joined with three companies very similar to Ro-Na, three buying groups that were active in English Canada: Hollinger Hardware in Ontario, Falcon Hardware in Manitoba, and Link Hardware in Alberta. Together they formed United Hardware Wholesalers Limited / Les Quincailliers Grossistes Associés Ltée. Under this company name they would purchase products that they would then sell exclusively to their retail dealers.

Still, it took some nerve to make a pact with the "English" just as Quebec was undergoing its great economic emancipation. And when one recalled the problems that Les Marchands en Quincaillerie Ltée had had with the Toronto establishment up until the early 1950s, it seemed even more audacious. But to Napoléon, who considered

---

The Beauséjour kids

Claude Beauséjour

M.C. Beauséjour & Richard, Rona Le Rénovateur, Saint-Michel-des-Saints, Quebec

The Beauséjour brothers' Rona adventure began over a family supper in 1973. Claude, 21, had recently completed a college diploma in finance and was working at the Provincial Bank of Canada in Sainte-Agathe-des-Monts. Maurice, 20, was studying nuclear physics at Université de Montréal. Their father, Gérard, who owned the five-and-dime store in Saint-Michel-des-Saints, announced that he had bought the old bowling alley opposite his store. It had been vacant for some time, and youths had begun loitering there, so he wanted to do something before there was an accident. This was a great opportunity for Claude and Maurice, who decided to open a Sports Experts and a hardware store on the site. They joined Rona right away. They were affectionately known as "les p'tits Beauséjour!" (the Beauséjour kids) by neighbouring merchants, and the moniker stuck—36 years later, some people still remember them by that name!

Local residents welcomed the arrival of Rona with open arms. With their innovative ideas and excellent customer service, the brothers built themselves a solid reputation. In the summer of 1976, they created the "braderies," or discount sales, which were so successful that tourists flocked in from miles around. In those days, people would drive up to their cottages with their trailers loaded with supplies, but as Rona's reputation grew, so did that of the Beauséjour brothers, and vacationers soon realized that they could find everything they needed at the local store. No more burying the kids under bags on the back seat! The local chamber of commerce took an interest, calling Claude to know the date of the next sale, and soon many other stores were running sales of their own. The brothers' involvement in the community and their love of sport put a special slant on their fundraising activities. With Rona's support, they organized a BMX event for kids, building an outdoor track and providing medals, trophies, and hot dogs for everyone!

After 36 years in the trade, it's clear that Claude has business in his blood. His recipe for success? "First off, hard work. If you're only interested in working nine to five, do something else!" A company manager also needs to have people he can delegate to. "Of course, in the beginning, you run around like a headless chicken trying to do everything yourself! But having a good team behind you frees up valuable time to think." Second, a flair for business. "Whipping up sales is all fine and well, but you've got to be profitable, otherwise your banker will see you don't stay in business for long!" And Claude is not about to let that happen!

In 2004, he bought a second store in Saint-Zénon that already had a good reputation with major building contractors. One more feather in his cap—and so the story continues!

1966

Early in 1966, China launched what would become known as the "Great Proletarian Cultural Revolution." Over a period of three years, fanatical militant Maoists, the Red Guards, spread throughout the country, brutally purging Chinese society, closing universities, and destroying art treasures thousands of years old, all the while brandishing the "Little Red Book" of Mao Zedong's thoughts and ideas. Official figures produced in 1979 put the death toll at 8 to 10 million and estimated that some 200 million people suffered varying degrees of persecution.

In the United States, a cultural revolution of a completely different kind was brewing, with the emergence of the first hippie communes, where the values and lifestyle of industrialized Western society—materialism, consumerism, professional "success"—were rejected wholesale.

It was a year of firsts in the space race: first soft landing on the Moon (U.S., June), first satellite to orbit the Moon (USSR, August), and first space rendezvous with docking in orbit (U.S., March).

The Canada Pension Plan came into effect on January 1. Quebec, exercising its newly acquired right to opt out, which was granted to the provinces and territories, and established the Québec Pension Plan, whose funds are managed by the Caisse de dépôt et placement du Québec.

In Quebec, the Union Nationale, led by Daniel Johnson, unexpectedly wrested power from the hands of Jean Lesage's Liberals, even though it had clearly lost the popular vote (the electoral map at the time was weighted heavily in favour of rural regions). For the first time in an election, two pro-independence parties fielded candidates and received more than 11% of the vote.

1967

The year 1967 was especially eventful for Quebec and Canada. It marked the 100th anniversary of Canada's Confederation, and, on April 27, Expo 67 📷, the first world's fair ever to be held on Canadian soil, opened in Montreal, with its theme of *Man and His World*. In six months, Expo would welcome more than 50 million visitors in an atmosphere of non-stop celebration shared with the entire world.

Many visiting heads of state passed through Montreal, and one in particular left an indelible mark on our history. Greeted with great pomp, the president of France, Charles de Gaulle, travelled the historic "Chemin du Roy" from Quebec City to Montreal, accompanied by Premier Daniel Johnson. He concluded his journey on the balcony of Montreal City Hall where, before an electrified crowd, he uttered the famous words, *"Vive le Québec libre!"*

A realignment of political forces in Quebec led to the creation of the Mouvement Souveraineté-Association (Sovereignty-Association Movement) by René Lévesque and other dissident Liberals.

During this same time, in the Middle East, a brief war of six days' duration enabled the State of Israel to gain control of the Gaza Strip, the West Bank, and the Golan Heights, further exacerbating the plight of the Palestinians. With 300 000 new refugees, military occupation, and Jewish colonization in the occupied territories, resolution of the Palestinian issue seemed practically impossible.

1968

What a year 1968 was!

April saw the beginning of the "Prague Spring," when Czechoslovakia's new leaders replaced the Stalinists and announced radical reforms aimed at establishing "socialism with a human face."

In the United States, the charismatic leader of the civil rights movement, Martin Luther King, Jr., was assassinated on April 4, igniting a wave of terrible riots in the black ghettos of several major cities.

Then came the events of "May 68." For the entire month, France was turned upside down by the student uprising, which was eventually joined by workers everywhere in a general strike. There were occupations at universities and factories, huge demonstrations, and nights of violent rioting,

all of which would take on an almost mythic quality for an entire generation. Galvanized by the actions of their French counterparts, students everywhere began to rise up, in the East as well as the West; their fervour extended even as far as Quebec, where, in the fall of that year, the very first brand-new CEGEPs became the scene of student occupations.

Robert Kennedy, brother of the assassinated president and candidate for the Democratic nomination for the presidency, was himself assassinated in June.

The Prague Spring was brought to an abrupt close in August with the "Summer of Tanks": Warsaw Pact tanks invaded Czechoslovakia and put an end to socialism with a human face.

Also in August, violence erupted between protesters and police during the Democratic National Convention in Chicago.

The Olympic Games in Mexico began in October, after the Mexican Army had killed more than 300 people when it opened fire on anti-Olympic demonstrators. Two American medalists raised their black-gloved fists and lowered their heads during the playing of their national anthem, an unforgettable image that appeared on television sets the world over...

1969

The space race scored a major achievement in 1969. On July 21, the Americans took a decisive lead with an image that reverberated around the world: a man walking on the Moon 📷! One more moon landing took place on November 19. The U.S. had "won the race," meeting the incredible challenge set by John F. Kennedy in 1961 of putting a man on the Moon before the end of the decade.

Meanwhile, back on Earth, it was a shining hour for anti-establishment youth: in August, 400 000 young people gathered in Woodstock, New York, for "three days of peace and music." The

Woodstock Festival would become a reference point, a symbol of the aspirations held by a majority of youth for new values and new ways of living.

These aspirations largely found their expression in the widespread opposition that existed to the war in Vietnam, which was now in its fifth year and had already claimed more than 10 000 American lives. In November, 250 000 people assembled in Washington to stage the largest anti-war demonstration ever held. President Nixon, who had taken office earlier in the year, finally announced a partial withdrawal of the half-million troops then present in Vietnam.

The government of Prime Minister Pierre Elliott Trudeau passed the "Omnibus Bill," reforming many key provisions in Canada's Criminal Code. While it touched on issues as diverse as divorce, gambling, gun control, and impaired driving, it would go down in history for having decriminalized abortion and a variety of sexual acts between consenting adults—notably those associated with homosexuality.

1970

In Quebec, 1970 was the year of the "October Crisis."

On October 5, members of a cell of the Front de libération du Québec (FLQ) kidnapped a British diplomat in Montreal, James Richard Cross, and issued demands that included the release of 23 FLQ members who were being detained by police and the broadcast of the group's Manifesto.

When the Manifesto was read on television, it created quite a stir; but when the governments of Quebec and Canada refused to negotiate, a second cell kidnapped the province's Minister of Labour, Pierre Laporte, five days later. On October 16, the Canadian government invoked the *War Measures Act*, suspending civil liberties across the country, and sent the army into the streets of Montreal. The following day, Laporte's body was found next to a military base.

The crisis ended in December with the arrest of Pierre Laporte's abductors, the release of James R. Cross, and the departure of his kidnappers for Cuba. More than 400 people were arrested, most of whom would never be charged with any kind of offence at all...

In Chile, meanwhile, socialist Salvador Allende was elected president and proceeded to set his country on the path to "socialism in freedom."

himself a "proud French Canadian" (the term "Québécois" was still not frequently used), this alliance was not at all radical. On the contrary, it just happened to demonstrate that a "French Canadian" business could deal very comfortably and on equal terms with its Anglophone counterparts and shine brightly outside Quebec—two notions that were not self-evident at that time.

The association was formed to increase purchasing power in order to secure better prices from manufacturers. United Hardware Wholesalers Limited represented a combined purchasing power of $25 million, and the four member companies together had more than 800 retailers.

The company's head office was established in Calgary, and Napoléon Piotte was its vice-president.

The partners had other plans in mind as well. They proposed joint advertising programs, and they even floated the idea of having private label products—a concept that Ro-Na was quick to turn to good account...

This was the second of the three key projects undertaken by Napoléon and his partners: clearing the pathways to growth that would subsequently be travelled again and again by their successors.

Providing Ro-Na with the means to grow

The third of Napoléon's key projects would cast the young André Dion in the central role. In the opinion of this accountant, trained in all the latest management methods, there were two major issues in the company's funding and operations that needed to be corrected promptly to ensure it would have the resources required for further development.

First problem: the rebates. The group's cupboard, one might say, was bare. Each year, the company paid out almost all of its operating margin in the form of rebates. André Dion pleaded the urgency of ensuring that the group was well-capitalized. This was how he described the attitude of the dealers at that time: "They had to make money. So the group had to help them make money. But when it came to the group itself making money... not a chance!"

Dion set about changing a culture that had already existed for a quarter of a century. He would enjoy the full support of Napoléon Piotte who, let us not forget, had previously criticized the weaknesses of the cooperative business model.

To begin with, André Dion had to convince the members of the board of directors, who were themselves all dealers. Of course, they were not keen on the idea of leaving money just sitting around. But to win their agreement, Dion devised a way to build profit into it.

He suggested creating a "security deposit" in the name of each member dealer. This deposit would consist of amounts withheld on the discounts given on each member's purchases and half of the rebates, which until then had been paid in cash. The deposits would be left

Affiliated dealer recruitment ·

THE RONA GROUP INCLUDES MORE THAN 400 INDEPENDENT STORES IN CANADA. THEY ARE IMPORTANT, AND SO IS GROWTH. TO EXPAND THIS NETWORK, TWO SOLUTIONS ARE FAVOURED, AND SOMETIMES COMBINED, AMONG THE INDEPENDENT DEALERS: RECRUITMENT AND MARKET CONSOLIDATION.

❶ From the very beginning, recruiting new dealers played an essential role in Rona's development. In the 1970s, Charles Morency and the company's officers were already making a point of meeting members to talk about their concerns.

There is an entire team dedicated to these strategies, consisting of more than 20 recruiters and development directors for Western Canada, Ontario, Quebec, and the Atlantic Region. It is through their efforts that the chemistry between the retailers and the administrative centre is established and sustained.

The regional directors each manage a specific territory in which there are 40 to 50 retailers. Their main responsibility is to visit them on a regular basis, resolve issues, assist them with developing their plans, making better investments, better purchases—in short, they help them to operate as efficiently as possible.

To stay connected with what is happening in the region, there are also banner committees in which dealers can get together several times a year to discuss the programs that have been implemented, how to improve them, etc. Annual conventions and interbanner meetings are additional ways to keep in touch with the dealers.

When it comes to surviving the current economic downturn, independents have a major asset they can count on: creativity, combined with Rona's support, which enables them to develop new market segments and new services, to be flexible, and to make the most of the opportunity to provide additional training and improve service. In a practice that is somewhat unusual, but a clear expectation at Rona, each independent dealer sends their annual financial statements to the group. This is essential in order for the business development staff to be able to provide the dealers with in-depth assistance and make informed recommendations, and for the administrative centre to better manage the growth of the group.

Market consolidation can take several different forms, but all have one specific goal, and that is to secure a position, keep it, and grow. Serge Vézina, senior director, Affiliate Dealer-Owner Network Development, provides some examples:

Market consolidation

- There is a competitor with three stores in the same region as a Rona dealer who wants to sell. The competitor is approached to buy the Rona store and join the group. Result: one Rona store is maintained and three are added, with the potential for consolidating another market.

- While surfing the Internet, an investor comes across the business model and finds it interesting; knowing that there are always issues around succession, he calls Rona. "Do you have any stores for sale? I have some money to invest..."

Serge continues:

"I get up in the morning, and I just can't wait to go to work. I love what I do. Because the world of the independents is a world of conviction, of connections, of trust. It's a fascinating world. If there's someone who's not in a good mood, we check it out right away. We find out what's going on. You can't say it's nothing serious and just let it drop. We get right on it."

Among the recruiters, John Longo, who has been with Rona since 1993, was the first employee whose mission focused on expansion in Ontario. Rona was ready, its reputation in Quebec was solid. But it was 1993 and the Bloc québécois had arrived on the federal scene with 54 seats; then, in 1994, the Parti québécois won the provincial election, and 1995 saw the second referendum on Quebec sovereignty. The political context, combined with economic habits that were more north-south than east-west, sharpened his patient determination. At that time, the tendency was for business in Ontario to see itself as the big brother of little Quebec, rather than the other way around. There was resistance, even anxiety. What was going to happen?

Well, Rona's business model, while built with pride over decades in Quebec, was at its heart a cooperative model which, from the outset, emphasized sound values such as the common good. It was therefore a universal culture, one of people helping people to succeed, that was presented to prospective dealers. "Presenting the values of society, but acting locally," says John. As the company

❷ Every year, newly recruited dealers are introduced during the Spring Show in a "parade" held during the dealers' breakfast. In November 2008, 31 new dealer-owners were welcomed into the Rona family.

❸ John Longo, director of Development, and Claude Bernier, executive vice-president of Marketing and Customer Innovations, with Bill and Christine Corbett, affiliate dealer-owners from Parry Sound, who were recruited in 2007.

had always done. This is how bridges are built in business matters.

Each new addition is the result of a formal process in which the parties take the time to get to know one another; it involves introductions, listening and understanding, identifying issues, developing an optimal scenario, defining a business plan, making an offer, establishing a bond. Like most endeavours in life, it can take anywhere from a few months to a few years.

Without a doubt, these new dealers contribute significantly to the economic strength of the group.

Changing times

Dave Lavallée
Rona Cashway, Sault Ste. Marie, Ontario

"I spend 20% of my time with my clients and 80% in my office, but I'd rather it were the other way around!" When you've been working with the public for 40 years like Dave Lavallée has, you miss that personal contact... even when you're a busy 2008 Store Manager of the Year finalist!

Dave's long love affair with retail sales began in Niagara Falls. Later, his parents decided to move to Sault Ste. Marie, in Northern Ontario. He had only intended to spend a few years there before heading back south, but the warmth of the people—and of one special girl in particular—won him over, so he stayed and remains there to this day! He has never looked back. And now, after all these years, his days simply wouldn't be complete without a friendly chat with his clients, who stop by the store to say hello, catch up on the latest news, and—of course—talk hockey!

Over the years, Dave has seen many changes, large and small. Snail mail turned into email, cheques disappeared, Air Miles points appeared... and Cashway became Rona. Cashway was a small company, with small stores and a Support Centre of just 60 employees. "Everybody knew everybody, and we all talked to one another. It was very friendly!"

And even if the changes weren't always easy to adapt to, Dave is convinced that were good for the company. "We're part of a very big group now. Rona wants the business to grow as much as we do." As for the people at Rona, they're not just friendly, he says, it's "like they seem to want to reach over, to follow you into the pit just to help you!"

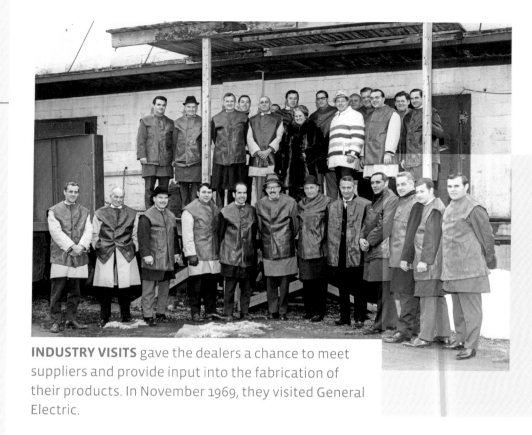

INDUSTRY VISITS gave the dealers a chance to meet suppliers and provide input into the fabrication of their products. In November 1969, they visited General Electric.

to accumulate for five years. In the sixth year, the dealer would get back his first-year deposit, and so on.

The proposed plan was accepted, and after that the Ro-Na group saw a rapid increase in its capitalization... and its capacity for growth.

The security deposits would bear interest, initially at a rate of 4.5%. In 1968, when the deposit system was introduced, the prime rate for business loans varied between 6 and 7.5%. Over the years, the rate on the security deposits would increase as a result of inflation and the general rise in interest rates, reaching 12% during the 1980s. A few years later, half of the security deposit would be converted to preferred shares.

The other problem that André Dion would soon address was the issue of retail prices. These tended to vary from one store to the next. They were established not on the basis of what the consumer was willing to pay—on the basis of the competitive environment—but rather on the price that the dealer himself paid and the profit margin he hoped to realize. This was disconcerting for consumers who expected at least some measure of consistency between two stores operating under the same Ro-Na banner. It was clear that this price structure needed to be reworked.

Dion suggested a gradual approach. They would start with a few products, the ones that were in the flyer. But for some members, even this was too much, it encroached too much on their independence as dealers. This difference

IN THE EARLY 1970s, representatives of Sylvania demonstrated how their lamps work to Charles Morency, Jean-Paul Pion and his wife, and company representative Roger Charest.

of opinion would persist for several years, recalls André Dion today:

> "At that time, some people withdrew from the group. They took down the banner. They said: 'We don't want to be identified with the group.' We accepted it and we carried on that way, to keep our volumes up, until the late 1970s, when some strict rules were brought in. If you want to take down your banner, you're out. End of story. It was very difficult, this shift to a new policy. It meant one year, at least, of stagnating sales, quarrels, the formation of new groups..."

But that was what had to be done in order to ensure credibility for the group and give meaning to the banner. The dealers retained some independence when it came to setting prices for many products; they could purchase goods from other suppliers up to a certain level; and of course, they exercised complete control over the running of their businesses. Dion's initiative, backed fully by the board of directors, struck just the right balance between the idea of "every man for himself" and the "all for one" attitude that made Ro-Na unique.

And those were the three key projects of Napoléon Piotte.

Five years after he took up the reins of command at Les Marchands en Quincaillerie Ltée, advertising was part of day-to-day operations at the company, which now had its

Never floored by a challenge!

Isabelle Giguère

Flooring Expert, Buyer, Administrative Office, Boucherville, Quebec

At 16 years old, Isabelle was already working as a sales clerk and was the best on the floor. Watching the buyers in action fascinated her. Her talent prompted her to study fashion marketing and international business. She was working for a shoe importer when a position as a buyer in the decorating department opened up at Rona.

The connection to fashion was obvious, but more importantly, Isabelle was ready for a challenge. And challenges are never in short supply at Rona. After a while, she left decorating to help create the department of merchandising analysts, under the direction of Luc Nantel. Once it was up and running, she moved on to paint buying, where she remained for four years, happy to be learning so much. "Everything evolves quickly at Rona; there are always new ways to do things, and it's gratifying to be able to evolve along with the company." When she found out about a buyer's position that was open in the flooring department, she saw it as an opportunity to learn a new aspect of the business and to return to her first loves: imports and trends.

It takes many qualities to be a buyer. First, you need to use your sense of aesthetic and listen to clients to find out what will be in vogue... in 35 weeks! That's how much time elapses from the selection of a product and the supplier to when the client is able to see, touch, and, ultimately, decide if it's a winner or not!

Then, you need strong analytical and negotiation skills to find the right product and the best supplier, at the right price and in sufficient quantity to stock all the stores. "It's not easy to find people who are both Cartesian thinkers and artists at the same time. Here, we're a bit of both. And it requires a solid team effort!" Nothing would be possible without the support of the operations, marketing, finance, and IT departments!

And, just to add one more challenge to the mix, she has to follow Rona's progressive green policy, which she does gladly, choosing suppliers and products with care. Isabelle derives enormous satisfaction from knowing that, like she and her clients, Rona also strives to be a good global citizen!

Weathering the storms

David Yurchesin

Joneljim Investments, Rona Building Centre,
Sydney, Nova Scotia

At the tip of Cape Breton, just steps from the Atlantic Ocean, you'll find the Sydney, Nova Scotia Rona. Established in 1919, the company was bought by the current owners, one of whom was John Yurchesin, in 1979. At the time, John's son David had just returned from Western Canada, where he had been working in the forestry business, and, in 1981, David joined the team as sales director. With his experience in lumber and construction, and a degree in commerce under his belt, he had the skills the company needed. As a young man, he had always dreamed of owning his own business; today, he is the general manager and really appreciates the freedom and leeway his two partners give him.

The country was in recession when David arrived, and to keep afloat they had been forced to restructure the company. In fact, they'd had to start over from scratch—which makes today's success all the more impressive. In 1988, they opened a second store in Sydney Mines, a few years later, a third in the small scenic community of Ingonish, and, in March 2008, a fourth in Irishat.

During that time, the arrival of a Home Depot, a Wal-Mart, a Canadian Tire, and a Central Home Improvement—their direct competitor—threatened to take the wind out of their sails. They would have to reinvent themselves to stay competitive, so they started to take a serious look at Rona. Although the company was little known in the region, its marketing strategies, flyers, TV ads, and Air Miles promotions were enough to convince them that they would have the support of a solid distribution network. In December 2006, they left the Castle Building Centres Group to join Rona. The stores were redesigned and restocked, and they were well equipped to brave any future storms!

Indeed, turbulence is a part of life in Nova Scotia, where heavy industry, steelworks, and coal mines have all closed in recent years. David says that they're used to downturns, "so we're optimistic, but I guess you've got to be realistic too... everybody's in the same boat right now." And each time things pick up again, he is just that little bit prouder for having weathered another storm!

LES MARCHANDS EN QUINCAILLERIE LTÉE followed the wave of change that could be felt near the end of the 1960s. Expo 67 provided a window onto the world.

own brand image; the business had opened new avenues for growth by forming a strategic alliance and making its first acquisition; and a significant shift in philosophy took place to ensure sound funding for the group and a consistent structure for store prices.

The deaths of Rolland and Napoléon

This series of reforms was well under way on April 2, 1967, when a grand banquet was held in the ballroom of the new Château Champlain Hotel to celebrate the 5th anniversary of the new administration of Les Marchands en Quincaillerie Ltée and the founding of Gestion La Savane Inc., the holding company that now headed the group. The guest speaker was none other than the former Minister and MNA for Laurier, René Lévesque. Business was good. Sales had doubled in five years, rising from $3 million to $6 million.

Just over a week later, on April 13, 1967, the annual general meeting was held. Rolland Dansereau was there. He came only to express his congratulations to the board of directors and to wish its members all the best in "continuing their achievements with the same good fortune." Over the previous two years he had kept himself up-to-date on the company's affairs and had received the documentation that was sent out to all shareholders. He still cared deeply about the company he had founded, but he opted now for discretion, and went no further than offering his encouragement. He had, nonetheless, allowed himself one

THE MARCHANDS CELEBRATED THE 5TH ANNIVERSARY OF THEIR NEW ADMINISTRATION in the banquet hall at the Château Champlain Hotel, in 1967. Sitting at the table in the foreground is Pierre Piotte.

LES MARCHANDS EN QUINCAILLERIE LTÉE welcomed a distinguished guest to the celebrations of the 5th anniversary of their new administration: René Lévesque, the former Liberal minister, delivered a speech at the Château Champlain Hotel in 1967.

extravagance the year before: when he attended the 1966 annual general meeting, he showed up in a shiny black chauffeur-driven Cadillac.

A regular meeting of the board of directors was held on July 15, 1968. The following is reported in the minutes of that meeting:

"Item 9: The president feels the time has come to change the name of the company Les Marchands en Quincaillerie Ltée to Ro-Na. A possible merger of the two companies is to be investigated."

For Napoléon, it was simply a matter of formally recognizing that which had already been sanctioned by use: it was the Ro-Na name that people saw and heard, that everyone in Quebec was familiar with. Surely it was time to make it official.

The 11th item on the agenda for that board meeting was more troubling: "Mr. Piotte wishes to remind the directors that he has not been in the best of health for some time now..." There was reference to some earlier discussions that had taken place concerning the granting of a pension to him, or to his wife if she survived him: "He intends to retire at the age of 70 if God grants him life and health enough until then."

Unfortunately, it was not to be. A few weeks later, Napoléon collapsed at his desk. The date was September 30, 1968. He died of emphysema a week later.

His funeral was held in a packed church, with at least a dozen flower cars lined up outside. Rolland Dansereau was in attendance, himself weakened and spent.

Napoléon Piotte was buried on October 12, 1968. Upon returning from the cemetery, the board of directors held an impromptu meeting. The minutes of the meeting read as follows:

Present: J.O. Roberge, Charles Morency, Philippe Dorval, Hector Durand, Aimé Lord, Raymond Goyer.

"Overcoming their deep sorrow at the loss of this true friend who had devoted himself tirelessly to the cause of both companies, and who had made himself their loyal champion in the last six years especially, the directors wished to pay him a final tribute by coming here to hold this meeting under his portrait, in which his brotherly smile still radiates the warmth we felt when he was with us, such a short time ago. It was therefore out of loyalty to his memory that the directors met in a spirit of harmony."

Charles Morency was appointed president of both companies.

Then, it was adopted that Piotte's salary for the week be paid to his wife, and that the pension that had been discussed at the previous meeting be paid to her as well.

Morency was charged with making an inventory of Piotte's personal effects and documents, and handing them

TO MARK THE APPOINTMENT OF CHARLES MORENCY AS PRESIDENT IN 1968,
the dealers in the Beauce region organized a reception in Sainte-Marie on November 13.

IN 1971, CHARLES MORENCY SURROUNDED HIMSELF WITH A DYNAMIC LEADERSHIP TEAM:
Marc St-Pierre in advertising, controller André Dion, Maurice Michaud in purchasing, Laurent Héon in accounting, Suzanne Duchesneau in ordering, and André Galarneau in the warehouse.

over to the spokesperson for the executrix... all, that is, except for the portrait of the late president, which the company wished to acquire.

It was then resolved that Morency would make the necessary arrangements for taking back possession of the company car that Piotte had for his personal use.

Rolland Dansereau passed away a few months later, on March 1, 1969. He died in his home in Outremont at the age of 63. His funeral was a very quiet affair, attended by family members only.

From Piotte to Morency

And so the torch was passed to Charles Morency. Here was another man who would leave a lasting mark on the company. He was the eldest of a family of 13 children. His father, Édouard, was one of the first hardware store dealers in Quebec City to join Les Marchands en Quincaillerie Ltée, in 1946. Charles took over from his father, and some of his brothers founded their own hardware business. In 1962, he was one of the nine dealers who, with Napoléon Piotte, took a considerable risk by buying up Rolland Dansereau's share of the business.

His appointment to the position of president was favourably received. It might even be said that he was the obvious choice. Morency was a natural leader, a man with a very warm personality who had a gift for connecting with people, employees, clients... A dealer through and through,

he was truly a product of Les Marchands en Quincaillerie Ltée, as it was the only business environment he had ever known. This business was in his blood. And he in turn would help it to take a giant step forward, a step into the modern age.

He began his term as president by acting on the wish Napoléon had expressed shortly before his death. The company Ro-Na Hardware Inc. was dissolved on August 31, 1969 and, at the same time, the company Les Marchands en Quincaillerie Ltée changed its name to Marchands Ro-Na Inc. Gestion La Savane Inc. now had only one subsidiary, its financial statements would appear consolidated, and it would be known by the name that would immortalize its founders: Ro-Na.

Consolidated key figures – 1971
(Gestion La Savane Inc. / Marchands Ro-Na Inc.)

		Year-to-year change
Net sales	$14 656 877	+68%
Net earnings	$158 411	+88%
Share capital	$399 700	–
Shareholders equity[1]	$784 836	+20%
Long term debt	$951 690	+65%[1]
Working capital	$1 178 918	+76%[1]

1: This increase results primarily from growth in the dealers' security deposits.

ANDRÉ DION brought a fresh approach to Les Marchands en Quincaillerie. He met with André Gagnon and Aimé Lord in 1971.

1971

The Vietnam War had now raged for more than eight years. In the United States, after the shock of the 1968 Tet Offensive, after the election of Richard Nixon—considered to be a "hawk"— as president, after the disclosure of the grim details of the massacre carried out by American soldiers at My Lai, the outcry against the war reached a peak when more than half a million demonstrators marched on Washington in April 📷. Nixon announced a gradual partial disengagement of American troops.

In the Cold War, tensions eased somewhat in the wake of a key event: the entry of the People's Republic of China into the United Nations. Ever since the Communist victory in 1949, the United States and its allies had worked to block China's entry, leaving that country's UN seat to the "nationalist" government in Taiwan. After more than 20 years, the West finally seemed ready to yield to reality...

International monetary stability had been achieved at the end of the Second World War through the Bretton Woods agreements, which made the U.S. dollar the only currency directly convertible to gold, but that stability was profoundly shaken in August with the announcement that the United States was suspending the convertibility of the dollar. In future, currencies would "float" freely according to the laws of supply and demand, a situation that would put the global economy on a fragile footing.

The Canadian government established the Metric Commission to oversee Canada's conversion to the International System of Units (SI), the modern metric system. It would effectively begin in 1975 with the implementation of the Celsius scale to measure temperature.

1972

The normalization of U.S.–China relations entered a new phase in 1972 with a groundbreaking event: Nixon's historic visit to China, which he described as "the week that changed the world." Taking a course diametrically opposed to the policy his predecessors had followed for 25 years, Nixon acknowledged the legitimacy of Mao Zedong's regime, re-established normal relations with it, and withdrew his previously unconditional support for the "nationalist" regime in Taiwan. The Soviet Union did not look kindly upon such a sweeping realignment of world power.

On September 2, the world of hockey was thrown into turmoil when, in Game One of the first Canada/Russia hockey series, being played at the Montreal Forum, the Soviet team crushed Team Canada with a score of 7 to 3. Canada would go on to win the "Summit Series" in the dying moments of the final game, but its supremacy in its national sport had been dealt a hard blow.

Also in the world of sports, but on a far more serious note, members of the Black September Organization, a Palestinian militant group, took nine Israeli athletes hostage on September 5 at the Olympic Games in Munich, demanding the release of Palestinian prisoners jailed in Israel. The incident ended in tragedy, with 16 people killed, including five of the terrorists. The Games resumed the following day...

1973

1973 opened with a huge sigh of relief, as a cease-fire agreement was reached on January 27 between the United States and the Democratic Republic of Vietnam (North Vietnam). The U.S. would withdraw its troops from South Vietnam within 60 days, while the North Vietnamese would release their prisoners of war. Elections would be held in South Vietnam under international supervision.

In April, the infamous Watergate scandal erupted; it would eventually lead to the fall of President Nixon, despite his triumphant re-election the previous November, when he carried 49 of the 50 states. Small-time crooks working for members of the president's inner circle had broken into Democratic Party offices. Nixon persisted in denying any wrongdoing on the part of his men and obstructed the investigation for months before resigning in August 1974.

But it was probably events in Chile that etched 1973 in the world's memory forever. On September 11, a military *coup d'état*, secretly supported by the United States, overthrew President Salvador Allende, who committed suicide in the presidential palace as it was being bombed by the air force. General Augusto Pinochet assumed power and established a dictatorship of torturers that would endure for close to 20 years.

1974

His reputation in tatters as a result of the Watergate scandal, U.S. President Richard Nixon resigned in August, just as Congress was preparing to launch impeachment proceedings against him.

The conflict between Greece and Turkey over the island of Cyprus, which had seen constant clashes between its Greek and Turkish communities since the attainment of independence in 1960, descended into open war when Turkish armed forces invaded the northern part of the island, creating the Turkish Republic of Northern Cyprus, an entity not formally recognized by the international community.

November 13 was the date of an event that held great symbolic importance for the people of Palestine. For the first time in its history (with the exception of a speech by Pope Paul VI in 1965), the General Assembly of the United Nations allowed an address by a speaker who did not represent one of the UN member states. That individual was Yasser Arafat, the chairman of the Palestine Liberation Organization (PLO), which was given observer status at the UN, while the people of Palestine had their right to national independence and sovereignty reaffirmed.

In Quebec, at its Fifth Congress, the Parti québécois adopted the strategy referred to as *étapisme*, or gradualism: accession to sovereignty would have to be preceded by a referendum.

Happiness begins at home

Jules, François and Martin Riopel

Centre de rénovation Jules Riopel et fils, Rona Le Rénovateur,
Sainte-Adèle, Quebec

The Riopel brothers started working for their father, Jules, at the tender age of eight or nine. Jules would bring home loose nails, and their job was to weigh them and package them up... for five cents a box! François says, "Our dad had us hooked—even if we didn't know it!" When Jules attended trade conventions, the boys would jump in the car without being asked. François remembers the first one, at Place Bonaventure... All the suppliers were there; everyone wore a suit and tie. He even remembers seeing Robert Dutton, Rona's current CEO. At 12, he was most impressed! He loved looking at all the products and always asked himself, "I wonder how you would sell this." Later, he would specialize in purchasing. From the age of 14, his older brother, Martin, would spend his summers in the yard sorting wood and dipping six-by-sixes in hemlock resin. Materials were definitely going to be his passion. Over the next few years, guided by their father, the two young men found their place in the business.

But the story of the Riopels' involvement in the lumber trade had begun many years before that. Their grandfather had owned a small sawmill in Chertsey and was one of the co-founders of Dismat. Jules worked there as a young man before opening his own construction materials store under the Dismat banner in 1969. The company eventually operated two outlets, one in Saint-Sauveur and one in Sainte-Marguerite, but these were sold in the mid-1990s with the goal of centralizing activities under one roof in a new hardware store to be built in Sainte-Adèle. They needed permission from the city and neighbouring businesses, though, before they could go ahead with the renovations. In 2006, just two weeks before Christmas, they found themselves out in the middle of a snowstorm knocking on doors to drum up support for the project. "You're saying to yourself, 'What on earth am I doing out here? It's Christmas!'" François adds, "That's when you realize you're a true entrepreneur!"

Today, succession is their number one priority. For the past six years, the brothers have been working to ensure a smooth transition when their father retires. They have hired external consultants to guide them through the process. "Each week we make a little more progress." Roles and structures will change, but the key is to be properly organized and to have every base covered before Jules goes. François adds, "I think it's really important for companies to go through this sort of exercise if they want to remain strong and in reliable hands. For us, that has meant moving out of our comfort zones on more than one occasion. It's been hard work!"

NEW FACES BEGAN TO APPEAR WITHIN THE ORGANIZATION. A member of the Ro-Na advertising committee from 1962 to 1967, André Gagnon joined the board of directors of Marchands Ro-Na in 1971.

At the end of 1971, Ro-Na had the wind in its sails. It was doing close to $15 million in business, its net earnings had nearly doubled in the space of a year, and the working capital it had available meant that the group could turn its thoughts to future development.

With Ro-Na's success and renown came an increase in the number of applications for membership. This was encouraging to see, of course, but it put the directors and the dealers in a rather tricky situation... one that would arise time and time again: what was to be done if a dealer who wished to join Ro-Na was located in what an existing member considered to be *his* territory?

At its meeting on January 10, 1972, the board of directors tackled this issue for the first time. The minutes of the meeting give some indication of the directors' predicament:

> "It is a matter of determining which business discipline to adopt as regards existing members, from the viewpoint of sales figures, discipline, identification, etc.
>
> Is the company going to become a general-purpose wholesaler with no restrictions, or will it have selective standards?"

At the time of this meeting, competition legislation in Canada was undergoing major reform; the outcome was a bill entitled *An Act to Promote Competition*, which was met with intense criticism—so much so that it would not be

IN 1969, ANDRÉ GAGNON UNDERTOOK THE CONSTRUCTION OF AN 18 000-SQ. FT. STORE IN SAINT-HYACINTHE, making it one of the 10 largest hardware stores in Quebec at the time.

passed until a few years later. The regulatory framework that would apply to companies wishing to "choose" their clients therefore remained unknown.

Following a laborious discussion on what the directors acknowledged was a "thorny problem," the board decided to approve "any dealer who meets the company's standards, irrespective of any protection of territory." However, the standards adopted then and there were much less categorical. One of them stated the following:

> "3. Acceptance of a new member on the condition that his establishment is a reasonable distance away from another member, taking local circumstances into account;"

There is no denying that this is less than clear. In other words, decisions were made on a case-by-case basis. "Local circumstances" could mean the size of the market, the number of competitors in the area, the progression of the current member's sales figures, etc. The uncertainty surrounding future legislation on competition undoubtedly contributed to the lack of precision, as did the serious difficulties inherent in defining specific and unvarying conditions for the admission of new members.

With time, Ro-Na would develop tools and methods for performing such analyses with precision, thereby ensuring the growth of the group and of each of its dealers.

Two's company!

Dianne and Dwight Clarke
Rona Building Centre, Fort St. John, British Columbia

Situated midway between Vancouver and Whitehorse, Fort St. John, in northern British Columbia, is a world apart. Established as a trading post in the 18th century, the oldest community in Western Canada is now thriving thanks to the oil and gas industry. Business is booming!

In 2001, not long after selling their restaurant, Dianne and Dwight Clarke took up a suggestion to contact Rona. At the time, they didn't know the company, the nearest store being an eight-hour drive away in Edmonton. But after some lengthy research and negotiations, they decided to make a go of it. The opportunity was too good to pass up. Rona, a rapidly growing Canadian company, immediately welcomed them into their large family, and, in June 2006, the Clarkes proudly opened a newly built 35 000-sq. ft. store! At first, their lack of retail sales experience posed a challenge in terms of store organization, but Rona dispatched a team to help them out, and everything was soon running like clockwork!

Dianne and Dwight Clarke form a winning partnership. During their 37 years of life together, they have travelled the world, launched several companies, and raised a family. The couple met at a rodeo. Following a marathon motorcycle trip that took them from London to Afghanistan, they returned to settle in Fort St. John. Before long, Dwight, a truck driver, realized that his family life was suffering from his long periods away on the road. So he decided to give it up and go into business with his wife. Their first venture was innovative; they converted gasoline engines into natural gas engines. But frustrated at constantly having to find funding for research, they decided to explore other options. One day, over lunch at a Wendy's restaurant, it suddenly occurred to them: why not open a Wendy's in Fort St. John? Easier said than done—they were turned down five times before eventually obtaining their franchise. Their perseverance and hard work paid off, and when they sold a few years later, the restaurant was the best-performing Wendy's in Canada.

Partners in life and in business, the couple say task-sharing is essential. Dwight is the builder, Diane, the "controller." Dwight says he provides the money, and Dianne looks after it. His wife says "men are builders; we're nurturers...we want to fix anything they wreck!" In any case, the Clarkes are certainly used to working as a family. The kids were taught to answer the phone for their parents from a young age, when they would holler, "Dad! Get line one!" Today, Dwight's brother Brian, the couple's son-in-law, Dan Wuthrich, and their son Bob are now partners at the Rona store.

Advertising campaigns •

IT WAS THE 1960S, AND THE TIME HAD COME TO ADOPT A COMMON BRAND IMAGE. WHILE THE RARE BIRD LOGO WAS THE FINAL RESULT, THE ORGANIZATION'S ADVERTISING CAMPAIGNS CONTRIBUTED SIGNIFICANTLY TO ITS BRAND IMAGE AS WELL.

❶ In 1965, the advertising firm of BCP won a special mention for this ad it created for Quincaillerie Ro-Na Inc.

❷ In the 1970s, the "man in red" was joined by several well-known Quebec personalities, including Jean Lapointe, Gilles Latulippe, and Jacques Godin.

Among them:

1964. Les Marchands en Quincaillerie Ltée celebrated its 25th anniversary by launching a major advertising campaign with a budget in excess of $100 000. The twin objectives were to recruit new member dealers and to familiarize the public with the Ro-Na name. Radio, television, and newspapers were all used in the campaign. Journalist Claude Beauchamp, writing in the October 19, 1964 issue of the newspaper *Les Affaires*, had this to say:

> Les Marchands en Quincaillerie Ltée currently has 300 clients, all of them French-Canadian. Of that number, approximately 125 belong to the Les Quincailleries Ro-Na Inc. chain of independent stores. However, the upcoming advertising campaign is expected to boost that number to close to 300 by next year.

1965. Publicité Club de Montréal gave a special mention to the ad *"Êtes-vous cet oiseau rare que nous cherchons?" (Are you the rare bird we're looking for?)*, created by the advertising firm of BCP. It was published on the cover of the magazine *Le Quincaillier*.

1969. The man in red greeted shoppers at more than 250 hardware stores throughout the province. The cheerful pasteboard figure welcomed customers and highlighted current promotions.

1989. The Ro-Na Dismat Group turned 50. To celebrate, there were specials in all 600 stores. This was the year of the television ad that showed Napoléon and Rolland as children building a tree house. What people did not know was that because the ad was filmed in winter, the tree, and the actors, were actually in Florida!

2000. Three bilingual campaigns featuring consumers were aired on television:

- "It's easy, it's only until Tuesday at all Rona stores"/*"C'est simple, c'est jusqu'à mardi dans tous, tous, tous les Rona."* Each 15-second spot presented a feature product and created a sense of urgency.
- "It's easy, it's always Rona" / *"C'est simple, c'est toujours Rona"* promoted the strength of the network and the proximity of the dealers.
- "Yellow means Rona L'entrepôt" / *"Le jaune, c'est Rona L'entrepôt"* encouraged people to think yellow when they had a project to do.

2003. "My name is still Bob, Karen, Shelly, Brenda..." was a striking campaign. Developed as a collaborative effort between Revy's marketing team and Rona's, it reassured regular customers of Revy and Revelstoke that with the name change from Revy to Rona, 99 years of service and expertise would not suddenly disappear, that the employees they knew and trusted would still be there. It placed the employees and the individual at the centre of the company-consumer relationship. It was heard on radio and seen in newspapers throughout Western Canada.

2003. "The How-To People" / *"Vous voulez. Vous pouvez."* was a bold campaign in that it combined a broad range of media outlets: television, radio, internet, in-store banners, targeted sponsorships, and public relations. The campaign showcased the talent, expertise, and accomplishments of its customers with the theme "I am a handyman"/*"Je suis un bricoleur, une bricoleuse."* This theme would be reprised over several years.

Putting Rona in the spotlight

RONA DISMAT
UNE FORCE ÉCONOMIQUE DE 1 MILLIARD

LE QUINCAILLIER
LE RÉNOVATEUR
DISMAT
LE QUINCAILLEUR
AMBIANCE
LE CHANTIER
PODIUM
BOTANIX

MY NAME IS STILL BRENDA

EVEN THOUGH REVY & REVELSTOKE MAY BE CHANGING THEIR NAME TO RONA

You are a handywoman

RONA
The How-To People.

Je suis un bricoleur

RONA
Vous voulez. Vous pouvez.

2003. "If it exists, we've got it" - "Réno-Dépôt: driving down the cost of renovation" / *"Si ça existait, on l'aurait"* - *"Réno-Dépôt : celui qui fait baisser le coût de la rénovation"* was another campaign that drew praise from the advertising industry. Normand Brathwaite is still the spokesperson for the banner's publicity campaigns.

2003-2004. "Rona Dream Home" / *"Ma maison Rona"*, a 10-episode series broadcast on TVA and Global, won gold in the Television category at the 2003 Media Innovation Awards presented by *Marketing Magazine*. Home renovation reality TV had arrived.

2009. The Bos advertising agency came up with some original ideas to attract the public's attention to paint recycling.

2010. More recently, during the Vancouver Winter Olympics, 14 remarkable "Made in Canada" / *"Fabriqués au Canada"* television spots were aired, including the inspirational ad of a tape measure rapidly retracting from one coast to the other, passing through iconic Canadian landscapes along its way.

❸ In 1989, Rona's 50th anniversary advertising campaign was entirely themed around two children who represented Rolland and Napoléon. They were featured in both newspaper and TV ads.

❹ From March 3 to 17, 2003, the goal of the so called "transition" campaign was to reassure customers that the quality of service would remain the same in spite of the name change from Revy to Rona.

❺ Rona launched a national campaign in March 2003. According to a survey carried out three months earlier, the favourite ad was the one featuring a young woman looking into her mirror, who had to repair a tile.

❻ "Doing it right" was the theme of the 2009 advertising campaign, which placed Rona by Design projects and sustainable development at the forefront.

❼ Claude Bernier, the executive vice-president of Marketing and Customer Innovations directed the company's marketing operations from 1988 to 2001, and from 2008 to today. From 2001 to 2008, he oversaw the development of the network of proximity and specialized stores.

CONSTRUCTION on the new 225 000-sq. ft. distribution centre progressed quickly during 1973.

THE MODEL OF THE NEW DISTRIBUTION CENTRE on Nobel Street in Boucherville, which, it was hoped, would solve the problems due to lack of space.

That year, 1972, also marked the official arrival of the computer age at Ro-Na. The new president, Charles Morency, was the great champion of this cause. To him, computerization meant efficiency, productivity, and profitability. While others hesitated over the investment required, he could already see the time coming when inventory management and the coordination of deliveries would be decisive factors for success, and when technology would play a key role in competition among large retailers. The first computer was installed at the beginning of the year, but by the fall, it was at maximum capacity and had to be replaced by a more powerful machine.

Daring to think big

Ro-Na was therefore growing rapidly, in every possible way. Space was becoming tight. In the building on De la Savane Street, people were literally treading on one another's toes. The company rented a neighbouring building, adding 40 000 sq. ft. (3 700 m²) of floor space to house the shipping department. Pierre Forget joined the company at that time. As he recalls:

> "We had a sort of little tunnel, and we could go through the tunnel to take our boxes over to shipping. Going and picking up merchandise in the warehouse was a problem because there were so many pallets in the aisles that you had to walk over them..."

This was a temporary solution. Arrangements were already being made for a big move. Management was looking toward the suburbs, where there was no shortage of available land.

On October 25, 1972, the board of directors decided to make an offer on five adjoining lots running along Nobel Street in Boucherville, just a stone's throw from the Trans-Canada Highway. "It will also give us good visibility," said Morency, the president, adding that it was time for Ro-Na to start thinking big. What an understatement! The land in question totalled nearly a million square feet (93 000 m²), enough to meet the company's immediate needs three times over.

The transaction was finalized the following April. The building at 5200 De la Savane Street was put up for sale, and the lots in Boucherville were purchased for $228 000. But there was not a moment to lose. The municipal by-laws required them to act quickly: they could have no more than nine months before starting construction and no more than nine months for construction to be completed.

A year and a half from start to finish!

Plans for the future building were drawn up internally for the most part, mainly by André Dion and André Gagnon, who, assisted by an engineer, devoted long hours to the project after their own workday was over. It was an immense undertaking. What they wanted to build went far beyond a brand new building for a hundred or so employees and a

DURING THE OPENING OF THE DISTRIBUTION CENTRE IN 1974, the Marchands Ro-Na make a contribution to the Campagne des Fédérations du grand Montréal (the precursor to the United Way), represented by hockey player Jean Béliveau.

THE NOBEL STREET DISTRIBUTION CENTRE maximized the use of space: the area of the warehouse that stores high-volume inventory had a double deep pallet racking system.

million pieces of merchandise; what they wanted to create was in fact the nerve centre of a flourishing company, a company that had the ambition to expand its market and that was already preparing to do battle with the heavy hitters. So, they looked at what was being done elsewhere; they went to Texas to tour a revolutionary distribution centre that was fully computerized. That was exactly the sort of thing Ro-Na aspired to!

The budget for the project as a whole—construction, outfitting, moving—was $2.4 million. This amount would be financed in part by a $1.5-million mortgage loan with the Caisse de dépôt et placement du Québec, amortized over 15 years at an annual rate of 9%.

It was a thrilling prospect for all employees of Ro-Na, who felt they had a personal stake in a wonderful adventure. Everyone lent a hand with the move, recalled Pierre Forget: "We'd work at the building on De la Savane. Then on Friday around noon we'd go over to the building on Nobel and stay there until midday on Saturday."

The grand opening of Ro-Na's new administrative centre and distribution centre took place on March 3, 1974, attended by 900 guests who had never seen anything like it before. The building had 20 000 sq. ft. (1 850 m²) of office space, and the giant warehouse covered 160 000 sq. ft. (14 850 m²). In the administrative section, visitors stood awestruck in front of the large glass panels that enclosed the computer room, which even boasted the very latest computer, the amazing NCR 101, with a memory capacity of... 32 KB! The distribution centre offered an equally stunning glimpse into the future: 33 double rows of shelves standing three stories high; 10 lift trucks; 250 computer-controlled carts that moved on their own from section to section—some of them were even set up to run on a mini-rail system. And the tour ended in a huge cafeteria where people raised a glass and said to one another that, really, there was no stopping progress!

Ro-Na's move to its new facilities on Nobel Street marked its transition from what might be called the minor leagues to the major leagues. Ro-Na was now a major company, with 388 member dealers across Quebec. Its sales had nearly tripled in four years, rising from $9 million in 1970 to $26 million in 1973.

It was the dawn of a new era, one that would bring its own share of trials and triumphs, but one that would take the associated dealers even farther along the road to success...

A family portrait · The extended clan

1974

Sales: $32 369 000

Net earnings: $266 493

Shareholders' equity: $1 502 779

Affiliate stores (members): 411

VISITORS ENTERING THE NOBEL STREET RONA IN BOUCHERVILLE were awed by the avant-garde and modern facilities.

Stepping onto the big stage
1974 - 1990

4

In 1975, the first Ro-Na dealers' strategy conference was the starting point for a major development offensive. The pace of growth was so rapid that new stores, larger and better designed, were needed. It was during this exciting time that I started my career at Ro-Na, when I quietly joined the marketing department. In five years, from 1975 to 1980, sales more than quadrupled, jumping from $45.1 million to $204.5 million. The trusty old catalogue was replaced by an electronic order management system, and new banners were introduced.

In 1981, Charles Morency retired. By that time, he had propelled Ro-Na onto the big stage. He passed the torch of chairman of the board to Henri Drouin, who would remain in the position for 21 years. André Dion took over reins of command in 1983. Ro-Na acquired the Botanix nurseries. To finance its vigorous growth, Ro-Na became listed on the stock exchange for the first time in 1984, in a highly successful debut. They achieved a great coup in 1988 with the acquisition of a direct competitor, Dismat, and Ro-Na subsequently became the Ro-Na Dismat Group. But in the shadow of this triumphant march, labour relations at the Boucherville distribution centre were deteriorating. A union was formed and a strike was called. It would continue for three months. When the conflict ended, André Dion left Ro-Na and I was promoted to the head of the company.

It was now the mid 1970s. Ro-Na had the wind in its sails. Quebec was buzzing with excitement. Soon, the world would be meeting in Montreal for the 1976 Olympic Games. For two weeks, Quebec would be the centre of the world. And our guests would barely have taken their leave when all of Canada would be rocked when René Lévesque's Parti québécois would be elected to power for the first time.

My humble beginnings at Ro-Na

It was around that time, in 1977 to be precise, that I arrived on the scene… treading softly all the way. I had just completed my business administration studies at the HEC business school in Montreal, and my path seemed to be laid out before me: working with my father at the family hardware business in Laval and then eventually taking over from him. He had said to me: "You can buy me out when you're able."

One day, I was in the basement of the store. I was putting away some black plastic piping. I was covered in dirt. My father called out: "Robert, telephone!" I went upstairs, dust flying everywhere, and he held the phone out to me.

— It's André Dion.

— You're joking, right?

I had met him a few days earlier. My father introduced him to me at a meeting of Ro-Na dealers on the South Shore of Montreal. He practically dragged me there, hoping that I might learn something and that it might help me to lose the shyness that kept me on the sidelines.

I remember that I found André Dion to be very imposing. He was someone you called "Sir," a man who exuded great confidence and great authority. I couldn't understand why he was calling me.

I took the receiver. It was indeed André Dion who was at the other end. He said: "We're looking for someone in marketing. I'd like you to meet with my director of human resources." I answered, "Okay." I didn't really want to, but I was too intimidated to tell him no.

The meeting was not a success. And that's putting it mildly. I waited out in the hallway for nearly an hour and a half, only to find myself being introduced to a gentleman who told me straight off that he was not feeling up to doing interviews: "I had a bit too much of a good time with the foremen yesterday."

Ro-Na was everything to my father, but I myself did not yet understand the pride that pulsed through these dealers, nor the delight they felt in getting together for their rather boisterous parties.

André Dion called me again. This time I summoned up every bit of my courage. I thanked him for his interest and told him that the job was not for me. But Dion was not a man who would take no for an answer. He said: "Come back in to see me, and bring your father."

HALF OF THE MARCHANDS RO-NA MEMBERSHIP
made the trip out to Hôtel Le Chantecler in Sainte-Adèle in the Laurentians for the very first Ro-Na convention in 1975.

THE CONVENTION'S PRESIDENT, Pierre Piotte, and organizer Lise Pichette flank Me. Gaétan Raymond at the microphone.

— Yes, Mr. Dion.

So there I was in his office in Boucherville, with my father. André Dion spoke firmly and enthusiastically. I could clearly see that he was still a young man—he was 36 at the time—but he had the bearing and assurance of a general. He had been promoted to executive vice-president not long before this. Apparently, nothing happened at Ro-Na without him having a hand in it.

— What would you like to do later on, Robert?

— Well, I'm going to work with my father and eventually take over from him and open another store.

— Another store? You want to open another store, Mr. Dutton?

My father was a proud man. A second store was not something that we had ever discussed seriously, but he was not going to show any loss of confidence in front of Dion. So he answered assuredly:

— In the next two years, we're going to have a second store.

André Dion then turned to me:

— Listen, Robert, working in your father's store and taking over from him, that's great. That could be a very good plan for you. But we need some talented and well-educated young managers here to coordinate Ro-Na's growth. I want you to be one of them.

I did not feel that I fit this description. Nevertheless, a few days later, I started working at Ro-Na.

My first task: develop a pricing policy for price-sensitive items, those for which the price had to be the same in all Ro-Na stores—basically, the flyer items. For this, it was necessary to consider our cost price, the desired profit margin, and also what our competitors were charging. The price had to be competitive, but attractive for the dealers. I had to make this type of decision for approximately 350 products. I was learning retail... right down to the details!

I had a small office next to André Dion's. From there I could see the line that formed every day and stretched beyond my door, often 10 or 12 people long, all of them waiting to speak to André Dion. His office was a real hive of activity.

Gradually I was won over by the spirit that existed within this company: the camaraderie, the daring, the pride at having built a business like this with just a handful of neighbourhood dealers and a few thousand dollars. Those forerunners who were always mentioned with such veneration: Rolland Dansereau, Émery Sauvé, Napoléon Piotte, Charles Morency...

After a few months, I came to understand my father's pride; I understood the fervour of the associated dealers. I wanted to earn my place among them.

In fact, if I feel this kind of attachment to Ro-Na today, 33 years later, it is because, in a certain sense, it was there that I was born again.

André Dion • Working together

ANDRÉ DION WAS PRESIDENT OF RONA FROM 1983 TO 1990. HE BEGAN WORKING FOR THE COMPANY IN 1966 AT THE AGE OF 24.

❶ The arrival of André Dion in accounting was noted in the internal newsletter *La Ronde Ro-Na*, 1966.

In those days, Rona was looking to hire a controller. Originally from Lac Saint-Jean, André was living in Quebec City and had just finished his studies as a chartered accountant at Université Laval. One of his fellow students mentioned that a position was opening up, so, even though he was somewhat intimidated by the prospect of travelling to Montreal, he went to meet Napoléon Piotte. Their discussions lasted a week because Napoléon wanted enough time to assess his skills, which he evidently felt were suitable as he ended up offering him the position. A known member of the Ordre de Jacques-Cartier, Napoléon welcomed his newest employee with even greater enthusiasm when he learned that André's father was also a member of the order.

Back then, Rona operated in the spirit of the cooperative system. André's first challenge—which would last several years—was to persuade the administrators one by one to consider managing the business differently. For starters, he proposed that the retail price should not be determined based on the cost price but on what the consumer was willing to pay. He also suggested that the administration should hold back a portion of the earnings for the group, rather than returning it to the members in the form of rebates. On learning this, several merchants threatened to separate from the group and demanded that all the shares be distributed among the hardware store merchants. André later said that he reached his goal by learning to work with the most dynamic merchants, by convincing them to work together.

At that time, the office was run by a small group of 60 employees. Michel Gendron, who was single-handedly responsible for keeping the hefty catalogue up to date, remembers that it was not unusual for André to join him at 5 p.m., at the close of the working day, to give him a hand with the printing. He has fond memories of a kind-hearted man whose contribution helped build a more dynamic company. In the space of a few years, André worked his way from controller to assistant chief executive officer, before becoming assistant to the president—Charles Morency—until Charles stepped down. Charles supported and championed André every step of the way, and, when the time came, he encouraged André to take his place.

When André arrived at De la Savane Street, everything was still being done by hand. Charles and he began to prepare for the move to Nobel Street. They travelled to Texas to see how things were being done elsewhere and discovered, to their astonishment, that customers there were placing orders directly through the computer system, without an intermediary; instantaneous inventory management... a system that would, once again, transform the new corporate headquarters into one of the most advanced of its day.

Then, in the fall of 1983, André took over the helm of the company. At the 1975 conference, the new president stated, "The time is ripe, because in these difficult economic times, people are tightening their belts. It is essential that Rona evolve from being just a purchasing group to being a sales group." Construction of model stores, the relocation of stores, modern retrofitting of existing stores, well organized and increased publicity, client-oriented training for the staff, financial support provided to contractors, "Carte Clé" credit cards for members: there were some of the myriad ways they would achieve this goal. Various outfits operating under the Rona banner appeared: Le Quincaillier, le Rénovateur, le Chantier—which became Rona L'entrepôt—the Ambiance Boutiques, Podium, integrations such as Botanix, the merger with Dismat... All those years spent meeting merchants, increasing his knowledge of the industry, coupled with his burning desire for cooperation and his strong administrative skills, made him the right man for the job. He was the president who could be approached, whose door was always open.

Progress was remarkable, although management began to lose some degree of contact with the employees. Mechanization necessitated a clear-cut separation of tasks, which was partly responsible for the strike of 1989. If it united the merchants, who had to come and fill their orders themselves, and management, who pitched in as well, the strike also highlighted the need for a revitalized collective project.

Under André's leadership, the company became seriously committed to its mission of social involvement. Rona had always been a catalyst for solidarity among the merchants, and, consequently, within the community. But now, Rona's corporate headquarters became actively involved too, working, for example, with Intégration Jeunesse, teaching society's marginalized youths to build houses, or bringing seniors who had lost their independence to the Montreal Botanical Garden. This last activity, which was deeply moving for everyone involved, created a major logistical challenge and required the participation of a number groups: the *Journal de Montreal* advertised it; the merchants provided the buses that rolled in from all corners of the province, packed with seniors who were thrilled to be going on such an adventure; and the Canadian Boy Scouts provided helping hands and smiles, as they ushered along the crowd that had descended upon the Botanical Gardens. Back at Rona, people like Marc St-Pierre and a young Robert Dutton were busy working furiously. André adds, without attempting to hide the tears that welled up in his eyes at the memory, "I had never seen elderly people looking so happy. It was extraordinary."

When André left in the early 1990s, he was 49 years old. The integration was now complete. He had led the company to a stage it had never reached before and now wanted to heed the call of new challenges. Soon after, he created the micro-brewery Unibroue, which would become a huge Quebec success story... and one more way to bring people together!

❷ A dynamic businessman involved in a wide variety of projects, André Dion took part in the creation of the brewery Unibroue, and is currently writing a book about the experience.

❸ Voted "man of the month" in September 1984 by the publication *Commerce,* André Dion attended the gala in his honour, held a few months later, with Charles Morency and Henri Drouin.

Investing in human capital

François Marcil

Marcil Centre de rénovation, Saint-Sauveur, Quebec

When he was young, François preferred to drive the tractor on the family farm than to help his grandfather, Arthur, at the store. Sorting lumber into different lengths seemed like a long, tedious job to a little kid!

A few years later, though, he was the one who would yell to his two younger brothers, "Quit playing and come and help me!" Though François, Yvon, and Normand are now the third generation of Marcils to run the business, the true founder was their mother, Marie-Cerylda. She was the one who bought supplies for Arthur, persuaded her husband to buy the store, and subsequently encouraged her sons to work there. Today, at 87, she still likes to know what's going on! In 1972, the three brothers purchased the business. Within 10 years, sales grew from $60 000 to $2 million! During the 1982 recession, their competitor went bankrupt, and François promptly bought them out. It was the beginning of a period of significant expansion. Today, Marcil Centre de rénovation includes nine stores, all recovered from owners in financial difficulty or who had lost interest.

Today, having experienced another economic slowdown, many businesses have adopted a more cautious approach. For François Marcil, that just means more stores will be available for him to buy! "I like rescuing unsuccessful ventures, because in the end, what really matters is the people who work there—the human capital." Ranked one of the 50 Best Employers in Canada in 2005 and 2008, François Marcil has certainly proved that he cares about the human capital. And his employees are behind him all the way; they often ask him, "So, boss, when are we opening the next store?"

When the Dismat Group was experiencing difficulty in 1985, they offered François the position of president. At the time, a merger with BMR or Sodisco was on the cards. As Rona was their direct competitor, they told François, "Anyone but Rona!" But André Dion, who was leading the negotiations, was "as tough a guy as you'll ever meet. He never gave in, and he was right, because he finally won me over!" François was convinced that a merger with Rona was the right thing to do, although persuading his members was a different story: Dismat's people were all about materials, Rona's, about hardware. Nonetheless, in 1988, Rona-Dismat was finally born. A few years later, after the initial culture shock subsided, they began to grow together.

François later sat on Rona's board of directors for several years. In fact, he arrived just in time to vote on two of its most important decisions: appointing Robert Dutton as president and opening the first big-box store. He's proud to have had a hand in both of those.

RO-NA CONVENTIONS INSPIRED MUCH THOUGHT AND DISCUSSION, as this 1977 workshop led by Gaston Tétreault, Guy Nantais, and Réal Chevrier shows.

A pivotal conference

When I joined Ro-Na, there was an excitement in the air, an energy that could be traced back to a major conference that had taken place some 24 months earlier, in 1975. In a way, what came out of that conference was the company's first true strategic plan.

Ro-Na, with its modern facilities, its 460 dealers, and its sales of more than $45 million, had stepped out onto the big stage. Its competitors were bonafide institutions: Pascal, Beaver Lumber, Canadian Tire...

These were rock-solid organizations, well structured and highly developed. Whereas at Ro-Na there still reigned what you might call a sort of "creative anarchy." Ro-Na had gone through the years in perpetual survival mode, its history marked by constant friction and conflict. Then, after 25 years, the wind picked up. Suddenly, the little galleon that was Ro-Na, with its undisciplined crew, who often tried to row in opposite directions, was forced out into the open sea where it sailed alongside grand ocean liners. Beautiful vessels that commanded respect and even admiration.

I find it a little bit crazy, the idea of these dealers trying to play at being businessmen. But life can give me no better gift than to be able to share in their enthusiasm.

"We had to start from the ground up," recalls Henri Drouin today. Here was another man who was larger than

TO OPEN THE 1984 SPRING SHOW, 2 360 dealers and employees gathered at Place des Arts in November 1983. During the event, Le Group Ro-Na launched its advertising campaign and projects for the upcoming year.

THE ORGANIZING COMMITTEE FOR THE 1977 RO-NA CONVENTION poses for the camera in front of Le Manoir Richelieu, in Charlevoix, where conventions were held toward the end of the 1970s.

115

life. This hardware store owner from Abitibi would chair the board of directors for over 20 years. At more than six feet tall, he easily towered over whomever he happened to be speaking to, and although he was always pleasant and reserved, almost self-effacing, he commanded respect.

As he tells it today: "There was no obligation to display a Ro-Na sign, to advertise, to distribute catalogues, to comply with retail prices, to keep our stores in order, etc." They had been given red jackets, which looked great in photos, but behind the scenes, there was still a general lack of organization.

Ro-Na therefore found itself up against some fundamental choices: grow or perish; get organized or go under.

These were the challenges facing this first major strategy conference, which took place at the Hôtel Le Chantecler in Sainte-Adèle on September 28, 29, and 30, 1975. The participation rate was impressive. No less than half of the member dealers had made the trip. In his opening address, the president, Charles Morency, spoke of his ambition for the group: "The success of the nationals and multinationals lies not in what they are doing, but in what we are not doing."

There followed three days of intense work led by Pierre Piotte, son of the late Napoléon, who kept the proceedings rolling along at a brisk pace. Participants were spoiled for choice, with four workshops conducted by experienced speakers. "Prospects for growth in the hardware business" and "Marketing issues" were facilitated, respectively, by Gérard Virthe and Gaétan Bouchard, both from the marketing consulting firm Cogem. Notary Gilles Larose conducted the workshop on "The problem of business succession," a topic which was already at that time, and still is today, a central issue for RONA, many of whose stores are family-run businesses. And Gérard Blondeau, then director of deposit services at the Caisse de dépôt et placement du Québec, instructed participants on "Operating costs and business processes."

For three days, the dealers were once again schoolboys, studious, hard-working... but always ready to have a good time. After all, this was a gathering of Ro-Na dealers, let's not forget!

The conference proved decisive for a number of reasons. First, it brought the dealers closer together, and more importantly, it helped them to realize that they were now part of an elite team. It was no longer just a slogan. It was a fact. Each of them was indeed "a rare bird." Together they could legitimately aspire to the loftiest ambitions. This conference marked Ro-Na's official arrival on the big stage, and the transformation of what had primarily been a purchasing group into what would in future be first and foremost a selling group.

On an operational level, this realization of what Ro-Na had become, this appropriation by the dealers of a shared destiny which, far from threatening each one's independence, seemed impossible without it, led to a number of

1975

The Vietnam War truly came to a close in 1975. Following the U.S. withdrawal two years earlier, the conflict between North and South continued, with the tide turning markedly in favour of North Vietnam and the Vietcong insurgents, who seized Saigon on April 30. The dramatic evacuation of the last remaining American nationals from the embassy roof seemed to symbolize for the whole world the greatest military defeat in U.S. history.

In the Middle East, it was Lebanon's turn to be drawn into turmoil with the outbreak of a protracted and bitter ethnic-religious civil war of extreme complexity between two camps qualified, respectively, as "progressive Palestinian" and "conservative Christian," themselves rife with internal divisions. It was a conflict in which neighbouring Syria would become increasingly involved.

In June, Quebec adopted its Charter of Human Rights and Freedoms, seven years before the adoption of the federal Charter. In November, the province signed the James Bay and Northern Quebec Agreement with the Cree and the Inuit, affirming their ancestral rights to more than 645 000 km² of land, while at the same time opening the door to hydroelectric development.

In December, Pierre Elliott Trudeau's Liberal government introduced wage and price controls to battle spiraling inflation.

1976

After Expo 67, Montreal became the focus of world attention once again when it hosted the 1976 Olympic Games, which opened there on July 17 📷. The highlight of the Games was without question the dazzling performance of a 14-year-old Romanian gymnast named Nadia Comaneci, who received seven perfect scores of 10 out of 10. This unprecedented achievement would result in a revamping of the entire scoring system, as the scoreboards were not capable of displaying a score of 10...

The Games were, however, boycotted by most African nations in protest over the presence of New Zealand, which they criticized for its sporting links with South Africa, the land of apartheid. Originally estimated at $310 million, the final price tag of the Games was over $1.3 billion, and the debt incurred for construction of the facilities would not be paid off until 2006!

The Quebec election on November 15 shook all of Canada, when the Parti québécois, led by René Lévesque, swept to victory with 71 seats, compared to the 26 won by Robert Bourassa's Liberals. Bourassa himself was defeated in his own riding, and he stepped down as leader of his party four days later. The election of a sovereignist party to power in Quebec seemed likely to plunge Canada into the gravest political crisis in its history.

1977

On the international scene, the most sensational event of the year took place in November, when the president of Egypt, Anwar El Sadat, a key figure in the Arab world, made an official visit to Israel 📷 and delivered an important speech before the Knesset (the Israeli parliament) in Jerusalem. While insisting that Israel withdraw from the territories it had occupied since 1967 and give up its "dreams of conquest," he proposed that peace negotiations begin immediately. Sadat thus became the first Arab leader to give *de facto* recognition to the existence of the State of Israel, sparking controversy in the Arab world, with some countries condemning Egypt's initiative.

In Quebec, the Parti québécois government set in motion a "second Quiet Revolution" when it passed several key pieces of legislation, including the landmark Bill 101, which constituted a true Charter of the French Language. Following suit with Saskatchewan (1945), Manitoba (1971), and British Columbia (1973), Quebec brought in a public automobile insurance plan. The Quebec legislation placed under government responsibility all matters relating to bodily injury resulting from automobile accidents, regardless of who is at fault, leaving property damage matters in the hands of the private sector. Under another law that was passed, for the first time in Canada the use of strikebreakers (scabs) was prohibited in labour disputes.

ALL THE BOUCHERVILLE EMPLOYEES ATTENDED THE "DEMAIN EN MAIN" MEETING held in March 1986. Robert Dutton, André Dion, and Henri Drouin each gave riveting speeches.

reforms, reforms which in the past could not even have been attempted, so strong would the dealers' resistance have been.

And so, in the months that followed the Sainte-Adèle conference, significant action was taken to reassert and strengthen the cohesion of the associated dealers.

- The Ro-Na name would need more space than what was available on a little poster. It was neither a secret nor an incidental bit of information. It was now a statement of identity, a rallying cry. The hardware dealers would have to devote 50% of their outdoor signage to displaying the Ro-Na name.

- All would have to contribute their share to Ro-Na advertising.

- A minimum of 80% (and, later, 90%) of their supplies would have to be purchased with Ro-Na in order for them to be eligible for the full benefits of membership, such as rebates.

- Members would have to submit their financial statements to Ro-Na. This measure gave the group not only a means of verifying loyalty rates in terms of purchasing supplies, but also a basis for acting as an advisor to the dealers on matters of management, financing, merchandising, set-up, and so on. The soundness of the company's

management would thus be extended across the entire group.

- The requirements for joining the group were standardized. The terms at that time were as follows: the dealer must purchase a minimum of $2 000 in shares, and pay a fixed annual contribution of $500 and a variable contribution based on the amount of his purchases; he must leave a security deposit with the group consisting of a portion of his rebates, interest on his deposits, and discounts and dividends payable to him. The deposit for a given year was locked in for five years and was returned to the dealer in the sixth year. This profit-sharing and loyalty-building plan was a continuous circle that both helped to fund the group and ensured that each member would benefit from the growth of its business overall.

In the months that followed the Sainte-Adèle conference, there was such rapid growth that the network of dealers struggled to keep up. Around that time the magazine *La Prospérité*, published by the Conseil d'expansion économique—an advisory body created by the Quebec government in the 1960s—featured an analysis of Ro-Na that read as follows: "Operational capacity at Ro-Na is greater than the members' capacity for absorption. [...] Their establishments have become too small for what they want to sell."

Like a fish to water

Georges Lanouette
Quincaillerie Notre-Dame, Rona Le Quincaillier, Montreal, Quebec

The Lanouette family's love affair with the trade began in 1889, when Georges's grandparents opened a general store on Saint-Jacques Street in Montreal's Saint-Henri neighbourhood. When his grandfather died in 1929, in the midst of the economic crisis, Georges's father took over with his grandmother, Albertine. At five feet tall, what she lacked in stature, she more than made up for in character, remembers Georges. "We probably have her to thank for getting us through that period. With her, we always knew where we were going!" The Lanouettes lived right above the hardware store. "That had its downside, because clients always knew where to find us!" he adds.

In 1945, after completing a year and a half of studies at business school, taking classes at night and working at the store during the day, Georges finally entered the family business full time. "The only thing I learned at school was that some people think they're smart when in fact they're not. I used to say to the teachers, 'Come and work in the store for a week, then you'll see how things work in the real world,' but they didn't like that much. I think they were glad to see the back of me! It just goes to show that being good at school doesn't necessarily make you good at business!"

Georges has had his share of trouble at the store. One day, in the middle of fall, he discovered the basement flooded under two metres of water. He recalls having to swim through the basement fully clothed to unblock the drain! A few years later, his neighbours were digging some foundations, but didn't realize that the work was endangering the structural integrity of the store. Georges was behind the counter, when a client came in and told him the door wouldn't shut. It took a few seconds to click—then he realized something was very wrong. "Everybody out!" he yelled. Five minutes later, half the building collapsed. Miraculously, no one was injured. And, by chance, there was a vacant store across the street that they were able to move into the very next day!

Today, Georges's sons, Marc and Jean, are the fourth generation of Lanouettes to be at the helm of the business. And Georges is finally enjoying a well-earned retirement—at the helm of his magnificent yacht!

55 years and counting

Gérard Harvey
Replenishment Expert, Rona Le Rénovateur,
Sainte-Adèle, Quebec

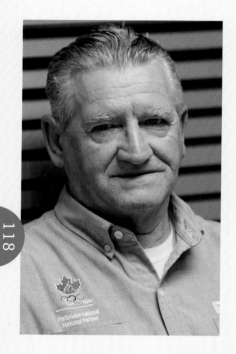

Gérard Harvey has been the buyer for the Riopels' Rona store for the past 14 years. It's a job that keeps him on his toes. A typical day starts with a tour of the warehouses, where he takes note of what needs to be reordered and makes sure everything is in its proper place. He then places his orders and serves his clients, while keeping one eye on the lumberyard.

Gérard started working in 1953, when he joined his father, a bricklayer in Amos in Abitibi. But after falling from the scaffolding one day, he decided he wasn't really cut out for that line of work! He went on to find a job in a lumberyard, receiving orders for materials. In those days, a 60-hour week was the norm, and a typical order of cement was a thousand 90-lb. bags—all of which had to be carried and loaded by hand. Gérard stuck it out, but it was when he started working in the store that he knew he had found where he wanted to be. At last, he could serve his clients while learning more about new materials. It wasn't as well paid as production line work, of course, but he says, "That sort of work is for robots!"

Work methods have changed considerably over the years. In the early days, it could take a whole morning to place a hardware order—the stock catalogue was 12 inches thick! The arrival of microfilm was revolutionary; a single eight-inch-square sheet could contain 200 pages of catalogue. And when computers finally made their appearance, Gérard found working with this new work tool a real pleasure.

Gérard can't say what he enjoys most about his job; he just loves it, plain and simple! At 71, he still works a 40-hour week and isn't yet thinking about quitting. What about slowing down? Perhaps... that would give him time to write a book—about his work!

TOWARDS THE END OF THE 1970s, the company introduced new concepts in product merchandising and layout, such as this model paint department. Prototype stores would follow the models to the letter.

A retail expert

Ro-Na therefore found itself in a situation where its growth was limited by the size of its members' stores. From buying group to selling group, Ro-Na would take yet another step towards becoming a retail expert. Because there was no other solution. It had to come up with the "perfect hardware store."

Management then created a 10-member team, with a special budget of $100 000, to take urgent action on this problem. For a few weeks there was a steady stream of specialists advising the company on presentation, architecture, decoration, and even consumer psychology! Ro-Na was undoubtedly one of the first retail businesses in Canada to seek this sort of expertise in the development of its store concepts.

Ro-Na's arrival on the retail scene proved highly successful. The special team proposed the construction of new facilities, buildings ranging in size from 8 000 to 12 000 sq. ft. (750 to 1 150 m²). Stores that were modern and up-to-date. Well-designed. Attractive. Stores whose products were displayed in a carefully planned layout to make life easier for customers.

All these stores would have to conform to a single model, so that Ro-Na customers would always be able to find their way around, whether they were at home or away. A pilot store was even set up inside the Boucherville

ONE OF THESE PROTOTYPE HARDWARE STORES was J.P. Lauzon, in Chambly, which opened in 1976.

administrative centre. Many dealers would visit each day, with dreams of being able to swap their sometimes antiquated little shops for this store of the future.

Still, many seemed hesitant. And it is not difficult to understand why. For so many years, they had fought to keep themselves afloat. Many of them were more survivors than conquerors. They were proud to belong to Ro-Na. They were proud to be able to say that they, too, were "rare birds." But although they needed to take that step forward, they had to be convinced. They had to be told: "The challenge is no longer to just hold fast; the challenge now is to grow."

To encourage these dealers to get on board with the new stores, Ro-Na set up financing for its dealers. Through agreements established with the Provincial Bank and the Caisse de dépôt et placement du Québec, Ro-Na started offering credit, loans, and mortgages at attractive rates. Teams of specialists travelled the length and breadth of Quebec, assisting the dealers with negotiating their financing, and with building and setting up the new stores.

The first "perfect hardware stores" opened their doors before the end of 1976, less than a year after the conference in Sainte-Adèle, and every time, it was an occasion for the whole neighbourhood, even the whole town, to celebrate.

The wheels of growth were turning ever faster. The new stores drew more clients whose needs had to be met. Ro-Na added two new product lines: plumbing supplies and construction materials, which until that time had been

The *dépanneur*

Gerardo Marasco

Quincaillerie Jean Hébert, Rona L'Express, Montreal, Quebec

Quincaillerie Jean Hébert is nestled between a cosy little café and a trendy boutique on Mont-Royal Avenue in Montreal.

Entering this cheerful pell-mell, located in the heart of Montreal's hip Plateau area, you immediately feel at home. In fact, it is literally steps away from home for many of the customers, who do most of their local errands on foot.

This is a no-frills store: they sell paint, the basics for beginner do-it-yourselfers, and anything you might need when moving house. Oh, and they also rent bikes! The owner, Gerardo Marasco, jokingly refers to it as his "dépanneur," or convenience store.

Just as this part of the city has changed over the years, so has the clientele. Once a working-class neighbourhood, it is now home to a trendier, wealthier set, and it's not unusual to see well-known faces in the store.

Gerardo recalls when he started working here as a young student. His father, who ran a shoe repair shop across the street, had heard they were looking for someone. New to the hardware business, Gerardo learned on the job, and his interest grew with every new exhibition or trade show that he visited with his boss. "It was really exciting!" he remembers. He was promoted to manager/buyer in the mid 1980s and finally acquired the business in 1990.

In 2001, Gerardo updated the inside of the store, which involved major renovation work. But he had a lot of support from Rona. He adds proudly, "Rona has a special place in my heart!"

Last year, he won the paint booking contest, which earned him a trip to the Vancouver Olympic Games. Three exciting days of hockey, curling, speed skating, and medal ceremonies. The atmosphere was electric; in short, "the experience of a lifetime!"

1978

In 1978, a faint glimmer of hope dawned in the Middle East. Following Anwar El Sadat's audacious visit to Jerusalem the previous year, peace negotiations were entered into between Israel and Egypt, the first Arab nation to embark on such a path. In early September, U.S. President Jimmy Carter invited Sadat and Menachem Begin to Camp David, the presidential country retreat. After 13 days of tense negotiations, accords were signed stipulating the withdrawal of Israel from the Sinai, and the establishment of a rather vaguely defined "Palestinian national entity." Sadat and Begin would go on to receive the Nobel Peace Prize, but Egypt would find itself isolated in the Arab world and would eventually be expelled from the Arab League, as it was felt that Sadat had abandoned the historical claims of the Palestinians.

November 18 was the date of the Jonestown massacre in Guyana, an event that shocked the world. More than 900 members of a U.S.-based cult led by Jim Jones, including 276 children, died after ingesting a drink laced with cyanide. It was considered to be a mass suicide, although the extent to which the victims had consented could not be established with any certainty, as some of them had clearly been shot.

1979

International attention was focused on Iran at the start of 1979. In the face of huge public demonstrations, the Shah's regime crumbled, allowing his fiercest opponent, Ayatollah Khomeini, to establish in Tehran a particularly austere and rigid Islamic republic. In November, Islamic militants stormed the U.S. embassy in Tehran and took about 50 people hostage.

Iran's neighbour Afghanistan captured the headlines at the end of the year, when Soviet tanks rolled into the country to support a shaky pro-Soviet government. This event signaled the beginning of a "second Cold War," with the United States suspending deliveries of wheat and technology to the USSR, resuming deliveries of arms to dictator Zia-ul-Haq's Pakistan, and supporting the Afghan rebels in their struggle.

At the same time, the U.S. saw what it deemed to be a Soviet threat in dangerous proximity to its own borders. In Nicaragua, the Sandinista National Liberation Front overthrew the bloody dictatorship of Anastasio Somoza in July and established a junta government that represented a broad spectrum of political ideologies, ranging from moderate to communist.

All these events would play a role in the rise of Ronald Reagan to the U.S. presidency the following year.

1980

The big story of the year, in Canada, was, of course, the referendum on sovereignty-association, held on May 20, in Quebec. The Parti québécois government had unveiled the question the previous December, at a time when the minority Conservative government in Ottawa, led by Joe Clark, appeared to be rather weak. In February, however, Pierre Trudeau's Liberals returned to power with a majority, winning 74 of 75 seats in Quebec. It was in that context that the referendum campaign got under way, and it was characterized by citizen engagement on an unprecedented scale, on both the NO and the YES sides. The ballots were cast on May 20, with the NO side winning close to 60% of the votes. Speaking in front of an impassioned crowd, René Lévesque declared, "*A la prochaine fois!*" (Until next time!)...

In January, Canadian ambassador to Iran Ken Taylor and the embassy staff helped six American diplomats escape from the American embassy, which had been in the hands of Iranian revolutionaries for 14 months. Taylor was immediately hailed as a hero in the United States.

On April 12, Terry Fox, a young Canadian athlete who had a prosthetic leg as a result of a battle with cancer, set out on his "Marathon of Hope," which was to take him from one end of the country to the other. However, illness forced him to stop after 143 days, by which time he had travelled 5 373 kilometres, an average of more than 37 kilometres per day. His extraordinary feat touched the hearts of Canadians everywhere and inspired them to take up his cause.

July marked the opening of the Moscow Olympic Games, which were boycotted by more than 50 nations over the Soviet invasion of Afghanistan. The United States and many of its allies, including Canada (but few European countries), as well as most Arab countries, participated in the boycott.

On a much more serious note, an Iran-Iraq war erupted in September. Amid concerns over fallout from the Iranian Revolution, both the USSR along with the U.S. and its allies supported Iraqi dictator Saddam Hussein, while Israel, Syria, and China sided with Iran. The war would last eight years.

ONLY A FEW YEARS AFTER IT WAS BUILT, the Nobel Street distribution centre was no longer big enough! It underwent several expansions, including this one in August 1976.

the exclusive domain of the lumber dealers and specialty businesses. But space was in short supply. This time, it was the distribution centre that was struggling to keep up with demand. So, the facility was expanded again. From 180 000 sq. ft., it grew to 286 000 sq. ft., then to 450 000 sq. ft. (16 700, 26 600, and 41 800 m^2, respectively) in the late 1970s, when a warehouse for construction materials, designed to allow trucks to drive right in so that they would be sheltered from the weather for loading and unloading, was added on to the main building.

Dazzling progress

In five years, from 1975 to 1980, the group's annual sales more than quadrupled, surging from $45.1 million to $204.5 million. Average sales per member grew at a similar rate, rising from $110 000 to $490 000 per year. Returns to members, consisting of annual rebates, interest on deposits, annual discounts and dividends, skyrocketed from $3.7 million to $12.1 million. The administrative and distribution centre on Nobel Street had become the nerve centre of a major company. With a staff of 360, it had five times more employees than when it opened.

This growth impacted every aspect of Ro-Na's activities, and the company also had to improve its management methods. The entire ordering system had to be redesigned. The dealers had always had a reference catalogue to use for placing their orders, in the form of a loose-leaf ring

binder. But the company now had 25 000 products, with more being added all the time. The catalogue had grown into a massive volume more than 30 cm thick, with a dozen different sections. Managing the catalogue was a cumbersome task for all concerned. On the one hand, new pages had to be produced constantly, and at an ever-faster pace. On the other, the dealers regularly had to replace outdated pages one by one. Gérard Harvey, a hardware dealer in Sainte-Adèle, recalls: "Placing an order would take up about half a day."

So, the old catalogue was retired and, in record time, a microfiche system was set up in all the stores. Each microfiche, which could be viewed with the help of a very easy-to-use device, contained 200 catalogue pages reduced to miniature size. The entire Ro-Na product range fit onto 20 of these microfiches. The method by which orders were sent was also revolutionized with the introduction of Telxon devices, a harbinger of the era of electronic data transmission to come. The Telxon device recorded data on a magnetic cassette then, using the phone line, transmitted orders that might include up to several hundred items in just a few seconds. It was estimated that for the average hardware store, the new system represented a time savings of 20 hours per week!

This dramatic development also turned Ro-Na into a major transport company. Shipments and deliveries to the dealers were now made by a fleet of close to 70 trucks,

The nuts and bolts of the job

José Jackman

Hardware Expert, Derrible SPM,
Saint-Pierre and Miquelon

When you hear the word "hardware," the first things that come to mind are probably nails, screws, nuts, and bolts. And if you're looking for any of these, José Jackman's the man who can help you—he's been in them for the past 27 years! It all began when his brother Jérémie, who was working in the auto parts department at the time, persuaded him to leave his job at the Saint-Pierre post office and come to work at Derrible.

Hardware might seem like a pretty straightforward business, but in Saint-Pierre it requires fluency in two languages: metric and imperial. On this island, where Europe meets and mingles with North America, you have to cater to everyone's needs. Apparently, repairing a Citroën can be quite a challenge when you only have imperial screws. Clients from France are stumped by the square-headed variety and sometimes come looking for José to ask him for "normal" ones!

The salty sea air presents a challenge, too, because it makes things rust. And being cut off from the rest of the world means having to keep more inventory on hand in case a storm rolls in and delays the boat—especially when the standard delivery time from mainland France is a month and a half! Happily, all orders from Rona arrive within a week.

There are days when it seems as though the island's residents have all conspired together to ask José for things he doesn't have in stock. But these are the small day-to-day challenges that make his work interesting, and, when you enjoy serving customers as much as José does, moving heaven and earth to meet their needs is a pleasure!

ONE OF THE ENORMOUS ORDER CATALOGUES used by the dealers, dating back to the 1960s, preserved by the Morency family of Quebec City.

A FLEET OF RONA TRUCKS, IN 1975. Employees of the shipping department and truck drivers strike a pose.

including 25 tractor trailers that criss-crossed Quebec. Each of these trucks proudly displayed the rare Ro-Na bird, like so many mobile billboards, and each year the distance they travelled was the equivalent of 40 trips around the world.

The excitement in the air at Ro-Na was contagious. I could feel it too. I had been there for seven or eight months, and I wanted to do more than just find the most attractive price. I wanted to be in on this adventure, but at that point I felt more like a spectator than a player. I therefore requested a meeting with André Dion, and I confided to him that what I wanted to do was market research. But I had barely had time to produce a few studies before he suggested that I take on the role of managing a new department dedicated to member services and staffed by specialists such as store planners, display designers, architects, and retail price and market analysts. I was 23 at the time.

New banners and a private brand

Back then—it was still the late 1970s—hardware stores were still a sort of hodgepodge where you would find building and renovation products jumbled up alongside sporting goods and even housewares. To make it easier for consumers to find their way around, and to counter the competition, Ro-Na decided to clean house. So it was that in 1977, the decision was made to create two new specialized banners. Ro-Na Hardware would remain the group's flagship, but two new divisions were added: Ro-Na Sports and Le Rénovateur Ro-Na.

Approximately 30 dealers who had a large quantity of sporting goods in their stores adopted the Ro-Na Sports banner. Others opened a second store under the banner, while continuing with their hardware operations. Le Rénovateur Ro-Na, on the other hand, was intended for renovation professionals. By 1978, it would have more than 80 outlets. To stay in step with these changes, Ro-Na's board of directors was expanded to include 12 members.

In the meantime, the Ro-Na dealers' conventions had become something of a tradition, and each year's event was bigger and more lavish than the last. In 1979, the Manoir Richelieu, perched high above the St. Lawrence River, provided a magical setting for their meeting. That convention, too, would lead to some important measures being taken to increase visibility for the group. At that time, the decision was made to distribute promotional catalogues in every region, to quadruple payments to the advertising fund, and to place special emphasis on the private brand.

As will be recalled, the idea of a private label had been put forward by Napoléon Piotte some years previously, when a purchasing alliance was formed with four partners in English Canada.

The introduction of Ro-Na brand products, such as tools and accessories of all kinds, was a demonstration of

IN 1978, FRENCH REPRESENTATIVES OF SAPEC visited the Marchands Ro-Na during an annual meeting of the Quincailliers Grossistes Associés held at Château Frontenac in Quebec City.

Ro-Na's power; it was proof that the business had achieved the size and credibility needed to turn its name into a brand that inspired confidence and stood as a synonym for quality. When the first Ro-Na brand products were released, they were an immediate success, and their number would continue to grow.

Morency passes the torch

In the early 1980s, Ro-Na entered a new period of growth. Up until then, the company's development had been essentially organic, in that growth had occurred autonomously, through the recruitment of new members, through the expansion of its distribution capacity, through its dealers' investments, and through enhancements to their stores. Only one very modest acquisition had been made several years earlier, that of Delino, a small distributor in the Quebec City area.

"We are going to have to be more active in terms of acquisitions if we are to continue to grow," said the president, Charles Morency. That was the thought he expressed when he resigned from his position. The year was 1981. At the age of 68, he wanted to step down and allow the next generation to take his place. During his 13 years at the helm, Ro-Na underwent remarkable development. Charles Morency would be forever known in the company's history as the man who propelled Ro-Na into the modern age, transforming its culture, its organization, and its management

A decorator's touch at your service

Sylvie Bourbonnais

Decorating Expert, Centre de Rénovation Île-Perrot, Rona Le Quincaillier, Île-Perrot, Quebec

Sylvie has always loved beautiful things. She enjoys painting, drawing, photography, and, of course, decorating. Her former career as a nurse didn't provide her with enough of a creative outlet, so she changed direction to focus on her passion: other people's decor! For the past seven years, she has been putting her talent to work for the clients of the Île-Perrot Rona store. She splits her time between in-store consultations, which are usually fairly short—clients ask for her advice on colours, styles, window treatments—and visits to people's homes—where she might have to redecorate the whole house!

Sylvie says that a decorator's work often consists in simply helping people to make choices or adding small details that make a big difference. In general, she finds that people have more taste than they think. And if she occasionally has to act as a mediator between husband and wife, or parent and teenager, the secret to creating a classy decor is always... knowing how to listen well. She finds that her experience as a nurse comes in useful when dealing with the different dynamics between people!

Sylvie draws inspiration from the world around her. A sun-kissed golden wheat field against a trendy charcoal-grey autumn sky might become her palette for a living room. The most rewarding aspect of her job is when she establishes a good relationship with a client and is invited to come back and design another room. Her dream is not to decorate a sumptuous home with an unlimited budget but to use her creative flair to offer clients a well-designed space that reflects their personality and tastes. A place they can call home.

Social involvement •

PHILANTHROPY HAS ALWAYS EXISTED AT RONA. IT DERIVES ITS ESSENCE FROM THE COMPANY'S VALUES OF SHARING AND OF SOCIAL GOOD. IT COMES NATURALLY. THE MERCHANTS SUPPORT NUMEROUS LOCAL CAUSES, AND THE COMPANY IS INVOLVED WITH LOCAL AND NATIONAL CAUSES.

❶ For more than 15 years, Rona has been supporting Les Impatients, an organization that provides a place for therapeutic artistic expression.

❷ The Rona Foundation helps Toujours Ensemble, a community organization that provides support to youth through a variety of initiatives, including homework help, lunch, and bursary programs, to help young people follow their dreams and reach their full potential.

❸ In 1986, on an initiative by Rona, more than 5 000 seniors living in residences in the Montreal area and in the Centre-du-Québec region visited the Montreal Botanical Garden.

The Rona Foundation has been making a difference since 1998. The Foundation combats school dropout rates and illiteracy among youths between the ages of 12 and 30. It promotes employability for youths from underprivileged backgrounds by, for example, supporting organizations that provide vocational training to youths so that they can go on to practice a trade or profession, or by creating homework club programs, scholarships, mentoring opportunities, etc. The Foundation raises funds, mainly from its suppliers, and redistributes them among registered charitable organizations whose activities reflect the Foundation's mission, to encourage these young people to believe in themselves and in life, for their own benefit as well as that of their communities. Golf Days and chocolate sales in the hardware stores are some of the other initiatives, and the list keeps on growing. In 2008, an internal campaign was launched to encourage employees to contribute either to United Way or to the Rona Foundation through deductions made at the source.

In addition to these activities are donations to various institutions, such as Les Impatients, an organization that has held a special place at the heart of the Foundation for over 15 years. Les Impatients offers art-therapy workshops for people with psychiatric disorders. Their mission is to help people living with mental health issues express themselves through art and to promote exchanges with the community by sharing their creations. Still incredulous, managing director Lorraine Palardy describes how, "In 1994, Robert Dutton, the picture of elegance, walked into our semi-basement with its orange-painted pipes. He decided to stay and support us." The first fundraising initiative was intended to be a one-shot deal; Rona would supply shovels and tools with which Les Impatients would create an exhibition to be presented at the Musée d'art contemporain de Montréal. One thing led to the other, and many projects later, their relationship continues. "Robert forced me to enlarge my scope. To express and fulfill my dream." This dream was for

Philanthropy at Rona

Les Impatients to establish a presence everywhere where mental health was an issue, in psychiatric hospitals, throughout Quebec. And Lorraine adds, "We can do far more through the freedom that Rona affords us than within the limits imposed by traditional sponsorships."

In the areas of education and research, among the institutions Rona supports are the Chair in Ethical Management at HEC, the International Chair in Life Cycle Assessment at the École Polytechnique de Montréal, and the Chair in Logistics Management at UQAM; institutions whose research closely reflects the core concerns of the group.

Each year, the Multiple Sclerosis Society of Canada's Rona Bike Tour attracts a wide participation. In 2009, Rona was able to raise $165 923 in donations. Over the last 10 years, including all the money that has been collected through all the teams' sponsorship and fundraising activities, Rona has donated a total of $1.6 million.

Rona's social involvement also extends to the field of health, through their support of the Montreal Heart Institute and the Sainte-Justine UHC Foundation.

Various heritage organizations also benefit from Rona's assistance, including Saint Joseph's Oratory, who receive funds for the preservation of their sites.

Going back several years, but still fresh in many people's memories, was the support given, in 1986, to the La fleur de l'Âge d'Or organization, which, over a seven-day period, brought thousands of seniors on outings to the Montreal Botanical Gardens, and, in 1989, the assistance provided to homeless people through the Dernier recours organization.

While it is impossible to compile an exhaustive list of all of the causes the company has been involved with, it is even more difficult to enumerate those that have received support from the broader Rona community. Hats off to all the local merchants in neighbourhoods throughout Canada for the unceasing commitment they have shown since the outset! The Shaved Head Challenge for Leucan, the sale of holiday cards for UNICEF by all the merchants in Canada, Réno-Dépôt dream teams that carried out renovation projects for neighbourhood organizations, help with the construction of a local skating rink, the Relay for Life event for the Canadian Cancer Society... just some of the thousands of actions each year, involving thousands of Rona employees.

❹ In 2007, to brighten the lives of young patients, Calgary's Rona Home & Garden store donated tables and chairs to the Alberta Children's Hospital to furnish the gazebos and gardens of the facility.

❺ André Dion receives a scouting award from Governor General of Canada Jeanne Sauvé for Rona's "La Fleur de l'Âge d'Or" project in 1986.

❻ With support from the Rona Foundation, the Vancouver YWCA's Emma's Child Care centre provides assistance to teen mothers by caring for their children while they complete their high school education.

❼ In May and June 2008, the Durand hardware store in Quebec City took part in the Shaved Head Challenge to benefit Leucan. In all, 43 heads were shaved and $26 000 was raised!

Lifestyles •

REFLECTING TODAY'S LIFESTYLES AND SOCIETY, THE NEW STUDIO BY RONA STORES BEAR NO RESEMBLANCE WHATSOEVER TO THE VERY FIRST HARDWARE STORES, EXCEPT, OF COURSE, THAT THEIR GOAL IS STILL TO BETTER RESPOND TO CUSTOMERS' NEEDS!

❶ In 1983, Pierre Piotte opened a 900-sq. ft. prototype Ambiance Boutique in his Quincaillerie Modelectric hardware store in the Town of Mount Royal. It offered curtains, wallpaper, decorative objects, and a fully equipped bathroom. A decor professional divided her time between the boutique and visiting clients in their home.

When Nicole Plamondon joined Rona in 1987, the concept of combining home decor within a hardware store was unheard of. Nicole was the first woman hired as a director at Rona. Her mission: to develop home decor boutiques. These would eventually become the Ambiance boutiques, located within the hardware stores themselves. With her colleague Michel Mérineau, she began by setting her sights on people buying paint. If they wanted paint, it had to be because they were renovating or decorating. They would also need advice, materials, and perhaps even accessories and furniture. Ambiance thus became not only a shop in itself, but also a service boutique that created spin-offs throughout the store.

Today, although Nicole chooses products that reflect an emerging trend within a theme she has devised, she works with the designers as a group to select products and make decisions, particularly when it comes to promotional material, since each designer knows his or her market best. There are

about 50 Ambiance boutiques. They all provide interior decoration and design services. This, once again, is what sets Rona apart from its competitors: service. And trust. "When I go to my hairstylist, I trust her. I know she'll give me a good cut. The same relationship of trust has to exist between the decorator and the client. And it also applies to the person selling the materials," she adds.

The stores also have decorating tools and elements to inspire customers. They are called Rona by Design. As Normand Dumont says:

"In Canada, people are not as homogeneous [as in Europe]. There are people who live in the city, there are people who live in the country. But there are major trends that can be identified each year. We look at this with specialized trend-watchers. Then we have to find things that will reflect the overall needs of our customers. Everyone is different, everyone has a personality, and it's precisely through Rona by Design that we can express Rona's personality."

Of course, not all trends can be accommodated in one store. Choices have to be made. The Rona by Design concept is like an off-the-rack clothing collection that offers three distinct looks to suit three different lifestyles: one is ultra modern, another, more classic, and the last has a country flavour—or Global Village Style, Oasis Style, and Spirit Style.

The concept being offered is a turnkey solution. The mission of the Marketing and Customer Innovations sector is to create projects that, through the choice of objects and materials, express the essence of each of these lifestyles.

Bathrooms, kitchens, and living rooms are first developed as rough layouts. A lot of information has to be collected and compared before they begin to take form. Trips, visits to shows, reading, and internet research turn up elements that, at first glance, might seem like a real mixed bag: colours, materials, transparency effects, wood,

Keeping pace with the evolution of the home

ceramic tiles, glossy finishes, lacquered effects, sustainable development, metals, gilding, contrasting colours, a dominant vibrant yellow, the return of electric blue...

Then the styles thus articulated and detailed are presented to the merchandising team so that the merchandisers can locate the products the style team needs. Usually, buyers specialize in a product category, such as fittings and faucets, lighting, etc. But, in this case, things work differently. Everyone has to work together towards a common goal, the goal that each style team is seeking to achieve.

For the last five years, the Spring Show has provided a sneak peek at Rona by Design's latest creations. Like a cake recipe, on the backs of the cards is a list of all the accessories and materials needed to carry out the project. The challenge is to offer fashionable combinations at affordable prices.

In 2009, a new concept was born: the Studio by Rona stores. Professional painters, interior designers, and customers alike would all receive a personalized service. Clients would be offered free consultation, while professionals could take advantage of shipping areas, exclusive access to paint and stain services, and adapted opening hours. Paint, wallpaper, floor coverings, mouldings, window treatments: every decorating need could be found under one roof. The colour centre lets customers mix and match thousands of colours, identify the best possible combinations, and manipulate large-size colour swatches. A first in Canada!

❷ The first Ambiance Boutiques were officially launched in 1988. They offered a full range of decorating products as well as advice from professional designers.

❸ One of the first 30 Ambiance Boutiques in the early years of their existence.

❹ A Rona by Design "Spirit Style" bathroom, set up at the 2009 Spring Show, held in November 2008, in Toronto.

❺ The "Global Village Style" is one of three looks offered as part of the Rona by Design concept. The two others are "Oasis Style" and "Spirit Style."

❻ The new Studio by Rona boutiques.

IN AUGUST 1981, THE MARCHANDS RO-NA HONOUR THEIR OUTGOING PRESIDENT, Charles Morency, with a bronze plaque and a recital by Jean Lapointe at the Château Frontenac.

FOLLOWING THE DEPARTURE OF CHARLES MORENCY IN 1981, Henri Drouin took over as chairman of the board, and André Dion became the CEO.

in a way that equipped the group with everything it needed to rival the largest companies of its time.

The role of president then fell to Henri Drouin, the dealer from Abitibi who joined the movement in 1965 and who had been a member of the group's board of directors for the previous six years. The role of chief executive officer was entrusted to André Dion, who continued his meteoric rise within the organization.

On August 22, a huge celebration was held at the Château Frontenac in Quebec City to honour Charles Morency. No fewer than 425 guests attended. When he walked onstage to thank the organizers for the many glowing tributes that had been paid to him, Morency said with his typical modesty: "Looking at the few accomplishments that you have credited to me, are they not in reality the fruits of the collective endeavour to which you all have contributed?"

Ro-Na makes its first major acquisition

The torch changed hands, but the company's path continued in the same direction: straight ahead.

In 1981, Ro-Na created a subsidiary that would handle operations for the group's credit card, the Carte Clé. In less than a year, more than 53 000 cards were issued, generating sales of more than $10 million.

The acquisition in 1982 of Botanix, a group of 36 nurseries with annual sales of $18 million, was a major coup. The idea was seen as a natural extension of Ro-Na's customers' home improvement projects. Indeed, interior renovation often led to outdoor design and landscaping work.

The project was an ambitious one. It was not simply a matter of adding a banner or integrating another dealer. It meant dealing with another organization, another corporate culture, another line of business with substantially different characteristics, including activity that was seasonal in nature.

The acquisition would prove to be a valuable learning experience in how to integrate another organization while preserving its unique character. This was stated clearly in the 1982 annual report:

> "These dealers are different in the sense that they work in a different line of business. Consequently, Ro-Na does not plan to impose the same business methods as those that apply to the other banners. On the contrary, we must respect this difference and find a certain autonomy in their market penetration strategy."

In the meantime, the Ro-Na Sports banner underwent a name change to become Podium. Experience had shown that the name "Ro-Na" was too closely associated with hardware to lend itself to the sale of sporting goods. (As it turned out, the sporting goods line would be dropped in 1991).

BOTANIX WAS BOUGHT BY LE GROUPE RO-NA IN 1982.
Through this acquisition, Ro-Na took over thirty-six nurseries, including Ferme Florale in Saint-Bruno-de-Montarville.

The successful rollout of the "perfect hardware store" prompted Ro-Na to look for ways to constantly improve its stores in order to reach out to a broader clientele and meet the new needs of consumers. And so it was that, in 1983, Ro-Na developed its Ambiance boutiques. These were self-contained areas set up inside existing stores, and their focus was interior decorating. The boutiques sold wallpaper, draperies, and curtains, with decor specialists to provide expert advice. This was another concept that was instrumental to Ro-Na's growth. Like the Botanix garden centres, the Ambiance boutiques helped the company to connect with female consumers. Ro-Na was evolving in terms of its positioning. Hardware could be more than just a "guy thing." The company now sought to appeal to women and couples as well.

Stock market debut

Ro-Na was experiencing torrid growth. It exceeded even the grandest dreams that Rolland and Napoléon may have had. But, once again, capital was needed to sustain that sort of pace. In the spring of 1984, the board of directors was given the task of restructuring the company's share capital.

The project was championed by André Dion, who had recently been appointed to the position of president. After two years in that role, Henri Drouin wanted to lighten his workload so that he could devote more time to his own store, and he then embarked on a lengthy tenure as

1981

At least three assassination attempts made the headlines in 1981. In March, Ronald Reagan, the newly-elected president of the United States, was targeted by a mentally disturbed man who made an attempt on his life as a way to get the attention of movie actress Jodie Foster. In May, before a crowd of 20 000 people who had gathered to see him, Pope John Paul II was struck by three bullets fired by a far-right Turkish nationalist who was hiding in the throng and whose motives remain a mystery. Then, in October, Egyptian President Anwar Sadat was assassinated during a military parade by soldiers with Muslim fundamentalist affiliations.

There was widespread surprise in Quebec on April 13: after losing its referendum the year before, René Lévesque's PQ government was returned to power with close to 50% of the popular vote (it garnered 41% in 1976) and twice as many seats at Claude Ryan's Liberals. Ryan would step down as leader of the Liberal Party the following year.

December saw a military *coup d'état* in Poland. Faced with a massive popular opposition movement spearheaded by Lech Walesa's Solidarity, General Jaruzelski seized power, with Moscow's support. Solidarity was banned, and its leaders imprisoned. Clashes between the army and strikers claimed many lives. The United States imposed economic sanctions on the Polish government.

1982

On April 2, 1982, Argentina invaded the Falkland Islands (or Malvinas), a British possession that it nonetheless considered part of its own national territory. Great Britain sent a fleet to take back the chain of islands, located 13 000 kilometres from London, and Argentine troops surrendered on June 14. This bitter defeat signaled the beginning of the end for the dictatorial military junta in power at the time, at whose hands Argentina had suffered a reign of terror lasting several long years.

On June 6, Israel sent 60 000 troops and hundreds of tanks into southern Lebanon, for the purpose of driving out the Palestinian fighters responsible for the

relentless commando raids being staged on Israeli territory. Besieged in West Beirut under heavy shelling, Yasser Arafat's men admitted defeat on August 21 and fled into various Arab countries.

But Israel's military victory was tarnished by the moral step backwards taken by the Jewish state, whose troops allowed the massacre of more than a thousand Palestinian civilians by Lebanese Christian militias in refugee camps under Israeli control.

In Canada, the Trudeau government "repatriated" all constitutional powers from London and called a vote on a Charter of Rights and Freedoms 📷. The Quebec government would continue in its refusal to agree to these amendments, which had been made against its wishes.

1983

Once again, the world seemed to be plunged back into the Cold War. U.S. President Ronald Reagan, a neo-liberal Republican, described the USSR as an "evil empire," and in so doing, prompted the resumption of the arms race 📷. In addition to the Strategic Defense Initiative, a missile defense program almost straight from the pages of science fiction and aptly nicknamed "Star Wars," Reagan set up missile bases in Western Europe (the "Euromissiles"), despite massive protest demonstrations. He vigorously supported the anti-Soviet rebels in Afghanistan and the anti-Sandinista *Contras* in Nicaragua, going so far as to proceed with the mining of Nicaraguan harbours, in clear violation of international law. He sent the Marines to the island of Grenada to overthrow a pro-Cuban government.

There was further bloodshed in the Middle East. The UN peacekeeping force that had been sent to civil-war-torn Lebanon suffered a devastating blow when a horrific suicide bombing in October claimed the lives of close to 300 soldiers, 241 of them American. The international peacekeeping force withdrew, leaving a sorely divided country to descend into chaos.

A dash of flair

Grant McKinnon

Pacific Building Systems, Rona Building Centre,
Duncan, British Columbia

Pacific Building Systems celebrated its 50th anniversary along with the opening of its fourth Rona store in 2009. It all began when Grant's grandfather, a Scottish immigrant, arrived on Vancouver Island and started building houses there. His son and six associates opened a small store in Cobble Hills. It was a gamble—they only had around 18 potential customers at the time! Though there were days they didn't ring up a single sale, he managed to build a strong reputation based on good service and eventually bought out his partners. In the early 1970s, he began to expand his activities and opened a truss plant, which today exports around the globe, as far afield as Japan, Israel, Chile, and Iceland.

The first buying group Pacific Building Systems joined was Howden, where they stayed until the mid 1980s. The following decade, they teamed up with Timber Mart. Then, in 1994, Beaver Lumber approached them with a proposal to buy a store in Duncan. It was a great opportunity, so they changed groups. When Molson sold Beaver Lumber to Home Hardware, the McKinnons didn't have much of a choice; they stayed with Home Hardware for five years, but it wasn't the best structure for them. In 2006, they moved on to Rona, whose model was closer to their neighbourhood store concept, and this took them to a new level in retail sales. Not only were Rona's stores much more oriented towards women but, as Grant says, the move also brought with it "some French-Canadian business flair to a bunch of BC contractors."

Grant started out in the trade as a young boy, doing all sorts of odd jobs in his father's factory. He went on to earn a degree in Forestry at the University of British Columbia and continued to work in that field as an engineer until 1992. When the opportunity arose to buy the family business, he grabbed it. Grant hates routine and loves the freedom of owning his own company. Above all, though, he is tremendously proud of what they have achieved!

chairman of the board of directors, during which time the company continued to benefit from his wisdom and sound business sense.

Dion was perfect for the position of president and chief executive officer. He was the driving force behind the reforms that were introduced under Charles Morency and continued by Drouin. His appointment was seen as confirmation of what was already an established fact.

His share capital restructuring plan was an organization-wide revolution. The minutes of the meeting held on May 17, 1984 stated unequivocally:

> "Ro-Na is going to have to use profits to operate, its shares are going to have to be profitable, unlike the current situation; [...] it may therefore prove necessary to completely change the philosophy that has guided Ro-Na's destiny thus far."

After what the minutes describe as "extensive discussion," the board gave its agreement in principle to the project. The plan consisted of two parts. First, Ro-Na would issue some $2 million worth of common and voting shares that would be available exclusively to member dealers, executives, and employees of the company. The proceeds from this issue would be used to refund members' security deposits and redeem a portion of the preferred shares they owned. For the second part of the plan, Ro-Na would proceed simultaneously with a public issue of $15 million

IN 1983, THE RO-NA SPORTS BANNER BECAME PODIUM, as seen on this Royaume du Sport store on the South Shore of Montreal in Longueuil.

worth of preferred shares. The proceeds from that issue would help to reduce the company's bank loans.

Both issues would qualify for the Stock Savings Plan (SSP), introduced a few years previously by the Minister of Finance, Jacques Parizeau, to encourage investment in Quebec businesses by the people of the province, through tax reductions applicable to the purchase of shares.

The project was ratified by the board of directors on September 12 and, six days later, a communication went out to "all members of all banners":

> "Your board of directors has approved [...] a resolution that will allow not only the shareholders among our members, but also their staff and the staff at our head office, to acquire shares. The success and the future of our companies depend on greater involvement by all those who work to ensure that success and that future. As our staff's participation in the share capital of our group is facilitated by the tax advantages put in place by the Quebec government, there is every reason to encourage it."

On November 14, 1984, André Dion and Henri Drouin were on the floor of the Montreal Stock Exchange for the ceremony to launch the new Ro-Na preferred shares.

The operation was a manifest success. "It took 45 years to accumulate $16 million in our company, and only a

1984

India was the focus of considerable international attention in 1984. In June, Prime Minister Indira Gandhi sent the army to storm the Sikhs' holiest shrine, the Golden Temple in Amritsar, which had been occupied by Sikh separatists. The operation claimed hundreds of lives and caused extensive damage. In retaliation, two of Prime Minister Gandhi's Sikh bodyguards assassinated her on October 31.

In December, one of the worst industrial disasters of all time occurred in the city of Bhopal, where a toxic gas leak from a Union Carbide pesticide plant claimed thousands of victims and would continue to affect people to this day. The official death toll was set at more than 20 000, with hundreds of thousands of others suffering varying degrees of injury.

In Canada, the September 4 federal election catapulted Brian Mulroney's Progressive Conservative Party to power with a landslide majority government, the largest in Canadian history (211 out of 282 seats). It was the first election to be held since the repatriation of the Constitution, against Quebec's wishes, in 1982, and the Liberals were crushed in Quebec, winning only 17 out of 58 seats. Mulroney pledged to bring Quebec into the Constitution "with honour and enthusiasm."

Marc Garneau became the first Canadian to fly on a mission to space, aboard the Challenger space shuttle.

1985

In March 1985, Mikhail Gorbachev became General Secretary of the Communist Party of the Soviet Union. His emergence as leader ushered in a period of profound change, the greatest in the country's history, and would eventually lead to the complete dissolution of the Soviet Union. In November, international tensions eased suddenly when Gorbachev and Reagan held their first meeting in Geneva, where they discussed the arms race.

On March 21, Canadian Paralympic athlete Rick Hansen set out from Vancouver on his world tour, travelling the globe in a wheelchair to raise funds for spinal cord research. Over a period of 26 months, he would cover 40 000 kilometres and raise $26 million.

One of the most terrible tragedies in aviation history occurred on June 23, with the crash of an Air India jumbo jet travelling from Montreal to Bombay (Mumbai). A bomb placed on board by Sikh terrorists exploded when the plane was 9 500 metres above the Atlantic Ocean, killing 326 people.

In Quebec, the political scene was in turmoil. Premier René Lévesque resigned

and was succeeded as head of the Parti québécois by Pierre-Marc Johnson. Former Liberal leader Robert Bourassa, who had suffered a humiliating defeat in the 1976 election, made a spectacular comeback and won a decisive victory in the election held in December.

1986

The worst nuclear accident in history occurred on April 26, 1986. A meltdown in a reactor at the Chernobyl Nuclear Power Plant in Ukraine, then part of the Soviet Union, caused an explosion that lifted off the 2 000-tonne concrete slab covering the reactor 📷. Although an extremely dangerous radioactive cloud was spreading further and further out from the accident site, people living in the area were not alerted until 24 hours later, when an emergency evacuation was ordered, while hundreds of firefighters, miners, helicopter pilots, and other workers were dispatched to the site, without adequate protection, to contain the disaster. In the months that followed, 600 000 "liquidators" worked on the decontamination efforts, of whom close to 70 000 would die and 170 000 would be left with permanent disabilities. More than 250 000 people were evacuated. The radioactive cloud spread as far as Western Europe, although no one there was affected.

In October, a second summit meeting between Ronald Reagan and Mikhail Gorbachev on arms reduction, held in Reykjavik, Iceland, ended in failure, with the United States refusing the Soviet Union's demands to halt development on its Strategic Defense Initiative ("Star Wars").

Expo 86, a world exposition on transportation and communication, was held on a 173-acre (70-hectare) site in Vancouver from May 2 to October 30. It was a huge success, attracting more than 22 million visitors.

QUINCAILLERIE LACROIX ON MONK STREET IN MONTREAL.
The Le Quincailleur banner began
appearing on storefronts from 1984.

LE CHANTIER, the forerunner to Rona L'entrepôt.

few days to double that amount," read the annual report. Employees were the subject of a special appeal, and they were enthusiastic in their response. More than 60% of them became shareholders. President Henri Drouin wrote:

> "Among the general public and in the business world, the image projected by our group is so highly regarded that it is equalled only by the pride each one of us feels in belonging to it. If Ro-Na stirs us, as it sometimes does to the depths of our being, it is because Ro-Na is not only an organization, it is a veritable movement."

With this influx of funds, the company's working capital swelled that year from $14.3 million to $31 million, and shareholders' equity doubled, climbing from $16.0 million to $33.6 million. This public issue of shares heralded a change in philosophy and the emergence of a true business mindset focused on growth and the creation of value. That is the idea Henri Drouin would express when he spoke of the "transformation of our traditional buying group, with its emphasis on maximum returns to its members, into a distribution business that is both competitive and profitable, providing a maximum return on its shareholders' investment."

Nonetheless, while the operation was a great success, this first venture by Ro-Na into the stock market would be of relatively short duration. In 1991, the company would redeem all of the preferred shares listed on the stock exchange

and, for a time, Ro-Na would again be owned by its dealers and its employees exclusively.

This initial foray into the stock market demonstrated the lively interest that Ro-Na sparked among investors and the potential that existed with a public offering of shares. Next time, Ro-Na would go all the way, and instead of issuing non-voting preferred shares, it would issue common shares. But the situation at that time would be completely different, involving as it would a sharing of control by the dealers. We're not quite there yet...

The spectre of the big-box stores

While work on the share capital restructuring was progressing, also in 1984, two new banners were introduced. The distinction this time centred around the physical area of the stores: Le Quincailleur, for the small local hardware stores, and Le Chantier, for large-scale projects. With 45 000 sq. ft. (4 200 m²) of floor space, these were the first stores to which the "big-box" term could be applied. Ro-Na now had seven banners.

Here was an expression that was gradually making its way into the vocabulary of the trade—"big-box stores." The idea was as chilling as it was inspiring. It was said that these stores were popping up all over the United States. They were the big American retailers' answer for consumers in search of savings during the recession of the early 1980s. Just think of it. Gigantic stores. Measuring over

1987

1987 is a year that will long be remembered in the stock markets. In January, the Dow Jones Industrial Average surged to close above 2 000 points for the first time in its history, and it continued to ride this upward trend in the months that followed, topping 2 700 points in August. But then: crash! On October 19, the Dow Jones fell 22%. It was the largest single-day loss in the history of the New York Stock Exchange, and its effects were soon felt the world over (46% in Hong Kong, 42% in Australia, 11% in Toronto).

The United States and the Soviet Union reached an agreement on disarmament and would begin—finally!—to destroy their arsenals, under mutual supervision, as per the Intermediate-Range Nuclear Forces Treaty, signed on December 8.

In Canada, the Meech Lake Accord, signed in June by all provincial premiers and the prime minister, sought to bring Quebec back into the Canadian fold by recognizing it as a distinct society, and by granting to all provinces a constitutional veto and the right to opt out of any federal program in an area of provincial jurisdiction, with compensation.

In October, Canada and the United States reached an agreement on creating a free-trade area to liberalize the flow of goods and services between them. The Canada–United States Free Trade Agreement entered into effect on January 1, 1989.

1988

The 15th Olympic Winter Games were held in Calgary between February 13 and 28. Freestyle skiing made its debut as a demonstration sport. Despite the unbounded enthusiasm of its supporters, Canada failed to win a single gold medal, in a repeat of its performance at the Montreal games in 1976.

Global tensions would drop a few more notches in 1988. The Soviet Union announced in March that it would withdraw it troops from Afghanistan, putting an end to a conflict that had poisoned

international relations for close to 10 years. But Afghanistan's troubles were not over yet, as the anti-Soviet resistance was soon replaced by a war among competing Afghan factions.

Iraq and Iran signed a cease-fire in July after eight long years of ruthless war characterized by lethal gas attacks, the use of child soldiers, and bloody hand-to-hand fighting. Iraqi dictator Saddam Hussein was at that time a great friend of the West, which supplied him with the very chemicals needed to produce the deadly gases, then turned a blind eye when he used them on the Iraqis themselves. Worn out, the two belligerents reverted to their prewar positions, no further advanced after a conflict that had cost $500 billion and claimed a million lives...

Scandal erupted at the Seoul Olympic Games in September, when Canadian athlete Ben Johnson, world record holder for the men's 100-metre sprint, was stripped of his gold medal after failing a drug test.

1989

January ushered in what is perhaps the most important year in the second half of the 20th century. To everyone's amazement, the entire Soviet empire in Eastern Europe suddenly crumbled. Following Russia itself, where, in March, the first free elections since 1917 saw the reformers making huge gains, Poland held similar elections in August, which brought the Solidarity movement to power; in November, the Communist regime in Czechoslovakia was subsequently overthrown in the "Velvet Revolution." Also in November, in a dramatic turn of events, the East German government opened all the gates in the Berlin Wall, allowing a veritable, and unstoppable, tidal wave of people to stream through, amid unforgettable scenes of elation and emotion broadcast live on television to the entire world. The year ended with the brutal overthrow of Romanian dictator Nicolae Ceausescu, who, with his wife, was executed by a firing squad in December. Hungary would hold its own free elections the following year.

On the other side of the world, another significant, but far more violent, event occurred on June 4, when the Chinese government sent tanks to clear Tiananmen Square in central Beijing, which had been occupied for several weeks by thousands of protesters. An exact death toll has never been established, but estimates range anywhere from 300 to 2 000. The image of a protestor standing alone and unarmed before a column of tanks will forever be etched in our collective memory.

On March 23, the supertanker Exxon Valdez ran aground on a reef after setting out from Alaska, spilling 40 000 tonnes of

crude oil that eventually covered 7 000 km² of ocean and polluted 800 kilometres of coastline. It was one of the worst oil spills in history.

On December 6, the entire country was shaken to its core by the massacre of 14 women at the École polytechnique de Montréal, shot at point-blank range by a madman for no reason other than that they were women.

1990

The international spotlight was on South Africa in 1990. Following the legalization of the African National Congress (ANC), an organization that advocated armed struggle against apartheid, its leader, Nelson Mandela, was released after 27 years in prison. In June, apartheid in public places was, for all intents and purposes, abolished, and, in August, Mandela announced the end of the armed struggle against apartheid.

In Canada, the Meech Lake Accord was defeated when the provinces of Manitoba and Newfoundland refused to endorse the agreement by the deadline.

The infamous Oka Crisis erupted in July. An officer of the Sûreté du Québec was killed in an attack on the barricade erected by the Mohawks of Kanesatake to block expansion of the Oka golf course, which threatened to encroach on an ancestral Mohawk burial ground. It would take nearly three months of ongoing tension and the intervention of the Canadian Army to restore order.

On August 2, Iraq's army invaded Kuwait. Saddam Hussein, who had enjoyed the support of the West during his country's war against Iran, was roundly condemned by his erstwhile allies, who soon raised half a million troops to save Kuwait's oil reserves, while the United Nations Security Council authorized the use of force.

There were further astonishing developments in Germany. Less than a year after the fall of the Berlin Wall, the German Democratic Republic (GDR, or East Germany) ceased to exist, and Germany regained the unity it had lost in 1945.

ANDRÉ DION, PRESIDENT OF LE GROUPE RO-NA, and Élizabeth Murdoch, director general of Fercomat, during the acquisition announcement in Chicoutimi, in 1987.

PREPARING THE ORDERS.

150 000 sq. ft. (14 000 m²). The most basic of physical layouts, but more than 100 000 products on the shelves. A logistical and technological tour de force. And it was coming. Sooner or later, it would be here. If we did not prepare, we would be swept away by the groundswell.

In January 1985, accompanied by André Dion and Henri Drouin, I left for the southern U.S. to visit these giant stores. I would return fascinated by what I had seen… and convinced that Ro-Na would have to come up with a way to construct and manage similar renovation superstores. The companies behind the big-box stores were giants, businesses worth billions of dollars, next to which Ro-Na looked like no more than an insignificant handful of shopkeepers…

But shopkeepers who were bold and daring, as I well knew. I knew that the Ro-Na dealers were willing to venture off the beaten path in order to innovate, to find ways to set themselves apart from the rest of the market, and to continue to attract consumers to their stores. In any event, we had no choice. We were fundamentally different, and we had to own that difference and use it to our advantage. We would have to devise our own ways of doing things, even if it sometimes meant making mistakes.

In 1987, Ro-Na acquired Fercomat, an 85 000-sq. ft. (7 900 m²) distribution centre located in Chicoutimi. As a result, Ro-Na's sales grew by $25 million and its market share in the Saguenay-Lac-Saint-Jean region more than doubled, jumping from 11% to 25%.

The acquisition of a direct competitor: Dismat

It was, however, in 1988, on the eve of its 50th anniversary, that Ro-Na made the most important acquisition in its history thus far. Ro-Na struck hard. This was a direct competitor, a large company. A name that was almost an institution: Dismat. It was also a company in dire financial straits. Either it would be taken over, or it would go under. The fruit was ripe and it fell right into Ro-Na's hands. The transaction was finalized through a share for share exchange.

The Dismat dealers would have a 15% ownership stake in Ro-Na, whose sales shot up by $165 million. The 1988 annual report had this to say about the transaction: "The Ro-Na Group could not have given itself a more wonderful 50th birthday present. […] We must now build bridges between the fierce competitors of yesterday and the shareholders of today."

That was certainly an understatement…

On paper it was a monumental project, and it would yield the expected results. But it would not be easy. Dismat was a network of 97 dealers specializing in construction lumber, from framing to finishing, and in doors and windows. The transaction would put Ro-Na on a firm footing in this market, and would also put it in possession of one of the largest lumber and materials distribution centres in

TRACKING INVENTORY.

Full speed ahead, right to the top!

Henri Drouin
Former Merchant and Chairman of the Board

Twenty-one years as chairman of Rona's board of directors is quite an achievement. Henri Drouin's impressive track record is proof not only of his commitment to the company but also of the high esteem people have for him. Looking back, his was a fairly rapid rise to the top...

When Henri was a child, his father's family worked in the food wholesale business in the Abitibi region. In 1964, he completed his studies in business and was immediately hired by Loeb in Ottawa. He had just married. Less than a year later, however, his father, a Superior Court judge, told him of a hardware store up for sale in the town of Amos. What to do? Return to Abitibi... to the hardware business... with hardly any money? Curiosity finally got the better of him, and off he went, just to check it out. And there he stayed.

At that time, the store was being supplied by wholesalers in Montreal, Abitibi, and Ontario. But Henri and his associate soon got wind of Les Marchands en Quincaillerie Ltée. They met with Napoléon Piotte, who told them membership was out of the question... unless they could reach an agreement with another small hardware outlet in Amos who was already a member. As it turned out, the owner was happy to sell to them, and, in 1966, Drouin Allard Inc. became a Rona merchant.

Henri asked Napoléon to point out some stores on which he could model his own. One of the first he visited was a large store in the Plateau area of Montreal. What a disappointment! Drawers lined the walls from floor to ceiling and could only be reached by a rolling ladder, bare light bulbs hung from the ceiling... this store lagged behind the retail food industry—which understood how to attractively package, merchandise, and market products—by a good 15 or 20 years. André Dion, Rona's president at the time, used to say, "The hardware industry is like a car drawn by horses on a highway!" So Henri went ahead and invented his own store concept, a few years before Rona was to launch its now-famous prototypes.

In 1966, Henri also became co-owner of a food store; in 1971, when his associate in the hardware business died, he bought up his partner's shares; in 1973, he purchased a large retail space in downtown Amos, which he turned into a 15 000-sq. ft. Rona store, complete with a large sports section.

Perhaps it was the young man's passion that compelled Charles Morency to offer him a seat on the board of directors in 1976. Whatever the reason, things again moved quickly for Henri. In 1980, he was appointed vice-chairman of the board, and in 1981 he took over as chairman until 2002. During those years he also stood in as acting company president between André Dion's departure in 1990 and Robert Dutton's official nomination in 1992.

What would Henri say makes him most proud? "Seeing and being able to help individuals grow." He noted that "The ones who made it have become pretty competent businesspeople." And perhaps also "to have given a guy like Robert Dutton the chance to take charge of the business and to fully exploit its potential."

135

RECEIVING GOODS.

CHECKING GOODS BEFORE
THEY ARE SHIPPED OUT.

Canada, a warehouse covering more than 225 000 sq. ft. (21 000 m²) in Sainte-Catherine, a suburb to the south of Montreal, near the St. Lawrence Seaway. The place was enormous—no fewer than 15 railway cars could fit inside. This would be Ro-Na's distribution centre for its building materials.

The transaction was of such great significance, and the Dismat dealers' attachment to their name so strong, that the decision was made to change the name of the company to the Ro-Na Dismat Group. The first stirrings of resistance were felt. It had been only a few years since the Ro-Na dealers had invested thousands of dollars in signage displaying the image of the rare bird, and now they would have to get new signs at considerable expense.

But that was nothing compared to the hostile feelings that would soon surface. In countless neighbourhoods and towns, enemies found themselves having to work together as a result of this marriage of convenience. You wouldn't believe the stories of local rivalries that came to light then! I don't know how many times I heard dealers tell me things like: "If you want me to work with him, it'll be over my dead body." "His grandfather swindled my grandfather." "I've been fighting him for 20 years, and now his prices are going to be the same as mine." On both sides, the transaction proved very difficult to swallow. Some Dismat dealers saw it as a defeat. And for some Ro-Na dealers, it was practically a betrayal.

It would take months, and, in some cases, years, for the situation to calm down in certain regions. Often, members of Ro-Na's executive would have to go in person to act as mediators and attempt to unravel long-standing quarrels.

For many dealers, this first major acquisition of a competitor left a bitter taste. The company would have to do better next time. A better job of laying the groundwork, a better job of handling people's feelings, a better job of taking each organization's unique culture into account. And most of all, taking greater care of the individual people involved.

A painful labour dispute

Growing is a never-ending learning experience. That holds true for all aspects of management. During the 1980s, there were countless developments, of the kind that typified a company striving tirelessly for success. But behind the scenes of this fast and furious race to the top, labour relations were deteriorating on Nobel Street.

Things had, however, started off well. In 1978, management and employees had set up a liaison committee "whose primary role is to communicate to Management the opinions and suggestions of the employees, with a view to constantly improving labour relations and working conditions."

Everyone was acting in good faith. Everyone was willing to make it work.

DISTRIBUTION UPON RECEPTION.

Mr. Fix-it

José Desautels

Tool Expert, Ferronnerie Houle,
Saint-Jean-sur-Richelieu, Quebec

137

José Desautels calls himself a "Mr. Fix-It." It's a fitting description for this 27-year-old mechanic and tool expert who works at the Ferronnerie Houle tool rental centre. With eight years at the hardware store under his belt, this resourceful young man loves what he does and does it well. He learned his trade on the job, first by cleaning the tools and then by watching the mechanics repair them. And though one day he intends to take more training to perfect his skills, for now he's happy to keep his hands busy fixing equipment and putting pieces back together. In any case, he enjoys being up to his elbows in grease! So much so, in fact, that after his 50-hour week at the store, he goes home to repair more tools and do renovation jobs for his friends. After all, how can he give his clients good advice if he hasn't tried something first-hand?

The store offers a wide choice of tools and equipment, from pneumatic nailers and industrial vacuums to lawn tractors and aerial work platforms. José is lucky to have a great team behind him to ensure everything is working properly. And if he doesn't have a part on hand, you can bet he'll find a creative solution.

Though he likes to work quietly in his corner of the workshop, José also loves the contact he has with his clients. In the winter, the store rents out temporary car shelters. Many of the clients who use this service live in a nearby retirement community for independent seniors. It takes José a day to install the shelter at their home and, because he simply can't refuse the offer of a cookie and a chat, half a day to sign the contract! Sometimes, he goes back to visit the friends he has made and takes his children along with him.

But the company was booming. Many new employees and new managers were hired in quick succession. The family feeling that pervaded the work environment started to fray. Ill-advised decisions were made that upset the employees. Conflicts developed.

In the early 1980s, one issue in particular brought this dissatisfaction to a head. The employees wanted to be assigned to a task that would be theirs alone and would give them some job security. Management, on the other hand, wanted each employee to be able to perform a variety of tasks so that the organization could be more agile, more effective, and able to constantly improve its operations.

The employees viewed management's insistence on this point as sheer stubbornness. They felt threatened. They expected that any day, word would come down that jobs were being eliminated. And yet, with the company's expansion, there was certainly no shortage of work! But when the bond of trust is broken, dialogue becomes difficult and people believe what they want to believe.

In addition, we had just implemented a new logistics system, and the transition had not been easy. All of this fostered feelings of insecurity and dissatisfaction among the employees.

In retrospect, I am convinced now that there would have been no such feelings if we had communicated with the employees the way good companies do these days, if we had explained the reason for the new logistics system,

Windows of opportunity

Ian Sullivan

Door and Window Expert, Chester Dawe,
St. John's, Newfoundland

As soon as he was old enough to work, Ian would tag along with his father to the building sites. Obviously, at seven, mostly he was just asked to watch the truck! Later, when the family business he was working for, Stokes Building Supplies, ran into difficulties, he was hired by The Window Shop, where he continued to broaden his experience. After a few years, he and his business partner launched their own doors and windows company, Windows Unlimited. They were young, full of energy, and convinced there was a niche for their business. They were right, but their different visions eventually led them to part company in 2001. It was then that Chester Dawe offered Ian a job that suited him to a T: he would be in charge of their doors and windows division. And this department continues to grow year after year!

Contractors are early birds, so Ian is up at dawn every day. First he has to deal with any emergencies that have come up, and then he moves on to his daily duties, humouring the builders he already works with and finding others to take on new jobs. Of course, in this business, contractors don't come easy, but since everyone knows everyone, Ian says, "If I pester them enough, they'll end up giving me an hour or so, just so they can get rid of me!"

But what he likes best is spending time guiding new home-owners. When they go away happy, with the right information and confident they are in good hands, Ian is happy too.

When Rona bought Chester Dawe in 2006, Ian admits he was a little worried. He had full confidence in his team and the quality of their work, but would things change? In the end, nothing did. After all, if it ain't broke, why fix it?

EMPLOYEES of the Nobel Street distribution centre in Boucherville, in 1987.

the reason for the changes in the way the work was organized. But we never manage with hindsight... at best, we manage with our experience, and that experience often derives from errors.

On both sides, the parties dug in their heels.

The employees at the Boucherville distribution centre signed membership cards to join a union, one that until then had been largely absent from the areas of commerce and distribution: the Energy and Chemical Workers' Union, based in Western Canada and affiliated with the Fédération des travailleurs du Québec (FTQ) in Quebec.

Management saw this as an act of repudiation, a provocation.

Negotiations were very difficult. Many times, the parties were within a hair's breadth of a strike. Nonetheless, an initial collective agreement was signed in 1983.

But the climate did not improve.

When I reflect on those difficult times for Ro-Na, I think that no one knew the right way to handle matters. This was a new situation for all of us. For most of the union members, it was their first such experience. They thought they had to hate the bosses. As for the bosses, they thought they had to play the tough guy in order to win out over the union.

I came to understand later on that both sides should have taken a much more constructive approach to dealing with the situation. As bosses, we should have viewed the

138

employees' intention of joining together under a union as the legitimate aspiration of a group of workers that had grown in number within a company that had grown large. And the union should have been able to present its demands to the employer as an expression of the workers' desire to reframe their partnership with the company.

But we had not reached that point. No one had. The errors made on both sides left only one path open, and that was the path to confrontation.

As a result, after the first collective agreement was signed, the climate continued to deteriorate. Many senior staff members flatly refused to go down to the warehouse, which had been rechristened the "Bronx." Management tried to demonstrate its good faith by rehiring employees who had been fired for intimidation. Senior staff saw this as disloyal. It seemed to them that management was putting the running of the distribution centre right back into the union's hands. The feeling of unrest started to spread.

Productivity fell drastically. The Ro-Na distribution centre, the most modern in all of Quebec, was running at a third of the North American average. Some employees were bullied for appearing to be too "chummy" with the bosses. And the union bombarded management with grievances, which would eventually number close to 1 300.

In 1986, partly to get around the problems at the Boucherville distribution centre, Ro-Na moved up the scheduled opening of a new distribution centre in Quebec

Roots and shoots

Jean Paquin
Comptoir Richelieu, Botanix, Sorel-Tracy, Quebec

The Paquins' Botanix store is a small ecological marvel, designed with maximum energy efficiency in mind. The superb lighting shows off the plants beautifully and consumes very little electricity. In 2004, when the store was being built, Jean Paquin wanted to create something out-of-the-ordinary with his children, who had strong ties to the family business. "They're going to spend their whole lives in there," he explains. His innovative project paid off, winning him first prize in the Energia Competition of the Association québécoise pour la maîtrise de l'énergie (AQME) two years running, in 2005 and 2006. "In any case," he adds, "I would have really regretted doing it any other way!"

Botanix merchants have always been environment-conscious. In 1955, Joseph-Adélard Paquin purchased a pet food company. His son Jean joined him in 1958, and they quickly realized there was a growing demand for gardening products. At the end of the sixties, four merchants—Jasmin, Dion, Cléroux, and Paquin—decided to band together to increase their buying power. Botanix was born. All stores were welcome, large or small, in a spirit of collaboration and individual participation. In 1982 Botanix experienced financial difficulties, and Rona purchased the stores: it was the first step in their diversification process.

Today, Jean is slowly but surely preparing the transition from himself to his daughters, Éloïse and Sophie. His son, Marc-André, worked for the family business until 2004 but then decided to branch off... into landscaping. Now he comes into the store as a client!

DURING THE 1989 STRIKE,
managers like Pierre Piotte
took over duties in the
warehouse to make sure
orders continued to be
filled.

140

City. The decision was made to test out a popular new management philosophy, the philosophy of "total quality." The 1987 annual report presented the concept in this way: "[...] the aim of this approach is to eliminate the errors and waste that can occur at every step of our operations. [...] It is a strategy based essentially on mobilizing staff and involving them in all phases of operations."

To the workers, there was not a shadow of a doubt as to what management intended. It was right there in black and white: management wanted to make employees perform whichever tasks they decided, and even cut staff if they so wished.

Attempts to bring the two sides closer together were in vain. On June 9, 1989, to everyone's surprise, the union launched the first strike in the history of Ro-Na. Only a few weeks earlier, the president, André Dion, had assured the board of directors that a strike would not take place. This came as a serious blow to a man who had always been able to forge cordial relations at every level of the company.

The strike polarized the two sides. There were the strikers, of course, who turned out in great numbers to sing on the picket lines during those beautiful summer days, and then there was everybody else: the managers who did the work in the warehouse, the dealers who came to take delivery of their supplies themselves, and even a number of suppliers who agreed to make deliveries, at no extra

charge, to the dealers directly instead of the warehouse, to lighten the workload at the distribution centre.

During the strike, which would last three months, I was in the warehouse, in the "Bronx," every day. After a week, I went up to see André Dion. I said to him: "André, if I had to work every day under those foremen, I'd be out there on the picket lines too!"

Tired of the fight, the strikers returned to work on September 9. But the underlying problem was still there. I did not know it yet, but I was the one who would be asked to take the matter in hand. Because after 24 years with Ro-Na, André Dion announced a few months after the strike ended that he was going to step down. It was easy to see that there was a cause and effect relationship here, that he saw the strike as a personal failure. Perhaps. But he would say instead that he wanted to experience other things before thinking about retirement. He was 50 and had other projects in mind.

Whatever the true source of his feelings, I was greatly saddened at the departure of the man who had been my guide and my mentor. I had learned everything from André Dion, and never would I have been able to aspire to an executive role had I not crossed his path. Thank you.

In the game of musical chairs that followed André Dion's departure, I was appointed executive vice-president and chief of operations. In other words, the head of the company. Henri Drouin, who was still chairman of the

AFTER 24 YEARS WITH RONA, André Dion stepped down as president. His chief associates organized a tribute to him in 1990.

board, temporarily took on the additional title of "chief executive officer." I knew full well that this was intended to reassure anyone who had doubts: don't worry, young Dutton, who has only just turned 35, will be supervised by Henri Drouin.

Thank goodness, because I myself was one of the doubtful.

A family portrait · The extended clan

1989

Sales: $560 247 000

Net earnings: $3 737 000

Shareholders' equity: $35 922 000

Affiliate stores (members): 616

A busy elf

Lise Pichette
Retired Executive Assistant, Administrative Office, Boucherville, Quebec

At 18, Lise started to work at the Rona Administrative Office. That was in 1965. She stayed there 40 years.

Her first job was as a secretary/receptionist, "out front" where the merchants and suppliers came in. An efficient multi-tasker, she typed up orders and did secretarial jobs between answering phone calls. And, of course, she couldn't afford to make mistakes—that was the era of the cumbersome manual typewriter, long before the days of the correcting ribbon and word processing!

Over the years, she has worked in three different locations—De la Savane in Montreal, Nobel, and Du Tremblay in Boucherville—in several departments and for a variety of different managers—including St-Pierre and Thibault—and directly for three presidents—Morency, Dion, and Dutton. Not surprisingly, she knew just about everyone, and thanks to her, we were able to put names to hundreds of unidentified faces in the photos you see in this book!

Lise was there for all the events that shaped the company's development over the years: the growth of the merchant trade shows, the arrival of computers, maintaining services during strikes, and the group's expansion into the rest of Canada. She was also a devoted and enthusiastic contributor to the Rona Foundation and helped out with various office moves and reorganizations. Helping, adapting, providing good service—these are words that recur frequently throughout her story, and they are qualities that made her such a pillar of strength in the organization.

Both Lise and her sister, Marie-Thérèse (on the right in the photo), who arrived at Rona a few years after her, left the flagship at the same time. But the Pichette pair are still very much involved in the company's activities. They take part in volunteer initiatives and organized outings. And every year, at the end of November, they don their Santa's elves costumes for the annual Christmas party, to the delight of one and all!

Lise adds, "We contributed a lot to the company, we gave a lot of ourselves—we were happy here." By all accounts, they also spread a lot of happiness to those around them.

Computer technology •

WHEN RONA SET UP OPERATIONS ON NOBEL, THE ORGANIZATION ALSO MADE THE MOVE TO THE COMPUTER AGE. NEEDLESS TO SAY, COMPUTERS BACK THEN LOOKED VERY DIFFERENT FROM THOSE OF TODAY!

❶ During the 1979 policy conference at the Manoir Richelieu, André Dion, the then executive vice-president and CEO, and René Gauthier, the director of Computer Services, presented Rona's new computer equipment.

The invitation to the opening of the new facility in March 1974 read: "Come and admire the most modern computer centre of its kind in the country!" And, indeed, visitors seemed awestruck by the technology on display behind the glass panels. This was the era of large computers, mainframes. Twenty-two people worked in the computer centre alone.

The November 1986 issue of *L'Associé* magazine described their duties as follows:

- The encoding of invoices, purchase orders, credit memos, and shipping charges is carried out by data entry operators who key in all the information.
- The operators run the computer [*sic*] and manage the storage media (magnetic tapes): general billing, order preparation, the "Carte Clé" credit cards, direct billing, etc.
- Member services supports TELXON (dealer terminal) and data communications users.
- System services is responsible for making sure the equipment works and for monitoring systems and equipment.

- The programmer-analysts draw up the specifications for programs that are to be modified or created.
- The programmers code the programs.

All of this took place under the watchful eye of René Gauthier, who at the time was the coordinator of computer services.

It all seems so very long ago, and yet... Below are some of the milestones along the journey:

1975. TELXON terminals were installed for the dealers.

1981. The "Carte Clé" credit card was a new loyalty tool for dealers. It would be managed by the National Bank starting in 1989.

1983. At a time of economic difficulty, and to make renovation jobs easier for people, Rona introduced its "cash premium" (Rona money). In the same spirit, and during the same period of time, Canadian Tire money was also accepted.

1984. Data communications made it possible for 110 member dealers to access the warehouse directly.

1986. A pilot project at Modelectric in Montreal meant that an inventory control system would soon be widely available. For the first time ever, a sale entered at the checkout would automatically deduct the item from the quantity of merchandise in the store.

1992. "This was the year of the big revolution," said Linda Michaud, who was then the newly-appointed vice-president of Information Technologies. The organization had just acquired the SIDMA integrated system, and the decision had been made to keep the employees who were already there and train them on an entirely new technology. The software package was a thing of the past; it was time for new computers and methods. The impetus came from the technology itself, and also from the needs of the evolving organization. Up until this point, the

From cash register to integrated system

primary focus of information technology (IT) was distribution: the dealers ordered merchandise, and the order was processed up to delivery. But with the advent of the big-box stores, Rona's role changed, and so did the role of IT. There was a new emphasis on the management of retail stores—very large retail stores.

1993. In concrete terms, this meant developing a number of new systems: cash tills in the stores, merchandise receiving, labelling, management of flyers, inventories, promotions... It was a huge effort. It took one year to develop the system for the first big-box store, in Laval.

1994. June 28. It was 4:00 a.m., and the doors of the first big-box store would be opening very soon. It had just been discovered that a few adjustments still had to be made to the equipment so that it would be able to read the Universal Product Codes (UPC) needed to make sales, and they spent the night working on this final issue, which was resolved in the nick of time. Two days before, 6 000 prices—and therefore labels—had been changed.

1999. The distribution centre moved to a new location on Du Tremblay. With the change to a new environment, the time was right to switch to a new distribution system. It was quite a challenge. The warehouse employees had to learn how to interact with a keyboard instead of putting a check mark on a worksheet, and they had to overcome any fears they might have. The computer specialists had to explain how to dialogue with an information-sensitive computer; they had to understand the mechanics of how human beings work. But they stuck with it, and in the end their extraordinary teamwork paid off.

The year saw the arrival of eCat, the first catalogue on CD, which replaced the microfiche system.

2000. This year saw the launch of the rona.ca website, which today gets 700 000 visitors every month, a number that jumps to 1 million in the spring. Here, people can search for decorating ideas, prices, style suggestions, and Rona by Design projects. Although they can buy online, most consumers go to one of the network's some 700 stores to make their purchases and get information and advice.

2001. The company introduced eRONA, the electronic catalogue for dealers.

2002. EDI (electronic data interchange) was implemented. It handles invoices totaling more than $1 billion annually at Rona. Over 820 000 transactions are conducted with about 1 000 suppliers.

2000-2007. Consolidation tools were developed for the purpose of harmonizing the analysis of results and operations for new acquisitions without having to bring operations to a standstill.

2008. The year marked the beginning of a changeover to a new system and new applications at the administrative centre, which, in the coming years, would be extended throughout the stores.

2010. 300 people work in the organization's IT sector.

❷ At the Nobel Street head office in Boucherville, massive computers were cloistered behind a glass wall. They increased the efficiency of the company's operations.

❸ In 1975, the Telxon telecommunications system was set up in 87 stores. A cassette recorder allowed orders to be placed by telephone and then relayed to the main computer located at Rona's head office.

❹ Rona took advantage of the move to its new distribution centre on Du Tremblay Road in Boucherville to set up a new computer system. It was a formidable task, but one that bore fruit!

❺ In Penticton, British Columbia, like everywhere else in the Rona network, computers were now fully integrated into store operations.

143

THE NEW RONA L'ENTREPÔT BANNER flew over stores that were 125 000 sq. ft. in size, offering 45 000 products in five categories, with a workforce of 150 to 200 full-time employees.

Change or disappear
1990 - 1999

5

In 1990, labour relations had hit rock bottom. I would spend two years at the distribution centre attempting to rebuild bridges with the employees. But an illegal strike broke out in the fall of 1991. It would last for two weeks. When it was over, 26 employees would be dismissed. An agreement satisfactory to both sides was signed in 1995. Concurrently with this labour dispute, Ro-Na was hit by the recession. The company's results for 1990 were poor. Sales and net earnings fell by about 20%. A vigorous plan to streamline the organization helped to rectify the situation. Ro-Na then spent a year developing a strategic plan to make it the leader in each of its market segments. This would result in Ro-Na launching its own big-box stores. The first Ro-Na L'entrepôt outlets would open in 1994, one year after the opening in 1993 of the first hardware-renovation superstores in Quebec, the Réno-Dépôt stores. It was a brilliant success. But this kind of growth put the company under severe financial strain. A French partner, ITM Entreprises, invested $30 million in Ro-Na. The Ro-Na Dismat Group Inc. became simply RONA and moved into a new distribution centre, still in Boucherville, but twice the size of the previous one. RONA took its first steps towards establishing itself in English Canada, and the last remaining sparks of the labour conflict were extinguished as the 1990s came to a close, when 60 employees who had lost their seniority had that seniority reinstated after their co-workers voted overwhelmingly in their favour.

Cécile Laquerre, Gilles Normandin, Andrée Allaire, Claude Forget, Carole Racine, Jacques Bérubé, Lise Pichette, François Lauzon, James Martin et Lise Jacques assistaient à la rencontre.

PRÉOCCUPATIONS...

01. L'inquiétude face aux mises-à-pied
02. Le très haut volume d'information aux membres qui n'ont pas le temps de lire
03. L'orientation de l'entreprise
04. Le service aux membres
05. La gestion des palettes
06. L'information entre les secteurs de l'entreprise
07. Les communications, les lourdeurs administratives, la longueur des processus
08. Le manque de formation
09. Les transits

SUGGESTIONS...

09. Réunions par service, par secteur, inter-secteur
10. Créer un centre téléphonique d'information aux marchands
11. Installer un système de suggestions qui soit vraiment suivi
12. Que les p'tits déjeuners-rencontre aient lieu toutes les semaines et qu'il y ait des suites
13. Créer un centre d'information interne par l'intermédiaire des écrans cathodiques
14. Faire connaître le plan de restructuration à tous les employés le plus tôt possible

Les p'tits déjeuners... un huis clos pour plus d'ouverture

LE PROCHAIN P'TIT DÉJEUNER... VENDREDI, LE 27 JUILLET 1990

It was 1990. A dozen years earlier, I would have been the last person to bet on my chances of rising up the corporate ladder. I joined Ro-Na at a time when its little story was starting to explode. There was everything to do. Or redo. Caught up in a non-stop whirlwind, the group of dealers who had welcomed me in had become a Quebecois and Canadian entrepreneurial success story. And in that whirlwind, I had been swept towards the top.

I would have liked, at that point, to step back for a moment to reflect on the unlikely chain of events that had taken me from a shy young man to a man in charge, but this was not the time for introspection. Behind Ro-Na's success lay some very serious internal challenges that threatened to undermine the company and its potential.

Two years in the "Bronx"

When I took up my new role in May 1990, nothing had been resolved. Labour relations at the Boucherville distribution centre had hit rock bottom. A collective agreement had indeed been signed some months earlier, but it did nothing to improve the poisoned work environment that existed in the "Bronx," the distribution centre. In addition, shortly before my promotion, an employee had been fired for "assault and attempted injury" against a co-worker using a conveyor trolley. A few weeks later, on April 30, an arbitrator ordered the reinstatement of five employees who had been terminated for cause a year previously, not because the dismissals were unjustified in themselves, but because they had not been carried out according to the rules.

Restoring a healthy work climate became my absolute priority. But what was the best way to tackle the problem? Acting the tough guy was out of the question. That approach would be destined for failure. But Ro-Na's nerve centre could not be left to the mercy of a handful of troublemakers. I had no experience as a chief of operations, and even less with handling this type of situation. I followed my instincts. I put on some work boots and went down to the "Bronx." And for two years, that was where I would spend a good deal of my time.

Every day, I was in the "Bronx." At first, people avoided me, people I had known, in some cases, for 13 years, with whom I'd shared a drink and laugh, and who now saw me as an enemy. I would hear them murmur, "Don't talk to him." But bit by bit, one day at a time, one person at a time, communication resumed and smiles started to reappear.

If there was one thing that was clear to me, it was that in a situation like that, you have to look for solutions, not for someone to blame. My approach was not to take sides and stick up for either management or the employees, but to stick up for the company and its vision. I knew my decisions would have value in the medium term only if they were made for the sole purpose of furthering Ro-Na's progress. After all, that was our common goal.

BREAKFAST MEETINGS were organized to improve efficiency at Rona. Résumés of the July 13 and 27, 1990 meetings.

However, it was unacceptable that employees who had been terminated for cause were back working among us simply because of a procedural error. Ro-Na paid them severance to ensure they would leave. Then, I eliminated the foreman role to encourage more direct contact between management and the warehouse employees.

I started holding breakfast meetings. After a few weeks, despite threats from the union, a dozen or so employees were taking part. Every Friday morning, in an out-of-the-way room with no windows, I served coffee, I explained the company's plans, I asked for suggestions. Each week, I reported back to the employees on the suggestions that had been tried out and the results they had produced. I encouraged the managers to implement as many of the employees' suggestions as they possibly could. It was important to send the signal that management was listening. In the first year, 267 employee ideas resulted in the company saving $2.5 million in operating costs. This, at last, was a success we could share.

But while relationships with the employees were becoming easier for us, the union leaders were taking a hard line, as though they could feel their influence over the employees slipping away. Sixteen months after the collective agreement was signed, in late 1990, the union filed more than 600 grievances and the employer issued some 15 disciplinary notices, mainly against union leaders.

1991

The year opened with a campaign of horrific bombings, which looked like so many fireworks when they were broadcast on television. In response to Saddam Hussein's invasion, a few months previously, of neighbouring Kuwait for the purpose of seizing its oil, a massive international coalition led by the United States, under the aegis of the UN, attacked Iraq on January 17 📷. After 42 days of intense aerial bombing, the Iraqi army crumbled following four days of fighting on the ground. But the coalition forces stopped short of entering Baghdad, allowing Saddam Hussein to brutally crush both the Kurds and the Shiites who rose up against him.

The disintegration of the Soviet empire continued throughout 1991. One by one, the republics that made up the Soviet Union, including Russia itself, declared their independence, while an attempted *coup d'état* by a conservative element on August 19 failed in the face of popular resistance mobilized by Russian President Boris Yeltsin. Finally, on December 31, the Union of Soviet Socialist Republics, the champion of communism for three quarters of a century, dissolved.

Yugoslavia, too, was breaking apart. After the republics of Croatia, Slovenia and Bosnia-Herzegovina declared their independence, Serbia tried to take them by force, and a chaotic and fierce ethnic-religious civil war broke out between Serbs, Croats, Slovenes, and Bosnians, some of them Eastern Christians, others Catholics, and still others Muslims...

1992

In June 1992, Rio de Janeiro hosted the "Earth Summit," a key event in the struggle towards achieving sustainable development, which is based on the principle that we must pass on to future generations an earth that has at least as many resources as the earth that we ourselves inherited.

Also in 1992, two major political-economic treaties were signed. In February, the Maastricht Treaty created the European Union, with the introduction of European citizenship, a European Central Bank, and, ultimately, a single currency, all of which were the starting points for a common foreign and social policy.

In October, Canada, the United States, and Mexico signed the North American Free Trade Agreement (NAFTA), with the goal of eliminating barriers to the free movement of goods, capital, and people among the signatory countries.

The year also saw the demise of one of Canada's retail and commercial real estate giants, the Steinberg empire, whose grocery stores in Quebec would eventually be absorbed by its competitors, the Métro-Richelieu and Provigo chains.

On October 26, a Canada-wide referendum rejected the Charlottetown Accord, which was to take the place of the failed Meech Lake Accord. Quebec still would not sanction the 1982 constitution.

1993

There were a few glimmers of hope on the world scene in 1993.

The year opened with the signing, in January, of the Chemical Weapons Convention, according to which the signatory States undertook not to produce, acquire, or use chemical weapons, and to destroy any such weapons in their possession. (Israel, Egypt, Iraq, Syria, and Lebanon did not ratify the treaty.)

There were hopeful signs also in the Israeli-Palestinian conflict: in September, the prime minister of Israel, Yitzhak Rabin, and the chairman of the Palestine Liberation Organization, Yasser Arafat, exchanged an historic handshake in Washington. For the first time, there was official mutual recognition between the two adversaries, and the accord they signed provided for the creation of a Palestinian Authority in the Gaza Strip and West Bank, although with somewhat reduced powers. Would this crucial first step finally lead to peace?

In Canada, the year saw a major electoral upset. After winning the 1984 election with the largest majority in Canadian history, the Progressive Conservative Party suffered its most crushing defeat, sliding from 151 seats...to 2! Jean Chrétien's Liberals formed a majority government, while a sovereignist party, the Bloc québécois, led by Lucien Bouchard, won 54 seats in Quebec and became Her Majesty's Loyal Opposition in Ottawa!

147

Robert Dutton • The strength of a dream

ROBERT DUTTON HAS BEEN AT THE HELM OF THE COMPANY SINCE 1992. BOTH OMNIPRESENT AND UNASSUMING, HE IS A MAN ON A MISSION. IT IS ONE THAT PUTS PEOPLE AHEAD OF NUTS AND BOLTS, AND OCCUPIES HIS EVERYDAY; IT IS HIS MISSION IN LIFE.

❶ At the helm of Rona since 1990, Robert Dutton is a strategic leader and an inspiration, a visionary with myriad plans for Rona's future.

Robert's parents owned the Quincaillerie Laval in Sainte-Dorothée, and, as a child, he never expected he would choose hardware to fulfil his professional aspirations. Like any kid, he spent much of his time playing, only his playground was the hardware store. Following an uneventful adolescence, when it was time for further education, he hesitated between history or economics, before deciding to study at the HEC (Hautes Études Commerciales) business school in Montreal. Upon his graduation in 1977, on an invitation by André Dion, to whom he had been introduced by his father, he was hired by Rona as a marketing analyst for what was to be a two-year internship. He was 22 years old at the time.

To his surprise, he was smitten. He discovered a vibrant world where work and human relations intermingled. The inspirational force that had been Dansereau and Piotte could still be felt everywhere. Encouraged by André Dion, and spurred by an insatiable curiosity and an equally great capacity for learning, Robert advanced within the company with determination and speed. Within just a few years, he had analyzed the stores and made recommendations to the group, created and managed the Dealer Support Department—retail prices, store locations, and layout—and, still bursting with project ideas in addition to his increasing responsibilities, Robert succeeded in breathing new life into the marketing and advertising department.

When André Dion decided to retire in 1990, the board of directors officially named Robert executive vice-president—he was only 35 years old—though, for all intents and purposes, he was already calling the shots. Henri Drouin assumed the position of acting president in the interim. The context was serious: the demoralizing strike had just ended and the economic situation was catastrophic. It would be necessary to act quickly, otherwise all would be lost. A dream that would mobilize everyone and re-establish healthy relations, productivity, and finances was desperately needed. But what?

Robert looked around to see was happening elsewhere, but, mostly, he spent time with his people, the merchants as well as the employees. And he asked questions. He observed. His ability to listen and to analyze, his daring and his creativity allowed him to impart renewed pride in the work, productivity, and solidarity within the team, to turn around the general trend. The figures began to reflect the changes being made, and Rona soon was well on its way to prosperity.

The remarkable rise in popularity of big-box stores was rapidly emerging as another major challenge to face. The first Rona L'entrepôt opened its doors in 1994, in Laval. This new concept made the merchants anxious, but they didn't really have a choice about coming on board, as the major competitors had opted for this format and were fast gaining ground. But Robert Dutton, Henri Drouin, André Gagnon, and their close partners had to expend vast amounts of energy in first developing a solution and then convincing the merchants of its strength. The idea was to offer each one the opportunity of selling their store to the group, and, in turn, establish a tangible, financial participation in the bigger project. Over the years, not only has this option proved beneficial, but the changes have occurred with the utmost respect for all involved.

Human decency has always been the focal point of Robert's concerns. At 42 years of age, at the height of his success, he began to question everything. It all went so fast. He had the feeling that he had arrived... as if by chance, without having made the choice. He felt he had led a privileged life and needed to give something back. All of it—developing the company, generating profits—couldn't be just about the money. There was no value in that. He dreamt of doing more, doing better.

❷ In 1960, young Robert could already be found admiring the shelves of merchandise in the family hardware store in Sainte-Dorothée.

❸ Richard Dutton and his wife ran the Quincaillerie Laval. An article published in the April 1960 edition of *Le Quincaillier* described the establishment as a "masterpiece of good taste," blending modernism with an attractive layout.

❹ At the end of the 1970s, Robert Dutton started his career with Rona as a retail price analyst. He soon became very involved in the company and took on the responsibility for members services.

In 1997, after numerous conversations with Henri Drouin, he decided to take a leave of absence. It wasn't a hasty decision, and he kept in touch with the company. Like many people in their forties, he began to re-evaluate his life, his ambitions, and his goals. He surrounded himself with silence. He took the time he needed to refocus, until he knew what he wanted to do. "That's when I became passionate about the study of ethics," he said. The project to define the company's values was born. And all the members of the team would be brought into play when he returned.

From then on, Robert would put his know-how, his people skills, and his great talents for strategy and courage to work growing the company, mobilizing its people, providing them with work, and encouraging them to achieve their goals. And ever since, with a re-vitalized spirit and an energy renewed daily by the clarity of his vision and his convictions, he has never stopped developing the company.

Many challenges have arisen to test the solidarity of the hardware store dealers as well as the creativity and talent of each of the team members. But they have only served to bring Robert's immense leadership and management capabilities to the fore. One only has to think of the company's unprecedented expansion across Canada; the relocation of corporate headquarters in response to the phenomenal growth; the new up-to-date warehouse; the raising of capital that provided the group with remarkable financial resources—which nonetheless required orchestration by the hand of a master, while maintaining respect for the members' values; and the rivalry between Réno-Dépôt and Rona that would result in an integration, which, though fraught at the outset, would result in an unqualified success.

And we can safely say: it's not over. Robert Dutton still has dreams...

Sales and service in his blood

Jean Prud'homme

Rona L'entrepôt, Charlemagne, Quebec

When Jean was at boarding school, he couldn't wait for the Friday bus to take him home so he could finally do what he loved most: selling to customers! He dreamed of the day when he would have a big store with lots of employees. Today, he's living his dream.

In 1957, Ange-Albert Prud'homme left his home town and bought a store in Repentigny, on the north shore of the St. Lawrence River, to the east of the island of Montreal. The 1 500-sq. ft. ground floor space housed both the general store and the family kitchen. That way, Jacqueline could serve clients and make supper for the kids at the same time! Right from the get-go, Jean says, his parents "worked hard to keep the business in the family." Even though Jacqueline was expecting every year, she nevertheless devoted her energy to running the store, lifting boxes of nails until the last minute! In doing so, she and her husband passed on their work values, their energy, and their passion for customer service to Jean and his six siblings.

In 1980, Jean joined Rona. He could tell it was a forward-looking group; it had a well-structured network and offered its members good marketing tools. While their first expansion in 1975 had meant moving the family upstairs, the opening of a 65 000 sq. ft. Rénovateur home improvement centre in 1989 signalled the beginning of an entirely new era of expansion. Twenty years later, in 2006, they would leave it for an immense Rona L'entrepôt in Charlemagne, not far from Repentigny. Even in such a huge retail space, the Prud'hommes' values are tangible. The employees evidently love working there, and, like Jean, they are Rona people through and through.

The larger the business, however, the harder it is to keep in the family. So Jean intends to invest in his employees' future. He would like to cut down on his 55-hour week and focus on training and mentoring all the young upcoming managers around him. Meanwhile, the projects just keep on coming: in 2011, he'll be opening a new 40 000-sq. ft. proximity store in Repentigny, and creating 85 jobs in the process. After all, he says, he wouldn't want "his" clients having to drive 12 kilometres just for a gallon of paint!

SANTA CLAUS, THE ICE FAIRY, AND ELVES entertained the little ones during the children's Christmas party, one of the activities organized for the children of employees at the head office in Boucherville.

Another strike!

In June 1991, the situation deteriorated further when the union's vice-president was suspended, then fired. On August 15, I asked all the unionized employees to gather in the cafeteria. I gave them a rundown of all the things that had been done to restore a climate of trust. I told them that we were headed for failure because certain people had no other goal than to stand in the way of progress. I told them that, for reasons of efficiency and cost-cutting, the Quebec City warehouse had just been closed and the transport service had been subcontracted. The union leaders stormed out, overturning chairs as they went.

But the employees stayed. I knew we had reached a turning point.

The union leaders no doubt felt that as well. In early September, I was in Henri Drouin's office when a small group of employees, led by the president of the union, burst in, shouting their disapproval over a new series of disciplinary notices and suspensions. The insults rained down. Two days later, the president of the union himself tried to pick a fight with an assistant manager. He was suspended. He then proceeded up and down the aisles of the distribution centre, shouting to anyone who would listen: "You're walking out with me." About a hundred people ended up out on the sidewalk.

The date was September 11, 1991. And it was starting all over again.

THE ANNUAL SHAREHOLDERS' MEETING at the Sheraton on Île Charron, in Boucherville, in 1992.

THE SON OF NAPOLÉON PIOTTE, Pierre Piotte had long been a part of Rona's history, as both a hardware dealer and a member of the board of directors. In 1992, he received a special tribute.

However, the union's leadership was weakened. More than 40% of unionized employees refused to walk out. An illegal strike. The union members divided. This time, clearly, we had every reason to take a firm stand.

Tensions were running high. But as the saying goes: "You never want a serious crisis to go to waste." It was suggested that I obtain a court injunction to force the illegal strikers back to work. I opted instead to give the employees the opportunity to bring their illegal action to an end themselves. I was asked to arrange for a bus and escort to bring in the employees who were still working. I refused. This was an illegal strike, so they were not scabs! I told the loyal employees and the managers that if they suffered any damage, if their cars were vandalized, we would pay for the repairs. Allowing themselves to be bullied was not an option. Friends were pitted against each other, families were divided. But each day, some of the strikers went to join their fellow workers on the job and were reinstated in their positions.

The uprising was running out of steam. After two weeks, the strikers prepared to return to work. But there would be consequences. Approximately 50 of them were served notices of indefinite suspension by a bailiff. All those who took part in the illegal strike lost their seniority. That was the penalty specified in the agreement for three days of unjustified absence. After due consideration, 22 employees were fired, essentially all those who belonged to the union executive and those at the top of the disciplinary notice list.

Finally, after months of talks, some common ground for agreement was found with the terminated employees. We were able at last to turn the page.

A true settlement

Now that the skies had cleared, the employees changed their union affiliation and chose to join the Teamsters. In 1995, a six-year contract was signed. At that time, it was highly unusual for a collective agreement to cover so long a period! The contract gave Ro-Na the flexibility it needed to organize the work efficiently. It provided for full cost-of-living indexing of wages, plus a small real wage increase. But we would go beyond those terms. We introduced a two-tier incentive system: a bonus if budget targets were exceeded and a share of the profits, all of which could add up to about two weeks' wages. I wanted good work to be rewarded. Productivity at the distribution centre underwent a spectacular increase.

To mark the signing of the contract and symbolize the end of the conflict, I had a waste container shipped to the distribution centre. I said to the employees: "Any souvenirs you have from the two strikes, just throw them in there." So, amid much laughter and backslapping, in went photos of the strikers, vests that had been worn during that time, and a quantity of miscellaneous items that each employee associated in some way with those dark days. Then, to general applause, tar was poured onto the pile. "Everyone is a winner. Now let's move on."

ROBERT DUTTON became the vice-president and chief of operations early in 1990, and was appointed CEO soon after.

Chairman of the board since 1981, Henri Drouin occupied this position throughout the 1990s.

IN THE 1990s, THE RO-NA DISMAT GROUP began publishing the magazine *Le Maître d'œuvre,* which consisted primarily of construction plans for do-it-yourselfers.

Those years of labour conflict were a tough learning experience, for both the managers and the employees. Of course, I was not prepared for anything like that. No one was. Throughout that time, I acted in accordance with what my conscience told me was best, I learned from my mistakes, and I depended every day on the advice and support of Henri Drouin. But this was also a decisive time in Ro-Na's history. These trying experiences served to shape the relationship that would exist between management and staff in what was no longer a group of dealers burning with ambition, but a large company focused on performance. For this organization that had grown too quickly to step back and think, this period of conflict was something akin to a teenage crisis.

While Ro-Na was addressing these internal issues, the business environment around it posed some significant challenges. On the one hand, economic conditions were deteriorating sharply, and on the other, it seemed clear that the arrival of the big-box stores was now just a matter of time.

The recession takes its toll

Hopes for a new world, stirred by the spectacular fall of the Berlin Wall and the implosion of the Soviet Empire, were brought up short by a severe recession that sent the developed countries of the world into an economic tailspin. Unemployment was high. So were interest rates. Worried consumers curtailed their spending. Businesses everywhere struggled to stay afloat.

The company's results for 1990 were poor. Ro-Na's net loss was close to half a million dollars. Indicators were down across the board: sales, 18%; operating profit, 21%; shareholders' equity, 8%; working capital, 23%. The banks were nervous. The board of directors was, too.

In June 1990, the board adopted a restructuring plan. Ro-Na's survival depended on it, and we knew it; the plan would therefore be put into operation without delay. In early 1991, we sold the Podium banner, which specialized in sporting goods. That enabled us to refocus our efforts on our core business, with its emphasis on housing products. Operating costs were reduced. The closure of the Quebec City warehouse and the elimination of foreman-level jobs—as mentioned above—were two of the measures taken; in all, 50 supervisory positions were cut. Inventories were reduced by more than a third. As a result, the recession lessened the impact of the conflict somewhat; in a period of robust growth, the disruptions at the distribution centre would have been more damaging to the company. And particular attention was paid to dealers who had overdue accounts. These measures had an immediate effect. Ro-Na was back to showing a profit in 1991, largely as a result of productivity gains. And by the end of the fiscal year, Ro-Na's debt had shrunk by $20 million.

The recession and advances in computer technology were the two main drivers behind the spread of the big-box stores in the United States. And they were coming here. There was no doubt about it. It was like the distant rumbling of thunder. An American giant was gaining ground, it was growing at a phenomenal rate, and it was already looking north of the border.

From survival plan...

In 1990, shortly after my appointment as chief of operations, Claude Bernier, the director of marketing, and I spent a few days touring some stores in the United States. When I made my first reconnaissance trip, in 1985, the big-box stores were an attraction, an anomaly. They drew crowds of both do-it-yourselfers and the simply curious who were amazed by these veritable temples of renovation. But five years later, they were everywhere. These immense stores imposed their rules and their prices. They redefined the standards of the business. They had developed inventory management into a science. In fact, they understood the importance of managing the entire supply chain. They had elevated it to an art form.

Clearly, this was a revolution, the biggest in retail trade since the post-war years, since the time when food stores took down their counters and allowed customers to walk through the aisles among the products.

I returned fascinated. Impressed.

Towards a common goal

Steele Curry
Former President and CEO of Revelstoke

In the spring of 1971, Steele Curry was working for a Toronto-based firm that advised SMBs on mergers and investments, when he spotted a golden opportunity. Revelstoke's president and two of its directors wanted to sell the business and retire. To take advantage of the low market value, Steele assembled a group of buyers and together they purchased 50% of the company's shares. In December that year, he moved to Calgary as Revelstoke's new president.

For 10 years, business boomed and the company grew. But they were caught off guard when the economy went into decline in the early 1980s. In an effort to maintain their growth, they decided to diversify their activities. On top of their sawmills, cement plants, and hardware stores, they purchased a clothing chain—Coconut Joe—as well as a chain of video rental stores. Steele then became convinced that The Home Depot's business model would dominate the home improvement market and set about creating his own based on what he had learned from the owners... but his lack of expertise in the domain showed through.

At the end of the 1980s, they were the target of several takeover bids. Steele and his partners had learned from their mistakes; they seized the opportunity to sell off various sector-specific components of the company to businesses around the world. Revelstoke went to West Fraser Timber... and would later be taken over by Rona.

From then on, Steele turned his attention to mentoring. When he was young, his father used to say, "Businessmen should devote between 20% and 25% of their time to community work!" In the 1970s, he was already president of the Salvation Army's Red Shield campaign and of their advisory board. In 1999, encouraged by his wife and daughters, he joined the Alberta Mentor Foundation For Youth (AMFY), which provided him with training and assigned him his first student... then another, and another. In 2003, after three years of service on the board of directors, he was appointed chairman.

To reach out to even more young people, the foundation joined up with Big Brothers and Big Sisters of Calgary, and, together, they created the mPower Youth Mentoring program. It was there that Steele first came into contact with the Rona Foundation, which has been supporting their activities since 2006. Two years later, AMFY and BBBS Calgary officially merged. Steele is currently writing a series of guides for 18- to 30-year-olds to help them learn life skills and overcome their difficulties.

His business vision is based on the principle that "A successful company is one that is able to strike a delicate balance between its employees' strengths and weaknesses and cultivate their ability to work together towards a common goal." In this respect, he says, Rona is a "Canadian success story."

153

IN 1992, RONA RENEWED ITS ASSOCIATION with Home Hardware and Hardware Wholesalers Inc., collaborators since 1984 and 1990 respectively, to create Alliance Internationale LLC, a North American alliance Rona would remain a member of until 2004.

HENRI DROUIN

And very worried.

Firstly, our independent dealers were not in a strong enough financial position to invest the many millions of dollars that would be required to construct such huge stores.

Secondly, our members were for the most part local hardware dealers; the largest stores measured 30 000 sq. ft. (2 800 m²) and had 30 to 50 employees; nothing could have prepared them for managing a monster of 100 000 or even 150 000 sq. ft. (9 300 to 14 000 m²) with 150 to 200 employees.

Thirdly, the Ro-Na Dismat Group Inc. could not open its own big-box stores itself; to do so would be to fly in the face of the principle on which it was originally founded and to compete with its own dealers.

Everything seemed to be against us. The trade publications carried articles forecasting Ro-Na's imminent demise.

... to strategic plan

The 1991 restructuring enabled the company to address its most pressing concerns. But as soon as it was completed, it was time to move on to the next phase. Our next project would be a comprehensive and structured strategic plan. Like everything else, this would be done "the Ro-Na way." The process would involve many of the executives and managers, as well as the dealers.

For a good year, everyone at the administrative centre pitched in: finance, marketing, legal, purchasing, and shipping. Each area worked on its piece. The management team met regularly to talk about context, our strengths, our vulnerabilities. We went over every aspect of our operations with a fine-tooth comb in an effort to bring forth a company-wide vision that would meet new challenges while remaining true to Ro-Na's philosophy and spirit. All the cards were on the table. It was—again!—a question of survival.

At this same time, Henri Drouin and I went on the road with other members of Ro-Na's executive team. We met with the dealers region by region. We shared with them our observations and our thoughts as we went along. We asked for their opinion. We had, of course, studied the major trends affecting our industry in North America, and we had to take them into consideration. But the dealers had a much better understanding than we did of their immediate reality: the customers and their expectations. That ability to think simultaneously on two levels, globally and locally, was already apparent as one of Ro-Na's strengths. What grew out of it was an original world view. A capacity for venturing off the beaten path.

Times were changing, challenges were changing, but Ro-Na remained first and foremost a group of independent dealers.

The outcome of this collaborative effort was a 17-point strategic plan. Yes, the plan called for our expansion into the big-box store segment. But it was much more than that.

From five-and-dime to hardware

Richard Allard

Centre de Rénovation Île-Perrot, Rona Le Quincaillier, Île-Perrot, Quebec

In 1956, Fernande and Jean-Paul Allard opened a small five-and-dime store in Île-Perrot, which sold everything from underwear to boxes of nails. As the town and the family expanded, however, so did the business, and in 1960 they joined the Rona network. In 1972, they moved into a Rona prototype store and their son Richard began working with them. But when his father died, the 23-year-old had to take over as boss. At first, clients who came in asking to see the owner were a little confused when he answered that they were speaking to him! But after their initial surprise, Richard's clients soon grew to know and trust him, and the store's reputation grew steadily, thanks to the hard work of the entire family.

Seven of the eight Allard children have worked at the store. Four are still there. Lise, the eldest, came back to the business after raising a family. Denise, Claire, and Jean hold the fort full time with Richard. Yves worked there for about 20 years before setting up his own company, and Denis, the youngest, works in the lumberyard. Roger was also involved in the company for a while—that is, before he became a "black sheep" and turned to dentistry!—but he still has a say in important decisions and brings an outsider's viewpoint to the discussions. And until recently, their mother, Fernande, the store's co-founder, helped with the ordering and the Christmas displays. She is still the company president and stops by to visit regularly—when she's not out on the golf course, that is!

The Allards have business in their blood. All the management positions are held by family members, whose leadership is esteemed and trusted. The next generation will undoubtedly do things differently. Though Richard has two sons and one nephew working there, running a store is more complex and demanding than it used to be, and young people nowadays are less willing to devote the 70 or 80 hours a week their parents did. Richard adds, "40 hours a week isn't much, but it's OK!"

Local residents are proud and grateful to have this 50-year-old family store to serve them. And clients also know that if they speak to one of the managers, the rest of the family is going to know about it!

155

Sponsorships at Rona •

❶ **Rona is a good sport! En 2001, the company sponsored the 37th edition of the Jeux du Québec, held in Lachine, and awarded thirteen cash prizes to young medal winners.**

In the late 1990s, Rona sponsored the Tour de l'île, Tour des enfants, Tour de la ville, and Tour la nuit cycling events.

Then, in 2000, still in the world of cycling, the company became the main sponsor of then Olympic hopeful Geneviève Jeanson and of the Rona Cycling Team, made up of eight young women. It was a sponsorship that would continue for three years. "What we liked was that these athletes had a real desire to excel," says Claude Bernier, the executive vice-president of Marketing and Customer Innovations, who has been with Rona for 22 years.

Cycling also features prominently in fundraising events for multiple sclerosis, a cause Rona became involved in at around the same time. It began with the family of François Lespérance, a dealer living with this illness. His son André, who was running the family business, was the president of the Quebec Division of the Multiple Sclerosis Society of Canada, and he turned to Rona for help. From bike tour to bike tour, the story was repeated, growing and spreading across the entire country, in tandem with Rona's expansion in Canada. Since 2002, many stores have joined in, forming teams and organizing fundraisers the minute the nice weather returned. The official tally of people who have taken part in the event since 2004 is 1 271. In 2009, there were 21 teams and as many different routes. And the tradition continues...

A major sponsor of the Montreal Alouettes since 2000, Rona went on to became the lead sponsor of the entire Canadian Football League (CFL).

Rona's relationship with the Olympics began when it sponsored the television presentation of the Summer Games in Atlanta (1996) and Sydney (2000), and the Winter Games in Nagano (1998) and Salt Lake City (2002). Its involvement with the 2010 Olympic Games in Vancouver had been in the works since 2002. Rona's vice-president of Marketing, attending the Games in Salt Lake City on the company's behalf, was awed by so much self-giving, such dedication to excellence. "Nothing is perfect in this world of ours. But the Olympic values... there is nothing more fundamental. We have to sponsor those values," he says. Later he would return from Beijing, deeply moved once again, after attending the Paralympic Games there.

Since 2006, Rona has held the title of National Partner, meaning that it has the right to use the prestigious Olympic logo in its in-store promotions. The organization announced the news to the network in these words:

"As the primary symbol of the Olympic Games, the flame heralds the beginning of the games as well as representing and expressing its values: unity and peace among the nations, loyalty, courage, kinship, and solidarity. We have our own flame to carry. At Rona, we inherited a culture of service, unity, and determination from our founders and those who followed in their footsteps. These Rona forerunners also gave us the

Participating in emergence

discipline of working day after day and the confidence and courage to dream big. This is the flame they left and the one that we now must keep burning brightly. Today we carry this flame proudly and pass on our values and the baton to future employees."

A special program was launched in 2006 to support high-performance athletes who are current and future Olympians. Entitled "Growing With Our Athletes," the five-year program was developed to help prepare 100 Canadian athletes for the 2008 Beijing Summer Games, the 2010 Vancouver Winter Games, and the 2012 London Summer Games. In a letter he sent to Rona in March 2009, John A. Furlong, chief executive officer of the Vancouver Organizing Committee for the 2010 Olympic and Paralympic Winter Games (VANOC), wrote:

> "We have all been extremely impressed with Rona's "Growing With Our Athletes" program. It is one of the most ambitious support programs ever undertaken for athletes, and it is an initiative that will help our Olympic hopefuls to offset living, training, and competition expenses, while at the same inspiring Canadians from coast to coast who have the success of our athletes at heart."

One of the projects associated with the event was the Rona Vancouver 2010 Fabrication Shop. Near the end of 2007, Rona and VANOC together launched this training program for the disadvantaged and unemployed of Vancouver. Developed in cooperation with several local community organizations, the 30-week program provided carpentry training for some 64 underprivileged young people. During their time at the Shop, trainees produced more than 10 000 items that were be used at the 2010 Games, including podiums, wheelchair access ramps, signage, barricades, and much, much more. Rona supervised the planning and set-up of the Shop, recruited the instructors, and supplied all the required tools, equipment, and materials. It was one more way that Rona demonstrated its commitment to sustainable development.

❷ Having himself competed at the international level in several sports, John Furlong distinguished himself through his involvement in the organization of Canadian Olympic sports. He is the chief executive officer of the Vancouver Organizing Committee for the 2010 Olympic and Paralympic Winter Games (VANOC).

❸ The Olympic Flame on the waterfront.

❹ Catherine Girard is one of the approximately 100 Rona volunteers who worked alongside the organizers of the Vancouver 2010 Olympic and Paralympic Winter Games. She had been posted to the entrance to the site of the ski competitions at Cypress Mountain.

❺ The Canadian Football League (CFL) has received funding from Rona since 2002. Today, Rona is the promotional partner ot the CFL, sponsoring all its teams.

157

ARENA • For increased purchasing power

AT RONA, PURCHASING IS CENTRALIZED IN BOUCHERVILLE, WHERE NEGOTIATIONS ARE HANDLED BY THE ADMINISTRATIVE CENTRE. THE LOGIC UNDERLYING THE PURCHASING FUNCTION IS BASED ON OPTIMIZING THE NUMBER OF SUPPLIERS WITH WHOM THE COMPANY DOES BUSINESS.

❶ The opening of this strategic office brought Rona closer to its manufacturers and provided them with access to a wealth of products. The goal was to meet the changing needs of its customers by drawing on Chinese expertise and knowhow. Manon Bouchard left her position as merchandising director, Plumbing, in Boucherville to head up the Shanghai office.

From left to right:
Luc Nantel, vice-president, Merchandising (Hardware); Isabelle Shen, merchandiser; Manon Bouchard, general manager; Stéphane Rousseau, Product Development manager; Jessica Chen, administrative assistant; Dominic Bélanger, merchandiser; and James Dong, merchandiser.

Here again, sustainable development is key. As Normand Dumont, with Rona since 1989 and the executive vice-president of Merchandising, explains:

"The more products you buy from a single supplier, the more you optimize your supply chain. When you buy from 5 000 suppliers (as was previously the case), with each of them providing a small part of your selection, it means more deliveries, more trucks on the road, and so on."

Currently, Rona has close to 2 500 suppliers, of which 1 500 are very active.

Sustainable development also means buying more products locally. Not only is this important to consumers, but each time we buy locally we reduce our environmental footprint, and that ties in directly with Rona's mission. So, given this context, what is the role of the international purchasing group ARENA? First, a bit of background...

Before the advent of Access to Retailers in Europe and North America (ARENA), Bricomarché in France had formed an alliance with Hagebau in Germany, which later became Zeus. These two founded ARENA in 2000. They then started recruiting worldwide. In 1997, Rona had already formed an alliance with Les Mousquetaires, a major purchasing group in the hardware business, so, in 2003, an association with ARENA was a natural fit. Today, ARENA includes the Groupement des Mousquetaires (France), Zeus (Germany), Rona (Canada), Ditas (Denmark), Mica Plus and Mica Hardware (South Africa and England), Mitre 10 (Australia), Bricostore (Romania, Hungary, and Croatia), Homemart (China), Bricofer (Italy), and Jumbo (Switzerland). With operations in 17 countries, it is the fourth largest buying group in the world (12 billion euros) after Home Depot (first), Lowe's (second), and Kingfisher (third). In 2008, Rona's sales figures were the highest of the lot.

ARENA is, therefore, a platform for negotiating contracts with supplier companies. Take light bulbs, for instance. Companies like Philips and Sylvania are multinationals. They offer products that differ from country to country. But when several buyers together, through ARENA, go looking for a supplier, it becomes possible to negotiate directly with these companies. Each partner can then proceed with selecting its products.

Flooring products are another example. When it comes to laminate flooring, the big producer is Europe. Whereas individually it is difficult to achieve any significant savings, a rigorous process and intense negotiations have resulted in a 12% savings for Rona, which greatly benefits both the company and its customers.

It also translates into a forum for sharing ideas, comparing methods, and exchanging visits in the context of business meetings. The purchasing group functions as a council. Meetings are held several times a year and rotate from one host country to another across five continents. The largest display centres are now in China. The facility in Shanghai is gigantic, and yet you'll see people there bringing their materials in on carts…

But it's not possible to purchase everything locally. Not so very long ago, as people will no doubt recall, Santa Claus lived in Canada! Well, not anymore. These days he has taken up residence in Asia. And presents are always made wherever the jolly old fellow lives…

Rona's responsible purchasing policy, developed in 2005, pertains to all its suppliers, both here at home and around the world.

> "Rona encourages joint-action initiatives in the Canadian and international industry to develop shared approaches that meet stringent credibility criteria to ensure that all products sold are manufactured under conditions that respect both human rights and the requirements of sustainable development."

That is where ARENA comes into the picture: when it is a question of products manufactured outside Canada. If you think about it, it is exactly the same principle as that followed by Rona's founding merchants, who, one day, decided to join forces to be able to secure better prices, except that ARENA's scope is international.

Over the last few years, Rona's challenge has been to get through the recession by drawing on increased effectiveness and creativity. In all sectors, Rona used this opportunity to raise its team's awareness of process review. For the 200 people working in the merchandising sector, this has also meant tracking down and offering out-of-the-ordinary or exclusive products. "And then dreaming. That's what really makes things happen," adds Normand Dumont.

Among the creative, essentially strategic, ideas the company implemented was the opening of a Rona office in Shanghai, in March 2009. Its goal is to be able to double its direct imports from Asia, which would allow the company to expand the lines of private and controlled brands it offers.

A.R.E.N.A.

A.R.E.N.A. sas: *Total Purchasing Turnover*

A.R.E.N.A. Alliance Purchasing Turnover € 6 682 000 000

ITM
€0.80 Billion

Jumbo
€0.219 Billion

Zeus
€1.51 Billion

Homemart
€0.37 Billion

A.R.E.N.A. Sas
€6.682 Billion

Ditas
€0.83 Billion

Bricostore
€0.15 Billion

Mica UK
€0.017 Billion

Rona Inc.
€2.2 Billion

Mitre 10
€0.50 Billion

Mica SA
€0.086 Billion

❷

❸

❷ Made up of 10 hardware industry firms, and established in 16 countries, ARENA is the fourth largest buying group in the world.

❸ In October 2008, Rona attended the Canton Fair in Pazhou, China.

Sharing the passion

Roy Perkins

Perkins-Caron Home Centre, Rona Home Centre, Cornwall, Ontario

A fierce snowstorm is raging in Cornwall. A client calls the Rona store in a panic; the snowblower he recently bought at the store refuses to start. No problem—we'll take the one from the store's lumberyard, deliver it to his home, exchange it for the one that won't start, and bring his back as soon as it's repaired!

That's Roy Perkins' way of doing business. He was 17 when he started working at Claude and Gaétan Ménard's lumberyard. Under those two entrepreneurs, he quickly learned the secret of success: love what you do and serve your customers well. At 25, he was promoted to manager; then, with the help of the Ménards and a loan taken out on his home, he became a co-owner before he had even turned 30. Walking into the store 32 years later, you can still feel this man's enthusiasm and concern for his customers. Roy adds, "Being passionate about your job is a commitment to yourself to make an extra effort, to do more than what's expected of you!"

At the Cornwall Rona, this passion takes several forms. Employees are chosen first and foremost for their positive attitude and willingness to get involved: everyone takes part in the annual fundraisers for the hospital and other charities. Their motivation has a ripple effect on the whole community. "And that commitment," Roy says proudly, "is found everywhere at Rona, from the top floor of the head office to the aisles of the store…" The customers feel it. And they are always right.

THE HEAD OFFICE OF THE VAL ROYAL COMPANY has been located at the corner of Jean-Talon and Waverly in Montreal since 1936.

In fact, it was at this time that Ro-Na decided it would not be obsessed with store size. This exercise in planning made us realize that there are no right or wrong surface areas, no right or wrong retail sales formulas. There are good dealers, and then there are the rest. And it is better to be the best local store than a mediocre megastore. Ro-Na would be the place where the best dealers were found. Period.

We decided that we would not specialize in one particular store format. Instead, we would specialize in consumers and their needs. And those needs could not be met with any one store format. The spirit of the plan was that the Ro-Na dealer would be the leader in his market segment. And that Ro-Na would not overlook any market segments, and would even create new ones.

Once it was ready, the plan was presented to the dealers at meetings held in each region. The script varied little. We reviewed the context. We presented the plan. We answered questions. And we offered each of the dealers an opportunity to play a part in the execution of the various components of the plan. They could pick and choose among them. Their support had to be freely and fully given. The result: the dealers got behind each of the points in the plan in massive numbers.

With that kind of strength, I knew we would succeed.

Big-box stores: confounding the skeptics

Those who did not know Ro-Na, however, were skeptical on at least one point: our plan to open big-box stores. Being

IN 1987, the Val Royal Group, which already owned the Brico Centre stores, acquired the Castor Bricoleur home centres.

the leader in all market segments meant having big-box stores—the emerging segment in Quebec. According to some observers, this spelled the end for Ro-Na. Once again, their predictions were premature.

It is true that in this instance, as in past endeavours, the company did not do things in the usual way. In 1939, some dealers got together to buy; in 1960, they got together to advertise; in 1993, they got together to open big-box stores!

Local dealers would band together to raise $1.5 million. That would be their initial investment. Ro-Na would finance the rest of the approximately $20 million it would cost per store. Ro-Na and the group of dealers would be fifty-fifty partners in these new joint ventures. The dealers would decide for themselves what they would do with their existing stores. Either they would keep them as neighbourhood stores, or they would close them, in which case Ro-Na would buy back the inventory and look for buyers for the fittings.

The plan was presented to the dealers with no beating about the bush, and each time, one point in particular was emphasized by Henri Drouin: "The success of each store displaying the Ro-Na banner depends on proximity to the customer, on quality service, in short, on being committed to the role of dealer; that is the road we have to take to stay alive, but we are going to travel it in our own way, the Ro-Na way, the dealers' way."

1994

One of the most abhorrent episodes of the 20th century unfolded between April and July 1994: the genocide in Rwanda 📷. For a hundred days, the Tutsi ethnic group, which, although a minority, had dominated the country for much of its past, was systematically slaughtered by gangs of killers of Hutu origin, while the Hutu government clashed with Tutsi rebel forces. Close to 800 000 people were killed in three months, making this the worst genocide in history after the Jewish Holocaust during the Second World War.

The Arab-Israeli conflict swung from horror to hope. In February, an Israeli settler killed 29 Palestinians and injured 150 more during prayers at a mosque in Hebron, prompting the first suicide bombings by Hamas on Israeli territory. The Palestinian Authority, however, was finally established in Gaza in July, while Israel signed a peace treaty with a second of its neighbours, Jordan, in October.

In Quebec, the Parti québécois, now under the leadership of Jacques Parizeau, defeated Daniel Johnson's Liberals, with the electoral system translating a slim majority of the popular vote (0.35%) into a total of 77 seats to 47. A new referendum on sovereignty was expected within the year.

1995

January 1 was a key date for the global economy, as it marked the creation of the World Trade Organization (WTO), the successor to the General Agreement on Tariffs and Trade (GATT) established in 1947. Like its predecessor, the WTO is a forum where the countries of the world can negotiate international trade, but, unlike GATT, the WTO recognizes all member states as being equal, it operates essentially by consensus, and it provides for a multilateral dispute resolution mechanism with which its member states are bound to comply. The scope of the WTO is also much broader and covers not only trade in goods, but also investments, cultural property, and intellectual property.

Sparking what would come to be known as the "turbot war," Canadian authorities seized a Spanish fishing vessel, arresting its captain. The fishing rights dispute was resolved six weeks later by the conclusion of an agreement between Canada and the European Union.

In Canada, the big political story of 1995 was the second referendum on sovereignty, held on October 30. Over the course of a highly-charged campaign, the YES side garnered increasing support, even coming out on top in some of the polls, especially after Lucien Bouchard's appointment as chief negotiator with Ottawa in the event of accession to sovereignty. Worried, Canadians from across the country held a huge rally in Montreal on October 27 to proclaim their great love for Quebec and Quebecers. The NO side eventually won with 50.6% of the vote against the YES side's 49.4%.

1996

The Palestinian question continued to seesaw between hope and disillusion in 1996. The year opened with the first Palestinian elections to be held by universal suffrage. The Islamic group Hamas refused to take part in the electoral process, allowing Yasser Arafat's Fatah party to win an easy victory; Arafat was elected president of the Palestinian National Authority, and his party won 55 of the 88 seats in the Palestinian Legislative Council. However, immediately thereafter, Hamas resumed their suicide bombings, while Israel embarked on a bombing campaign in southern Lebanon intended to put a stop to Hezbollah rocket attacks.

In April, the Palestinian National Council repealed the articles of the Palestinian National Covenant (Charter of the PLO) that denied Israel's right to exist. But this crucial overture was soon cancelled out by the election in Israel of Benjamin Netanyahu's Likud, a far-right anti-Arab party that immediately authorized the expansion of Jewish colonies into Palestinian territory in a move that could only have a disastrous effect on the peace process.

In September, the Taliban emerged victorious after the long civil war that followed the Soviet withdrawal from Afghanistan in 1989. From Kabul, they instituted a particularly oppressive Islamic regime that would provide a haven where militants with Al-Qaeda, Osama bin Laden's terrorist organization, could train and plot their deadly attacks.

ON APRIL 1, 1993, VAL ROYAL OPENED ITS FIRST RÉNO-DÉPÔT, in Brossard, with an area of over 120 000 sq. ft.

THE FIRST RONA L'ENTREPÔT opened its doors in Laval as planned, on June 29, 1994. Comedian Yvon Deschamps, who was the spokesperson for the advertising campaign that year, joined the managers for the opening ceremony.

And there was no time to lose. In 1993, a Quebec-based group, Val Royal, which owned the Brico Centre stores, was the first to join the megastore movement in Quebec, when it opened Réno-Dépôt, a big-box store patterned after Home Depot in the U.S. At that time in Canada, big-box stores were primarily the domain of Ontario's Aikenhead chain, a subsidiary of Molson. Val Royal had signed a sort of "non-aggression pact" with Molson that prohibited Val Royal from expanding into Ontario, and Aikenhead from expanding into Quebec, until 1998. This agreement would survive the takeover of Aikenhead by Home Depot in 1994. As a result, only Ro-Na could prevent Réno-Dépôt from monopolizing the big-box store segment in Quebec.

The first Réno-Dépôt opened in Brossard, on Montreal's South Shore. Its grand opening was an event. The attendant hubbub was so great that traffic on the Champlain Bridge was backed up for hours. It was a runaway success. Sales of $60 million were expected in the first year, and plans were in place to open four more Réno-Dépôt stores almost immediately.

The enthusiasm sparked by the opening of the first Réno-Dépôt silenced the few remaining skeptics at Ro-Na and galvanized everyone into action. The Ro-Na dealers were proud individuals. They were not going to let themselves be outstripped by a competitor.

Ro-Na's response was not long in coming.

THE AD ANNOUNCING the opening of the store in Anjou, Quebec, in 1979.

GILLES LAMOUREUX AND HIS ASSOCIATES were the first to take on the challenge of the big-box store at Rona: they transformed a former Club Price into a Rona L'entrepôt in 1994.

"It was bigger than any of us!"

Gilles Lamoureux
Rona L'entrepôt, Laval, Quebec

Gilles hasn't slept for the past six months. He's got 300 employees to hire and 45 000 products to find, buy, and put on the shelves. His team is working around the clock. It's April 1994, and he's opening the very first Rona L'entrepôt, in Laval.

The big-box frenzy in Quebec began with the opening of the first large Réno-Dépôt in Brossard. Rona knew they had to act quickly—but how? Who would have the guts to embark on that sort of adventure? Gilles was on Rona's board of directors at the time. He realized that they were all small merchants and that even the newly opened 30 000-sq. ft. store in Place Versailles was tiny compared to their competitor's 150 000-sq. ft. warehouse. But he was willing to give it a go, and Head Office was behind him. "In the first few years, I'd get nervous and scared, then they'd get nervous and scared... but we pulled it off!" Later, Réno-Dépôt's president, Pierre Michaud, told him, "If you hadn't been there, all that business would have come to me!" Today, Gilles feels privileged to have been part of this pivotal event in Rona's history and is proud to see how much the company has expanded since then.

But all of this would never have happened had it not been for a bold decision taken a few decades before. In 1967, after 17 years as a sales clerk in a Val Royal hardware store, Gilles's father, Joseph, branched out on his own, and with his meagre savings he bought the Quincaillerie Delorimier. Gilles joined him in 1977. Two years later, in 1979, they acquired their competitor, a Rona on Mont-Royal Avenue, and, in doing so, obtained the right to call themselves Rona merchants. No doubt about it—Rona was already a leader, especially in advertising. The formula was simple: their stores had to make money from the very first year of operation. They purchased more stores: A.D. Leblanc in the "Village" in 1987, and Charleroi in Montreal North and Latendresse in Pointe-aux-Trembles in 1989. Then, in 1991, the Pascal chain went under, and Gilles jumped at the opportunity that offered him. With the help of Rona and brothers Serge and Jean-Marc Legault, he bought two Pascal stores—the one in Place Versailles and the La Promenade location in Verdun. 1994 saw the creation of a big-box store in Laval, and 2010, the transformation and expansion of the Saint-Eustache Rona Le Régional into a big-box store.

His modus operandi has always been pretty much the same: find failing businesses, spot their most committed people and get them on board as partners—then bring them all along on the next adventure. One of Gilles's great strengths is that he trusts the people he works with: "You can't give people responsibilities, then go above their heads. I get really upset when I see that!"

163

THE RONA L'ENTREPÔT STORES WERE A SUCCESS. Many more were being opened at the end of the 1990s, including one in Mascouche on May 7, 1998, and another in Anjou on March 24, 1999. Construction of more Rona L'entrepôt outlets were forging ahead, including the 12th one in Brossard, which opened in 2000.

The operation proceeded at a brisk pace. Eight dealers in the Greater Montreal area joined forces. With Ro-Na's support, they converted a former Price Club store with an area of 140 000 sq. ft. (13 000 m²) located in Laval, in Montreal's north end. It was a colossal job, with a timeline that was far too ambitious. There were kilometres of shelving to install, 20 cash registers to set up, 45 000 items to prepare for sale; employees had to be hired, trained, and given some idea of the future location of the products that were still sitting in the distribution centre...

Would they make it?

At the new store, deadlines were too tight. And Boucherville was not ready either. They had recently changed over to a new computer system, and even the most resourceful among them were still learning how to use it. There was nothing in place to connect the administrative centre with the store's cash registers, to track sales, to coordinate deliveries. The labelling system was practically non-existent. For 55 years, each store had done things its own way. The new computer system did not even recognize UPCs (Universal Product Codes) yet. In short, the technology and logistics infrastructure to support a big-box store was simply not ready.

It was all so rushed that the day before the grand opening, the prices on 6 000 items had to be changed!

But no one would have guessed any of that on June 29, 1994. This was a day to celebrate. The first Ro-Na L'entrepôt caused a sensation. For a week, the store was packed from

morning to night. In anticipation of its opening, a major advertising campaign had been rolled out highlighting the difference between Ro-Na L'entrepôt and Réno-Dépôt: a more pleasant environment, better-designed stores, and most importantly... incomparable service.

And it would be easy for people to compare, as this first Ro-Na L'entrepôt was less than a kilometre away from a Réno-Dépôt!

Gilles Lamoureux, the owner of several hardware stores and a member of the board of directors at that time, states categorically: "If Ro-Na had not started up those stores, Ro-Na would no longer exist; Ro-Na would be dead."

I could not agree more.

An overseas investor

The impact on the company's business was dramatic. The annual report was jubilant: "1994 has been one of the most successful years in our history. [...] Our sales, our earnings, and the returns to our shareholder dealers have reached a level unprecedented in the history of our group." In 1993, net sales totalled $477 million. In 1994, they shot up by $90 million. Five years later, in 1999, they would approach the billion-dollar mark, and there would be 12 RONA L'entrepôt stores open in Quebec.

That kind of growth requires a huge amount of capital. It was then that the company had a stroke of good fortune. It was the fall of 1996. A human resources consultant from

Working with people you love

Jules St-Georges

Building Materials Expert, M.C. Beauséjour & Richard, Saint-Michel-des-Saints, Quebec

Jules St-Georges worked at the Beauséjours' Rona for a decade before embarking on a 20-year career as a carpenter. But during all those years, whenever he dropped by the store, customers would still stop him and ask for advice. "I must've had 'Rona sales associate' stamped on my forehead!" he laughs. When he finally decided to quit the construction world, it was only natural that Claude Beauséjour would invite him back to work at the store. As it turned out, this suited them both, as Jules couldn't see himself going to work for another banner. So, for the past two years, he has been running the materials department and, most importantly, guiding clients through their building and remodelling projects.

Jules will assist you through every stage of your venture, from the foundations to the finishing touches. He'll help you find the materials you need and make sure to order the right quantities for you at the right price. But mostly, he's there to give you good advice! And while he considers every renovation project interesting, what Jules enjoys most is when a young person just starting out comes to him for help in building a first home.

His best advice, "Before embarking on any renovation project, enlist the help of a friend or relative who knows what they're doing, like an uncle or a retired grandfather. Not only will they be able to pitch in with the construction work itself, but more importantly, they'll know what questions to ask." Plus, it's so much more enjoyable working with people you love!

On the go year round

Lyne Lanouette

Seasonal Expert, Quincaillerie Beaubien,
Rona Le Quincaillier, Montreal, Quebec

IN THE 1990s, Rona's directors and dealers, and Les Mousquetaires met in France in front of a Bricomarché store.

When you're in charge of a department that's constantly changing, like the seasonal section, you have to be well-organized, with both feet planted firmly on the ground. Lyne Lanouette has these qualities and then some: her sense of humour helps her see the positive side of every situation and she's only happy if she's done a good job. Before carving out a niche at the Quincaillerie Beaubien, 12 years ago now, she earned her stripes in another male-dominated field: garages! So, a word of advice to any guy who might doubt what she says: you'd better believe that Lyne knows exactly what she's talking about and knows the products like the back of her hand!

To be happy in the seasonal department, you have to enjoy working hard. With each new order, you have to find space in the warehouse and on the shelves. It's a never-ending challenge. You also have to be able to anticipate trends and clients' whims. Lyne says her favourite time of year is the end of winter, "because everything arrives at once!" The summer products start coming in, but you never know if there'll be another snowstorm, bringing with it a sudden rush on shovels!

Lyne is happiest when she is ahead in her work, knowing that if she had to take time off, her colleagues and clients would have everything they needed. She loves dealing with the public and really appreciates it when regular customers call her to let her know how their plants are getting on, or simply to thank her for her help. And as she puts it, "A day without talking to anyone would be a dull day indeed!"

Quebec, Charles Dupont, saw a connection between Ro-Na and a French company called ITM Entreprises S.A. It operated along much the same lines as our company. It too had "members," dealers who were independent, but who stood united. These associated dealers were known in France as "Les Mousquetaires": all for one and one for all. It was an imposing group, with operations in the food, clothing, restaurant, and service station industries and, of course, in hardware, under the Bricomarché banner. The group's sales totalled more than 135 billion francs, which at that time represented some $33 billion Canadian.

At first, a strategic alliance was a long way off. Initial contact took place in the context of a cultural exchange, a project designed to give youth from Quebec and from France an opportunity to work on the other side of the ocean for fun and adventure.

But discussions soon broadened beyond these educational trips for young people. There was real chemistry between the two companies. We found common ground in our philosophy, our values. An initial meeting in Boucherville, originally scheduled for 20 minutes, lasted more than two hours. Not long after that, representatives from the companies got together in Paris and, over a fine meal, talk turned to Ro-Na's reluctance about initiating a public offering of shares as a way to raise capital. The Frenchmen's hearts skipped a beat. At the time Jean Émond, now retired, was Ro-Na's senior vice-president, People and Culture: "The

IN DECEMBER 1997, Henri Drouin and Robert Dutton were introduced to the Les Mousquetaires community by directors Boris Blache and Pierre Gourgeon at their major international convention.

French were dealers through and through, even more so than we were; they were true, dyed-in-the-wool merchants, they were musketeers. They said it was not an option for fellow dealers to sell themselves to the public. They said: we'll advance you the funds!"

And that is exactly what happened.

Around the middle of May 1997, Ro-Na announced that ITM Entreprises would be investing $30 million in the Ro-Na Dismat Group Inc., consisting of $10 million in preferred shares and $20 million in common shares, which would give it a 16.67% voting interest. In the edition of the French group's newsletter that was published on June 14, Henri Drouin made the headlines: "This is the most wonderful transaction of my life."

The general meeting of Ro-Na dealers would ratify the transaction with the French group on... July 14, and the issue of new shares would be completed in December. We certainly had a sense of occasion...

Tentative beginnings in English Canada

In the early 1990s, while Ro-Na was dealing with the labour dispute, the recession, and the development of a format for its big-box stores, another avenue for growth was slowly emerging. Soon it would become the leading factor in Ro-Na's expansion, but for the moment, we were, so to speak, still at the introduction stage. The idea was to take Ro-Na beyond Quebec's borders.

From the warehouse to the vice-president's chair

Allen Cheney
Former Vice-President of Operations, Surrey, British Columbia

When he retired at the end of 2008, Allen Cheney was vice-president of operations for the big-box stores in Western Canada. His job was to ensure maximum profitability for around 15 stores with 4 000 employees and annual sales of up to $500 million.

He had been on the job for 33 years. Hired by the Revelstoke operation as soon as he completed his commerce degree, he had started off sweeping the warehouse floors. But he firmly believed that "always doing your best, no matter what the job, just might get you promoted," and that philosophy helped him climb the ladder, one rung at a time.

In 1988, West Fraser Timber bought Revelstoke. Following a transition period, Allen was appointed district manager for Alberta and Saskatchewan. In the space of five years, Revelstoke went from "small lumberyards" to "warehouse stores." Known affectionately by its clients as "Revy," the company officially adopted this name in 1993.

1994 was both a decisive year for Revy and an exciting one for Allen, as they made their first foray into the world of warehouse stores together. There were four people on the project, and Allen recalls that none of them really knew what they were doing! If someone had said to them, "Hey, guys, you can't do that, it won't work!", they probably would have believed it. So they looked at how Home Depot and Aikenhead's were doing things. Finally, they bought some land and established the purchasing team—and that's when Aikenhead's began to make overtures to Revy. They held two or three months of negotiations, during which Aikenhead's went ahead and opened a store in Edmonton! War had been declared, and they had to act quickly, especially since Eagle was also starting to build in Edmonton. Revy put its plans for Calgary on hold and entered the fray. It was make or break. One year later, they had opened stores in Edmonton and Calgary, and bought out Eagle Canada. In 1996, they purchased Lumberland in Vancouver, and, in 1998, they acquired Lansing in Toronto. In 2001, the last of Revy's four warehouse stores opened its doors in Toronto, the very same day Revy went up for sale.

When Rona bought Revy, everyone felt it was predestined. The two organizations had known each other since 1998 and had similar business values. As Allen says, "It's so much easier when everyone's pulling together in the same direction."

Because of the recession, Allen knows that his successor will face many challenges. Given Vancouver's atrocious traffic as well as an aging population, he thinks the pendulum is swinging back to neighbourhood stores. "But change is good," he says with a twinkle in his eye; "It keeps you on your toes!"

Behind everything we do • Ethics

BUSINESS, PROFIT, WORK; SOLIDARITY, ETHICS, SPIRITUALITY. WORDS THAT YOU WOULD NOT SPONTANEOUSLY LINK TOGETHER, EXCEPT PERHAPS TO HIGHLIGHT THE FACT THAT THEY ARE MUTUALLY EXCLUSIVE, SUCH AS BUSINESS AND ETHICS; PROFIT AND SOLIDARITY; WORK AND SPIRITUALITY.

❶ In May 2007, Rona made a donation to and formed an association with the Chair of Ethical Management at the HEC. Robert Dutton presents the cheque to Thierry C. Pauchant, to his left, professor and holder of the Chair, along with three other representatives of the establishment.

In one of his speeches, Robert Dutton explains his vision in this way:

"But such systematic opposition reveals a poor understanding of what business is—or at the very least, confusion between a business's reason for being and a business's way of being; confusion between motivations and behaviours; confusion between the life *of* a business and life *in* a business. [...]

A business is a place of efficiency. That is the primary and only reason for its existence. [...] Efficiency, not profit. Profit is what motivates investors; it is a measure of efficiency. [...] Business exists because it simplifies the organization of work, decision making, investment. It simplifies the management of resources towards achieving one or more common goals.

[...] It is by definition a place of solidarity—that is, a place where two, two hundred, two thousand, or two hundred thousand individuals coordinate their activities towards achieving one or more shared objectives. [...] A place of efficiency, a place of solidarity, a business is also a place of life. And it is on this point that confusion often arises. Because, while that is not the business's reason for being, it is here that we witness its way of being. And it is in this way of being that expression is given to its ethical and spiritual dimensions. [...]

There is nothing more dangerous than the belief that different rules of ethics exist for each facet of our lives: family life, relationships with friends, social life, life in the workplace. And yet, this belief is widely held. We all know people who live according to moral precepts that differ radically depending on whether they are acting in their capacity as head of a family or as head of a business. People who, like big-hearted mafiosi, jealously guard their daughters' virtue while exploiting prostitution on a major scale—with other people's daughters. [...]

A behaviour is either ethical, or it isn't. [...]

The spiritual dimension, the meaning of life, the search for meaning: these are individual processes. Groups can support the process, but spirituality lies completely within. [...] While the search for meaning does not under any circumstances form part of the business's reason for being, it can be facilitated by its way of being. [...]

And if it is not up to the business to give meaning to the life of individuals, then it is up to individuals to give meaning to the life of the business.

Here are a few of the basic values at Rona through which this vision is articulated:

- Service. Generosity. The real thing, true generosity of self.
- Unity, the unity that is based on the common good. It is the founding principle of our business, the heritage of our founders and of the cooperative spirit.
- Respect for the dignity of the human person. Employees are at the service of a plan, not an institution. The institution serves them, not the other way around. This can happen only if we listen.
- The search for the common good and the sharing of wealth beyond the boundaries of the business: customers, suppliers, social partners.
- A sense of responsibility."

For Robert Dutton, the drive to build a prosperous business, and the drive to create a more just society, are inextricably linked.

Thierry Pauchant, holder of the Chair in Ethical Management at HEC Montréal, says of Robert that he understands we are living in a "pluriverse," and that he is seeking to effectively manage paradoxes, including his own. Pauchant says:

"It's a paradox to say: I have to be the leader, but not a role model, I'm just one example... I think Rona has succeeded in finding a holistic approach. Rona does not make the mistake of saying that ethics is just something to play with. There are lots of people who say, "Tell me what's legal and not legal..." or "We're going to do this with a code of ethics..." They throw a code of ethics at you because it's required by law. Rona doesn't take that approach. Which is very interesting. And I think it stems at the same time from the

corporate system, the cultural environment in Quebec, and Robert Dutton's personality. [...] Rona sees it both at the collective level and at the personal level... it's reflected in the company's values... respect for the person, not respect for people. It's respect for the individual person. It is simultaneously individual and collective."

❷ In 2005, Rona entrenched its fundamental values in a code of ethics, which it distributed to its employees: "In respecting this code of conduct, founded on trust and respect, we will continue to enjoy harmony in the workplace."

The first Rona outside Canada

Romuald Derrible

Derrible SPM, Rona Le Quincaillier, Saint-Pierre and Miquelon

THE FIRST STORE OUTSIDE CANADA!
On June 5, 1998, the Derrible family inaugurated a Rona Le Quincaillier in Saint-Pierre and Miquelon.

An overseas territory of France, Saint-Pierre and Miquelon is a group of charming islands off the coast of Newfoundland, with a population of 8 000 and just 42 kilometres of roads. For Romuald, this small corner of Europe in the North Atlantic combines the best of both worlds. As he puts it, "We're French in North America; we've got both Camembert and Cheez Whiz!" You can sense his deeply rooted attachment to Saint-Pierre. Though the thought might have occasionally crossed his mind, he has never really wanted to leave. Even if he were the last person on the island, he'd fish for cod off the end of the pier; he wouldn't budge.

Romuald joined the family business in 1995. Their supplier at the time, Pro Hardware, was in trouble. Being leaders, the Derribles wanted to team up with an innovative company that was willing to take risks. They compared Rona and Home Hardware, and Rona came out on top. With Rona, they could work in French. It was also a forward-looking company that offered them the flexibility they needed to deal with the European quirks of life in Saint-Pierre, including culture... and voltage! The deal was signed in 1998.

Romuald is a visionary. He says it's his greatest quality but also his biggest weakness, because his brain works faster than what he's able to accomplish. His sister Séverine, who co-owns the business and is in charge of marketing, has to remind him every day to breath deeply and slow down!

A visit to several Rona stores in Quebec inspired Romuald to make some major changes. He wanted to completely restructure the company's 20-year-old practices by introducing innovative new work tools. His employees balked at the idea, but he took the time to explain what he had in mind; he is a pragmatic man who understands what his livelihood depends on. Entrepreneurs face all kinds of challenges in small communities like this. When Romuald got Rona's backing to carry out major renovations to the store, he was told it would be simple—all he had to do was hire 20 workers and a carpenter! But on this island, you have to work within the constraints of a 35-hour week, a small labour pool, and much higher wages. Added to that, everybody knows everyone else. His clients bump into each other every day at the supermarket or restaurant. An unhappy client who talks to 10 others can do serious harm; 10 people is a lot in Saint-Pierre! Here, you have to be tactful and always try to be the best at what you do.

When you thrive on challenges, like Romuald, you don't like geographical restrictions getting in your way. He has to have a new carrot dangling in front of him all the time and, at 37, admits he's unlikely to change. So, who knows, his next step might be to expand his activities outside the island. In which case, Canada had better watch out!

The company set its sights first on Eastern Ontario, because of its proximity to Quebec and the fact that the Ro-Na name was already known there. In November 1993, John Longo was hired; his mission was, literally, to knock on doors and recruit any independent dealers who wished to join Ro-Na.

The timing was not the best for promoting a Quebec-based company in English Canada. A second referendum on Quebec sovereignty was planned for October 30, 1995, and tensions sometimes ran high on both sides of the Ottawa River. But Longo was not a man who was easily discouraged. He persisted, and although he was many times rebuffed, he succeeded nonetheless in recruiting a good number of dealers, year after year. By the end of the 1990s, they would number around 30.

On the other side of Quebec, towards the Maritimes, the situation was quite different. Francophone dealers, Acadians and Brayons alike, were already very familiar with Ro-Na, and applications for membership arrived at a steady pace. On the Anglophone side, progress was slower... and it was partly our fault! At least, that is what we hear from Peggy Godfrey, a horticulture dealer from Bedford, Nova Scotia: "In November 1993, I got into my car and I drove all the way to Boucherville. At that time, they were only looking west; they didn't seem to be interested in anything to the east. So, I went and knocked on their door, knowing that we met all the criteria: we were a family business, we had

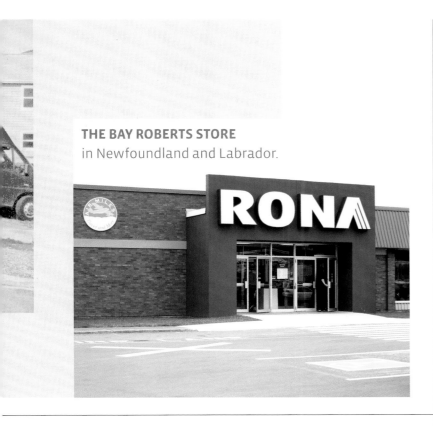

THE BAY ROBERTS STORE
in Newfoundland and Labrador.

a permanent structure, and we were second-generation dealers. [...] They had to turn to look in our direction then."

We took her advice and not long afterwards, John Longo's mission was expanded to include developing the Anglophone market in the Maritimes as well. An Anglophone dealer in Saint John, New Brunswick, was the first to join Ro-Na in 1999.

And thus were sown the seeds for Ro-Na's expansion through all of Canada.

A pause for reflection

In 1997, after the partnership agreement with the French had been signed, when the recession and the labour dispute were already far in the past, and the Ro-Na L'entrepôt stores were well on their way, I felt the need to take a time out.

My 20 years with Ro-Na had gone by in a blur. Since 1977, I had lived in a state of perpetual urgency, driven on as much by a desire to succeed as by the fear of failure. In this balance of extremes, I was soon entrusted with leadership responsibilities. Those responsibilities were for me a source of pride and of mistrust. It was no doubt due to my humble background, but I had always thought that there were three things a person should never trust, three things that shared the potential to completely alter one's relationships with one's fellow human beings: money, fame, and power. I had just turned 40, and I had all three! I needed to think, to contemplate something other than figures...

1997

1997 was a chaotic year for the world economy. The majority of Asian countries were hit by a financial crisis, with estimates putting the overall global loss at $600 billion. Meanwhile, Boris Yeltsin's Russia was heading straight for disaster. The brusquely undertaken transition from a centrally-planned economy to a market-based economy was turning into a nightmare, triggering a collapse in production and trade, capital flight, and galloping inflation.

The Bre-X affair would distinguish itself as the biggest financial scandal in Canada yet. This company's value on the stock market would plummet from $6 billion to zero when it was revealed that its worth was based on falsified results of test drillings.

In Canadian politics, the Chrétien government narrowly preserved its majority government, losing 22 seats in an early election. All but wiped out in the Atlantic provinces and the West, the Liberal Party won 101 of the 103 federal ridings in Ontario.

In December, under the aegis of the United Nations, the Kyoto Protocol set an overall target for the reduction of greenhouse gases to 5.2% below 1992 levels (or 29% below 1997 levels), to be met in 2010.

Also in December, a constitutional amendment allowed the Quebec government to abolish confessional school boards, which had been protected under the *British North America Act* of 1867, and to replace them with linguistic school boards.

A faint glimmer of hope appeared in the efforts to curb the savagery of war: the treaty banning anti-personnel mines was signed in Ottawa in December.

1998

The year began with a weather disaster that will not soon be forgotten in Quebec. From January 5 to 10, an ice storm lasting 80 hours pounded southern Quebec with freezing rain, depositing up to 100 millimetres of ice on the ground, trees, and structures. Power lines collapsed under the weight, leaving close to a million homes without electricity 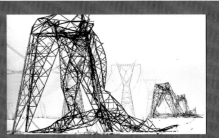. Some 100 000 people sought refuge in emergency shelters. At the height of the storm, there were even fears that the system that supplies drinking water to the entire city of Montreal would be shut down. The army deployed 16 000 soldiers to ensure safety and assist with evacuations. The hardest-hit area, Montérégie, was plunged into darkness for a month and a half.

In September, Swissair flight 111 travelling from New York to Geneva crashed into the sea off the coast of Peggy's Cove in Nova Scotia. The disaster claimed the lives of everyone on board.

Faced with an armed national liberation movement in the province of Kosovo, Yugoslavia embarked upon an extensive "ethnic cleansing" campaign, driving hundreds of thousands of Kosovars into neighbouring countries.

A general election was held in Quebec in November. The Liberals and their new leader, Jean Charest, former head of the federal Progressive Conservative Party, won the popular vote by an extremely narrow margin. However, the peculiarities of the electoral system meant that a large majority of the seats (76 out of 125) went to the Parti québécois, led by Lucien Bouchard.

1999

The situation in Kosovo degenerated into open war with NATO's aerial bombing campaign against Serbia, launched in March to put an end to the Serbs' ethnic cleansing operations targeting the Kosovars. After 78 days of shelling, Serbia withdrew its troops from Kosovo, which was placed under UN administration until an international agreement could be reached on its future status.

April 1 saw the birth of a new Canadian political entity with the creation of Nunavut, which would from then on constitute a territory distinct from the Northwest Territories.

On April 20, two students from Columbine High School in Littleton, Colorado, shot and killed 12 students and a teacher at their school before taking their own lives. The shooting, the most deadly at an American school up to that time, shook the country and sparked extensive debate about guns, and violent movies and video games.

A chapter in the history of Canadian retailing came to a close with the bankruptcy of Eaton's, a company that, having opened its first store in Toronto in 1869, had dominated the department store sector for many years.

In December, the meeting of the World Trade Organization (WTO) in Seattle was seriously disrupted by violent demonstrations and ended in failure over the irreconcilable demands of the United States, Europe, and the countries of the South.

A dream come true

Michel Perron

Quincaillerie Saint-Jean-Baptiste, Rona Le Quincaillier,
Quebec City, Quebec

Walking into the Saint-Jean-Baptiste hardware store is like stepping into the pages of a history book. With its high wood slat ceilings, round windows, and hand-painted signs, the boutique is in perfect harmony with the bygone charm of Aiguillon Street, where it is located. The walls are filled with nostalgic reminders of the past: old tools and photographs bear witness to the storied history of this 109-year-old business. The company that would remain in the family for 99 years was founded by Joseph-Arthur Dorval in 1901. His son, Philippe, became a Rona merchant in 1959.

Today, Michel Perron describes his store as a childhood dream come true. As a young boy, he would accompany his father, an army officer, to the Quincaillerie Corriveau, where they were always greeted with a warm "Good morning, Colonel!" Years later, after working in the tourism industry and for housing cooperatives, and after having bought and renovated two bars with some friends—the Foubar and the Zanzibar—Michel's flair for business brought him back to the hardware trade. A long-time client of the Quincaillerie Saint-Jean-Baptiste, Michel tried to persuade Claude Dorval to sell him the store. To no avail. Weary of waiting, in 1989, he bought a hardware outlet in Saint-Sacrement, not far from the Corriveau store he had known as a boy. But he left the door open for Claude should he change his mind. It was not until December 9, 1999, that he got the call he'd been waiting for. "You still interested?" were Claude's first words. Three weeks later, Michel and his business partner were the new owners of the Saint-Jean-Baptiste store. Since then, he has felt privileged to be able to walk "to his dream workplace" every morning.

But of course, running your own business is not just about dreaming. "It's like being called to the priesthood—it's a vocation!" The desire to be your own boss and be free to take your own decisions runs deep. What's more, Michel would rather hire employees he knows he's going to get along with, even if they have little or no experience, rather than people who've been in the hardware business all their life but can't easily adapt to a new boss's methods.

One day, while out hiking in the Appalachian Mountains, Michel met a young boy of about 12 or 13, who was spirited and full of energy and enthusiasm. He asked him to come back and see him at the store if ever he was looking for a job. No prizes for guessing where that young man is working today!

THE RONA FOUNDATION was officially created on May 12, 1998. The fourth Rona Golf Day fundraiser—the Foundation's second—was held in 1999, and 125 suppliers took part in the event.

I confided my feelings to Henri, who agreed to let me take a six-month leave of absence. Even today I still feel infinitely grateful to him for this. He acted as a true friend. He protected me. Thank you, Henri.

During those six months, I immersed myself in the study of ethics and philosophy, morality and theology. I took life at a slower pace. I drank in the works of those great minds whose wisdom has survived the centuries. I was not having a crisis. I was not searching for something. I was, in a manner of speaking, lying fallow. Like land that is left unplowed for a few seasons, so that it has a chance to recover and regenerate. Nonetheless, I continued to keep up with what was happening at Ro-Na, by attending board meetings.

One day, at the Grand Séminaire de Montréal where I was studying, a Sulpician father told me that, for the first time in 40 years, a jobless man had come knocking at the door looking for work.

I realized that the quest for growth and success in a company can take on a meaning that goes far beyond dollars and profit. Creating wealth, yes, but while providing work for willing hands at the same time. Work is not just earning a salary and getting ahead. Most of all, it is dignity. All those years, it had been right there under my nose.

I returned to work at the beginning of 1998. I was delighted to rejoin the management team. I felt at home here. We had barely finished exchanging greetings when I

IN 1998, construction began on the new, nearly 750 000-sq. ft. building that would house the head office and the distribution centre on Du Tremblay Road in Boucherville.

announced my objectives: "We have to double our numbers by 2002." Which meant increasing sales by $700 million in four years. It would be like nothing that had ever been seen before.

RONA on the move... again

The Ro-Na Dismat Group Inc. simplified its name. It would now be RONA Inc. All upper case, with no hyphen. The RONA Foundation was also created. It would provide financial support to community organizations that help teenagers and young adults complete their education and find employment. Then, preparations began for a colossal undertaking which we knew, just in discussing it, was going to be a nightmare. We had to move again. And we needed a new computer system.

With the company's growth, and especially the opening of the RONA L'entrepôt stores, the facilities on Nobel Street in Boucherville were strained to the limit. We had rented a large warehouse nearby, but this provided minimal relief. The distribution centre, which had looked so massive when it opened in the mid-1970s, was bursting at the seams, and its computer system seemed almost prehistoric.

RONA's new distribution centre and administrative centre would still be located in Boucherville, only a stone's throw from Nobel Street, on Du Tremblay Road.

The new main warehouse would cover more than 650 000 sq. ft. (60 385 m²). It would have room for 50 000 pallets instead of 22 000. Its computer system would be state-of-the-art. Intelligent conveyors would go and pick up cases of product anywhere in the warehouse based on an electronic code associated with their location and an order number. To accomplish this, every case of every product had to be measured and weighed—all 26 000-plus boxes.

While construction went ahead on the new building, employee training got under way. Staff would have to abandon paper and graduate to the optical bar code reader. It was incredibly fast and incredibly efficient, but completely unforgiving. The slightest discrepancy in a number when the data was entered, and the system would lock up. As an example, the job of measuring the cases had to be done three times over to get everything right!

The new facilities opened on April 6, 1999. The distribution centre was so large that employees used bikes to get around inside it, and many people got lost looking for the washrooms. Jean Émond recalls: "Not only are you moving your warehouse to a new location, and therefore all your products, which you have to locate and you have to identify, but at the same time as you're changing the physical appearance, you're also changing the brains of the operation, the computer system. You're also changing everyone's habits and all their points of reference at the same time."

IN ADDITION TO RONA L'ENTREPÔT STORES, a dozen Rona Le Régional (formerly Rona Le Rénovateur Régional) stores were opened in 1998 and 1999, including one in Châteauguay on May 13, 1998, and another in Saint-Hyacinthe on November 10, 1999. Each opening was cause for celebration!

The first few months were difficult. It was an extremely trying time for Pierre Forget, one of the stalwarts of the shipping department, who had been with RONA ever since its days on De la Savane Street. In his opinion, this move was the worst: "Everything, absolutely everything, changed. It took us eight months to debug the computer system. For eight months I worked seven days a week, twelve to fourteen hours a day; I had two Sundays off."

At one point, I was afraid we would never be finished with fixing all the little problems, and I asked Linda Michaud if it might not be preferable to backtrack and simply mothball the new system: "No way," she replied. "The physical environment is totally different, it can't be done."

Finally, with the help of Pierre Forget, Linda Michaud, and a host of other managers and employees, we got through it and were able to meet the constantly growing demand. Because that year, the company opened 10 RONA Le Rénovateur Régional stores—a new banner, an average-sized outlet for average-sized markets, presented as "a place that combines the advantages of the big-box stores with the personality of the more traditional stores."

Letting bygones be bygones

On December 10, 1998, I received a letter that moved me deeply. I was not expecting it. Not in the least. I had had no indication that anything like this was in the works. It was a petition. It was signed by some 60 employees, all of them workers who had taken part in the illegal strike in 1991 and who had kept their jobs with the company, but at the price of losing their seniority, the penalty that had been levied against them. The petition was addressed to me personally. Those who signed it acknowledged their error, asked for forgiveness, and expressed a wish to have their seniority reinstated.

The action was more than symbolic. At the distribution centre, where work volumes were subject to significant seasonal variations, many employees were on call. And the employees were called in on the basis of their seniority, within the meaning of the collective agreement.

I was not sure how to respond. This was a matter that went back seven years. But I could well imagine that the employees who had remained loyal would not appreciate a spontaneous reinstatement of the seniority their co-workers had lost under the terms of a collective agreement that was very clear on the matter. The union at the time had, furthermore, contested Ro-Na's decision to apply the agreement, and every court to which the case was referred, all the way up to the Court of Appeal, had sided with Ro-Na—and therefore, in a certain sense, with the employees who had decided not to participate in the illegal strike.

Personally, I had forgiven the whole thing long ago. But it was not my decision to make. The collective agreement was clear in 1991, and it was still clear in 1998. It was not a decision that even RONA's management could make. It

PIERRE FORGET, THE PRODUCTION COORDINATOR, AND HIS DAUGHTER CLAUDINE, a forklift operator, work with state-of-the-art technology in the Boucherville distribution centre.

is between union members, not between union members and management, that the issue of seniority takes on importance. It was not up to RONA to decide to let bygones be bygones. It was up to their co-workers.

What I could do, however, was start them thinking about it. I could encourage them to give it very careful thought.

I went down to the floor and broached the topic with a few of the unionized employees. Their response was rather frosty. One of them even made a veiled threat, saying: "Then we can't guarantee labour peace anymore, not here and not in your stores either!" Almost every day, I dropped by the warehouse and raised the matter with other employees. I knew that during breaks and lunch hours, every discussion revolved around the request made by the former strikers. I left the idea to take its course. I encouraged discussion.

Nearly a year later, in October 1999, I suggested that the union proceed with a secret ballot. The vote would take place over a 24-hour period, to accommodate all work shifts.

The union asked me to be present to help count the ballots. The result hit us like a bombshell. The unionized employees voted in favour of the former strikers... 81% in favour!

In the room, people cried, people laughed, people applauded.

In a voice choked with emotion, I said to them: "It's over, once and for all."

Yes, it is possible to build a big company, to aim for performance and growth, and to do it without losing sight of such values as respect for others.

On January 8, 2000, a letter of agreement was signed confirming that the seniority standing of all employees who had signed the petition would be fully restored to its 1991 pre-strike level. Eight years after the crisis, the last remaining sparks of the conflict were extinguished in a process that probably has no equivalent in the history of the union movement in Canada.

What a way to bid farewell to the 20th century!

A family portrait • The extended clan

1999

Sales: $960 548 000

Net earnings: $14 706 000

Shareholders' equity: $121 002 000

Affiliate stores (members): 413

Big-box stores: 12

Employees across entire network: 11 000

The Canada-France connection •

AS FAR BACK AS 1984, BUSINESS TIES WERE FORGED BETWEEN RONA AND EUROPEAN GROUPS SUCH AS SAPEC (LUXEMBOURG), COPAMÉTAL (FRANCE), MENOUQUIN (BELGIUM), AND UNIFE (SPAIN). BUT IT WAS WITH LES MOUSQUETAIRES THAT THIS HISTORY WAS TRANSFORMED INTO A FRIENDSHIP.

❶ The SITE program, an international work exchange program for businesses, has been offering workers from Quebec and France the opportunity to experience life abroad since 1997.

In the fall of 1996, the director of Human Resources at Rona received an invitation from his counterpart at Bricomarché (the ITM Entreprises hardware and home improvement banner) to set up a worker exchange program between France and Quebec. Bricomarché was a network of hardware dealers in France looking for a similar group with which to form a partnership. During a visit to Quebec, their representatives met with Robert Dutton and Henri Drouin. Their discussions were cordial, heartfelt. They were, in turn, invited to France. While there, Robert and Henri confided to them that Rona needed capital to expand its network and that consideration was being given to taking the company public... Once back in Quebec, Robert set aside his usual restraint and wrote to them. Enthusiastic and empathetic, Les Mousquetaires, who were operating under the name Bricomarché, advanced the $30 million needed for Rona's growth in late 1997.

In 2003, it was their turn to need capital. Rona helped them sell their shares on the market. Michel Pattou, chairman of the Société Civile des Mousquetaires, wrote:

> "Our common path—an original one, to say the least—will be forever engraved in the history of Les Mousquetaires, and we sincerely hope it will be similarly engraved in that of the Canadian dealers. One day, back in 1997, you needed us, and we were there for you. One day in 2003, we needed you, and you were there for us. The history that brought us together, that lives on today in the alliances between us, has forged indestructible bonds that will never be broken. And, who knows, perhaps tomorrow we will need one another once again."

Since that time, no legal obligation has existed between them, but they still belong to the international purchasing group ARENA for planning pooled purchases. Thanks to its partners,

A firm friendship

Bricomarché is part of the fourth largest buying group in the world.

Each year, representatives attend Rona's Spring Show, where they compare products and methods. Relationships grow ever stronger as they learn from one another. The companies, which operate in such vastly different ways, have in common the entrepreneurial spirit of their people and their commitment to the growth of the group. According to Christophe Bantquin, a member of Bricomarché:

> "The business values that are strong at Bricomarché are independence and inter-dependence. On the one hand, we are members, we are independent, we have our companies, we are each responsible for our operating statements, for our business. On the other hand, two days per week are spent working in our central office. Depending on each person's affinities, they might have important responsibilities within the group. They have a role to play in the central office, just as they do in the stores. We all help one another to succeed."

In France, the emphasis is on the lowest in-store price, not service. The situation is very different in Canada, and at Rona in particular.

Another difference is that "the government takes 55% of transfer costs, which means that transfers from one generation to the next are lost. Stores are often set up by two spouses, but then they get sold to other members. In a way, that is how succession takes place," adds Pierre Courbois, another member. At Rona, however, as we know, transfers between generations are encouraged and supported.

As for the SITE exchange program, it is still running. Since 1997, it has given some 100 young people from Canada and as many from France an opportunity to experience life abroad.

❷ The logo of the French group represents the ideals of the musketeer: the republican values of equality, Cartesian thinking, justice, and the rural and traditional values of roots, nature, and quality are evoked.

❸ In 1969, Les Mousquetaires was born with the founding of the food super-markets Intermarché, the first chain to operate under the Les Mousquetaires banner, which went on to specialize in seven different retail segments. Bricomarché, created in 1979, has slightly over 600 stores in Europe today.

❹ As a testament to their friendship, Les Mousquetaires offered this statuette to Rona in January 2004. It is prominently displayed at the Boucherville head office.

TODAY, EVERY NEW STORE PROUDLY DISPLAYS THE RONA SIGN EXCLUSIVELY.

All-out expansion
Since 2000

In 2000, RONA had the wind in its sails. But the inevitable consolidation in the industry imposed the following alternative on them: consolidate or be consolidated by someone else. And so began a phase of accelerated expansion. With the purchase of 60 Cashway Building Centre outlets in Ontario, RONA made its first large acquisition beyond Quebec's borders. Integration proved difficult. RONA learned from its mistakes and scored a major coup in 2001 when it purchased the Revy chain, which employed 5 000 people and posted revenues of $800 million. After 35 years with RONA, Henri Drouin retired. The mantle of chairman of the board passed to André Gagnon, a dealer from Saint-Hyacinthe. In 2002, to support its growth, RONA became listed on the stock exchange and issued $150 million worth of shares. The next year, Kingfisher, Réno-Dépôt's major shareholder, put the RONA L'entrepôt stores' great rival up for sale. RONA was the successful bidder. Further acquisitions followed across Canada, including Totem Building Supplies (Alberta), Chester Dawe (Newfoundland and Labrador), Matériaux Coupal (Greater Montreal), and Curtis Lumber and Mountain Building Centre (British Columbia). A new distribution centre was built in Alberta and the one in Boucherville was expanded. RONA strengthened its social involvement, incorporating sustainable development into its culture and entering into a partnership with the Vancouver 2010 Olympic Winter Games. Jean Gaulin took over as chairman of the board of directors, becoming the first person who was not a dealer to hold the position. The financial crisis slowed the pace of acquisitions. After more than 70 years in existence, the RONA network totalled 686 stores, with 30 000 employees, and was generating sales of $6 billion.

At the turn of the century and the millennium, RONA was at the top of its game. Its employees were united. Its facilities were modern. Its finances were sound. The grave threat that had been the big-box stores had been transmuted into a new momentum. All was well.

Consolidate or be consolidated

All was well, but we knew it could not last. Here, as in the United States, the media were abuzz with stories of "battles between giants"—specifically, big-box stores. In the U.S., all eyes were on the rivalry between Home Depot and Lowe's. In Canada, the competition between RONA L'entrepôt, Réno-Dépôt, and Home Depot eclipsed all other struggles, as though this format was the only one that existed in the marketplace.

Nothing could have been further from the truth. In the U.S., Bob Tillman, the president of Lowe's, Home Depot's rival, would explain to a reporter from *Forbes* magazine in January 2003: "Nobody seems to get it. It's not Lowe's against Home Depot. It's Lowe's AND Home Depot against 80% of the damn marketplace." This was already true in 2000.

His was a powerful formula and it hit the nail on the head of the true issue: market consolidation was inevitable, and it was far from settled. It would be on our industry's agenda for many years to come.

In this skirmish, there would be two types of players: the consolidators and the consolidated. The alternative loomed as a real possibility for RONA. Even with net sales approaching a billion dollars in 1999, RONA was far from what you would call a giant. But our leadership position in Quebec would make us a prize catch in the eyes of a bigger player. For us, slow and steady growth was not an option. Our choice was clear: we would be consolidators.

We had one huge strategic advantage going for us. Because we had elected, since 1993, to position ourselves in every market niche and offer a range of different store formats, we could envisage playing the role of consolidator in every market segment, and in a variety of ways: by recruiting affiliate stores, franchising big-box stores, or making acquisitions.

Recreating RONA?

The story of RONA is a story about dealers. Dealers who, in ever-growing numbers, had banded together to establish common leverage for purchasing, distribution, and growth. But RONA remained a group of dealers. Sixty years after its founding, the model was essentially the same. In 2000, the RONA stores still belonged to the dealers, and, to a lesser extent, RONA's managers. Only in some instances, in the cases of the big-box stores where these dealers were grouped and associated with RONA Inc., did the formula diverge from the original model.

1999 SAW THE CONSTRUCTION AND INAUGURATION OF SEVEN NEW STORES. The Rona Le Rénovateur banner was designed to meet the needs of consumers in peri-urban areas. The banner would later be renamed RONA Le Régional.

Could we do the same thing outside Quebec? Could we bring together dealer owners so they could create a common platform for themselves on which to build? Dealers who were as Ontarian in Ontario and as Manitoban in Manitoba as they were Québécois in Quebec.

We had to give it a try. In 2000, we created a division called RONA Retail Canada, which was managed in Toronto. Its mandate was twofold. First, it would develop a network of big-box stores in Ontario, and, second, it would rally independent dealers around a corporate cooperative project. A made-in-Ontario RONA.

It flopped. The dealers who had been approached did not climb aboard. Not only was there a difference in culture but, mostly, there was a difference in context. When RONA had been formed, at the time of Les Marchands en Quincaillerie Ltée, the arguments for imposing a union had been clear: the economy was in a depression, dealers faced enormous obstacles when it came time to purchasing, and a few wholesalers had an unacceptable stranglehold on the hardware sector. In 1939, an element of necessity and even urgency had attended the birth of RONA. But 60 years later, these conditions did not exist in Ontario. Dealers who were approached were pragmatic; they wanted to know "What's in it for me?"

We soon realized that it was futile to try to recreate the same trajectory that RONA had followed in Quebec. RONA would only interest independent dealers outside Quebec if

Flower power

Peggy Godfrey
Atlantic Gardens, Botanix, Bedford, Nova Scotia

In 2008, Atlantic Gardens celebrated its 40th anniversary and its 15th year with Rona.

The Rona adventure began in 1993, when the Godfreys were in San Francisco looking for garden centres to do business with. When they mentioned they were also planning a trip to Quebec, their American counterparts suggested some gardening stores they could check out while they were there. As she toured the province, Peggy was surprised to find that all the stores on the list were Botanix merchants. Among them were the Jasmin family, who had co-founded Botanix. They told her more about the company—and Rona. This piqued Peggy's curiosity, and she did some more research when she got home. As an independent merchant, she realized the importance of belonging to a buying group, and from what she had learned about Rona she was sure she would be able to rely on them. So, one November day, she jumped into her Jeep and drove all the way to Boucherville! Coming from the Maritimes, she surprised everyone, as Rona's attention was largely focused on Western Canada at the time. The rest, as they say, is history...

Things have certainly changed since 1968, when Peggy and her husband, Jim, set up a small roadside stand selling plants and flowers. In those days, as there were no specialized horticultural retailers in Nova Scotia, if you wanted to buy plants you usually headed to the local farmers' market. Their first season came to a rather abrupt end on October 29: the next day, Peggy was in hospital, and their son Robin was born! Today, Atlantic Gardens serves customers at three locations in Nova Scotia. The Bedford outlet is just a stone's throw from the site of the original roadside stand. The one in Sackville, which started life as a nursery in 1977, became a seasonal store in 1986. And in 1972, Jim's brother Ross joined the family business and opened a garden centre in Dartmouth—Lakeland Garden Supply—which is now run by none other than its new owner... Robin!

Members of the International Garden Centre Association, the Godfreys travel widely, drawing constant inspiration from the centres they visit in the Netherlands, Switzerland, New Zealand, South Africa, the United States, and elsewhere in Canada. Peggy says that each store is unique and reflects the personality of its owners. In the Godfreys' case, quality, attention to detail, and their passion for the business have become their trademark!

A change worth making

Wayne Filsinger

W. Filsinger & Sons, Rona Cashway, Guelph, Ontario

Wayne grew up in a small rural community in Ontario. As a young man, however, he decided that although he enjoyed farming, it was not what he wanted to do for a living. So he took a job with Beaver Lumber, where he was offered training to become a manager. "It was Beaver Lumber University: the chance to learn without having to set foot in a classroom—although we did have to sweep the warehouse floors!" He climbed steadily up the company ladder and ended up not only owning his own store but also becoming regional manager for 12 cities in Ontario.

By 1995, however, Wayne had lost interest in the retail trade, so he sold his store and bought a lumberyard in the town of Elora, close to the city of Guelph. He knew how important it was to belong to a buying group, so he arranged a meeting with Craig Graham, one of the owners of Cashway, and teamed up with the company. The following year, he acquired a store in Guelph, then became vice-president of Cashway, a position he held from 1997 to 1999. Until then, the stores had always been managed as individual units, so he felt he could do more to develop the company as an insider. Selling mainly construction materials, these were ultra-practical stores that operated with a unique "cash and carry" concept, where you paid for your materials in cash and carried them away with you.

Wayne's initiatives proved successful, attracting Rona's interest in his stores. In 2000, he and the small group of co-owners to which he belonged agreed to sell. When Rona bought Cashway, they were taking on board not only 66 retail outlets across Ontario but also 117 years of history. And while to their clients everything appeared to go smoothly, behind the scenes it was a madhouse! Wayne had to move the whole administration team, get used to working with new suppliers, and adapt to Rona's brand image. It was quite a program—but well worth it!

RONA AQUIRES CASHWAY. Jim Pybus, president of Cashway, Robert Dutton, president and CEO, Henri Drouin, chairman of the board, and Rick Blickstead, chief of operations, Retail, during the acquisition of Cashway in 2000.

we could achieve a critical mass. For the banner to have some marketing appeal, it needed a minimum density in any given region. And density was crucial to being able to supply stores in an effective and cost-efficient manner. Our recruitment efforts had not yielded the critical mass that, in turn, would have enabled us to recruit more dealers. Yet, somehow, we had to find a way to create this virtuous circle.

We would have to go the route of acquisitions. To say that we contemplated this scenario with caution would be an understatement. The experts all concurred: it is difficult to create value through acquisitions. Especially given that RONA had little experience in these matters. Certainly, we had successfully integrated 36 Botanix nurseries, in 1982, but because, in this case, they had not been in the hardware business, we had told them: you know your trade, so carry on with what you've been doing. Botanix had operated alongside RONA, rather than having been truly integrated. The one real competitor takeover dated back to 1988 with the acquisition of Dismat and its hundred some dealers. Ten years later, bitter memories still lingered in the minds of many. It was undeniable that, from a business standpoint, the operation had generated the expected gains, but, for some of the dealers involved, integrating had proved an ordeal.

During the Dismat merger, the problem had been that we had not paid heed to the animosity that pitted dealers in small Quebec markets against one another, dealers who,

October 2000

WHEN IT WAS BOUGHT BY RONA, Cashway was already a century-old company. The third largest player in the industry in Ontario, its image had wide public recognition.

IN JUNE 2000, Henri Drouin attended the official opening of the Rona Cashway in Exeter, Ontario.

for generations, had been competitors and rivals. But, of course, such a problem could not exist in areas that were still, for us, untapped markets.

The first acquisition outside Quebec

It was time to make inroads. And, as throughout RONA's history, there would be no half measures. The first acquisition outside Quebec would be significant. We had to achieve that all-important critical mass in the targeted region. And we wanted to send a message: RONA will be a consolidator; it will not be consolidated. And RONA already knew whom to acquire: Cashway Building Centres, in Port Hope, Ontario.

This was a very old and respected company. In 1883, Charles A. Larkin founded a lumber wholesaler in Brandon, Manitoba. In the mid 1950s, the company moved to Ontario and set up shop as a building materials' dealer under the name Cash and Carry Lumber, which would become Cashway Building Centres in the late 1960s. In 1975, the company even broke into the Quebec market when it bought Dorval Builders Supplies and opened a new store under the name of Rénovaprix. However, Cashway's ambitions in Quebec soon cooled, and it sold its interests to the Beaver Lumber company.

In 1999, Cashway's sales reached $322 million, up 3.6% from the previous year. The company had just purchased Hensall District Co-op, an Ontario building materials sales cooperative, when RONA came knocking at its door.

After several months of negotiations, the transaction was finalized. RONA obtained the retail chain and its 61 stores for just shy of $50 million. With the approximately 50 RONA and Botanix stores already in Ontario, chiefly in the eastern part of the province, RONA doubled its foothold in the largest market in Canada. We now had over 100 stores in Ontario.

The Cashway stores, which employed 1 000 people, varied in size, from 12 000 to 30 500 sq. ft. (930 to 2 850 m²), and resembled many of RONA's hardware outlets. In this respect, integration would be easy.

But, in other ways, the two companies were very different. Only six Cashway outlets were dealer-owned affiliated stores. All the others belonged to Cashway. But we were convinced we would be able to transfer these stores back to the people who ran them.

A difficult integration

We organized a big celebration. Cashway's people were invited to come to Boucherville. Tour the facilities. The distribution centre. "Wow! Incredible! It's so big!" Then they arrived in the cafeteria, which had been decorated for the occasion, to hearty applause from RONA's employees. Welcome. Make yourself at home.

"Timber!"

Carl Grittner
Former President, Revy, Langley,
British Columbia

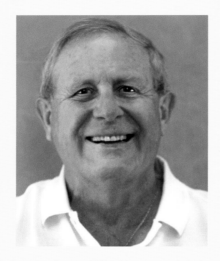

This year, Carl Grittner will celebrate 71 years of a full and active life. For the past 10 years, he has divided his time between his family in Kelowna and the golf courses in Las Vegas. And though he doesn't miss work for one minute, he often thinks about the wonderful colleagues with whom he shared the great Revelstoke adventure.

Carl started working in the lumberyard of a construction materials company at the age of 18. By the time he was 27, he was general manager of the company's three stores.

In 1977, West Fraser Timber was looking for a general manager for its 10 stores: the position was vacant and they needed to fill it, fast. One of their managers, who had already worked for Carl in Kelowna, suggested they call him. During the interview, Pete Ketcham, one of the brothers who owned West Fraser, asked Carl what his biggest weakness was. "Impatience!" Carl replied. It proved a quality that would serve him well for the huge challenges that lay ahead. In a few years, he turned things around. At that time, the company's activities were concentrated mainly in the forestry sector, though they did operate a few retail stores. Under Carl's management, retail sales expanded, new stores were opened, and, in 1988, the company bought up Revelstoke. Revelstoke's head office was located in Calgary, while West Fraser's was in Langley; Carl had the unenviable task of having to inform 51 of his 55 employees that they were out of a job—the hardest day of his life, he recalls. They kept the Revelstoke banner for the retail stores. The advent of warehouse stores posed the next challenge. Aikenhead's was expanding into the West and opening more big-box outlets; it was time to get in on the action. One of West Fraser's clients was Lowe's. Carl asked the American company if they could show some of his employees around their warehouse stores in North Carolina to see how things worked. "They really let us do what we wanted!" he says. The employees picked up plenty of practical tips, such as how many shopping carts to provide, how far apart to space checkouts, and so on. The initiative paid off: on the day of the grand opening of the Edmonton store, so many people showed up that Carl couldn't get out of the parking lot for two hours! He hadn't expected a store like that to make money the first year, and they haven't had a single bad month since. He thought, "My God! We'd better open a few more!" Which is exactly what they did.

When Carl was nearing retirement, West Fraser decided to sell its retail division to focus on the forestry business. The time was right from an economic point of view, and Rona was not only the right buyer but the only party interested in neighbourhood stores. It was a win-win situation for everyone!

IN 2001, West Fraser's internal newsletter announced the breaking news: Rona was buying Revy.

I said a few words. I spoke of RONA, of Cashway, of everything we had in common, of the way we would grow together. Everyone was in a good mood. Then I announced our intention to sell the Cashway stores back to their managers, who would, as a result, become dealer owners.

Well, that didn't go over very well. In fact, a decided chill settled in the room.

We quickly realized how we fumbled that one. But by then it was too late. So completely sold were we on our RONA model, we had assumed that everybody would want to be the owner of a RONA store!

We revised our position. RONA would henceforth be a retailer. We had 450 stores in Quebec, our board of directors was composed of dealers... we certainly had no shortage expertise in store management. And, in time, those who wished would become dealer owners. But we would not impose anything.

Our lack of experience complicated the integration process. It took close to 18 months for Cashway to get over the shock of the merger.

A major coup: the Revy chain

In the meantime, we soldiered on, learning lessons from our mistakes. The ink on the Cashway deal was barely dry when we set our sights on a vastly larger prize: the Revy chain, owned by West Fraser Timber Co. Ltd., an integrated forest products company. West Fraser wanted to divest itself

they were warehouse-type centres with over 40 000 products, serving the renovation market in British Columbia, Alberta, Manitoba, and Ontario.

EACH OF THE COMPANIES THAT WERE ACQUIRED RAN ITS OWN ACTIVITIES. Since 1988, employees of Revy have participated in the Revy Road Runners fundraiser. Teams made up of employees and suppliers run a 24-hour relay race, with the proceeds going to children's charities.

185

of its retail network so that it could concentrate exclusively on developing its core lumber business. Revy was in fact a chain operating under three banners: Revy, a network of warehouse-type home centres; Revelstoke, a network of smaller stores with a presence in Western Canada; and Lansing Buildall, a network of building materials stores acquired a few years earlier. A mix of formats that was anything but unfamiliar to RONA!

In all, Revy operated 51 stores, from the Pacific coast to Ontario, with 5 000 employees, sales revenues of over $800 million, more than 2.7 million sq. ft. of retail space (251 000 m^2). Purchase price: $216 million.

Announced in May 2001, the transaction was completed in July. From one day to the next, RONA had established a presence in 8 Canadian provinces; the pro forma retail sales of its corporate, franchised, and affiliated stores rose above $2.8 billion. We could legitimately announce the ascension to the throne of the new Canadian home-improvement hardware leader: RONA!

In less than two years, RONA became the parent company to five outfits: Cashway, Revy, Lansing, Revelstoke, and, of course, RONA. Five organizations; five corporate cultures; five internal newsletters; up to eight payroll, pension, and insurance plans; unrelated computer systems, each one of which was isolated from the next; unfamiliar coding systems; and 200 000 different products.

What now? We had learned some lessons from the Cashway acquisition. During the Cashway purchase, we had committed the classic errors of greenhorn buyers: we had underestimated the difficulties involved, underestimated how people would be affected, underestimated the importance of corporate culture; in short, we had underestimated the complexity of the operation.

We called in a Montreal management consulting firm whose clients included top corporations in America and Europe. They had already provided consultation services for a host of other organizations involved in acquisition ventures. With their help, we set up an integration program that would roll out gradually over two years. Priority was placed on communication. A merger is always traumatic for the personnel involved; we had to avoid compounding the problem by needlessly creating uncertainty. No surprises. Everything would be announced in advance.

We merged activities. We developed more efficient procedures drawn from the best practices of each company. It was a sharing of knowledge and of know-how. As far as technology was concerned, for the time being, we didn't touch the systems that were already in place, but we devised links that would allow us to create data warehouses. This provided us with a cost-efficient method of tracking inventory and sales in stores right across the country.

Later, new banners would appear on the Canadian landscape: RONA Lansing, RONA Revy Home Centre, RONA

Climbing ladders

John Kitchen
Former President of Lansing Buildall, Toronto, Ontario

In 1951, William Kitchen founded Lansing Buildall with his wife and a partner, Orvile Blackwood. The company name was inspired by its location, on the road between North York and, you guessed it, Lansing!

The business specialized in selling doors and mouldings to building contractors. But the company grew right from the start, and William found an increasing number of clients who were not builders coming through its doors; people had heard about his innovative in-store presentation, which allowed them to actually see and touch the products for themselves. In 1957, he also started to offer hands-on workshops such as "How to finish the basement," "Building a balcony," and "Do-it-yourself plumbing." These were all new concepts—a far cry from the traditional lumberyards of the time.

In 1963, William opened a second store, which is now a Rona, and in his honour, the street would later be named William Kitchen Road. And still more outlets were opened, until, in 1971, Beaver Lumber made an attractive offer to buy the business. Headstrong, and knowing full well that he could never work for anyone else, William refused. It was his children who, in 1997, would finally decide to sell.

William's son John was 16 when he started working for the company. After a hiatus during which he obtained a degree in Business Administration, he returned to the business. His father started him off on the first rung of the ladder, and from there he made his way up, slowly but surely, to the position of president, in 1989. Each time William thought his son was becoming complacent, he would encourage him to climb another rung. At each stage, John would look at what his boss was doing and think, "No way could I do that!" But then he'd jump in and realize that "it was a piece of cake and a lot of fun—as well as being a big challenge!" By 1997, the company had nine stores in all, with sales totalling $170 million. When The Home Depot arrived, the Kitchens approached Revy with a view to a merger, which was finalized in 1998. John and his four sisters were unanimous in their decision. They saw this as the only way to fully exploit Lansing's potential before it became either too big to sell or was crushed by the fierce competition they would suffer at the hands of the big boxes. John continued to work for Revy's Ontario division for several years.

Since then, after having taken nine months' leave—his domestic skills have surpassed those of his wife but he almost died from boredom—John is returning to the fold. His new business: luxury doors and mouldings!

REVELSTOKE WAS THE OLDEST COMPONENT OF THE REVY BANNER.
For over 100 years, it had been a part of the daily life of Canadians living in the West.

Revelstoke Home Centre, and RONA Revy Home & Garden Warehouse. Shortly after, however, we would integrate these banners into RONA's portfolio of banners according to the store's vocation.

I think that, this time, we did things right.

We forged a process for the future. Each acquisition had to meet four conditions: a) any company we sought to acquire had to be strategically in line with RONA's business model; b) its assets must be profitable from the outset; c) the integration of a new organization had to offer a high potential for synergies that would generate increased efficiency and savings; d) the company had to have talented, experienced managers. These four criteria are still today the principles that guide RONA's acquisitions.

As far as the integration process itself was concerned, we kept the systematic method we put in place for the integration of Revy, a method based on communication and an appreciation for people's needs.

The acquisitions of Cashway and Revy boosted the company's results. From 1999 to 2002, net sales shot up 135%, bounding from $988 million to $2.3 billion. Operating profit nearly tripled: $37 million in 1999; $129 million in 2002. Earnings per share rose from $0.46 to $1.12 and the total assets, from $288 million to $766 million. RONA now had 527 stores and held 11.5% of the Canadian market. We established that 83% of Canadians lived less than a 30-minute drive from a RONA store.

AT THE TIME OF THE ACQUISITION, there were some 30 Revelstoke stores in British Columbia, Alberta, and Saskatchewan, serving the retail market in both urban and rural areas.

THE LANSING STORES IN ONTARIO measured 40 000 sq. ft. on average. With their building materials and lumberyards, they catered mostly to the retail market and to contractors.

The acquisitions put the wind in RONA's sails. But they were not the only growth vector. RONA continued to pursue organic growth: increased sales in existing stores, recruitment of new dealers, and the construction of new stores were responsible for 50% of this accelerated growth. The 2002 annual report, for example, set building five to eight new big-box stores within 18 months and recruiting 250 new dealers over four years as a target.

This report also paid a glowing tribute to one of RONA's great builders:

"Henri Drouin did not merely witness RONA's growth. He was a driving force behind it. From the earliest RONA dealer-owner right up to the newest shareholder, from our most senior employee to our most recent recruit, we're all the beneficiaries of Henri Drouin's passion and efforts. We are all indebted to his vision, dedication, and wisdom."

Having joined RONA in 1966, as a dealer, Henri Drouin was appointed as a member of the board of directors 10 years later and went on to become its chairman for 21 years. It is a record that still holds today.

I was deeply saddened by the departure of Henri Drouin. On a personal level, he had been a mentor and a friend. I will be forever grateful to him.

The position of chairman of the board then passed to André Gagnon. He was another one of this second

The RONA banner •

TODAY, THE RONA BANNER FLIES ON THE MASTS OF AN INCREASINGLY GROWING FLOTILLA.

In 2000, when Rona was beginning to expand outside Quebec, the company was already operating under many banners, each with its own mission:

RONA L'entrepôt/RONA Warehouse: The warehouse store for hardware, renovation, construction, and horticulture; from 85 000 to 125 000 sq. ft. (7 900 to 11 600 m²); 45 000 products in stock; located in urban and suburban areas;

RONA Le Rénovateur: The store for renovation, hardware, and materials; 10 000 to 75 000 sq. ft. (900 to 7 000 m²); up to 25 000 products in stock; located in average-size urban centres;

RONA Le Quincaillier: The traditional-size store specializing in hardware; 5 000 to 25 000 sq. ft. (465 to 2 300 m²); up to 20 000 products in stock; located in a variety of communities;

RONA L'Express/RONA Hardware: The small-size store for standard hardware, electrical, and plumbing products; 1 500 to 5 000 sq. ft. (140 to 465 m²); up to 10 000 products in stock; located in small localities and in neighbourhoods;

RONA L'Express Matériaux/RONA Home Centre (outside Quebec): The specialized store for contractors, tradesmen, and handymen; 1 500 to 20 000 sq. ft. (140 to 1 850 m²); up to 15 000 products in stock; located in a variety of communities;

RONA Le Régional: A big-box store of 75 000 sq. ft. (7 000 m²), developed to serve populations of 50 000 to 75 000 residents; a hybrid between a Rona Le Rénovateur, with its neighbourhood store atmosphere, and a Rona Warehouse, with its wide variety of products.

Botanix: The store specializing in horticulture and in gardening products.

A period of transition, when many banners flew alongside each other, marked the 2000-2010 decade.

2000. Cashway Building Centres, in Ontario, was acquired in the first quarter. This enriched the group with 1 069 more people working in 66 new stores. Well integrated into their communities, these stores, often quite small, each had a lumberyard. As stores specializing in the sale of construction material, they were similar to the Rona L'Express Matériaux. Since the corporate culture was different from that of Rona, one rubbed off on the other. Thus, using the existing model, Rona experienced managing its own 'corporate' stores for the first time.

2001. The West Fraser Timber paper manufacturer sold their Revy chain to Rona. Revy was, in fact, made up of three companies. In the early 1980s, Revy had purchased Revelstoke, and, in the late 1990s, Lansing Buildall. But each of the chains operated using a different purchasing, sales, and inventory system; Rona needed to harmonize several companies and cultures at the same time. Here again, it was a valuable opportunity to learn. Moreover, this project, undertaken with great enthusiasm, resulted in 5 000 people being added to the momentum of the group, as well as approximately 50 stores, many of which were big-box stores. This group, similar to Rona's, consisted of warehouse stores in large urban centres as well as traditional stores in outlying regional areas. And again, the similarity to Rona was remarkable, except that these were corporate stores and not affiliates.

So as not to confuse customers, the 'Lansing Buildall' stores became 'Rona Lansing' stores; the 'Cashway' stores traded their name for 'Rona Cashway'; the 'Revelstoke' stores were converted to 'Rona Home Centres'; and the 'Revy Home and Garden' stores were henceforth known as the 'Rona Home & Garden' stores. The advertising

The standard for the group

campaign "My name is still Bob, Karen, Shelly..." aimed to emphasize the continuity and the stability of the employees.

As a result, the notoriety and the equity of the Revy brand were added to those of Rona. In addition, both companies were proudly Canadian, which has always been much appreciated by consumers in Western Canada.

2003. Rona bought Réno-Dépôt, its chief competitor in Quebec. Réno-Dépôt had started out as Val Royal, which went on to become Castor Bricoleur, then Brico. It was also the first chain to have established a big-box store in the province. Now, 4 300 people, distributed throughout 20 stores, joined forces with the Rona group.

Since both entities were well-known and appreciated, did not offer the same products, and catered to different clienteles, it was decided, then, that, for a period of time, the two banners would remain intact in Quebec. On the other hand, because the Rona banner had been present since the earlier acquisitions, the six The Building Box stores in Ontario became Rona Home & Garden centres. Today, there are 16 Réno-Dépôt stores.

2005. Totem Building Supplies joined the group, bringing on board 15 highly successful stores and some 900 people in Alberta. It was a market niche chain, recognized for the high quality of its construction materials and the excellence of its customer service. The key to its success: a highly innovative training program, which was quite different from Rona's. Employees were trained for two weeks before starting to work at the store. Rona picked up something new again.

The chain was so well-established and robust that it was decided to keep the Totem banner as it was, unchanged.

2006. In Western Canada again, other smaller chains were acquired, including Mountain Building Supplies, Dick's Lumber and Curtis Lumber, in British Columbia, and Noble Trade and Best-MAR, in Ontario. In the Atlantic Region, Chester Dawe in Newfoundland also rallied to Rona. The only hardware store chain in the province, it kept the name 'Chester Dawe,' but added 'a subsidiary of Rona,' which it kept only a short time before finally fully adopting the Rona banner.

2010. Today, customers from coast to coast recognize the Rona brand as the largest hardware dealer in the country.

Financing • Ensuring solid growth

FROM THE VERY BEGINNING, RONA HAS TAKEN A CAREFUL APPROACH TO FINANCING. AVOIDING THE HIGHLY LEVERAGED STRATEGIES THAT HAVE AT TIMES BEEN POPULAR IN THE BUSINESS WORLD, IT HAS ALWAYS FAVOURED EQUITY FINANCING AS A WAY TO FUND ITS GROWTH.

❶ In 1997, Rona secured crucial funding from the French group Les Mousquetaires, allowing them to continue their development by opening big-box stores.

For a very long time, Rona financed its expansion using the funds generated by its operations and investments from its member dealers in the form of share capital. Added to this, but on a more limited scale, were mortgage or term loans, and bank loans to provide working capital.

The company made a brief foray into the public markets during the 1980s. In 1984, in conjunction with an issue of voting shares made available exclusively to member dealers, executives, and employees of the company, Rona came out with a public issue of non-voting preferred shares that would be listed on the Montreal Stock Exchange. They were, however, redeemed from the holders between 1989 and 1991, using the proceeds from the sale of substantial non-operating assets. Rona was once again under the exclusive ownership of its dealers and employees.

Starting in 1994, however, the organization's accelerated growth prompted Rona to consider new and different funding strategies. This was the year that marked a change in direction for Rona with the introduction of its big-box stores. It called for the kind of significant investment that was impossible for a single dealer acting alone. Or, even if the dealer could come up with the funds, the risk was too great. For this reason, the dealers were given the opportunity to contribute time and money to the project, and bring their own clients with them. But it was up to Rona to supply the rest of the financing, in particular by securing loans, hence with the obligation to become profitable itself.

1997. With the relocation of its distribution centre, making it possible to serve big-box stores in Quebec, Ontario, and the Maritimes, the drive to step up the pace at which new big-box stores were introduced, and the development of the new regional store concept (Rona Le Régional), new capital was needed. Enter ITM Entreprises S.A., which in 1997 invested $30 million in Rona, consisting of

$20 million in voting shares in exchange for a 16.67% ownership interest—bringing Rona's total market value to an estimated $120 million—as well as $10 million in preferred shares. ITM Entreprises is a subsidiary of the Groupement des Mousquetaires, a French distributor and retailer that, like Rona, is owned by its member dealers.

2000. Major expansion across all of Canada began. In March, the acquisition of Cashway, with 66 stores, helped to significantly strengthen Rona's presence in Ontario, where it already had eight affiliated stores. The banks agreed to increase Rona's line of credit, following which the company took over Cashway's liabilities.

2001. Along the same lines, once the deal with Cashway was finalized, negotiations intensified with Revy in the West. Here again, a substantial investment was needed. The group, with its 51 stores, had over $800 million in sales, while the figure for Rona was $1.2 billion... The Société générale de financement (SGF), the Caisse de dépôt et placement du Québec, and ITM all lent their financial support. The three partners invested $100 million in common shares and subordinated debt, under conditions that boosted Rona's total market value to $260 million. The acquisition was finalized in July. To finance operations on this new scale, credit facilities were increased to $330 million.

2002. Rona decided to proceed with an issue of shares available to the general public and list its shares on the stock exchange. The market was not especially favourable, but, in October, Rona successfully issued $150 million worth of shares, which from that time on were traded on the Toronto Stock Exchange. The issue price meant that Rona's market capitalization was $625 million. The proceeds from the issue allowed the company to pay off its subordinated debts and increase its liquid assets for itself and for the dealers. In fact, up until that

THE NEW CANADIAN POWERHOUSE IN HOME IMPROVEMENT **❷**

point, the actual value of a share was difficult to establish, given the almost total absence of a market. The dealers were required to be shareholders and to renew their investment each year. As a result, a dealer who had been in business for 50 years owned a huge number of shares, but had no possibility of selling them. Once Rona became a publicly-traded company, dealers were able to realize the market value of their investment in the organization, which in many cases had grown over the years to a substantial amount, subject to restrictions based on their sales rate. This gave them the ability to recover liquid assets, often for the purpose of reinvesting them in their own stores. In exchange, they agreed to sign a contract with Rona for a period of 10 years, rather than 30 days as had been the case previously, in order to reassure outside investors as to the sustainability of the business.

2003. Rona acquired Réno-Dépôt, a subsidiary of Castorama in France, which itself was a subsidiary of the British multinational Kingfisher. Réno-Dépôt's sales totaled $850 million, while the figure for Rona was now $2 billion. Once again, new money was needed. An issue of $150 million worth of common shares was completed in June. Rona's market value was approaching the billion-dollar mark. The increase in the number of shares in

circulation meant greater liquidity, a fact that was beneficial for all shareholders.

2004. In November Rona proceeded with a $103-million leaseback transaction involving a number of its properties, primarily the Réno-Dépôt stores, in order to pay off part of its bank loans.

2005. Totem, in Alberta, was acquired in April for $100 million, financed from existing credit facilities.

2006. In April, Rona acquired Noble Trade, followed by Mountain Building Supplies in British Columbia and Chester Dawe in Newfoundland. In November, Rona entered into a new $650-million credit facility and issued debentures worth $400 million in the public debt market. The rating agencies assigned the issue a very high credit rating, a testament to the company's financial soundness.

2009. In June Rona completed the closing of a $172.5-million issue at a price that put the company's market value at $1.65 billion.

❷ In 2000 and 2001, Rona actively furthered its expansion with the acquisition of Cashway, Revy, and Lansing.

❸ Rona reached a new milestone in 2002 when it became listed on the stock exchange. On December 20, 2002, Robert Dutton received the official TSX listing certificate from Clare Gaudet, senior vice-president, Toronto Stock Exchange, and Barbara Stymiest, CEO, TSX Group.

❹ Claude Guévin (right), the executive vice-president and CFO, discusses development with Martin Lacroix, the vice-president of Finance and Corporate Development.

2000

The arrival of the year 2000 was greeted with spectacular celebrations around the globe, while the dreaded "millennium bug" that had been expected to affect computers worldwide did not materialize, a result of the hundreds of billions of dollars had been spent since 1995 on preventing it.

In Jerusalem, Ariel Sharon, the leader of Israel's right-wing political party and an ardent promoter of Jewish colonization in Palestinian territories, engaged in an act of deliberate provocation in September when he visited Temple Mount, sacred place of the Muslims, accompanied by hundreds of police officers. This would lead to the outbreak of the second *intifada* (Palestinian uprising).

The United States presidential election on November 7 is one that will long be remembered. Democratic candidate Al Gore won 550 000 votes more than Republican candidate George W. Bush, but it was not clear who had carried Florida's 25 electoral votes, the popular vote in that state being so close that a recount became necessary. The process dragged on amidst great confusion for more than a month. In the end, the Supreme Court decided in a 5-4 vote to halt the recount and give Florida's electoral vote to Bush, which meant that Bush finished with 271 electoral votes to Gore's 266. Bush would therefore become president of the United States by virtue of the wishes of a single Supreme Court judge...

2001

Major events in the alter-globalization movement took the spotlight in the first half of 2001.

In January, some 20 000 participants gathered in Porto Alegre, Brazil, for the first World Social Forum, under the theme of "Another world is possible." It was intended to be a popular response to the World Economic Forum held each year in Davos, Switzerland, which is open exclusively to business and political leaders.

In April, when the heads of state representing all the nations of the Americas (with the exception of Fidel Castro) met in Quebec City to discuss plans for a free trade area, police used tear gas and rubber bullets to disperse large groups of violent protestors.

In July, 300 000 demonstrators disrupted the G8 summit in Genoa, Italy, and one of them was killed by police fire.

But there is no question that the events of September 11 and their aftermath are what make 2001 such an unforgettable year. The suicide attacks carried out in New York and Washington by terrorists linked to the Al-Qaeda network claimed some 3 000 lives. As the network was based in Afghanistan, the United States retaliated against that country in October by initiating aerial bombings, sending in ground troops, and providing support for the Afghan anti-Taliban movements. The Taliban regime fell in December, but Al-Qaeda was far from being wiped out.

2002

On January 1, 2002, the euro (€) replaced the national currency in 12 countries of the European Union. This massive financial changeover, the first ever to be attempted on such a scale, went smoothly, the new tender embraced by the general public, a sign of the hope among Europeans that old national animosities might disappear.

July 1 marked the creation of the International Criminal Court, the first permanent international court responsible for presiding over cases involving war crimes, crimes against humanity, and genocide. The United States, Israel, China, and Russia are among the countries that still refuse to recognize the Court's jurisdiction.

This was also the year of the Bush administration's extensive national and international campaign against Saddam Hussein's Iraq. After identifying Iraq, along with Iran and North Korea, as forming an "Axis of Evil" that posed a threat to world peace, and after accusing Iraq of possessing weapons of mass destruction and having close ties with Al-Qaeda terrorists, Bush obtained a resolution from Congress authorizing him to go to war. In November, the UN Security Council demanded that Iraq allow international inspectors into the country to verify Iraq's compliance with its obligation to destroy its weapons of mass destruction. Iraq agreed. But matters would not end there...

generation of RONA builders, who, along with Henri Drouin and André Dion, had taken over the reins from Rolland and Napoléon. André Gagnon had joined the group in 1962. He had served as vice-chairman for 23 years. His family business, H. Gagnon et Fils, had shares in four RONA L'entrepôt stores. He was a dealer to the core and a seasoned businessman.

I knew I had his full support. I would need it; there was no dearth of challenges I would have to face.

Going public

RONA had grown tremendously and had become the Canadian industry leader. But the company had to pursue further growth, and, at the pace it had set, growth would require an infusion of fresh capital.

The previous acquisitions had been fueled by an injection of $60 million from three shareholders: ITM Entreprises, our France-based partner, who increased its interest in RONA; CDP Capital, a subsidiary of the Caisse de dépôt et placement du Québec; and the Société générale de financement (SGF), a public corporation set up by the Quebec government. However, the CDP Capital and SGF investments came with a condition: RONA had to go public within a maximum of five years.

So the question was no longer "if" but "when." The answer was "as soon as the market allows." Because there

A passion for people... and for business

André Gagnon

Former Member and Former Chairman of the Board

H. Gagnon et Fils; Rona L'entrepôt, Granby, Saint-Bruno, Saint-Hyacinthe, and Brossard, Quebec

NEW CONSTRUCTION WAS IN FULL SWING! IN 2006, Claude Bernier, executive vice-president, Mayor Gérald Allain, owners Ronald and Paul Cormier, and René Cloutier, director of Development, attended the groundbreaking ceremony on the site of the future Rona Le Rénovateur in Edmundston, New Brunswick, which would open its doors in July 2007.

André Gagnon left school at 15 to help his father in the hardware store—the "university of life," as he calls it. Even then, he could see that if the business was to succeed it was going to have to improve its supply and distribution strategy. Their three competitors in Saint-Hyacinthe had already grasped that notion, having joined Les Marchands en Quincaillerie Ltée.

It took him a few years to learn the trade, get to know the products, win people over, and build up a clientele. "It's simple—I like my clients, so they like me!" he says. When he turned 17, his father, Henri, put him in charge of purchasing. Nine years later, in 1962, Napoléon Piotte approached him. But joining the Marchands group required the endorsement of the other store owners; when Alphonse Vincent—hardware store owner no. 5—offered his support, the deal was clinched.

André's strategy was simple and effective: he singled out the most competent and experienced people in the group and befriended them. Jean-Jacques Latendresse, of Quincaillerie Notre-Dame in Pointe-aux-Trembles, particularly inspired him. He also joined the advertising committee run by Marc St-Pierre, which met once a week to choose which products to promote. Never missing a beat, he always had a copy of his competitors' flyers on him. And all the while, he was learning more and more.

He was also working increasingly harder, too. Each week, he would take his list of orders to Napoléon Piotte on a Saturday, to avoid the extra two or three mailing days that would have delayed his delivery confirmations—his "call fors." You have to remember that, at that time, the vast majority of wholesalers were Anglophones. "We received all our bills in English. We didn't speak the language, but we knew the jargon," he explains. His relative proximity to Montreal, his resourcefulness, and his limitless availability were all assets that propelled him up the ladder of success.

Gagnon's head for business and his attention to detail led him to buy shares in Gestion La Savane and then in Rona. From franchise in Saint-Bruno to affiliate in Saint-Hyacinthe, Granby, and Mont-Royal, he has experienced it all. Countless expansions, buyouts, partnerships... "It was fast and furious!" he says. Today, assisted by his son Stéphane, who sits in the vice-president's chair, he manages H. Gagnon et Fils, which owns shares in the four Rona L'entrepôt operations in Saint-Hyacinthe, Granby, Saint-Bruno, and Brossard. Since the age of 15, he has grown his sales figures from $38 000 to an impressive $165 million. Not bad!

In addition to an active and ongoing involvement in his local community, André Gagnon was also a member of Rona's board of directors of for 36 years, from 1971 to 2007. In 2002, he succeeded Henri Drouin as chairman of the board.

And would you believe that, in 1957, newlywed 19-year-old André travelled to New York for his honeymoon, arriving just in time for... the American hardware show! Happily, his new bride was not put out, and, 53 years later, they are still happily married!

The man with talent in hand

Michel Gendron

Retired Print Shop and Mail Manager, Administrative Office, Boucherville, Quebec

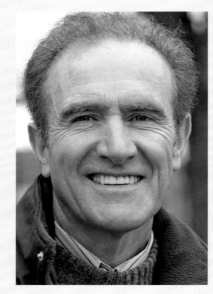

When the career advisor, René Piotte, Napoléon Piotte's son, walked into the Collège de Beauharnois classroom on June 13, 1966, he asked the assembled students, "Is there anyone here who's good at drawing?" Michel Gendron was about to take his final exams. He was a good student, but his father had already told him that after Michel finished high school, he couldn't afford to pay for further education for his son. At a mere 116 lb.—not much less than what he weighs today—young Michel wasn't big enough for the typical jobs in the region: the police force, the foundry, Northern Electric... So, he raised his hand timidly. That morning, he dedicated his professional life to Rona.

The next day, his father went into town with him, to De la Savane Street, to meet Napoléon. The merchants needed someone to replace their price catalogue management clerk—someone who could start the following Monday. The price catalogue was their bible; without it, the whole system would come to a screeching halt. In those days, to produce the catalogue, you had to cut things out with scissors, draw freehand, set your type using dry transfer sheets, then print the whole thing on a Gestetner spirit duplicator machine. And that was all done by one person. It was a huge responsibility... all for $47 a week!

If the merchants' orders were not all processed by five o'clock, the controller, André Dion, would come to give him a hand at the print shop. "There were only about 60 of us at the time. We all knew one another and helped each other out, and no one counted their hours, despite the fact that some of us had a two-hour journey home."

Technology progressed: first came microfilm, then computers. Michel took graphic arts courses to keep up with the latest techniques. He passed on what he learned to the merchants, even though that wasn't part of his job. They loved him—he was their front man; he kept in contact with them and knew their concerns. Always on the lookout for smart, cost-saving ideas, Michel would constantly come up with great deals and imaginative solutions, which he shared with everyone. "I was kind of my own boss all my life," he says. "It was a bit like having my own company."

Forty years at Rona is hard to sum up. Forty years of working together, sharing good times and bad, confiding in each other... There was a tremendous feeling of solidarity. On his last day, Michel went to see Robert Dutton, but was so choked up he couldn't speak. "I had such a huge lump in my throat... It was like losing a close friend!" he adds.

Michel may be retired, but he doesn't show any signs of slowing down! He still takes part in the company's fundraising events like the multiple sclerosis bike tour—pedalling 150 km in two days—and is fixing up a traditional home and its outbuildings... just to keep his hands busy!

were no lack of investment opportunities, and they had to be funded.

For several months, RONA prepared for its stock market debut. The operation was led by Claude Guévin, the executive vice-president and chief financial officer. First step: persuade the dealers that the time to go public had come. We had already opened the capital to non-members: ITM had held shares in the company since 1997. But ITM was a group of dealers, like RONA, a sort of extended family. In 2001, we had opened the capital to financiers. We were now at the next stage: we had to list the company on the stock exchange and share control with thousands of anonymous shareholders.

So, we took to the road once again, as had Napoléon, and Henri after him in 1992-1993, to explain our strategic plan.

We met with the dealers in each region. We explained that it was time to accept that we must relinquish a RONA hallmark, a tradition: the company would no longer be under the control of its dealers. The structure that had served us so well was no longer compatible with our size and our goals. But another hallmark had emerged. Achievement. "Understand all that you have accomplished. Your investment, your unity, your solidarity as a group, and your independence as individual dealers have built this company, which, today, is national in scope and has continental ambitions. Listing the company on the stock

THE BRICOMARCHÉ BANNER, which operates under the Groupement des Mousquetaires (ITM), is made up of 600 independent stores across France, Spain, and Poland. The Bricomarché chain specializes in household equipment.

THE COMPANY PROUDLY ANNOUNCES to employees its listing on the stock exchange.

exchange doesn't mean we are renouncing what we are, merely consecrating it."

The dealers were enthusiastic. They were ready to do what was needed to make the operation a success. And "what was needed" was huge. They had to commit themselves to RONA for 10 years. They had to buy an unprecedented 90% of their total purchases from RONA. They had to grant RONA the right of first refusal on the sale of their stores. In addition, they had to pledge their RONA shares as security for receivables owed to the company. Then, for a determined length of time, they had to accept strict rules governing the resale of their shares to reassure the new investors by offering a guarantee that there would be no massive sell-off of their shares by the dealers.

But they would obtain a direct benefit in the medium term. The dealers, who were already shareholders, would see the value of their stock rise considerably. As things stood, the value of their shares was determined solely by the book value of the company. But publicly listed, in an open market, the market value of their shares would be based on the profit and growth expectations of the company. RONA's growth and profitability was attracting a lot of attention.

The dealers subscribed unreservedly to the project: they all signed on. Each one, without exception, came out in favour of the company going public and accepted the rules put forward for the operation's success.

In September 2002, with the full and unqualified support of the dealers, we prepared the second step: convince potential shareholders and embark on a grueling tour to promote RONA to institutional investors and financial analysts.

The firm BMO Nesbitt Burns oversaw the syndicate of underwriters. In consultation with them, we finally reached the following decision: we would issue 11 120 000 common shares at $13.50 per unit, for a gross issue of $150 120 000.

Along with representatives of BMO Nesbitt Burns, Claude Guévin, the executive vice-president and CFO, Martin Lacroix, the vice-president of Finance and Corporate Development, and I spent three weeks making the rounds of investment companies. Montreal, Toronto, Vancouver, New York, Boston. We had to meet financiers who invested in the stock market on behalf of clients: they could make the difference between success and failure; they had the power to create popular demand for RONA stock or to let it be met with indifference. Hundreds of millions of dollars were at stake. It was a difficult exercise. Sometimes we had the impression that we were being looked upon with a hint of condescension. We were just one company among so many others trying to sell ourselves. "It was like a beauty pageant," said Claude Guévin. Everywhere we went, we touted RONA, its history, its development, its values, its plans, in front of people who sometimes appeared blasé and whose lack of interest was ill concealed.

People and culture •

NOBODY REFERS TO 'HUMAN RESOURCES' AT THE ADMINISTRATIVE HEADQUARTERS ANYMORE. NOT SINCE JEAN ÉMOND, THEN VICE-PRESIDENT, AND HIS TEAM OF ADVISORS CAME TO THE CONCLUSION THAT 'PEOPLE AND CULTURE' WOULD BE A MORE ACCURATE DESCRIPTION FOR THE DEPARTMENT.

❶ In 1969, the directors of Les Marchands en Quincaillerie Ltée were already mindful of providing appropriate training to its members: they offered courses in management and finance at its offices.

That was in 2002. "Changing 'resources' to 'people' was a gesture that went beyond words. It was very significant to the organization. We wanted to give that designation to people," said director France Rehel, who has been with Rona for 34 years.

With the growth of the company, the number of people increased so rapidly in ten years that it was essential to be able to adapt. Before, the group had been very homogeneous. New employees were hired based on their skills, of course, but recruits who were sought were those who would fit in with the rest of the group.

Then, everything changed, and it was suddenly necessary to look for different skills, to draw from different sources. "All this was happening without any of us having all of the answers, but we had unshakeable confidence in ourselves. It was strange: we were anxious, yet we were convinced we would succeed," said Jean. The challenge was to maintain the cohesion we had while hiring new people who would allow the company to grow, to open up. The new balance that was achieved was due in large part to acquisitions and the change to big-box stores. This forced the company to identify the best practices needed to succeed during each phase, then go out and find people who already had that type of experience. We had to go from homogeneity to cohesion, to accept to expand the culture, but never to the detriment of the company's values.

"Despite the tremendous growth, these values withstood the test because there were enough people to defend them and to convey them," added France Rehel. They stemmed from down-to-earth common sense, and were deeply anchored within the people who embraced them. They are values that are easy to understand: service, unity—everyone working together, common good, respect, and a sense of responsibility. There weren't five different models. Across Canada, new employees were evaluated using these criteria, those valued by the organization.

The common good, the balance between the needs of the employees, the consumers and the investors, is the foundation for all decisions.

A sense of responsibility appeals to the entrepreneur in people. New employees are hired on the basis of a job description, but they are welcome to develop it further. It is the new hire who sets the limits. As a matter of course, the organization offers a great amount of freedom—a natural way of doing things for a company that, it should be recalled, hails from a long line of businessmen and entrepreneurs. That is the strength of Rona. But it can be a weakness, too. It requires an enormous amount of mutual confidence, which is one more reason to select the right people, but also to let them make mistakes and to give them time to learn.

Cohesion and passion

Moreover, once a year, everyone is evaluated using a performance appraisal document. Each employee's commitment to the common values is measured against a first set of core objectives, and their mastery of certain skills, against a second. In this way, each employee knows where they stand.

And hierarchy may be sacrificed at any time for the benefit of efficiency. If someone needs an answer or a piece of information that they know someone else is capable of providing, they do not need to go through their boss, but may go directly to the person. And no one is offended.

An interesting and extremely revealing phenomenon is that growing numbers of retirees are looking for work in the stores. Their vast experience coupled with their passion for service and for people are of enormous benefit to the company.

A trend of remaining with the company for many years has developed among Rona employees. This is due in large part to the company's values, which are increasingly better known outside the walls of the company: life is good here. Respect, ethics, and service are embodied everywhere. The

Boucherville distribution centre offers a number of quality of life benefits due to its location away from the big city and its infernal traffic. In 1987 the company opened a daycare, right in the workplace. It has been unable to keep up with demand.

❷ The Centre de la petite enfance (CPE) Domisol daycare centre at the administrative office in Boucherville.

❸ From the Boucherville Rona's merchandising department, Marie-Josée Blais, Maxime Harvey, and Germain Voyer.

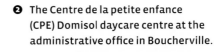

The president's tour •

THIS TOUR WOULD GENERATE SCORES OF ENCOUNTERS OF ANOTHER KIND, WHICH WOULD NOT SOON BE FORGOTTEN!

❶ At the Epcor Centre's Jack Singer Concert Hall, Totem employees learned of their official integration with Rona during the president's tour's stop in Calgary on March 23, 2005.

It was the fall of 2004. Robert Dutton was travelling the country to meet with store managers, to hear and see what was or was not working, and what could be done to make things better. He met with more than three quarters of the corporate store managers. From problems that were raised to the company's vision and emerging solutions, the discussions were promising. Things snowballed rapidly after that. He said, "I'd enjoy talking with the employees, too." And the president's tour was born.

In December, Daniel Richard was in Calgary with the Totem owners—the sale was not yet completely finalized—and he told them that if all went well, he planned to invite all of their employees to attend when the tour rolled through town the following March. On the very morning of the get-together, it was announced that the transaction had been approved by the Competition Bureau. Late that afternoon, there were a thousand people in the room, 450 of them Totem employees. It was truly a magical moment. The speaker asked them to stand, and the entire room welcomed them into the group with applause.

From 2005 to 2008, the president met more than 6 000 employees each year, in late winter, in Montreal, Toronto, Calgary, Edmonton, and Vancouver. How did he manage this? Mostly, the meetings took place in large theatres. People arrived from all over by bus. Often the date fell on a Monday or a Wednesday, days which tend to be quieter in terms of work. Some of the big-box stores sent up to 50 of their employees. According to Danielle Savard, a long-time employee:

> "When they arrived, they were welcomed and offered some refreshments. They were treated well. The president was there to greet them, shake their hands, and speak with them. These were wonderful, truly exceptional occasions."

The format for the first part of the evening was not always the same. One year, for example, the vice-presidents presented the Olympic program and related advertising. The president always gave an address. It was his opportunity to share his vision of things and the values of the organization to which they all belonged.

On the first tour, the second half of the evening kicked up a notch with the *Rona Star – Le rêve* show, an reprise of the November 2004 Spring Show presentation. In the same format, a new show, *Rona Star – La passion,* was presented in 2006; The *5th Season Show* in 2007; and the *Grand Cirque des couleurs* in 2008. Over a period of two weeks, the artists, all Rona employees, the president, and the entire team assigned to this massive project, travelled from city to city across Canada, performing four shows for their colleagues. So what is the *Rona Star* show?

Meeting people one by one

In 2004, Rona held a contest for store employees and staff at the distribution centres. The idea was to give employees a chance to live their dreams of being a star. The contest format chosen was solo performance. People signed up and sent in their videos. From the entries received, about 50 people were invited to take part in a preselection process. Of those, 10 were chosen. Throughout the fall, the finalists worked with professionals, who provided voice training and instruction on how to move on stage. So much talent, so much passion! With 13 musicians on stage, it was a show that would not soon be forgotten.

During the president's tours, this has become a gift that is given from one group of employees to their colleagues, and it is all made possible by the organization.

The president's tours have been a tremendous lever for mobilizing thousands of individuals, store managers, and employees, some of whom joined the group by way of successive acquisitions in which they did not play a part, to work towards a common goal. This original and powerful concept would not have been possible without the steadfast determination of a president for whom clarity, teamwork, and sharing are essential to lasting growth and development.

❷ On January 2006, approximately 1 000 Rona employees from Western Canada had a chance to meet their president at Edmonton's Winspear Centre. He received a warm and colourful welcome!

❸ In 2007, Rona's *Grand Cirque des couleurs* spotlighted the artistic talents of its employees in a major stage show featuring dancers, singers, and an on-stage painter!

❹ The grand finale of the first *Rona Star* contest took place at the President's Banquet in November 2004, during the Spring Show. The *Rona Star* shows then went on the road with the president's tour.

WHEN RONA TOOK IT OVER, Réno-Dépôt was a warehouse-style specialist, with advertising campaigns, store layouts, and products targeted to the male handyman clientele.

VAL ROYAL GOT A JUMP ON RONA
in being the first to open big-box hardware stores in Quebec. The Réno-Dépôt and The Building Box chain were bought by Rona in 2003.

While RONA was running its charm offensive, at the beginning of October 2002, the stock markets took a nose-dive. It should be said that global markets had been on a downturn since that spring. There had been the terrorist attacks in New York and Washington in September 2001, scandals had undermined investor confidence, the United States and Japan were going through difficult economic times... But the last few weeks had brought with them a rallying. We had reason to hope we were launching the RONA stock at the beginning of a wave. This scenario didn't quite materialize, however, and it was impossible to reschedule the operation. The train had left the station.

On November 5, 2002, RONA closed its $150-million offering. On December 20, 2002, its shares were traded for the first time on the Toronto Stock Exchange, under the symbol TSX "RON."

Initially, the market was cautious, and the shares generated only marginal interest, but very soon, everyone would be talking about RON, the new kid on the block...

Enemies yesterday, allies tomorrow

If the lukewarm stock markets were hardly conducive to a rapid surge in RONA stock, this situation would ironically provide us with another extraordinary opportunity for growth. And this time, the game would be played chiefly in Quebec. Our target: Réno-Dépôt!

The origins of Réno-Dépôt dated back to 1933, when Paul-Hervé Desrosiers opened a business called LaSalle Builders Supplies, in Montreal. Over the next years, he acquired several companies and grouped all his stores together under the name Val Royal.

In 1969, this company passed to the founder's grand-nephews, brothers Claude and Pierre Michaud. In 1970, with ten outlets now, the company joined the Marchands Ro-Na, though they were not obliged to identify with the banner. They were expelled, in 1978, along with other members whose purchasing volume was deemed insufficient to justify maintaining their membership in the group. It seems that Val Royal had been using Ro-Na as a "wholesale convenience store" rather than their primary supplier, as the group's philosophy demanded.

In 1986, Val Royal became a publicly traded company. It underwent a major expansion and, in 1993, launched the first warehouse-style stores in Quebec: the Réno-Dépôt stores—the company would adopt the name later. In 1997, control of Réno-Dépôt would pass to a French company, Castorama Dubois Investissements, which operated the Castorama chain in France and Europe. A British company, Kingfisher plc, became the majority shareholder of Castorama Dubois in 1998 and acquired virtually all of its shares in 2002.

At the start of 2003, because it wanted to reduce its debt and concentrate on its international development in

Europe and the Far East, Kingfisher announced the sale of its Réno-Dépôt / The Building Box division.

Was it possible that our rival would simply fall into our hands like ripe fruit?

The game would play out quickly. That was certain. Réno-Dépôt was a jewel. Twenty profitable stores, 14 of which were in Quebec; six The Building Box stores in Ontario, still in their infancy or in the developmental stages, in the richest and most competitive market in Canada; a solid reputation; a sales figures of $850 million, and poised to take off. If Kingfisher was willing to divest itself of such an asset, it was because it did not fit into the company's overall strategy.

The company was sold by auction through the Bank of America and the Toronto-Dominion Bank. We spent many nights crunching numbers, working out various scenarios, and formulating an offer. Then we crossed our fingers.

On April 23, 2003, a winner was declared. With a bid of $350 million, RONA was the victor! Accounting for closing adjustments, transaction fees, and Réno-Dépôt's cash flows, RONA ended up paying a net price of $328 million to clinch the deal. Not wanting to place too large a debt burden on RONA, we financed roughly $150 million of this amount with an issue of new shares, which was snapped up quickly enough.

2003

Throughout 2003, world headlines were dominated by the Iraq War 📷. Starting in January, ever more massive and ever more numerous anti-war demonstrations were held in cities across the United States, and in many other countries, including Canada. In Canada, they culminated on March 15, when close to 200 000 demonstrators gathered in Montreal, and 15 000 in Quebec City. It was without a doubt the largest protest demonstration in Canadian history.

Nonetheless, the U.S. government resolutely pursued its objective of going to war, an objective that seemed to have been set in the months immediately after George W. Bush became president, well before the attacks on September 11, 2001. After failing to obtain the backing of the UN Security Council, the "coalition of the willing," led by the United States, launched an invasion on March 20; Saddam Hussein's regime fell after six weeks, his armed forces, supposedly so formidable, having literally "vanished."

But the country's "liberation" by a victor that had almost no plans for what to do next resulted in a frenzy of pillaging that went on for weeks. And Iraqi insurgents were mobilizing, staging deadly ambushes against the occupation troops while the country descended into chaos.

In Canada, the SARS epidemic (severe acute respiratory syndrome) that originated in China in 2002 hit Toronto early in 2003. The city was practically under quarantine. There were 22 deaths out of 146 reported cases.

2004

Federal politics, especially in Quebec, were rocked by the "sponsorship scandal." A report from the Auditor General of Canada stated that the federal sponsorship program was being handled in a way that flouted even the most basic rules for awarding contracts. The new prime minister, Paul Martin, immediately established a commission, headed by Justice John Gomery, to conduct a public inquiry.

Then, the prime minister called an election. One of the major issues during the campaign would be the sponsorship scandal, along with corruption in politics in general, roundly condemned by the brand-new Conservative Party of Canada, which had been formed when the Progressive Conservative Party and the Canadian Alliance merged in December 2003. Paul Martin's Liberals won the election, but lost about 20 seats in Quebec, along with their majority in Parliament.

Another scandal, this one infinitely more serious and troubling, emerged on the world scene in April. Appalling images of the mistreatment of Iraqi detainees in Abu Ghraib prison at the hands of their American jailers were met with universal disapprobation and contributed significantly to eroding the moral standing of the United States.

The year ended with one of the worst natural disasters in history, when a gigantic tsunami struck the coasts of the Indian Ocean, claiming more than 225 000 lives and causing staggering damage to property.

2005

On March 3, four officers of the Royal Canadian Mounted Police were killed in a drug raid on a farm near Mayerthorpe, Alberta. It was the deadliest attack against the RCMP since the Métis uprising in 1885.

On July 20, 2005, Canada became the third country in the world, and the first in the Americas, to legalize same-sex marriage, after the courts in nine provinces had decided that the definition of marriage as the union of two persons of the opposite sex was a violation of the Canadian Charter of Rights and Freedoms. The bill introduced to Parliament sparked vigorous debate and was adopted on division by a vote of 158 to 133; one cabinet minister resigned his post in opposition to the bill.

July 2 saw a huge international musical demonstration: 10 concerts featuring 150 groups and 1 250 musicians were held simultaneously in 10 cities across the G8 nations in a bid to encourage their leaders, who were meeting a few days later, to cancel out the debt of the world's poorest countries. It is estimated that some three billion people watched the concerts, either live or on television. The G8 Summit would remain largely unmoved by the appeal.

Hurricane Katrina pummeled Louisiana on August 29, leaving New Orleans under water for weeks. The storm claimed close to 1 800 lives and caused more than $81 billion in damage, to say nothing of the political damage inflicted on the Bush administration, whose response to the disaster was woefully inadequate.

THE RONA HOME & GARDEN BANNER that appeared in 2001 offered, on a retail surface area of close to 100 000 sq. ft., over 40 000 products, a lumberyard, greenhouses, and an outdoor garden centre. The one in Langford, British Columbia, opened its doors in 2006.

Because of the rivalry that had existed between the Réno-Dépôt and RONA L'entrepôt stores, the Réno-Dépôt directors were, it has to be said, less than thrilled.

It was up to us to show them that we had learned our lessons from previous acquisitions.

First, reassure people. No one would lose their job. No store would close. Even in Sherbrooke or Quebec City, where the rivals of yesterday faced each other across the street. All of their stores were mostly profitable, like ours, proving that there was a need for them all. It also proved that those who managed and worked in these stores were competent. We would need everyone.

From the moment the acquisition was announced, integration teams were put into action to assess the practices of each organization and improve performance to the benefit of both companies.

We relaunched an internal publication, *Dialogue*, which had served us during the Revy acquisition. Its primary mission was to keep both RONA and Réno-Dépôt employees informed, and to foster reciprocal exchanges. We were no longer adversaries. From now on, we were partners.

Réno-Dépôt would continue to be Réno-Dépôt until further notice. There was no point in pushing things. It was a well-oiled machine, and any tampering would risk throwing it out of kilter. Réno-Dépôt was a centralized chain, whose managers were employees. It would stay that way. The Réno-Dépôt banner would remain part of the

Quebec landscape. It was strong. It had its own personality. It had a loyal market. You don't fix something that ain't broke. the only exceptions in this case were the six The Building Box stores in Ontario, which had not been in operation very long and whose brand was not yet widely recognized; there, the case might be made for adopting the RONA Home & Garden banner, which had already won consumer confidence.

All in all, we were able to unite these two fierce adversaries without major incident. We had welcomed Réno-Dépôt, its directors, and its employees in a respectful manner; we preserved the spirit and culture of this organization. And it made winners of us all. Ownership of a gem in both Quebec and Canada was returned home. We all won because the acquirer had not conquered; it had welcomed.

The day the Réno-Dépôt managers came to the Boucherville distribution centre, the employees formed a receiving line and welcomed the new arrivals with warm applause to what would henceforth be their home. Once inside, the roles reversed, and the newcomers spontaneously turned to salute the "veterans."

With the acquisition of Réno-Dépôt, who sales figure was 40% of RONA's, we were now the largest Canadian retailer and distributor of hardware, renovation, and gardening products. That transaction instantly added 20 big-box stores and 4 300 employees to our network.

BASED ON A NEW CONCEPT of specialized stores aimed at do-it-yourselfers and contractors, the first Rona Building Centre opened its doors in Midland, Ontario, at the start of 2003.

In all, RONA now owned 540 stores across Canada and employed 20 000 people. That year, in 2003, net earnings surged by 81%.

It was a prosperous year that was also marked by other events. In February, RONA strengthened its presence in some Canadian markets with the RONA Building Centre banner, which was aimed at home and garden professionals. And while the first nationwide advertising campaign in the history of RONA was in full swing, the company embarked on the construction of a new 320 000-sq. ft. (29 700 m²) distribution centre in Calgary, slated to open in 2004.

In 2004, under the RONA Le Rénovateur / RONA Home Centre banner, we reinvented the traditional local hardware store. About 40 000 sq. ft. (3 700 m²) in size, these stores were different because they had adjoining lumberyards. This format allowed us to gain a foothold in medium-sized communities with populations of 50 000 or less, and offer a variety of services that had, up until then, been largely available in the big-box stores. The positioning of this banner would lead several former Revelstoke stores to adopt it. Our big-box store competitors would later draw inspiration from what we had done when they attempted to penetrate new market segments.

Further west

RONA was increasingly looking westward. Alberta was in the middle of an oil boom and enjoying some of the

All for one and one for all

Hubert Robitaille
Materials Buyer, Administrative Office, Boucherville, Quebec

Any doubts as to the scale of the company are dispelled as soon as you walk through the main doors of the Boucherville administrative office. The energy is palpable in this hive of activity.

This is where Hubert Robitaille works, and it suits him well. With his firm handshake and honest smile, it's clear that this man knows where he's going. In fact, his three mottos are, "Do what you say you're going to do!", "Use your imagination—it's more important than anything else!", and "Be quick off the mark!"

The first has undeniably helped him advance on his outstanding career path. Straight after his business degree, he went into marketing. He worked for various companies and opened several stores before finally becoming the materials purchasing manager for Réno-Dépôt, remaining in the position when Rona took over.

He must also have used his imagination, because much of his career has been devoted to adapting the home improvement centre concept, first for the Quebec market, then for the big-box market. He visited a number of stores in the United States and Ontario before collaborating on the launch of the very first Réno-Dépôt.

And he's certainly quick off the mark because, as he says, "There's no time out at Rona!" Though relatively new to the company, Hubert has found it easy to settle in, thanks to his previous experience in the field and the fact that most of his team followed him. He remembers arriving on their first day: all the Rona employees had lined up outside to greet them, to the beat of tam-tams! They were then given a special welcome in the main cafeteria by Robert Dutton.

Hubert has since become a valued member of the team. When he is not away on one of the many trips his job entails, he also sits on the sustainable development committee, a working group that helps develop the company's environmental policies.

When asked what advice he would give to others, he replies, "The important thing is to be passionate about what you do. You don't want your passion to overwhelm others, but you do want to try to communicate it." Just looking into his eyes, you can tell Hubert has a lot of passion to share!

A Totem to watch over you

Jim Thorogood
Former President of Totem, Calgary, Alberta

In 2005, when Rona bought Totem, the Alberta-based company had 16 outlets (two of which sold only to building contractors), generated $260 million in sales, employed 900 people, and ran its own 107 000-sq. ft. distribution centre in Calgary. Not long after, Jim was inducted into the Industry Hall of Fame.

This success story has modest beginnings, however. Father and son team Cliff and Jim Thorogood worked together at the family lumberyard. In 1970, they sold the business and opened their first Totem in Calgary. Initially, their inventory consisted mainly of lumber and plywood. But the following year they took over Bow Valley Lumber and West Cloverleaf Building Supplies, and opened a second store north of the city. By 1980, Totem had five sales outlets and built its first, much-needed, distribution centre—which had to move six years later due to lack of space! And that wasn't the end of it; more stores were opened, and a special division was set up for residential projects of all sizes.

In 1989, Jim's son Ryan came to work with him a few years before the arrival of the big-box stores, which would revolutionize the home improvement market in the mid-1990s. For the Thorogoods, this was the beginning of a fight for survival; for Ryan, it strengthened his commitment to the business. It was a wake-up call that forced the family to put all their energy into rethinking their strategy, into breathing new life into the company. Knowing they could not compete with the wide selection offered by the big boxes, they decided to concentrate on their strengths: highly knowledgeable employees, top-notch customer service, and lumber chosen with Jim's scrupulous knowledge and expert eye. If they could not be the leader in a product category, they stopped selling it. They also decided to open new stores in towns with populations of under 100 000, staying under the radars while the big players contended for sites in Calgary and Edmonton. They also paid special attention to their staff's skills. All new employees would receive two weeks' training and have access to another 42 courses, as needed. The company even employed two full-time instructors. Today, Totem has a solid reputation with Alberta contractors for its excellence in building materials. What's more, there's fresh popcorn in every store—and it's really hard to resist!

TOTEM was founded in the 1970s and, from its beginnings in Calgary, spread right across Alberta.

strongest economic and demographic growth in North America. It was the perfect region to open new home and garden stores. RONA already had a brand new distribution centre and 20 stores there.

One company caught our attention. It wasn't its size, but its originality and culture, and the experience it offered its customers that impressed us. The company was Totem Building Supplies, founded in 1970 and specialized in building materials. It had 16 sales outlets, two of which were targeted to contractors; it had 900 employees and generated $260 million in annual sales. It grew quickly. The company set itself apart by its management and the quality of service in its stores. Store employees did everything; none of them stepped foot in a store without first following an intensive two-week training period. the Totem company was also known for its superb garages and sheds that were sold in kits, ready to assemble. But—and this is what made them so unique—each kit was prepared by Totem according to the measurements and style requirements supplied by the client, delivered to a customers' home usually within 24 hours!

On December 21, 2004, RONA announced the upcoming acquisition of Totem Building Supplies, for $100 million cash. The existing lines of credit were sufficient; we would not need to refinance at all. The Totem banner, and its strong personality, would remain unchanged. As far as integration was concerned, RONA now knew how to

WITH TOTEM, Rona acquired 16 stores in Alberta and increased its annual sales figure by about $260 million.

IN DECEMBER 2004, Robert Dutton and Jim Thorogood announced Rona's recent acquisition of Totem.

do things right. And this time, a happy coincidence accompanied this announcement.

I happened to be in Calgary on March 23, 2005, on my annual cross-country tour to meet the group's employees and directors. Close to 1 000 people, including 450 of Totem's employees, were assembled in an auditorium. The Totem personnel were sort of invited guests, as the transaction had not yet been finalized. The event had been organized several weeks in advance. Those in attendance had come from all over Alberta, some by bus, some by plane. By pure coincidence, the deal was closed that morning. The news was announced, and, in one wave, half the room stood up to applaud the new RONA employees. "It was utterly magical," recalled Daniel Richard, RONA's director of Corporate Communications. "Even we didn't know."

With that acquisition, RONA established a firm presence in the West, with 34 stores in Alberta and 28 in British Columbia.

One acquisition after another

There followed a crush of acquisitions. Early in 2006, RONA expanded into Newfoundland and Labrador. We bought the Chester Dawe chain of eight stores and one truss factory. The first building materials company in the province and one of the largest in the Atlantic Region, it generated annual sales of $80 million. We had to act with sensitivity and tact. The news was, as had been somewhat expected,

IN MARCH 2005, Robert Dutton and the president's tour were in Calgary, where he confirmed the acquisition, in person, to Totem's employees.

AGP • Acknowledge, Guide, Provide

THE AGP IMAGE HAS EVOLVED SINCE ITS INCEPTION IN THE FALL OF 2000, BUT ITS FUNDAMENTAL COMPONENT CONTINUES TO BE CUSTOMER SERVICE.

Customers First.

Le client. Ma priorité.

The recognition program, launched in 2000, was created in response to two major factors. First, Home Depot was moving into Quebec, reinforcing the need for Rona to differentiate itself. Also, within Rona there was an awareness that the quality of service in the big-box stores was inconsistent because of high staff turnover, which was due in part to the changing seasons. The question was how to take the quality of service found in a proximity or neighbourhood store and extend that across the entire network. The answer was the AGP program, with its emphasis on the service that is so important to Rona. The program is, of course, also available to independent dealers who wish to participate, and their employees.

It is based on nine behaviours that are just as important in day-to-day life as they are on the job.
- Acknowledge the customer (say hello, smile, make eye contact, be courteous);
- Guide the customer in his or her project (be available to orient the customer within the store, ask the customer about the project, listen);
- Provide a solution (offer all the products/ services required for the customer's project, thank the customer).

These behaviours, which have been adopted systematically by staff at the stores in Quebec, were adapted for the rest of the country in 2001.

The program itself has evolved over the years. While it still promotes exemplary behaviours and quality customer service, it has also become a recognition program in which appraisals are carried out not only by the store managers and supervisors, but by the customers themselves. As a result, every employee has a chance to accumulate points that can be redeemed for gifts, a highly motivating prospect in itself.

Then there is the group recognition aspect, culminating in the AGP Gala, which became the Excellence Gala. It takes place during the Spring

206

❶ 324 AGP Champions were honoured at the 2007 Excellence Gala, which took place at Montreal's Windsor Station, whose sumptuous decor evokes the days of railway travel in times gone by.

Show and is one of the three key events held in conjunction with the show. Josée Vachon, who handles the logistics for the evening, explains that it is an excellent opportunity for participants to meet the Rona management team. Service Champions from across the country get to know one another, and this, naturally, fosters a strong sense of belonging.

Also recognized at the event are the Builders of Excellence, the stores that have set themselves apart during the year in the big-box, proximity, and specialized store categories. The teams in these stores have distinguished themselves through their incomparable customer service and their store operations. Two Initia awards are presented to the managers who have demonstrated superior leadership, initiative, and daring—in short, vision. This prize is referred to as the go-getters award! And even though the manager accepts the award, everyone knows that the honour belongs to all the store's employees.

The following awards are presented at the Excellence Galas:

• The Builders of Excellence awards: to stores that have set themselves apart through exceptional performance. The awards recognize profitability, merchandising, human resource management, and incomparable customer service.

• The Initia awards: to recognize managers who have demonstrated a level of originality commonly found in ambitious entrepreneurs, who strive to surpass themselves and go the extra mile.

• The AGP Leader awards: to those store managers whose commitment to customer service and the AGP program has been exemplary.

2006

The Palestinian question was back in the forefront of international events in 2006. In January, the first Palestinian legislative election to be held since 1996 was won by Hamas, widely considered to be a terrorist organization. The election sparked a major internal crisis among Palestinian parties and factions, while the so-called democratic nations cut off all aid to the Palestinian Authority, deepening the already abject misery of the people living there. It was as though they were being punished for voting for the "wrong" party...

In July and August, after two Israeli soldiers were kidnapped by the Lebanese organization Hezbollah, Israel launched an intensive large-scale bombing campaign against all of Lebanon, systematically destroying infrastructure and indiscriminately shelling cities, where entire neighbourhoods were reduced to ashes. Hezbollah responded by launching thousands of rockets into northern Israel. International humanitarian organizations were unanimous in denouncing these flagrant violations of humanitarian law on both sides of the conflict, as both adversaries were targeting civilian populations directly, often with ball-bearing bombs or submunition-based bombs, especially cruel forms of weaponry.

In Canada, Paul Martin's minority government was overturned by a no-confidence motion, leading to a general election that put Stephen Harper's Conservative Party in power, albeit with an even smaller minority than the outgoing government.

2007

A massive financial scandal saw some initial closure in January, when the court handed the president of the Norbourg investment company the heaviest sentence in Canadian history for a case involving financial fraud. He was charged with diverting for his own use more than $130 million by fraudulent means from some 9 200 individual investors. A mere 10% of the defrauded clients were able to recover a portion of their investment; the others lost everything...

A general election was held in Quebec on March 26. Jean Charest's Liberal government won, but lost 28 seats and was reduced to a minority, while the Action démocratique du Québec (ADQ) made a spectacular breakthrough to become the official opposition. For the first time since 1878, Quebec had a minority government, with three parties practically neck and neck in terms of the number of seats they held in the National Assembly: 48 for the Liberals, 41 for the ADQ, and 36 for the PQ.

In June, in a small-scale civil war among Palestinians, Hamas took control of the Gaza Strip by force, while Fatah maintained its authority in the West Bank. The Palestinian people slid ever further into suffering and misfortune.

2008

The year saw a worsening of the financial crisis that had started in 2006-2007, as it spread to the entire world. Swelled by the practice of granting subprime mortgages, the real estate bubble burst, taking down a veritable house of cards founded on financial arrangements so complex that even the most knowledgeable experts were unable to make sense of them. Governments handed out many hundreds of billions of dollars in rescue packages, while the financial crisis soon spilled over into the real economy, resulting in millions of job losses.

While the economic storm gathered intensity, the federal election returned Stephen Harper to power with yet another minority government. When it seemed likely that he would lose the confidence of the House, Harper requested a prorogation of Parliament. Meanwhile, in Quebec, a snap election gave Jean Charest's Liberals a narrow majority in the National Assembly, due in part to the dramatic decline of the ADQ.

But it was the U.S. presidential election of 2008 that captured the world's attention. At the close of an extraordinary campaign, history was made when Barack Obama was elected to the presidency on an unstoppable wave of popular enthusiasm and hope 📷. A mere forty years after the end of racial segregation, the United States entrusted supreme power to an African American. Suddenly it seemed as though something had changed in the world...

ROBERT DUTTON AND PHIL BUDDEN, who had headed Chester Dawe since 1992, during the 2006 agreement.

coldly received. Chester Dawe was a Newfoundland institution; founded in 1941, the company had existed before the province joined the Canadian Confederation (1949). Gordon Kennedy, the general manager of Chester Dawe, recalls: "At first, people were shocked, because Chester Dawe had been a thriving business for such a long time. When they learned that Chester Dawe had been sold, I guess they must have wondered what lay ahead for them, if companies with roots in the very heart of the Newfoundland culture were passing into other hands."

We proceeded carefully. The directors remained in place, and the stores would keep their banner and their own flyer for at least two years.

Just a few weeks later, in April 2006, another acquisition: Matériaux Coupal, which operated nine outlets in the Greater Montreal area and generated annual sales of $125 million.

Then, in the middle of summer, Curtis Lumber: $80 million in annual sales, 6 stores and a roof truss factory in southwestern British Columbia. A few weeks after that, in August, the Mountain Building Centre chain, with $20 million in sales in three stores located in the Vancouver-Whistler corridor was added.

While these acquisitions were unfolding, the recruitment of dealers continued to play an essential role in RONA's growth. In 2006, we gained 37 new members—more than

IN 2006, Rona integrated Chester Dawe's eight stores and two plants in Newfoundland, which had sold building materials and hardware products.

100 since 2003—representing over half a billion dollars in annual retail sales.

The pace of this growth put great pressure on the organization. First, the facilities. We had already grown out of the new and gigantic distribution centre on Du Tremblay Road in Boucherville. So we built a 250 000-sq. ft. (23 200 m²) extension, bringing its total size to 900 000 sq. ft. (83 600 m²).

Furthermore, RONA's growth was straining its finances. In 2006, again, RONA issued $400 million in debentures as unsecured debt securities. The success of this issue would hinge entirely on the company's reputation. In the year before this issue, RONA's sales had risen by 13%, and its operating profit, by 15%. The company had enjoyed uninterrupted growth for the last 15 years. Its securities were attractive to investors because the company had maintained its growth and managed its finances soundly. RONA's reputation was impeccable, and this debenture issue was a success.

A company with values

RONA continued its dramatic growth, while at the same time affirming the values that set it apart. Our growth was invested with meaning. We wanted to provide work for people and improve the quality of life in the communities where we set up shop.

For instance, RONA established a purchasing policy that favoured Canadian suppliers. In 2005, 95% of our

From the ground up

Gordon Kennedy
General Manager, Chester Dawe, St. John's, Newfoundland

Gordon Kennedy says it was a series of events rather than a conscious decision that led him to becoming general manager of Chester Dawe. After doing a few internships with Phil Budden's construction company while taking his commerce degree, Gordon was offered a full-time job with them when he completed his studies. And things just took off from there. In 1993, his boss became general manager of Chester Dawe, and, in 2001, he bought the company. That same year, he purchased their local competitor, Hickman. From two stores, they expanded to eight. Today, Gordon is proud of having been part of the management team that helped the company grow to such a point that they attracted the attention of Rona, who, in turn, bought them out in 2006.

Rona's takeover of Chester Dawe took Newfoundlanders by surprise; they had never seen any stores like this on the island, and they had never heard of the Rona brand. Customers waited patiently to see what would happen. Gordon made sure the transition went as smoothly as possible. On the one hand, he had to reassure his clients by promoting Rona's excellent reputation in terms of know-how, broad market experience, and excellent service. On the other, he had to make the most of all the benefits Rona brought with it: flyer specials, marketing, and purchasing power. Gradually, the Chester Dawe hardware stores began to take on the Rona colours. By 2007, the Kelligrew store had been completely transformed. And with the addition of new lighting and colour boutiques, clients were completely won over!

Like Rona, Chester Dawe is deeply rooted in the fabric of the society of its home province. The company founded by Chester E. Dawe has been selling construction materials and building homes for Newfoundlanders since 1941. In those days, you could bring your mortgage papers into the store and order a whole house from the ground up! Today, the estimates counter is still as busy as ever—and the architecture of St. John's as diverse!

Something for everyone

Valmond Melanson

Melanson Eudore A. & Son Ltd, Rona L'Express,
Cocagne, New Brunswick

Many of today's hardware stores started out as general stores. But what a surprise to find one that has stayed that way! Wandering the aisles of Melanson Eudore A. & Son Ltd., one wonders why anyone would ever need to go anywhere else. Fruits and vegetables, natural products, sports equipment, decorating accessories, video rentals, a skate sharpening service, not to mention everything else you'd find in an "ordinary" hardware store... you name it, they've got it! The store has actually become something of a tourist attraction!

In 1954, when he founded his company in Cocagne, a small village of 900 homes on the coast of New Brunswick, Eudore Melanson was following in his father's footsteps. Well, almost. Instead of taking over the reins of the family store, he chose to open a new one a few kilometres away. His intention was not to compete with his father, but to meet other clients' needs. In those days, hardly anyone had cars, so you had to be within walking distance.

His son Valmond joined him after finishing his studies in accounting. Even though he had worked there when he was young, he hadn't considered taking over the family business. He soon realized, though, that he didn't want to sit behind a desk all day, so he returned to the store. His knowledge and experience served him so well that, before long, he became the owner. That was 10 years ago. Now, work takes up so much of his time that it is his wife Loretta who has to keep the books!

Valmond is proud to be able to offer such a wide variety of products and services. He is always on the lookout for items the local residents might need to add them to his inventory. In this community, word gets around fast: "If you can't find what you're looking for, go to Melanson's, they're bound to have it!"

PARTICIPANTS FROM QUEBEC
at the start line of the 2006 MS Bike Tour.

purchases were from Canadian sources. In addition, each RONA supplier had to pledge to respect a high set of standards for ensuring the protection of workers' rights and health, and also of the environment. In Quebec, since the end of the 1990s, RONA had been recovering old paint cans from its customers and sending them to a company that specialized in reconditioning this type of waste to subsequently put it back on the market.

RONA also strengthened its brand image across the country. In 2005, the company signed on as the national partner of the Vancouver Organizing Committee for the 2010 Olympic and Paralympic Winter Games. Its $68-million investment brought RONA extraordinary visibility. In addition to the Vancouver 2010 Games partnership, the agreement provided RONA with sponsorship rights for the Canadian team for the Torino 2006, Beijing 2008, Vancouver 2010, and London 2012 Olympic Games. RONA also adopted a five-year plan to support a hundred athletes, chosen by the Canadian Olympic Committee as strong prospects.

As part of this partnership with the Olympics, one project in particular moved me. It was launched in 2007. It was known as the RONA Vancouver 2010 Fabrication Shop. This workshop, located in Vancouver, produced the approximately 8 000 wood objects that would be used on the various sites, including podiums, various structures—such as picnic tables—and wheelchair ramps. What made it

THE RONA VANCOUVER 2010 FABRICATION SHOP
provided 30 weeks of training in carpentry to some
60 disadvantaged youth. They built the podiums and other
wood structures used during the Olympic Games.

**WITH FINANCIAL ASSISTANCE AND CLEAN-UP KITS
DONATED BY RONA,** the Canadian Red Cross is able to
help families displaced by disasters.

particularly special is that it provided work for people, and especially youth, who had faced barriers to employment because of personal problems or other challenges. It was a workplace integration program that took four groups of 15 trainees through a 30-week carpentry training program and taught them skills that they could later use to earn a living. I visited the shop, and I saw people who were down on their luck who had regained their confidence. It was the type of project that changes lives.

As RONA grew, so did the RONA Foundation. As new stores opened, the RONA Foundation would establish a base in the communities and build links with local organizations devoted to combating the school dropout problem and integrating young adults into the workplace.

As well, RONA took on a few causes that were close to its heart. Notably, support for research into the cause of and treatment for multiple sclerosis. In 2002, RONA formed an association with the Multiple Sclerosis Society of Canada Bike Tours, and became the title sponsor for their 22 RONA MS Bike Tours, a series of cycling events held in eight provinces to raise money for the Multiple Sclerosis Society of Canada.

RONA also supports post-secondary education by contributing to the funding of fields of study connected to its activities. It has established partnerships with the Chaire en management logistique at Université du Québec à Montréal, the Chair in Ethical Management at HEC Montréal, and the International Chair in Life Cycle Assessment, whose Canadian arm is at the École Polytechnique de Montréal.

RONA's involvement in the community is naturally rooted in the concerns of our people. Our employees. RONA acts in partnership with its staff, people who are not merely the executors of our success, but the heart and soul of the organization. Health and safety are management priorities. We are expanding employee training, primarily through the classes given by the RONA Academy, an idea we adopted from Réno-Dépôt. Thousands of employees receive ongoing training in a variety of subjects, ranging from new products and construction standards to management and customer relations. These classes are also offered online, so employees can take them on their own timetables.

Currently, RONA employs 7 000 unionized workers, mostly in Quebec. In 2007, a new collective agreement was signed in a spirit of harmony—a long-term, nine-year contract.

And RONA continues to expand. In February 2007, we acquired Noble Trade, one of the largest plumbing and heating wholesalers in Ontario, serving the commercial and professional market. In the wake of this acquisition, RONA created a commercial and professional market division, adding three more stores to this new niche a few months later when we bought Dick's Lumber, a Vancouver area lumber, building materials, and hardware specialist. The following year three Best-MAR plumbing, heating, and

Keeping the family busy

Raymond and Gaétane Fluet

A. Fluet & Fils, Rona Le Rénovateur, Stanstead, Quebec

The town of Stanstead is so close to the United States that the border runs right through some people's living rooms! But as Raymond explains, "Americans aren't foreigners; they're my friends, my family, and half my clientele."

The Fluets' Rona, situated just 50 metres from the border station, was a general store at the end of the 19th century. Mr. Fluet senior, who worked as a customs officer, was a risk-taker; he bought properties and liked to play the stock market. In 1947, he purchased the store with his colleague, Mr. Morin. The following year, during a cruise on the Saguenay River, Mr. Morin met Rolland Dansereau and Napoléon Piotte, who invited him to join their group. He took them up on their offer, and, not long after, sold his share of the business to his partner. At the end of the 1950s, Mr. Fluet's son, Raymond, began working with his father at the store. Raymond remembers going with him to pick up orders from De la Commune Street in Montreal. Later, as a young man, he would complete the return trip in record time, setting off at 6 a.m., collecting four or five deliveries, and getting back by noon! Father and son worked together for 20 years.

In 1977, Raymond decided that the time had come to stop selling groceries at the store. However, the transition did not go as smoothly as expected, and it was a year before he could bring business volume back to its previous level. Today, his sons, Yvan and Jean, work alongside their father, and Raymond tries to let them provide as much input as possible. For example, when Yvan was looking for a project for his certified general accountancy course, Raymond let him set up a computer system in the family business. In January 2009, the family banded together to buy out their competition, the BMR in Stanstead, and Jean now runs it.

Raymond's wife, Gaétane, began working at the hardware store shortly after they were married. Of course, when the children were young, she was busy looking after them, but today she's very much involved in all aspects of the business, both in the office and on the shop floor. After all, that's her "baby" too. And she finds it reassuring to know that, being a family-run company, their children and grandchildren will never be without a job. In any case, it certainly keeps her husband busy... As Raymond puts it, "Working keeps you out of trouble!"

RONA HAS BEEN RECOVERING CARDBOARD in its distribution centres and big-box stores since the early 1990s and introduced plastic recovery in 2008.

air-conditioning specialty stores in the Ottawa-Gatineau region joined our list of acquisitions.

During this vibrant period of activity, RONA implemented a number of initiatives aimed at developing customer service. Following our research, we introduced professional installation services, which are being offered in an increasing number of stores, for products such as doors, windows, and flooring. RONA further innovated with the "RONA by Design" concept, complete projects created by professional designers for seasoned do-it-yourselfers wanting to remodel their bathrooms or kitchens, revamp their exterior facades, or build a patio. The "Project Guide" companion program was created soon after. A customer was offered a personal guide for their project, to advise and provide assistance for the duration of the project, from concept to budget and completion.

RONA became an industry leader in the area of sustainable development. We carried out a number of environmentally responsible actions. For me, this was an inescapable reality that we had to address. A Sustainable Development Committee was formed, made up of representatives from every sector of the company's activity, because this was an issue that couldn't be confined to only one department within the organization; sustainable development had to be fully integrated into the company and in every aspect of its growth. Employees throughout the country were invited to suggest ways the company could reduce its environmental

RONA'S COMMERCIAL AND PROFESSIONAL MARKET DIVISION WAS CREATED IN 2007. It now includes Noble (formerly Noble Trade), Dick's Lumber (formerly Curtis Lumber and Dick's Lumber), Best-MAR and, in Quebec, Matériaux Coupal, Plomberie Payette & Perreault, and Plomberie LGC.

DICK'S LUMBER operates stores in the Vancouver, British Columbia region, such as this one in Burnaby.

213

footprint. We launched a new line of RONA ECO products. What distinguishes these products is that they are assessed through life cycle analyses, from resource acquisition to their end of life. We developed a set of specifications for our suppliers, which includes guidelines for protecting the environment and reducing packaging.

From an operations standpoint, RONA rapidly set up a program to recover and recycle plastic film and cardboard packaging in all of the distribution centres (in 2009, this represented just shy of 4 000 tonnes of cardboard and more than 400 tonnes of plastic); we have adopted a variety of strategies to reduce fuel consumption in our fleet of trucks, such as the revision of our routes; and, in stores, we have implemented a number of measures to reduce our heating and lighting needs. Protecting the environment is still a fledgling concern, but one that has already touched every one of the company's sectors of activity.

Welcome to Jean Gaulin

RONA never rests. Another major change loomed on the horizon. In May 2007, the chairman of the board, André Gagnon, announced he was stepping down to retire. The word 'retire,' however, was not entirely accurate, because, in reality, he was returning to his life as a dealer. It could be argued he had been born a hardware merchant, and was merely returning to his roots. I remember my father telling me, as a child: "Robert, if you want to learn the ropes of retail sales, we'll send you off for a stint with Mr. Gagnon." His reputation went back a long way...

The son of a Saint-Hyacinthe dealer, André took over from his father in 1966. At the same time as he was playing a leading role in RONA's development, he was guiding the family business through 19 phases of expansion, which saw the number of employees jump from 4 to... 700! He was able to achieve this because not only was he an innovator, he was also a cautious and thoughtful leader. While orchestrating one success after another in his own business, this man, an entrepreneur to the core, fired us all with his enthusiasm during his entire 35-year tenure on RONA's board of directors. The best of luck in all your future ventures, André!

Jean Gaulin took over. His appointment marked a significant departure from tradition: it was the first time in RONA's history that a chairman of the board was not a dealer. But what stellar credentials he brought to the table! A chemical engineer by training, he became an internationally recognized executive, successfully heading up Gaz Métropolitain, the Ultramar refinery in Saint-Romuald, on the South Shore of Quebec City, and then achieving world-class status at the helm of the Ultramar-Diamond group. The influence he brought to bear on RONA was new, and it would position the company as a major North American player.

2009

2009 was marked by an almost perilous deepening of the economic and financial crisis brought on by the collapse of the subprime-mortgage market in the United States in 2007. The developed world, and the United States in particular, was effectively mired in the worst economic recession since the Great Depression of the 1930s. Countries spent hundreds of billions of tax dollars in the form of stimulus packages to keep their financial systems from imploding, to prime the credit pump, and to help the most vulnerable—though many who were infinitely less vulnerable would profit from the bailouts, adding to their already vast revenues.

On January 20, in front of a crowd of almost two million people gathered on the National Mall in Washington, Barack Obama was sworn in as the 44th president of the United States of America, in a moving and symbolic ceremony.

In February, the Harper government tabled a budget that earmarked nearly $40 billion over two years for the economic recovery, resulting in a forecast deficit of $63 billion.

On June 11, the World Health Organization declared the H1N1 Influenza A virus to be a global pandemic and implored countries around the world to take whatever measures were needed to stem the outbreak.

Mahmoud Ahmadinejad was re-elected as president of Iran on June 13, under circumstances that sparked weeks of violent confrontations in the streets of numerous cities in Iran and even around the world.

On December 4, the storied Montreal Canadiens professional hockey team celebrated their 100th anniversary in a grandiose ceremony, bringing to a close a year of festivities.

2010

The earth shook as 2010 dawned. On January 12, a 7.3-magnitude earthquake rocked Port-au-Prince, the capital city of Haiti, and several other of that country's cities, leaving in its wake more than 200 000 dead and 300 000 wounded, destroying tens of thousands of buildings, and leaving over a million people homeless.

On February 27, it was Chili's turn to suffer an 8.8-magnitude quake, one of the most powerful ever recorded. The tremor set off a tsunami that wreaked havoc along the country's coastline before sweeping across the Pacific Ocean. The death toll was nearly 500, with two million more disaster victims and damage estimated at between $15 billion and $30 billion rounding up the tally.

Meanwhile, the Vancouver Winter Olympics dominated headlines in Canada. They ran from February 12 to 28, with the host country achieving spectacular results. With a medal haul of 26, including 14 gold, Canada broke a number of records: it was the first time this country had ever won a gold medal at an Olympic Games hosted at home, either in summer or in winter, and it was the most gold medals won by any country at a Winter Olympic Games.

On March 23, after more than a year of debate and manoeuvring, President Obama signed into law the most important piece of legislation in the United States in the last 50 years, which would see the reform of the most unfair and most costly health care system of any industrialized country.

At the end of 2007, the house of cards that had been built in the United States—on dodgy financial products—in an effort to stimulate residential construction and make property ownership more accessible, came tumbling down in a thunderous crash. That financial crisis would soon catch up to the real economy and sow the seeds of unemployment.

The sudden recession put a temporary halt to our acquisition projects, while consumer anxiety translated into a slowdown in sales. The time was right to review our operations and practices with the goal of improving our efficiency. In 2009, we launched a new banner, Studio by RONA, boutiques specializing in paint and related products, designed to meet the needs of both consumers and professional designers.

This is the portrait of RONA, in constant evolution, as it brings the curtain down on its 70th year of existence. By December 31, 2009, the company that had set sail many years ago as a fragile skiff has grown into a massive ocean liner, a major modern corporation that embodies the values of its day with confidence and that is well prepared to meet any future challenge head-on.

Long gone is the era when a handful of neighbourhood merchants banded together to make group purchases. But the spirit that spurred Émery Sauvé and his colleagues has endured through the years. The drive that characterized Rolland and Napoléon has remained intact. The ambition demonstrated by Charles Morency and André Dion has only

AFTER OVER 36 YEARS WITH RONA, André Gagnon officially stepped down as chairman of the board at a tribute by longtime friends in 2007.

Making his contribution

Jean Gaulin
Chairman of the Board

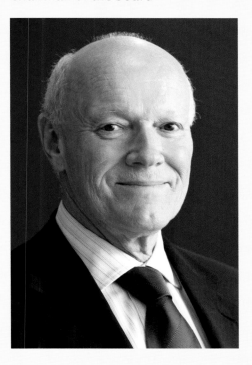

Rona's board of directors has always attracted exceptional directors, people whose expertise dovetailed with the challenges the group faced. Jean Gaulin, the current chairman of the board, is no exception.

Before joining Rona as a director in 2004, and subsequently succeeding André Gagnon as chairman of the board in 2007, he was the president and CEO of Ultramar Diamond Shamrock until it merged with Valero Energy Corporation in 2002. Before that, he had headed up Ultramar Plc (1989-1992), Gaz Métropolitain (1982-1985), and Nouveler (1980-1982). He served as Ultramar Canada's vice-president from 1977 to 1980, and its president from 1985 to 1989.

As if this impressive list of prestigious titles and positions was not enough, he also spearheaded large-scale financing projects and took part in a number of major causes, notably in the health sector. He currently sits on the boards of Rona, the National Bank of Canada, Saputo, and Bombardier Recreational Products.

In addition to his engineering credentials, his experience in being able to obtain financing for projects in a number of different ways, including through public offerings, had much to do with Rona wanting him to join its board of directors. How would he define his approach? His talent, he says, is being able to count on others while providing leadership through collaboration. An approach that lies at the heart of the Rona philosophy.

For him, one of Rona's strengths is its responsible social policy, which allows the organization to address the aspirations of its three key players: employees, clients, and shareholders. First, its employees are heard and supported, and they know that the company depends on them. Young people in particular appreciate this quality of relationship. Jean Gaulin points out, not without a smile, that a CEO can influence only those who report directly to him, so a company's social policy is the single most effective way to guarantee the respect and engagement of each individual, to ensure that the organization's values take deep root. And these are qualities that are also valued by Rona's clients, the second key component. By logical extension, the shareholders, in turn, stand to benefit from the resulting strong performance.

Among the socially responsible programs in place at Rona, the first that spring to mind are initiatives relating to the environment and the responsible use of resources, concerns that go back a long way with Rona. For Jean Gaulin, Rona's positioning is well thought out, intelligent, logical, and sustainable. It isn't simply based on the latest trends. Concern for the lifecycle, he adds, encourages the adoption of products with respect to available resources, resources that must be shared among a global population experiencing exponential growth in this finite area that is the earth. He is proud of Rona's vision and promotes it within all the boards he sits on. He says, "Look at what Rona has done!" and they are impressed.

He sees big things for Rona. "If we do things well here, we can do them elsewhere too," he says. "There is still great potential for growth while still respecting everybody's values. The planet is the limit!"

ON NOVEMBER 15, 2006, Rona opened a new Réno-Dépôt store in Rimouski—the 15th in Quebec. This 78 000-sq. ft. (7 240 m²) big-box store, with an entirely revamped store concept, represented an investment of over $20 million and created 125 local jobs. In 2010, there were 16 Réno-Dépôt stores in Quebec, and more will swell the banner's ranks in 2011.

swelled. The disciplined thinking of Henri Drouin and the enthusiasm of André Gagnon have become the pillars of our culture. The flame that burns brightly at RONA has always been fuelled by the same source: the unique balance between independence and solidarity; the idea that a company is also, and most importantly, a community of human beings that cares about its fellow citizens; and, at its core, the soul of a dealer, rooted in the heart of his community, always ready to lend his customers a helping hand in completing their projects.

For, in the end, RONA's success, in the past as today, is founded in one simple question, repeated thousands of time every day: "How can we help you?"

So long as this question continues to strike a chord within the hearts of the thousands of people who make up the RONA family, and so long as the organization resonates in unison, the doors to the future will be open to us always.

IN 2009, RONA opened two neighbourhood stores: a Rona in Saint-Georges-de-Beauce, Quebec, and a Totem store in Strathmore, Alberta.

IMPROVING THE PROCESS OF RECEIVING, STORING, AND DISTRIBUTING 90 000 PRODUCTS SOLD BY RONA is one of the components in optimizing the supply chain.

RONA at December 31, 2009		
Stores	686	26 in the Maritimes, 360 in Quebec, 171 in Ontario, and 129 in Western Canada.
		77 big-box stores, 40 stores serving the professional and commercial sector, 569 neighbourhood or specialty stores, including 431 affiliated stores.
Distribution centres	9	The largest is in Boucherville: close to one million sq. ft. (93 000 m²), with an additional 1.5 million sq. ft. (140 000 m²) spread over several outdoor lumberyards.
Employees	30 000	30% are over 50 years of age.
Assets	$2.7 billion	
Net annual sales	$4.7 billion	
Operating profit	$347 billion	
Network retail sales	More than $6 billion	
Estimated market share	17.5% of the Canadian construction-renovation market.	

Between blue and yellow: green •

AT RONA, WE NEVER SAY WE HAVE GONE GREEN. TOO MANY PEOPLE AND COMPANIES HAVE USED THIS CLAIM LIKE SO MUCH WINDOW DRESSING, WITHOUT ANY SUBSTANCE, AS A WAY OF GREENWASHING THEIR IMAGE.

❶ The Rona ECO line of products all bear the green logo that was created in 2008, which evokes nature and sustainable development.

At Rona we talk about eco-responsible products and choices, and, especially, about sustainable development. Behind these words is measurable scientific methodology that Michèle Roy, the vice-president of Communications and Public Affairs, explains with earnest conviction:

"Our raison d'être, and thus the mission of the company, is to continue to develop by offering products and services, but to do it through sustainable development, which is our way of being. The concept of sustainable development means developing a company without it being detrimental to people, but rather the opposite, by developing communities while respecting the environment."

This aligns with one of Rona's cherished core values: respect. Respect for people, for property and for communities. Respect for the future. Respect. Period. This is how Rona came to adopt the triple bottom line approach, which favours harmonizing the three pillars of sustainable development—economy, society, and environment—in every decision that is taken by the company.

An example? In 1996, Rona participated in the development of the first program in Canada to recover and recycle leftover paint. Not to be 'in,' not because it was legislated by the government, but because, to the largest paint retailer in the country, it didn't make any sense to be dumping all that excess paint in landfills. Under this program, leftover paint is collected and reconditioned, then put back on the market as recycled paint. As an added bonus, it has also given individuals being reintegrated into society the chance to be involved in the process. That's real sustainable development. And this gesture was taken long before society subscribed to today's prevailing life cycle methodology.

Thus, in 2007 Rona formed a partnership with the International Chair in Life Cycle Assessment at the École Polytechnique de Montréal, a research unit of CIRAIG, and a leading research centre in the field. It was a key event. The Chair works with Rona in two ways. The first is to measure the environmental footprint of the company and to act, where possible, to reduce it; the second is to select the finest quality products, using the life cycle approach, which endeavours to minimize the environmental impact of the product from the stages of resource acquisition, manufacturing, packaging and transportation, through to disposal, including its use.

The result was the Rona ECO line, which was launched in the spring of 2008 and already includes close to 400 products. These products are measured according to the life cycle method and a rigorous evaluation grid involving four key indicators, and their environmental performance must be outstanding. The indicators are: climate changes, the health of ecosystems, human health, and natural resources. The Rona ECO products have been added to the hundreds of eco-responsible articles offered in the stores.

And, of course, Rona's suppliers are all involved as well. The merchandisers identify products that could qualify as being eco-responsible or Rona ECO. All of those are evaluated. Next, proof is gathered (eco label, environmental attributes, etc.). Then, the baton is passed to the experts from the Chair.

Rona's Forest Products Procurement Policy from November 2008, states in its first lines:

"Rona is committed to becoming the sustainability leader in our industry in Canada. Product selection is a key component by which Rona can exercise such leadership. Our responsible purchasing policy already affirms that we will only do business with suppliers and partners who respect both the environment and workers' rights."

And it continues a bit further:

"Rona is committed to conducting business with suppliers who have a proven record of environmental awareness; are progressive in their environmental and sustainable forest management practices; can demonstrate that fibre used is sourced from legal and sustainable forests; do not contribute to deforestation; are committed to continual improvement and proactively address issues related to their activities. Rona values suppliers who integrate the life cycle assessment approach to develop and make products."

At the same time, in its Policy on the Sale of Pesticides Across Stores From the Rona Network, the company announced the removal of synthetic pesticides used for cosmetic purposes. Since 2009, these can no longer be found in their stores, under any label. This decision was consistent with the implementation of alternative solutions. Even more importantly, the change was supported by a vast awareness and information campaign directed at employees as well as consumers.

Internally, the statements were accompanied by actions. A program to recover plastic film and cardboard packaging was implemented in all of the distribution centres, and these materials are now reused or recycled. Everyone is happy.

Next came the flyers, the indispensible link between the company and the consumer, which are already 70% printed on recycled paper. The goal was to reach 100% as soon as recycled paper was available in sufficient quantities. It was an enormous challenge that was met in less than three years.

Added to this effort is the compact fluorescent light bulb recycling program, which allows people to bring their expired CFL bulbs back to the store. Most of the bulb components are then recycled: the fluorescent powder, the mercury, and the aluminum and glass base. The idea, of course, is to prevent millions of drops of mercury from making their way into the environment, polluting the entire food chain from fish to man, one drop at a time.

In fact, a great deal of emphasis is also put on the information given to consumers, so that they will be able to make more enlightened choices. Employees must therefore be trained accordingly, to be able to properly explain the differences between products.

And, in the interests of integrity, the book you hold in your hands is printed on FSC-certified paper. FSC certification guarantees that the paper comes from responsibly managed and sustainable forests.

❷ In April 2008, Rona organized their first Eco-responsible Day in Toronto, with a team of employees taking part in a clean-up operation. Other activities were also held in Montreal, Halifax, and Vancouver.

❸ In partnership with the International Chair in Life Cycle Assessment at the École Polytechnique de Montréal, Rona launched the Rona ECO line of products in April 2008. In the stores, aisle violators describe the environmental properties of each product.

Images of 2010

220

❶ In 2010, Rona opened four new stores in Sherwood Park, Alberta; Welland, Ontario; Aurora, Ontario; and Saskatoon, Saskatchewan.

❷ On the acquisitions front, the first half of 2010 was highly productive, with the addition of Plomberie Payette & Perreault in Quebec and the Pierceys chain of stores in Nova Scotia.

222

❸

❸ Moffat & Powell, a large independent Ontario dealer, joins the ranks of Rona.

❹ The annual Rona Foundation Golf Day raised $525 000 to help underprivileged young Canadians from 12 to 30 years carve out a place for themselves in the workforce and in society. Four Olympic medalists—Charles Hamelin, François-Louis Tremblay, Mathieu Giroux, and Caroline Ouellette—lend their support to the Foundation and to Nicolas Corriveau from the Centre résidentiel et communautaire Jacques Cartier, Québec, and Natasha Carter, from the Vermilion Energy/YWCA Skills Training Center, Calgary. They are accompanied by Robert Dutton, president and CEO of Rona.

Fondation **RONA** 30 août 2010

Fondation RONA **525 000$**

Cinq cent vingt-cinq mille 00/100 dollars

Aider les jeunes à atteindre
leur plein potentiel

❹

❺ Rona will invest close to $50 million in the construction of two Réno-Dépôt stores in Vaudreuil and in Sainte-Foy, Quebec. The two stores are slated to open in the spring and summer of 2011 respectively.

❻ Rona breaks ground, marking the start of construction of a new Rona store on Torbay Road. This project is one of a series of investments in St. John's and in the province of Newfoundland and Labrador.

❼ The second edition of the President's Forum was held at Kananaskis, Alberta, in August 2010.

THE PRESIDENT'S "CAMP" was a unique opportunity to work with the president and senior management of Rona. The forum brought together young leaders from the Rona network across Canada for discussions in a resort setting.

Projects galore

In 2008, RONA adopted a four-year strategic plan that will steer the growth of the organization until 2011. Short term goals include the relaunch of the organization by improving efficiency and profitability. This will be achieved through upgrades to our technological systems and improved inventory management and rotation planning.

In the medium term, a new expansion phase is in the works. The housing sector holds great appeal. It is in constant evolution. It is at the heart of the lives of people and communities, and it is influenced by all currents.

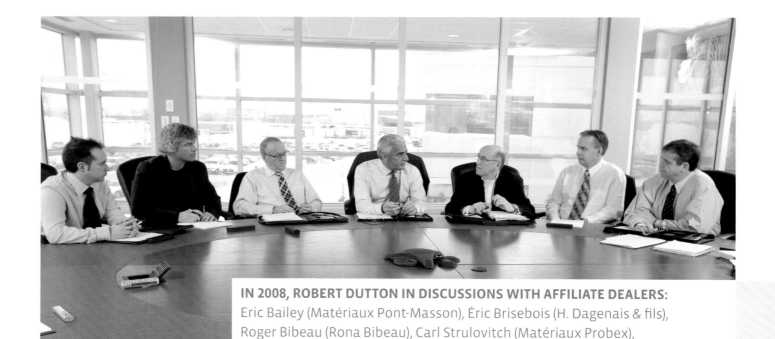

IN 2008, ROBERT DUTTON IN DISCUSSIONS WITH AFFILIATE DEALERS:
Eric Bailey (Matériaux Pont-Masson), Éric Brisebois (H. Dagenais & fils),
Roger Bibeau (Rona Bibeau), Carl Strulovitch (Matériaux Probex),
Yves Morel (Morel & fils), and Yves Lévesque (J.O. Lévesque).

**SOME RETIRED, SOME NOT, THESE BUILDERS OF RONA
PASS THE TORCH ON TO THE NEXT GENERATION.**
Michel Gendron, Marc St-Pierre, Pierre Forget, Lise Pichette (standing),
Pierre Piotte, Robert Dutton, André Dion, and André Gagnon.

A new era

The journey towards sustainable development has brought with it a revolution in people's everyday habits and a transformation in construction methods and the types of materials being used. We have to go with flow. It presents us with a training challenge. We have to be able to provide our employees with the knowledge required to respond to clients who are increasingly concerned about the environment and energy efficiency. For example, the plumbing/heating/air-conditioning sector, central to the environmental issue, is red-hot right now. Consumers are looking for clean solutions. They want solar panels on their roof, wind turbines in their backyards, and are talking more and more about geothermal energy.

Concerns changes, people themselves change. Generations X and Y are less interested in home improvement and renovation than their parents, but more concerned with quality of life. They attach greater importance to service, and seek solutions over advice.

This change in values and in generations will oblige us to revamp our stores and our notions of service. Big-box stores are going to remain the major shopping centres for do-it-yourselfers, but the spirit of the times dictates that we will see a return to proximity stores. A renaissance of neighbourhood stores is on the horizon.

THE PRESIDENT'S "CAMP" WAS A DISCUSSION AND LEARNING FORUM HELD FOR RONA'S YOUNG LEADERS, a platform for exchange for the succession of the network. For Robert Dutton, understanding youth and exploring what drives them and the issues related to their generation is not merely important, it is essential.

SUCCESSION PLANNING IS ROBERT DUTTON'S PRIORITY. In 2009, he invited the sons and daughters of dealers to the annual meeting. Some were still students who would eventually follow in their parents' footsteps, while others were already young entrepreneurs.

Through all this turbulence, major challenges lie ahead for RONA, and also excellent opportunities for growth. The issue of succession is a crucial one. Interesting young people in retail sales is an overriding concern for us. While the children of some our third or fourth generation member dealers have no interest in carrying on the family business, others cannot wait to do so. I spend time meeting this upcoming generation, young people between the ages of 20 and 35, who want to take the reins from their parents and whose ambition knows no limits. RONA must make sure it can meet their expectations.

South of the border

If the issue of succession presents a challenge, it also constitutes a certain leverage. Across Canada, independent dealers or small, local chains still occupy 50% of the renovation-construction market. For these local businesspeople, the temptation will be stronger than ever to join a larger group to ensure the survival of their business. For RONA, this will translate into both an acceleration in the recruitment of dealers and numerous acquisitions. Over a three-year horizon, RONA forecasts it will be able increase its share of the Canadian market from 17 to 20%.

Moving forward, we are hoping to soon expand south of the border. RONA's goal is to become a continental corporation, and the current context will help us achieve this. Everywhere in North America, the housing sector is hot and open to businesses that are able to respond to the changing needs of consumers. Increasingly, from a financial viewpoint, the appreciation of the Canadian dollar will facilitate future acquisitions in the United States.

That said, what will really open doors for us in the U.S. and, eventually, Mexico, is that we have learned a great deal. Our mistakes have taught us hard lessons about establishing footholds in new markets. We have learned to acquire, not conquer. RONA thus has the rare strategic advantage of being able to acquire both independent dealers and centralized organizations that operate corporate stores.

RONA is modest about its success, and wherever we expand, our first concern is to preserve the existing culture within an organization. Wherever our growth takes us, RONA is seen as a local business.

That is the dealer's spirit within us. This is the blood that courses through our veins. It is what 30 000 RONA employees have inherited from Émery Sauvé, from Rolland Dansereau, and from Napoléon Piotte.

Boards of directors •

Les Marchands en Quincaillerie Ltée (1939 - 1969)

October 11, 1939	J. Alphonse Lemay • Rolland Dansereau • Laurent Fauteux
October 12, 1939	Émery Sauvé • Rolland Dansereau • Sylva E. Bonneville
October 13, 1939	Émery Sauvé • Rolland Dansereau • Sylva E. Bonneville • Damase Desjardins
October 31, 1939	Émery Sauvé • Rolland Dansereau • Sylva E. Bonneville • Damase Desjardins • J.J. Girouard
November 21, 1939	Émery Sauvé • Sylva E. Bonneville • Damase Desjardins • J.J. Girouard • Henri Lemoine
1940	Émery Sauvé • Sylva E. Bonneville • Damase Desjardins • Henri Lemoine • J.J. Girouard • [Rolland Dansereau]
1941	Émery Sauvé • Sylva E. Bonneville • Damase Desjardins • J.J. Girouard • Henri Lemoine • Lucien Lamarre • [Rolland Dansereau]
1942	Émery Sauvé • Hervé Ravary • Damase Desjardins • J.J. Girouard • Henri Lemoine • Lucien Lamarre • [Rolland Dansereau]
1943	Émery Sauvé • Hervé Ravary • J.J. Girouard • Henri Lemoine • Lucien Lamarre • J.O. Roberge • [Rolland Dansereau]
1944, 1945	Émery Sauvé • Hervé Ravary • J.J. Girouard • Henri Lemoine • J.O. Roberge • Léopold Lamarre • [Rolland Dansereau]
1946	Émery Sauvé • J.J. Girouard • Henri Lemoine • J.O. Roberge • Léopold Lamarre • Olaüs Latendresse • [Rolland Dansereau]
1947, 1948, 1949, 1950, 1951	Émery Sauvé • J.J. Girouard • Henri Lemoine • J.O. Roberge • Olaüs Latendresse • Lucien Lamarre • [Rolland Dansereau]
1952, 1953	Émery Sauvé • J.O. Roberge • Henri Lemoine • J.J. Girouard • Lucien Lamarre • Olaüs Latendresse • [Rolland Dansereau]
1954, 1955, 1956, 1957, 1958, 1959, 1960, 1961, 1962	Rolland Dansereau • J.O. Roberge • Lucien Lamarre • Olaüs Latendresse • Ronald Dansereau • Médard Leduc

March 7, 1962	Napoléon Piotte • J.O. Roberge • Philippe Dorval • Charles Morency • Gaston L. Tétreault • Jean-Yves Gagnon
1963, 1964, 1965	Napoléon Piotte • J.O. Roberge • Aimé Lord • [Robert Tétreault]
1966, 1967, 1968	Napoléon Piotte • J.O. Roberge • Aimé Lord
1969	Charles Morency • J.O. Roberge • Aimé Lord • [André Dion]

Quincaillerie Ro-Na Inc. (1960 - 1969)

October 1960	Robert Tétreault • Gaston L. Tétreault • Claude Léveillé
1960	J.O. Roberge • Gaston L. Tétreault • Napoléon Piotte • Médard Leduc
1961	J.O. Roberge • Gaston Tétreault • Napoléon Piotte • Médard Leduc • Ronald Dansereau
1962	J.O. Roberge • Rolland Dansereau • Napoléon Piotte • Médard Leduc • Ronald Dansereau
March 19, 1962	Napoléon Piotte • Charles McKenzie • Jean Fortier • J.O. Roberge • Aimé Lord
1963	Napoléon Piotte • J.O Roberge • Aimé Lord • [Ida Riccio]
1964	Napoléon Piotte • J.O. Roberge • Aimé Lord
1965, 1966	Napoléon Piotte • J.O. Roberge • Aimé Lord • [Robert Tétreault]
1967, 1968	Napoléon Piotte • J.O. Roberge • Aimé Lord • [André Dion]
1969	Charles Morency • J.O. Roberge • Aimé Lord • [André Dion]

Gestion La Savane Inc. (1962 - 1982)

October 10, 1962 to January 28, 1963	Pauline Laplante • Jean L'Écuyer • Gaétan Raymond
1963, 1964, 1965	Philippe Dorval • Hector Durand • Jean-Yves Gagnon • Réal Gendron • Charles Jalbert • Olaüs Latendresse • Aimé Lord • Charles Morency • Napoléon Piotte • J.O. Roberge
1966	Philippe Dorval • Hector Durand • Jean-Yves Gagnon • Réal Gendron • Charles Jalbert • Jean-Jacques Latendresse • Aimé Lord • Charles Morency • Napoléon Piotte • J.O. Roberge

228

A convergence of experience

1967, 1968	Philippe Dorval • Hector Durand • Jean-Yves Gagnon • Réal Gendron • Charles Jalbert • Raymond Goyer • Aimé Lord • Charles Morency • Napoléon Piotte • J.O. Roberge
1969, 1970	Aurélien Campeau • Philippe Dorval • Hector Durand • Jean-Yves Gagnon • Raymond Goyer • Jean Hébert • Charles Jalbert • Aimé Lord • Charles Morency • J.O. Roberge
1971, 1972	Aurélien Campeau • Philippe Dorval • Hector Durand • André Gagnon • Jean-Yves Gagnon • Raymond Goyer • Jean Hébert • Charles Jalbert • Aimé Lord • Charles Morency
1973, 1974, 1975	Aurélien Campeau • Philippe Dorval • Hector Durand • André Gagnon • Jean-Yves Gagnon • Raymond Goyer • Jean Hébert • Arthur Leblanc • Aimé Lord • Charles Morency
1976, 1977, 1978	Philippe Dorval • Henri Drouin • André Gagnon • Jean-Yves Gagnon • Raymond Goyer • Jean Hébert • Arthur Leblanc • Gérald Lepage • Aimé Lord • Charles Morency
1979	Jacque Champoux • Philippe Dorval • Henri Drouin • André Gagnon • Jean-Yves Gagnon • Raymond Goyer • Jean Hébert • Gérald Lepage • Aimé Lord • Charles Morency • Pierre Piotte • Léonard Veilleux
1980	Jacque Champoux • Henri Drouin • André Gagnon • Jean-Yves Gagnon • Raymond Goyer • Jean Hébert • Gérald Lepage • François Lespérance • Aimé Lord • Charles Morency • Pierre Piotte • Léonard Veilleux
1981	Jacque Champoux • Henri Drouin • Roland Durand • André Gagnon • Jean-Yves Gagnon • Yves Gagnon • Gérald Lepage • François Lespérance • Aimé Lord • Charles Morency • Lionel Noël • Pierre Piotte
1982	Jacque Champoux • Jacques Deslauriers • Henri Drouin • Roland Durand • André Gagnon • Jean-Yves Gagnon • Yves Gagnon • Gérald Lepage • André Létourneau • Aimé Lord • Lionel Noël • Pierre Piotte

Marchands Ro-Na Inc. (1970 - 1981)

1970	Charles Morency • J.O. Roberge • Aimé Lord • [André Dion]
1971	Charles Morency • Philippe Dorval • Aimé Lord • [André Dion]
1972	Charles Morency • Philippe Dorval • Aimé Lord • Aurélien Campeau • Hector Durand • André Gagnon • Jean-Yves Gagnon • Raymond Goyer • Jean Hébert • Charles Jalbert • [André Dion]
1973, 1974	Charles Morency • Philippe Dorval • Aimé Lord • Aurélien Campeau • Hector Durand • André Gagnon • Jean-Yves Gagnon • Raymond Goyer • Jean Hébert • Arthur Leblanc • [André Dion]
1975	Charles Morency • Philippe Dorval • Jean-Yves Gagnon • André Dion • Raymond Goyer • Aurélien Campeau • Aimé Lord • Hector Durand • Arthur Leblanc • Jean Hébert
1976, 1977, 1978	Charles Morency • Philippe Dorval • Jean-Yves Gagnon • André Dion • Aimé Lord • Henri Drouin • André Gagnon • Raymond Goyer • Jean Hébert • Arthur Leblanc • Gérald Lepage
1979	Charles Morency • Philippe Dorval • Jean-Yves Gagnon • André Dion • Aimé Lord • Henri Drouin • André Gagnon • Raymond Goyer • Jean Hébert • Gérald Lepage • Pierre Piotte • Léonard Veilleux • Jacque Champoux
1980	Charles Morency • André Gagnon • Henri Drouin • Aimé Lord • Roger Côté • Bernard St-Charles • Jean Matteau • Jacque Champoux • Jean-Yves Gagnon • Raymond Goyer • Jean Hébert • Gérald Lepage • François Lespérance • Pierre Piotte • Léonard Veilleux
1981	Charles Morency • Henri Drouin • André Gagnon• Pierre Piotte • Aimé Lord • André Dion • Yves Gagnon • Gérald Lepage • Lionel Noël • Jacque Champoux • Roland Durand • François Lespérance • Jean-Yves Gagnon

230

Le Groupe Ro-Na Inc. (1982 - 1987)

1982 Henri Drouin • André Dion • André Gagnon •
Pierre Piotte • Aimé Lord • Jacques Deslauriers •
Yvon Cléroux • Gérald Lepage • André Létourneau •
Jacque Champoux • Jean-Yves Gagnon • Lionel Noël

1983 Henri Drouin • André Dion • Pierre Piotte •
André Gagnon • Aimé Lord • François Lespérance •
Jacques Deslauriers • Lionel Noël • Roland Durand •
André Létourneau • Raoul Grenier • Jacque Champoux •
Yvon Cléroux • Gérald Lepage

1984 Henri Drouin • André Dion • Pierre Piotte •
André Gagnon • Raoul Grenier • Jacque Champoux •
Jacques Deslauriers • Yvon Cléroux • Guy Champagne •
Roland Durand • André Létourneau • Lionel Noël •
François Lespérance • Gérard Mercier

1985 Henri Drouin • André Dion • Pierre Piotte •
André Gagnon • Raoul Grenier • Jean Rodrigue •
Yvon Cléroux • Gérard Mercier • Guy Champagne •
Jacques Deslauriers • André Létourneau •
Jacques Schmidt • Roland Durand

1986 Henri Drouin • André Dion • Pierre Piotte •
André Gagnon • Raoul Grenier • Guy Champagne •
Yvon Cléroux • Jacques Deslauriers • Raoul Durand •
Jean-Guy Hébert • Gérard Mercier • Jean Rodrigue •
Jacques Schmidt • Denis Sénéchal

1987 Henri Drouin • André Dion • André Gagnon •
Pierre Piotte • Raoul Grenier • Robert Chevrier •
Yvon Cléroux • Jacques Deslauriers • Roland Durand •
Jean-Guy Hébert • Gérard Mercier • Jean Rodrigue •
Jacques Schmidt • Denis Sénéchal

The Ro-Na Dismat Group Inc. (1988 - 1997)

1988 Henri Drouin • André Dion • Pierre Piotte •
André Gagnon • Raoul Grenier • Denis Sénéchal •
Jean-Guy Hébert • Robert Chevrier • Roland Durand •
Georges Lanouette • Gérard Mercier • Jean Rodrigue •
François Marcil • Yvon Cléroux • Clément Joncas •
Jules Riopel • Marc Bureau • Jacques Schmidt

1989 Henri Drouin • André Dion • Pierre Piotte •
André Gagnon • Marc Bureau • Gérard Mercier •
Gérald Harvey • Georges Lanouette • Clément Joncas •
Robert Chevrier • Jules Riopel • Denis Sénéchal •
Jean-Guy Hébert • Jacques Schmidt • Jean Rodrigue •
François Marcil • Yvon Cléroux • J. Gilles Nolet

1990 Henri Drouin • Robert Dutton • Pierre Piotte •
André Gagnon • François Marcil • Marc Bureau •
Robert Chevrier • Yvon Cléroux • Gérald Harvey •
Jean-Guy Hébert • Clément Joncas •
Georges Lanouette • Michel Nepveu • J. Gilles Nolet •
Jacques Schmidt • Denis Sénéchal

1991 Henri Drouin • Robert Dutton • Marc Bureau •
André Gagnon • Jean-Guy Hébert • Georges Lanouette •
François Marcil • Michel Nepveu • Gilles Nolet •
Claude Pichette • Jean-Paul Plante • Denis Sénéchal

1992 Henri Drouin • Robert Dutton • Marc Bureau •
André Gagnon • Jean-Guy Hébert • Georges Lanouette •
François Marcil • Michel Nepveu • J. Gilles Nolet •
Claude Pichette • Jean-Paul Plante • Denis Sénéchal

1993 Henri Drouin • Robert Dutton • Marc Bureau •
André Gagnon • Jean-Guy Hébert • Gilles Lamoureux •
Georges Lanouette • François Marcil • Michel Nepveu •
J. Gilles Nolet • Claude Pichette • Jean-Paul Plante

1994 Henri Drouin • Robert Dutton • Marc Bureau •
André Gagnon • Renelle Anctil • Pierre Brodeur •
Jean-Guy Hébert • Gilles Lamoureux •
Georges Lanouette • Michel Nepve • J. Gilles Nolet •
Claude Pichette

1995 Henri Drouin • Robert Dutton • Marc Bureau •
André Gagnon • Gérald Cusson • Renelle Anctil •
Pierre Brodeur • Jean-Guy Hébert • Gilles Lamoureux •
Georges Lanouette • Michel Nepveu • Claude Pichette

1996 Henri Drouin • Robert Dutton • Renelle Anctil •
Marc Bureau • Gérald Cusson • André Gagnon •
Jean-Guy Hébert • Gilles Lamoureux •
Georges Lanouette • Michel Nepveu • Claude Pichette

1997 Henri Drouin • Renelle Anctil • Marc Bureau • Gérald Cusson • Robert Dutton • André Gagnon • Jean-Guy Hébert • Gilles Lamoureux • Jacques Landreville • Georges Lanouette • Michel Nepveu • Claude Pichette

RONA Inc. (1998 to present day)

1998 Henri Drouin • Renelle Anctil • Boris Blache • Marc Bureau • Simon Cloutier • Gérald Cusson • Robert Dutton • André Gagnon • Jean Gauriat • Jean-Guy Hébert • Gilles Lamoureux • Jacques Landreville • Michel Nepveu • Jocelyn Tremblay

1999 Henri Drouin • Renelle Anctil • Boris Blache • Michel Caron • Simon Cloutier • Robert Dutton • André Gagnon • Jean Gauriat • Jean-Guy Hébert • Jacques Landreville • Robert Lévesque • Michel Nepveu • Louis A. Tanguay • Jocelyn Tremblay

2000 Henri Drouin • Renelle Anctil • Boris Blache • Simon Cloutier • Robert Dutton • André Gagnon • Jean Gauriat • Jean-Guy Hébert • Jacques Landreville • Robert Lévesque • Michel Nepveu • Louis A. Tanguay • Jocelyn Tremblay

2001 Henri Drouin • Alain Bouchard • Boris Blache • Simon Cloutier • Frédéric David • Robert Dutton • Wayne Filsinger • André Gagnon • George J. Heller • Jacques Landreville • L. Jacques Ménard • André Roy • Louis A. Tanguay • Jocelyn Tremblay

2002 André Gagnon • Boris Blache • Alain Bouchard • Louise Caya • Frédéric David • Simon Cloutier • Robert Dutton • Wayne Filsinger • Jean-Guy Hébert • George J. Heller • Jacques Landreville • L. Jacques Ménard • André Roy • Jocelyn Tremblay • Louis Tanguay

2003 Boris Blache • Alain Bouchard • Jacques Bougie • Louise Caya • Simon Cloutier • Frédéric David • Robert Dutton • André Gagnon • Jean-Guy Hébert • Monique F. Leroux • André Roy • Louis A. Tanguay • Jocelyn Tremblay

2004 Pierre Brodeur • Jacques Bougie • Louise Caya • Simon Cloutier • Robert Dutton • André Gagnon • Jean Gaulin • Jean-Guy Hébert • Monique F. Leroux • James Pantelidis • Louis A. Tanguay • Jocelyn Tremblay

2005 Robert Dutton • André Gagnon • Pierre Brodeur • Louise Caya • Simon Cloutier • Pierre Ducros • Jean Gaulin • Jean-Guy Hébert • Alain Michel • James Pantelidis • Louis A. Tanguay • Jocelyn Tremblay

2006 Robert Dutton • Louise Caya • Pierre Ducros • André Gagnon • Jean Gaulin • Jean-Guy Hébert • J. Spencer Lanthier • Alain Michel • James Pantelidis • Louis A. Tanguay • Jocelyn Tremblay • Jean-Roch Vachon

2007 Jean Gaulin • Robert Dutton • Louise Caya • Doris Joan Daughney • Pierre Ducros • Jean-Guy Hébert • J. Spencer Lanthier • Alain Michel • James Pantelidis • Robert Sartor • Louis A. Tanguay • Jocelyn Tremblay • Jean-Roch Vachon

2008 Louise Caya • Doris Joan Daughney • Pierre Ducros • Robert Dutton • Jean Gaulin • Jean-Guy Hébert • J. Spencer Lanthier • Alain Michel • James Pantelidis • Robert Sartor • Louis A. Tanguay • Jocelyn Tremblay • Jean-Roch Vachon

2009, 2010 Louise Caya • Doris Joan Daughney • Robert Dutton • Richard Fortin • Jean Gaulin • Jean-Guy Hébert • J. Spencer Lanthier • Alain Michel • James Pantelidis • Robert Paré • Jocelyn Tremblay • Jean-Roch Vachon

Legend: Names in square brackets indicate officers who were present but who were not elected as directors.

Features

Profiles

Photo credits

All photographs are from the RONA fonds except:

André Champagne fonds
p. 15, left; p. 53, left and right.

André Dion fonds
p. 125, No. 5; p. 166, right.

André Gagnon fonds
p. 166, right; p. 167, left; p. 190, No. 1.

Caroline Anctil fonds
p. 9, Nos. 5, 6; p. 33, right; p. 48, right; p. 51, No. 2.

City of Montréal archives
p. 18, Nos. 1, 2, 3; p. 23, right.

Claude Bélanger fonds
p. 8, Nos. 3, 4; p. 13, bottom; p. 33, left; p. 58; p. 59, left; p. 61, No. 6.

Claude and Pierre Michaud fonds
p. 16; p. 160, right; p. 161, left.

George Bird, The Gazette, 1985
p. 45, No. 2.

Georges Lanouette fonds
p. 40; p. 49, left; p. 61, No. 4.

Guy Morency fonds
p. 12 and 13, centre; p. 51, No. 4; p. 57, right; p. 68, top; p. 69, left.

Jean Dorval fonds
p. 8, Nos. 1, 2; p. 10; p. 15, right; p. 32, top and bottom right; p. 56, right; p. 57, left.

Jim Thorogood fonds
p. 204, left.

Judith Boulanger fonds
p. 54, No. 1.

Michel Perron fonds
p. 12, left.

Pierre Piotte fonds
p. 46, left; p. 126, No. 1.

Renelle Anctil fonds
p. 45, No. 3.

Richard Provost fonds
p. 47, left; p. 60, No. 1.

Rogers Communications, *Le Quincaillier,* April 1961
p. 19, No. 4;
Le Quincaillier, April 1960
p. 149, Nos. 2, 3.

Ronald Maisonneuve
p. 143, No. 4.

Susan Rapin fonds
p. 184, right.

Disclaimer: Every effort has been made to give proper credit to the contributors and to secure the necessary permission to reprint all copyrighted material. We would like to apologize should there be any errors or omissions, and we will be happy to make any necessary corrections in future printings.